Douglas Estes has written a very useful book. Not only will readers now see old questions in a new light, but they will also be prompted to ask new questions for the first time. The technical language and theoretical categories that drive the book are shown to have clear payoff in understanding the text of the New Testament in a new light. Especially interesting here are the case studies that conclude each section, where Estes shows us with great care and precision just how much is being asked by the different types of questions in the New Testament.

George L. Parsenios, Associate Professor of New Testament, Princeton Theological Seminary

Recognizing that questions are both central to ancient rhetoric and often overlooked in contemporary exegesis, Estes offers an expansive interdisciplinary treatment of questions in the Greek New Testament against the backdrop of grammatical theory, linguistics, and historiography, among other disciplines. He develops—in much greater detail—his previous research on the questions of Jesus in the Gospel of John, and in the process provides students, scholars, and pastors with an incredibly useful tool for exegetical research. Writing with the precision of an expert, the nuance of a skilled teacher, and the sensitivity of an exegete, Estes introduces the reader to the twenty-eight linguistic features of question asking, the four major formations of questions, and the thirty-six question types found within the NT. This impressive book represents an important achievement in the study of NT Greek and deserves to be among the required texts for advanced courses in Biblical Greek grammar. I cannot recommend this book highly enough!

Christopher W. Skinner, Associate Professor of New Testament & Early Christianity, Loyola University Chicago

Questions are powerful rhetorical devices, but surprisingly they have not been the subject of rigorous scholarly examination—until now. Estes, who has already established himself as an authority on the subject of questions in the Gospel of John (Brill, 2012), now extends his unique insights to the entire New Testament. Using a helpful taxonomic approach to the numerous questions in the Greek New Testament, Estes introduces his readers to the logic of questions in the text and their rhetorical effect, leading to a "rounder" reading of the New Testament.

Cornelis Bennema, Senior Lecturer in New Testament and Academic Dean, Union School of Theology, UK

Too often insufficient attention is paid to the logic of questions in the New Testament with the result that both exegesis and theological reflection are impoverished. Douglas Estes, in this interdisciplinary study, provides an excellent, user-friendly resource for analysing and understanding questions in the New Testament. I am sure it will prove to be an important exegetical aid for those engaged in a serious study of the New Testament, be they students, ministers, teachers, or established scholars.

RICHARD H. BELL, Professor of Theology,
University of Nottingham

This is an exceptional book. It addresses an issue that most of us do not spend much time considering, namely, the questions of the New Testament. But questions give shape to the rhetoric of the text in ways we fail to appreciate, not to mention the fact that fifteen percent of the New Testament involves questions of various kinds. Estes writes with linguistic and academic savvy while remaining very clear, offering helpful examples and illustrations. If you have never questioned New Testament questions — or even if you have — this book will prove enormously useful.

CONSTANTINE R. CAMPBELL, Associate Professor
of New Testament, Trinity Evangelical Divinity School

Just as questions bear significant rhetorical import within our conventional discourses, they play crucial roles within written texts. While Christian preachers and teachers may have learned well how to do exegesis of declarative statements, the rhetorical and semantic implications of questions have often eluded them, with detriment to their teaching and preaching. A conspicuous vacancy in exegetical studies is filled with *Questions and Rhetoric in the Greek New Testament*, a thorough, even if not exhaustive, exegetical guide concerning the rhetoric and semantics of questions in the Greek New Testament.

ARDEL B. CANEDAY, Professor of New Testament & Greek,
University of Northwestern — St. Paul

I'm delighted to see Douglas Estes deploy his considerable scholarly gifts and expertise in Greek rhetoric in this comprehensive yet accessible volume. This is a treasure trove for students and scholars alike. But I'm especially excited for pastors and Bible teachers to have this resource at their fingertips in sermon and teaching preparation. A wonderful resource.

TODD WILSON, Senior Pastor, Calvary Memorial Church

QUESTIONS AND RHETORIC

An Essential Reference Resource for Exegesis

DOUGLAS ESTES

ZONDERVAN

Questions and Rhetoric in the Greek New Testament

This title is also available as a Zondervan ebook.

Requests for information should be addressed to:

Zondervan, *3900 Sparks Dr. SE, Grand Rapids, Michigan 49546*

ISBN: 978-0-310-51635-4

All Scripture translations in the book, unless otherwise noted, are the author's own.

Cover design: Tammy Johnson
Interior illustration and production: Beth Shagene
Interior design: Matthew Van Zomeren

for Violet

Contents

Expanded Table of Contents

Abbreviations

ACNT	Augsburg Commentary on the New Testament
AJSL	*American Journal of Semitic Languages and Literature*
AS	*Aramaic Studies*
BDF	Blass, Friedrich, Albert Debrunner, and Robert W. Funk. *A Greek Grammar of the New Testament and Other Early Christian Literature*. Chicago: University of Chicago Press, 1961.
BECNT	Baker Exegetical Commentary of the New Testament
Bib	*Biblica*
BibInt	Biblical Interpretation Series
BNTC	Black's New Testament Commentaries
BRLA	Brill Reference Library of Judaism
BZNW	Beihefte zur Zeitschrift für die neutestamentliche Wissenschaft
CBQ	*Catholic Biblical Quarterly*
CCTC	Cambridge Classical Texts and Commentaries
CDL	*Cambridge Dictionary of Linguistics*
ClQ	*Classical Quarterly*
CP	*Classical Philology*
CSLI	Center for the Study of Language and Information
diss.	dissertation
ErIsr	*Eretz-Israel*
ESV	English Standard Version
GNT	Greek New Testament
GRBS	*Greek, Roman, and Byzantine Studies*
HCSB	Holman Christian Standard Bible
HSCP	Harvard Studies in Classical Philology
HTR	*Harvard Theological Review*

IE	Indo-European
JBL	*Journal of Biblical Literature*
JBQ	*Jewish Bible Quarterly*
JETS	*Journal of the Evangelical Theological Society*
JSNT	*Journal for the Study of the New Testament*
JSNTSup	Journal for the Study of the New Testament Supplement Series
JSOTSup	Journal for the Study of the Old Testament Supplement Series
JSS	*Journal of Semitic Studies*
JTS	*Journal of Theological Studies*
KJV	King James Version
L&N	Louw, Johannes P., and Eugene A. Nida, eds. *Greek-English Lexicon of the New Testament: Based on Semantic Domains.* 2nd ed. New York: United Bible Societies, 1989.
LCL	Loeb Classical Library
LHBOTS	The Library of Hebrew Bible/Old Testament Studies
LNTS	Library of New Testament Studies
LXX	Septuagint (The Greek Old Testament)
Mid.	Demosthenes, *In Midiam (Against Meidias)*
NA^{28}	Nestle-Aland Greek New Testament, 28th ed.
NAC	New American Commentary
NCV	New Century Version
Neot	*Neotestamentica*
NICNT	New International Commentary on the New Testament
NIGTC	New International Greet Testament Commentary
NIV	New International Version (2011)
NLT	New Living Translation
NovT	*Novum Testamentum*
NPI	Negative Polarity Item
NPQ	Negative Polar Question
NRSV	New Revised Standard Version
NT	New Testament
NTS	*New Testament Studies*
NTTS	New Testament Tools and Studies
OCM	Oxford Classical Monographs
Od.	Homer, *Odyssea (Odyssey)*

PhA	Philosophia Antiqua
PPI	Positive Polarity Item
SBL	Society of Biblical Literature
SemDial	*The Semantics and Pragmatics of Dialogue*
SHBC	Smyth & Helwys Bible Commentary
SP	Sacra Pagina
SPQ	Similar Polarity Question
SVO	Subject-Verb-Object
UBS^5	United Bible Societies, 5th ed.
VT	*Vetus Testamentum*
WBC	Word Biblical Commentary
WCCFL	West Coast Conference on Formal Linguistics
WGRW	Writings from the Greco-Roman World
WW	*Word and World*

Preface

Like our world, the world of the Greek New Testament is one that is full of questions. This book tries to understand these questions and take the exegete a little further down the road in their understanding of these questions. Thus, this book is more of a beginning than an end. In this book, I have not tried to be exhaustive in cataloguing and categorizing every question in the Greek New Testament. The reason for this is both practical and philosophical. Practically, there are too many questions with too many unique features for just one book. Philosophically, the idea of exactly identifying and categorizing a question goes against what it means to ask a question. There are always new logical angles and rhetorical effects for a reader to discover in questions asked. I also have purposefully limited the study to the questions in the New Testament and have not interacted (much) with questions in the Septuagint or other texts of Classical and Koine Greek. I believe that these kinds of investigations would be profitable, but they were beyond the scope of this work.

The reason for writing this book was simple: questions represent a numerically significant but largely overlooked feature of the Greek New Testament (GNT). Questions also play a much more important role in ancient discourse than modern readers assume. This book hopes to begin to address the imbalance. Even if the reader is not passionate about questions, I hope that at the least this will expose the reader to bigger questions about the style, discourse features, rhetoric, and aesthetics of the GNT—to move away from "flat" readings that are so common.

In this book, we explore twenty-eight linguistic features of question asking, the four major formations of questions, and thirty-six question types. We do so through more than forty in-depth case studies and hundreds of detailed examples. This book is by purpose and design interdisciplinary: I freely sample from such diverse fields as ancient and modern rhetoric, ancient Greek literary and grammatical theory, argumentation theory, linguistics, historiography, conversation analysis, speech act theory, psychology, and many more. Readers may notice, though, that the organization for this book is different from the organization of my previous book on questions, *The Questions of Jesus in John* (Leiden: Brill, 2013). This does not reflect a change in my thinking about questions as much as it has to do with the specific goals for each book. In *The Questions of Jesus in John*, my goal was solely to look at Jesus's questions in one Gospel, and the five categories I created for organizing those questions moved the reader from the less rhetorical in quality to the more rhetorical in quality. Those categories were descriptive categories, and while I could have used them in this book, I felt that the more exhaustive nature of this book required a less descriptive and more taxonomic approach to questions. Unlike my previous book, this book is intended as a ready reference for Greek exegesis; therefore, my hope is that this organizational style will make it easier for readers to get out of it what they need more quickly than if I had retained my descriptive categories. I have divided the questions of the GNT up into their more native categories as driven by their syntax, semantics, and pragmatics. I have tried to keep footnotes to an absolute minimum, choosing instead to rely on targeted bibliography sections at the end of each section.

I am thankful for the late Verlyn Verbrugge and for his desire to see this research reach a larger audience. Though he was unable to see the finished product, his early engagement with this book was both helpful and encouraging. The rest of the Zondervan team, including Ryan Pazdur, Nancy Erickson, Christopher Beetham, and Joshua Kessler were wonderful to work with as always. I am also thankful for the late Douglas R. Estes Jr., who also was unable to see the finished product. In so many ways, he made me the person I am today.

One does not get far in life without others who have believed in, supported, helped, prayed, and blessed one's work. While there are far more people to whom I owe gratitude than can be listed here, I name but a few: Nadine Estes; Eric and Morgan Estes; Jason, Su-Anne, Hudson, and Molly Wills Estes; David Estes; Ruth Estes; Ken and Emily Mears; Jason and Gretchen Woods; Matt and Jaime Reed; CJ and Jennifer Young; Jed and Crystal Smith; Sandy Kaiser and the rest of my Mesa staff; Vivian and Ross Oliver; Chuck and Marivic Mora, plus all the wonderful folks from BVC; Gary and Mary Appel; Charles "Cubby" and Lillie Boothe; Fred and Nita Boothe; Mary Ann and Ron Poythress; Terrell and Linda Boothe; Diann Cook; David Frees; all the folks that were a part of S2; and Joshua Paul Smith. Above all, my deepest gratitude goes to my children, Wyatt, Bridget, Violet, and Everett, and to my marvelous wife, Noël. Nawapenda na barikiwa. It is to my sweet Violet that I dedicate this book.

Chapter 1

Introduction

Why study questions in the Greek New Testament? Aren't biblical exegetes looking for answers, not questions, when they study the New Testament? Aren't the many powerful statements enough? The answer to these questions lies in our desire to interpret faithfully and accurately the Greek New Testament to the best of our ability—and not just the statements, but the questions too. This book will help you to understand and interpret the questions that the New Testament asks in a whole new way.

It is said that in order to find the answer to something, someone must first know the question that needs to be asked. The difficulty for most readers of the Greek New Testament is that they are not prepared to understand the questions. This is because their training, up to now, has been in understanding the statements of the New Testament (NT). This book will equip you to better think through what is being asked in the nearly one thousand questions found throughout the Greek New Testament (GNT).[1]

Whether readers of the NT realize it or not, it is as much the questions in the NT as the statements that make such a great impact on readers:

- "What is truth?" JOHN 18:38
- "What do you seek?" JOHN 1:38A
- "Who are you, Lord?" ACTS 9:5
- "Who is like the beast?" REV 13:4
- "Where then is boasting?" ROM 3:27A
- "Do you speak Greek?" ACTS 21:37B

These are just a few examples of questions in the NT that influence the reading of the NT. They influence the theology of the text, but they also influence the life of the reader through their persuasiveness. Thus, we must take care not to

1. There are 980 direct questions in the GNT that are either undisputed or largely acknowledged as questions. Beyond this number, there are a number of disputed questions—usually these are sentences that most often appear in modern translations as a statement but for which a scholar has argued somewhere along the way that the sentence is better served being treated as a question. This includes sentences that are formed as statements but may carry interrogative force (something easier to pull off in Greek than English). And beyond that number, there is a multitude of indirect questions that will not be treated in this book but still have some indirect interrogative force that an interpreter needs to account for in the interpretation of the text.

underestimate the importance of the questions in the NT for reading the NT. They are included in the NT for a reason—and now, thanks to modern linguistics and related disciplines, we have an opportunity to interpret them with greater skill and acuity than ever before.

Questions Greatly Affect the Meaning of the Text

Imagine for a moment that you were reading a book where someone cut every seventh sentence out of the book. Would you be able to understand the book? Yes. But would you understand or appreciate the book in the same way as you would as if all the sentences were included? No. Those extra sentences—even if they only make up 15% of the book—really make a big difference. In the GNT, questions make up about 15% of the sentences. Therefore, when we read the NT without understanding the questions, we are like the reader who skips over every seventh sentence in the book. Many of the important theological ideas developed in Scripture occur in proximity to, or in response to, a question. As a result, it is difficult to appreciate those ideas when the neighboring sentences are not fully included in the interpretation.

In the study of the NT, readers have overlooked the importance of questions. This problem has gone on for centuries, slowly worsening over time since the end of the patristic age. It is a problem that is prevalent today. We can illustrate this numerically. In the GNT, there are approximately sixty-eight optatives, and most GNT grammars take the time to cover this (unusual and interesting) grammatical phenomenon.[2] In contrast, there are nearly one thousand direct questions in the GNT, for which little is said in most Greek grammars. In fact, 8,650 words make up the questions in the GNT. For us to interpret those words correctly, we must understand them through the logic of questions, not the logic of statements. If we are unable to understand them as questions, then there is a large gap in our interpretation.

Questions Give a Whole New Perspective on the Text

Questions have a different logic than statements (propositions). That is, the way a person thinks about a question is different from the way a person thinks about a proposition. Questions, when interpreted as questions, give a whole new perspective on the GNT because they make the reader think with question logic instead of proposition logic. The difficulty for most readers of the GNT today is that their training only included approaches to the text using *alethic logic* (the thinking behind propositions).[3] Gaining experience in the use of *erotetic*

2. E.g., Wallace, *Greek Grammar*, 480.

3. *Alethic logic* comes from the Greek ἀλήθεια, which means "the quality of being in accord with what is true" (BDAG 42). The reason scholars refer to the logic of propositions as alethic logic originates with Aristotle (384–322 BC), who has had tremendous influence

logic (the thinking behind questions) allows the exegete to approach the text in a whole new way. Instead of constantly thinking about what the text is saying, the interpreter with a background in erotetic logic can also think more precisely about what the text is asking.

This plays out in important areas of interpretation for the GNT. One of the challenges in interpretation is to relate to others what the text is *saying*. However, should the interpreter not relate to others what the text is *asking*? In fact, what *is* the GNT asking of its readers? What are the characters in the GNT narratives asking each other? What is the text asking of itself? If we can better understand what the GNT is asking of its readers and asking of itself, it will give us a completely new perspective on what it is telling as well. In fact, it will help us to know what questions were asked to begin with that prompted the GNT to tell what it does tell.

Questions Are at the Center of the Rhetoric of the Text

When reading a book, it is not unusual for a reader to read for the most interesting part of the text. Sometimes we readers skip over the details to get to the "good stuff." This good stuff—in texts such as we find in the GNT—often functions as a *rhetorical peak* in the text. Often a persuasive or controversial utterance gets the reader thinking. The same thing happens when we read and interpret from the GNT; we gravitate toward the rhetorical peaks, and they heavily influence our reading. For example, we focus heavily on John 3:16 but less so on John 3:17. In the ancient world, however, it was not just statements that readers understood to carry a rhetorical peak but also questions. (Today people recognize this in some forms of communication, such as political speeches, but less so in other forms, such as written texts.) In a highly oral culture, such as the one in which the GNT was originally created and first read, many questions are grouped around the rhetorical peaks in many of its texts. The words of Pilate are a great example of this—he really knew how to ask questions to get the hearer's attention.

As a result, readers and exegetes of the GNT will want to get to the heart of the important parts of the texts. In order to do that, a better understanding of the logic and the rhetoric of the questions contained within is a must. One reason they are included is to introduce new or controversial information for the

---

in this area even up to present day. Aristotle believed the key differentiation between a proposition (ἀπόφανσις) and other types of utterances (e.g., prayers, wishes, questions) was that a proposition could be judged based on its truth content whereas other types of utterances could not (Aristotle, *Interpretation* 17a1–8). We see this reflected in modern debates over statements in the GNT, whether a statement is true or false, whether it was truly made or recreated by an author. Alethic logic is important, but it does not help in interpreting nonpropositional thought (which makes up a considerable part of the GNT).

reader. Another reason they are included is to persuade the reader in the direction they want the reader to go. As readers, our coming to terms with this new information and persuasion helps us understand the meaningful statements that are embedded nearby.

The study of questions in the GNT is more complex than it may appear at first glance. There are many different types of questions, each type with a distinct logic and rhetoric, and the great variety of types of questions found in as large a body of literature as the GNT points to the potential for tremendous complexity. A parallel situation to the study of questions is the study of prepositions; the complexity of prepositional usage in the GNT is profound.[4] In this book, we will look at the top thirty-six different question types, distributed among the four major formations for questions. And it won't be a neat undertaking; each question can fit into more than one type, and most fit into several—which means this book will only start the exegete on the journey toward understanding the logic and rhetoric of the questions in the GNT. In summation, the purpose of this book is *to help interpreters understand the logic of questions in the GNT so they can explain the rhetorical (persuasive) effect of these questions in their interpretation of the NT.*

A. The Question of Questions

What is a question? This is one question that is hard to answer. Questions are such an everyday part of life and communication that we intuitively know what a question is and how to ask a question, long before we ever know what word we apply to define the act of asking. Within the modern study of language, there are at least eighteen significant answers to the question, "What is a question?"[5] While it is beyond the scope of this book to try to answer this question with any precision, I will offer a simple working definition: *A* question *is any utterance with interrogative force that asks not says, that always applies some rhetorical effect, and that invites a reply of some sort.*[6] In most Indo-European languages, the question is the communicative act whose primary job is to gain information. Indo-European (IE) is a large family of languages (including Greek, Latin, English, German, French, and Spanish, but not Hebrew) that share many similarities. Sometimes these similarities allow us to look at one language to gain insight into another (close) language in the IE family (a process called *comparative linguistics*; *CDL* 88).

If we cannot well define the idea of a question, we can at least give some suggestions as to what it is not. It is not a proposition, statement, or assertion.

4. Harris, *Prepositions and Theology*, 26–32; and cf. Bortone, *Greek Prepositions*, 171–94.
5. Estes, *Questions*, 39–42.
6. This is true even of so-called "rhetorical questions"; see §2.E.

This doesn't mean questions can't assert things or propose things; what it means is that questions are formed primarily with the purpose of doing something different. Even if we cannot well define questions, we can reveal much about the way that they function when they are used by a speaker or writer. We can also show how a question functions within discourse. While we cannot always know when an utterance is a question—instead of a proposition—the surrounding discourse will often provide the reader clues as to what type of utterance one is reading.

A Thought Experiment

Let's do a thought experiment to consider how deep the bias against questions runs.[7] As we read the Gospel of John, we are trained to think about the statements that Jesus makes. Some of the most remarked upon declarations in John are any one of "the hour" statements. For example, Jesus says, "The hour has come for the Son of Man to be glorified" (John 12:23 NIV). Propositions such as this one are often considered a "peak" of the gospel text and are frequently taken from context and used as a naked proposition (as in the example, "God is love"). These "the hour" statements are critical utterances in John, and they are far more studied and discussed by scholars and readers than, for example, the preceding narrative statement, "Philip went to tell Andrew; Andrew and Philip in turn told Jesus" (John 12:22 NIV). Now for the experiment: *How do we really know that John 12:23 is a statement rather than a question*? At first blush this question seems ridiculous. Surely we *know* it is a statement. But how do we know it is a statement? Is it not possible to translate ἐλήλυθεν ἡ ὥρα ἵνα δοξασθῇ ὁ υἱὸς τοῦ ἀνθρώπου as "Has the hour come for the Son of Man to be glorified?" It is possible. However, this is not my argument.

In John 2, during the wedding at Cana in Galilee, Jesus's mother goes to Jesus to tell him that the wine is gone (though the wedding is still going). Jesus responds, "Woman, what do you want with me? My hour has not yet come." In all modern translations, we read John 2:4b as a proposition where Jesus continues to rebuke his mother after what appears to be a pointed or rude question.[8] Yet recent research by J. F. Coakley reveals a Syriac tradition going back to as early as the second century that reads John 2:4b as a question instead of a declarative due to the presence of an early Syriac form of punctuation for polar

7. For another similar thought experiment on the challenge of discovering questions in the GNT, see Estes, *Questions*, 7–8.
8. The question is not rude, it is phatic; thus it is misunderstood by students (and some commentators) who try to overliteralize the expression without recognizing its pragmatic function (§4.K). A related example would be if a modern American student asked a 19th century English gentleman or gentlewoman, "What's up?" It would sound vulgar to their ears; they would be unable to interpret the expression as another form of "How are you?"

questions.[9] Thus, it appears likely that some early Syriac Christians heard Jesus's response to his mother as "Woman, what do you want with me? Has my hour still not come?"[10] If we were to read Jesus's statement as a question today, it would change the timbre of the passage; rather than rebuking his mother, Jesus would be using a standard multiple-question combination common in the GNT (§5.D.1) to persuade his mother to think through the implication of asking him to do something about the lack of wine. A question here would also give the reader pause—was the mother of Jesus more aware of Jesus's purpose than readers assume? Was Jesus asking her blessing to move forward with his Father's plan? Substituting an interrogative force for an assertive force brings out new shades of meaning and depth of relationship between Jesus and his mother. The dramatic quality and persuasive feel of the passage increases substantially. Other overtones begin to emerge. End of the thought experiment.

B. The Use of Questions

Questions are as primitive and embryonic a feature of language as is any other feature of language. Long before there were participles or predicate nominatives, there were questions. In fact, questions may be one of the only aspects of language that is prephonological and, arguably, prephonetic. Human children know how to ask questions without any instruction at the earliest ages and before any formal language develops. Questions are *holophrastic* (*CDL* 212), which means that they can be asked in abbreviated form with only one word: "Food?" is asked and understood universally. Therefore, to fully grasp a language, a speaker or reader must grasp questions as well as statements.

Questions play an important role in texts such as the GNT for reasons that are often overlooked. Because the NT is often consulted for what it says—and often poorly, in snippets—the NT is often seen as a book of "answers" or "information" or "facts." Long before Wikipedia and its revolving buffet of factoids, modern readers started searching the NT to discover truths that they could apply to their lives. It was all very modern, factual, rational, didactic, and neat. However, the NT writers were not very interested in modern, factual, rational, didactic, and neat truths. They were very much interested in showing, persuading, encouraging, reasoning, and warning the reader. This is where questions come in—while propositions excel at communicating truth claims, questions excel at reasoning and persuading. In fact, while logic and reason in modernity

9. Coakley, "Early Syriac Question Mark," 211–13. Long before Coakley's discovery, Nigel Turner also wondered whether John 2:4b would be better interpreted as a question, given its place and function in discourse; see Turner, *Grammatical Insights*, 43; also Zerwick, *Biblical Greek*, §447.

10. For the use of οὔπω in questions in the GNT, see for example Matt 16:9; Mark 4:40b; 8:17b; 8:21; John 8:57.

focus on propositions, asking questions is truly "the first and foremost theory of reasoning."[11] Thus, if reasoning and debate are to occur, questions must be a major component of the discourse.

What a strange world it would be if language only consisted of assertions (and commands and exclamations, even more so). There would be no way to engage another speaker other than talking "at" them. Long before the GNT, the writer of the book of Job used questions to establish the facts of the matter (1:7–12), to launch an argument (4:2), and to dispute ironically with a reader (41:1–7). Long before the GNT, questions were a cornerstone of local Greek civic discourse, occupying the thoughts of Plato and Aristotle and becoming a staple of oral and rhetorical presentations.[12] It is, and as far as we can tell always has been, a widely used language pattern in all forms of human communication.

Human communication is highly dialogical—people don't seem to be as interested in speaking to themselves as they are in speaking to other humans. Questions are the form of human communication wherein people are able to identify a need they have, and share this need with other people *in the hopes that this need will be met.* Often this need or lack is informational, but sometimes it is an action. Thus, people ask questions when they want to know something and sometimes when they want someone to do something. In either case, the question of one person directly intersects the behavior of another person: either the person asked will be persuaded to impart something or to agree to do something. Therefore, in all cases questions attempt to persuade a hearer to change their next course of action. While it is true that all communication is in essence persuasive,[13] questions occupy a special persuasive role in engaging hearers. As we know from experience, asking for something is far more persuasive (in most cases) than simply making statements about things.[14]

To accomplish this special rhetorical role in information exchange and request for behavior change in the broader scope of everyday communication, there must be many different kinds of questions with many different persuasive effects and many different intentional outcomes. The near limitless situations in which one person needs to engage another person require near limitless types of questions. One important writer in the history of the study of questions is Marcus Quintilian (AD 35–ca. 95), a rhetorician and lawyer. With his practice in these areas, Quintilian understood that there was an infinite variety of question types.[15] Having said this, readers may begin to wonder how this fits in with the two "types" of questions that English speakers are most familiar with: informational and rhetorical. As we will discuss extensively below, these two categories

11. Hintikka, Halonen, and Mutanen, "Interrogative Logic," 295.
12. See for example, Carawan, "*Erotesis*."
13. Kennedy, *Classical Rhetoric*, 2.
14. Quintilian, *Institutio oratoria* 9.2.8.
15. Ibid., 9.2.10.

are not really categories; they are broad terms that have become almost meaningless. All questions—by their nature as questions—are *both* informational *and* rhetorical. The concept of the "rhetorical question" is a late invention; there is no similar all-inclusive category in thinkers such as Quintilian or in the rhetorical and grammatical manuals from antiquity.[16] So as to prepare the reader for later chapters: there is no such thing in ancient Greek (or the GNT) as a "rhetorical question." To be more accurate, there is no such thing as a "rhetorical question" as *all questions are rhetorical to some degree*. In fact, what English readers overlook the most is that "rhetorical questions" ask just as much as informational questions ask, *as all questions are informational to some degree.*[17] To say that a question is a "rhetorical question" is to say nothing at all about the question.

In English grammar, one of the primary characteristics of the "rhetorical question" is that they do not seek an answer. This perspective fundamentally misunderstands the act of asking a question. All questions are asked—and this includes questions asked in ancient texts—for someone to give some answer somehow. When dealing with "rhetorical questions," there is a difference between saying "rhetorical questions don't seek an answer" and saying "rhetorical questions don't need an explicit answer." When asked, the questions most often labeled as "rhetorical questions" are answered internally or are intentionally inapposite (§4.M) or create an i-predicament (§2.C.7) or one of any other rhetorical effects; hence, they do not encourage an explicit answer (or one may embarrass oneself by replying, in some cases). If there is really no such thing as a "rhetorical question," why do we so quickly label a question "rhetorical" in the GNT? Besides our training in English grammar, it is because the familiarity of the Bible coupled with the familiarity for how one is supposed to read the texts of the Bible means that most readers early on are pragmatically conditioned to see the texts in the Bible as "telling and never asking." The result is that we are not actually reading 15% of the NT.

Throughout this book, we will refer regularly to two primary qualities that shape the use of questions in language. These two qualities are the *logic* of questions and the *rhetoric* of questions. For the purpose of this book, we chose these two qualities to serve as umbrella terms to help the reader understand the two most important qualities for the way questions work within discourse. (1) The *logic* of a question covers how the writer forms the question and how that question works within its grammatical-linguistic constraints. So for example, when we encounter a question that starts with a π-word, we will see that its formation and logic will be (most likely) built around the π-word. The logic of the question indicates what answer it seeks or information it requests. (2) The *rhetoric* of a question encompasses the way in which the question affects the surrounding

16. Fahnestock, "*Quid Pro Nobis*," 198.
17. Slot, *How Can You Say That?*, 85.

narrative context as well as the effect the question might have on the reader. To be successful in interpreting a question in the New Testament, both of these two qualities must be recognized and addressed—one cannot simply jump to the rhetorical effect of a question without coming to terms with its internal logic. There are other qualities that questions possess beyond these two, of course, but I have found that these two are the most useful for an effective assessment of the meaning of a question within the GNT.

Key Bibliography

Allen, "Understanding," 437–48; Brueggemann, "Jeremiah's Use," 358–74; Johnson, "Rhetorical Question"; Kuntz, "Form, Location, and Function," 121–42; Moshavi, "Positive Rhetorical Question," 253–73; Moshavi, "Two Types," 32–46; Porter, "Argument," 655–77; Watson, "Corinthians," 301–18; Wellman, "Socratic Method."

C. Questions in the GNT

Before we turn to study the questions of the GNT in detail, we will start with an overview of these questions to gain a better idea of the bigger picture. By my count, there are approximately 980 direct questions in the GNT. This number is not a firm number, as there are several questions we include that may not be questions, and it is possible that some sentences were originally meant to be primarily interrogative in force but have, over time, lost their sense of interrogativity and are now read as propositions (e.g., John 2:4b). My estimation is that the exact number of questions could vary by as much as ±3% from our standard number of 980. However, we will use this number as a base on which to standardize our overview.

The first statistic we address in understanding the makeup of interrogativity in the GNT is the gross distribution of questions, meaning the raw number of questions per text. The gross distribution of questions in the GNT is presented in the chart at the top of page 26. As we can see, the gross distribution of questions in the GNT is illuminating in at least one aspect: Some texts are heavy in questions and some texts have few or no questions. On the one hand, all four Gospels, Acts, Romans, 1–2 Corinthians, Galatians, Hebrews, and James seem to have a sizable number of questions included in their texts. On the other hand, 2 Timothy, Titus, Philemon, 2 John, 3 John, and Jude have no questions in their texts! (Is this book unusable for interpreting those books? No, because as a primary communicative force, interrogativity can be found in nonquestions also; §2.C.1). Evaluating this information reveals several interesting points:

- *Genre is a strong indicator of question use.* All four Gospels are heavily dependent on the use of questions. Each of the four Gospels is a

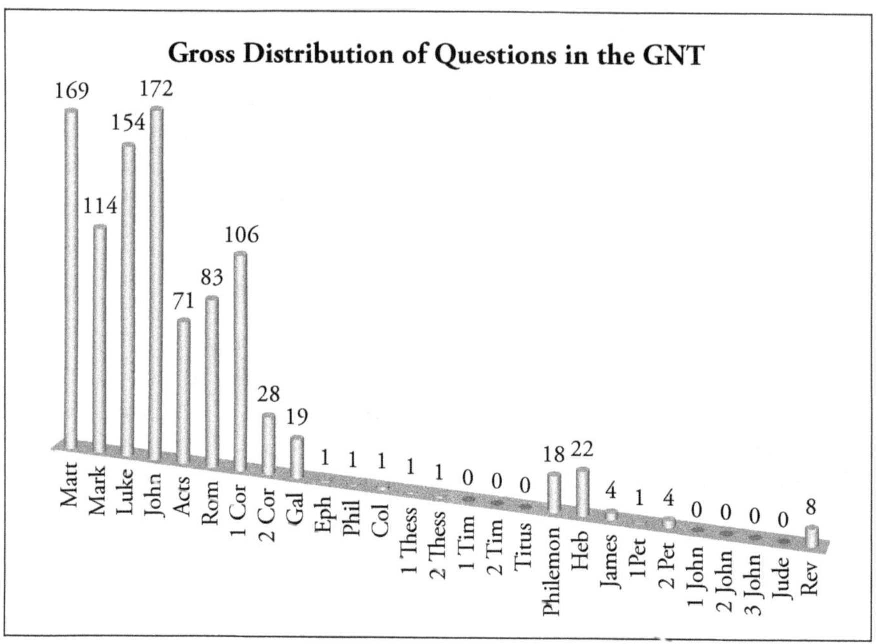

narrative, with strong interest in one protagonist and a great deal of direct discourse. Acts is also narrative, though it has less focus on one protagonist and less focus on direct discourse (choosing instead longer speeches), and—perhaps therefore—fewer questions than the Gospels. Among the letters, longer letters with more complex issues seem to possess more questions, whereas the very short writings seem to have few or no questions. Interestingly, Revelation does have a few questions, all of which occur during heavenly conversations and none of which are found in the epistolary sections. The relationship between genre and question usage is not limited to the GNT, as it is a notable feature throughout IE texts (see also §2.D.5).[18]

- *Questions are an important feature of narrative.* One important property of narrative, especially narrative with direct discourse, is *verisimilitude* (the quality of being lifelike). Since questions are an important fea-

18. In a related study, Andreas Willi tested a wide range of syntactical issues across three different text types in Attic Greek. When it came to direct questions, Willi found that the sample passages of Attic historiography had no direct questions, the sample passages of Attic rhetoric had a few direct questions, and the sample passages of Attic narrative-with-direct-discourse had numerous direct questions. While Willi's analysis is a small sampling, and ours is far more exhaustive, what is most interesting is the noninterrogative tendency of Attic historiography versus the tendency toward some direct interrogativity in Acts. It comes as no surprise that direct discourse in both Attic and Koine contains the most questions. For more details, see Willi, "Register Variation," 306–8.

ture of human communication, and since good narrative will portray human communication accurately, good narrative will make good use of questions.

- *Questions are an important feature of sustained rhetorical texts.* Rhetorical texts, or texts with a great degree of rhetorical emphasis and features, can employ questions effectively. It stands to reason that longer rhetorical texts are more likely to use a variety of rhetorical features, including questions, with more frequency and variety, than shorter, "to-the-point" rhetorical texts. In the GNT, this seems to be the case; longer, more complex letters with notable rhetorical development appear to make greater use of questions than shorter, less complex letters with much less rhetorical development. This is a general statement that deserves greater investigation at another time.
- *Questions are a weak indicator of authorship.* Authorship is of keen interest in the study of the GNT, especially among the various letters. However, the gross distribution of questions in the GNT does not appear to speak conclusively to this issue. The fact that 1–2 Corinthians possess a great deal of questions and 1–2 Thessalonians do not could be an argument for/against certain authorship, much in the same way as 1 John possesses some questions and 2 and 3 John possess none. However, questions are such a common and general feature of human communication that the divide between use/nonuse of questions seems much more distinguishable between genres rather than authors.

Next, we consider the breakdown of questions in the GNT by their formation. In IE languages, there are essentially four different ways that questions are formed: *polar questions* (§3.A), *variable questions* (§3.B), *alternative questions* (§3.C), and *set questions* (§3.D). In addition, there are also a few questions that are compounds or deviations of the four basic formations, and we lump those together as *composites* (§3.E). Since composite questions base their formations on the basic four, they are not distinguished as such in this chart. The breakdown of questions in the GNT by formation is presented in the chart at the top of page 28. As we can see, the texts of the GNT use variable questions and polar questions the most, and alternative and set questions far less. This breakdown conforms with common, direct discourse expectations for IE languages. Among the top two, variable questions are more prevalent than polar questions. While we want to be careful drawing conclusions from this data, we can offer a few tentative suggestions:

- *Questions in the GNT favor thought-provoking forms.* Variable questions, by their nature, gravitate toward information gathering and encouraging the reader to think deeply.

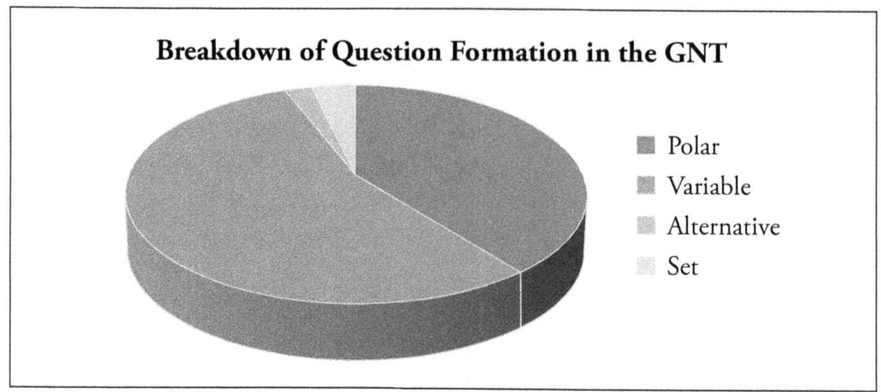

- *Questions in the GNT call for decision making.* Polar questions, by their nature, gravitate toward calls for decision and action. As a notable subset of questions in the GNT, the polar questions within do call for some response among audience(s).
- *Questions in the GNT do not favor intricate wordplays.* In a general way, set questions, alternative questions, and composite questions are less frequent in human communication than variable questions and polar questions due to the unusual situations they create and help maintain. The fact that there are as many of these forms of questions in the GNT as there are means the texts do not shy away from complex situations, but it is not the norm for these texts, either.

When we consider the breakdown of questions by formation within the individual texts of the GNT, interesting features emerge. For example, the book of Revelation contains only *one* type of question formation, the variable question. Although the gross number of questions is small, it is still statistically interesting. In conclusion, this overview to the questions in the GNT is valuable for general considerations but should not be used for drawing hard conclusions.

Key Bibliography

Babbitt, *Grammar*, §570–81; Estes, *Questions*, 33–56; Goodwin, *Greek Grammar*, §1600–1606; McKay, *New Syntax*, §11; Morwood, *Oxford Grammar*, 161–67; Thompson, *Usage*, 3–5.

A Note on Questions in Modern English Versions of the New Testament

In this book, we work from the presupposition that there are ±980 direct questions in the GNT. However, if we were to search modern English versions of the New Testament for questions, we would come up with a slightly different number than 980 and would also come up with a slightly different number for different versions. There are several reasons for this, but the most basic is that different translators have different criteria for rendering a sentence as a question or as a statement. Unfortunately, as with any translation process, some of these criteria are more harmful to questions than others. One of the greatest weaknesses in this process is when an English translation (unintentionally) changes the logic of a question, or worse, renders a question as a statement (which forces the unassuming reader to use alethic rather than erotetic logic to decode the utterance). For example, Hebrews 12:9 is sometimes translated as a statement rather than as a question:

> εἶτα τοὺς μὲν τῆς σαρκὸς ἡμῶν πατέρας εἴχομεν παιδευτὰς καὶ ἐνετρεπόμεθα· οὐ πολὺ [δὲ] μᾶλλον ὑποταγησόμεθα τῷ πατρὶ τῶν πνευμάτων καὶ ζήσομεν;
>
> HEBREWS 12:9

- We have all had fathers here on earth who disciplined us, and we respected them. So it is even more important that we accept discipline from the Father of our spirits so we will have life. (NCV)
- Moreover, we have all had human fathers who disciplined us and we respected them for it. How much more should we submit to the Father of spirits and live! (NIV)

In doing this, these English versions replace the original question asking with statement telling, which alters the original logic of the utterance for the English reader. The original question logic is more along the lines of:

- In fact, we have had human fathers who disciplined us, and we respected them; but will we not obey the spiritual father so much more, and live?

The NCV and NIV make a smoother translation than mine above, but at the expense of removing a question directed at the reader of the letter. For the interpreter of the GNT, we want to come to terms with the internal logic of the utterance as it was made, not as it is interpreted through translation.

Another example of this problem comes in 1 John 2:22:

> Τίς ἐστιν ὁ ψεύστης εἰ μὴ ὁ ἀρνούμενος ὅτι Ἰησοῦς οὐκ ἔστιν ὁ Χριστός;

- Who is the liar? It is whoever denies that Jesus is the Christ. (NIV)
- And who is a liar? Anyone who says that Jesus is not the Christ. (NLT)

However, if we want to see this question in English with a more accurate question logic, we could render it more like this:

- Who is the liar if not but the one denying that Jesus is the Christ?[19]

Here the English translations alter the erotetic logic of the sentence by simplifying the question, which reduces the impact of the original question's logic.

The issue here is not to quibble over translation strategy, which in my mind is not the issue, but over a change in the internal logic of the verses. In a few cases, it is really going from apples to oranges! The reason why this is a large concern is that the logic and rhetoric of the sentence was changed for the reader during the translation process. Sometimes, in translation, this type of situation is unavoidable; but for the exegete, we are able to restore a closer-to-the-original logic and rhetoric to the sentence. This situation is not common, but we note it at the outset.

Key Bibliography

Cohen, "What Is a Question?," 350–64; Estes, *Questions*, 39–42; Groenendijk and Stokhof, "Studies," 3–7; Hagstrom, "Questions," 478–92; Llewelyn, "What Is a Question?," 69–85.

D. How to Use This Book

This book is intended as a ready resource and reference for interpreting the questions found in the GNT (and may prove useful in other venues as well, such as the Septuagint or the Greek fathers). It is organized around a grammatical-linguistic approach to the questions within the GNT. In some ways, this book is different than other language resources because it is not "flat" but presupposes several levels to the study. To make the most of the study, each level should be taken into account by the reader. Therefore, as it is a resource book, the reader may skip around and use this book in whatever order they see fit as long as they understand how these levels work together.

This book utilizes insights from both grammatical studies and linguistic studies to study questions in the GNT. This is somewhat different from the way Koine Greek is often taught today, especially in the beginning stages where most focus is placed on the grammar of the language. However, grammar is but one subset of the larger linguistic enterprise. *Grammar* examines the morphology and the syntax of a language, whereas *linguistics* can cover every part of language from phonetics to sociolinguistics (including morphology and syntax). Sometimes scholars refer to linguistics as a science, but it is really no more of a science than grammar; it does tend to be more complicated because it covers larger areas (*CDL* 269). In order to understand best how questions function

19. Here I use "if not but" as a way to communicate in English the multiple bias words that are well-formed in Greek.

in the GNT, we need to expand our area of study to areas outside of grammar (morphology and syntax). With that being said, there is nothing in this book that cannot be understood apart from basic Greek grammar and the application of a little logic. A student does not need to be familiar with linguistics to profit from this book (though some basic knowledge of linguistics would add to the profit). In addition, because this book is about questions and question logic, many of the grammatical and linguistics ideas and terms will only be mentioned in light of the relationship to questions. Therefore, it goes without saying that many of these ideas and terms have different meanings and uses in other areas of grammar and linguistics (for example, polarity in §2.B.8).

Each question type will be broken down into six sections:

Subsection	Purpose
Intro	Defines the question type and provides an overview of its use in discourse.
Formation	Explains how this type of question is created, what is required of its type, and what tells are available to recognize this type.
Rhetorical Effects	Explains what effect this type of question has within the context in which it is found, and what effect it may have on hearers/readers.
Case Studies	Provides one or more detailed examples of this type of question as found in the GNT.
Further Examples	Other select examples of questions that display a similar erotetic logic to the question type.
Key Bibliography	Lists a number of resources for further study ("food for thought") on subjects discussed.

When working through the logic and rhetoric of a question in the GNT, it is important not to dislocate the question from its context. Each question in the GNT is an utterance that is one small part of a larger utterance. To extract a question from its context removes the question from its native environment and severs its logical and rhetorical ties meant to offer clues as to the interpretation of the question. While this is true of propositions, this is (if possible) even more true of questions.

Chapter 2

The Basics of Question Formation

The formation of questions in the GNT proceeds comparably to the formation of questions in most other Indo-European (IE) languages, in that questions only contain a few minor differences in construction that distinguish them from propositions or other types of utterances. In some situations, the difference between the formation of a question and of a proposition will be easy to distinguish, such as when the question begins with an interrogative variable (§2.B.10). However, it can also be at times impossible to clearly know when a sentence in Koine Greek is meant as a question and when it is meant as a proposition. In fact, writers of the GNT will at times form questions in the exact same way (without syntactical distinction) as they would a similar proposition, which makes identifying questions in the GNT a challenge. In this chapter, we cover numerous factors that affect question formation in the GNT, broken down into sections on where the effect is most felt.

One Positive Thing to Know about Question Formation

One positive thing to know about question formation in the Greek of the NT is that, as a rule, it makes sense and is logical. Furthermore, almost all the questions in the GNT follow a regular logic that is not hard to decipher (once one begins to think through questions as questions). This is great news, because language interpretation is hard enough without a great deal of irregularities making things more difficult. There are a few exceptions, but those are still not that exceptional. The value of this positive is that once one learns how Greek question logic works in the GNT, this logic will also work in the interpretation of the LXX, the Greek Apocrypha, the Greek fathers, and to some degree other texts within the IE language family. As we interpret questions throughout this book using erotetic logic, we will follow the rules for this type of logic even when this leads us to a disagreement with traditional interpretations.

One Negative Thing to Know about Question Types

One negative thing to know about question types in the Greek of the NT is that, as a rule, they resist easy categorization. This is not just a challenge for questions in the GNT—this is true of any attempt to categorize utterances within any natural language. It is the dynamic nature of natural language that resists and works against easy categorization. While the syntactical formations of questions in the GNT are relatively easy to master, the semantic and pragmatic values that need to be discerned from those questions are much more a challenge. It is those parts of interrogative logic that do the most to resist easy categorization. And the more complicated the question, the less easy it is to identify neatly. As a result, many of the questions of the GNT will fit more than one type of question. This is where your role as the interpreter comes in: Even as this book gives a start to understanding the questions in the GNT, there is still the vitally important function of interpretation that you'll need to apply to these questions in order to determine their primary purpose in biblical context. Knowing the information—acquiring the tools—in this book is only half the step.

When it comes to the basic formation of questions, almost all human languages have some type of indicator(s) for interrogativity. While every language is different, many of the indicators are universal (even if applied differently in different languages). Also, sometimes these indicators are more pronounced in some situations and less pronounced in others. We call these indicators *tells*, as they are signs of questions in natural language. The tells in natural language for interrogativity are:

- Interrogative force (including intonation/stress/rhythm/prosody)
- Interrogative adverbs/adjectives/pronouns (such as "why" and "when")
- Interrogative particles (such as the discourse particle ἆρα in ancient Greek)
- Positive-negative conjuncted clauses (in certain languages such as Mandarin, or certain formations such as tag questions)
- Subject-verb inversion (common in SVO languages such as English, French)
- Cleft construction for interrogative use (in certain languages such as French)
- Object-pronoun transformation (in certain languages such as Sanskrit)[1]

Looking over the list, the question may arise: "What about question marks?" Because of the unique challenges related to punctuation, we do not include it here as a tell for interrogativity (though it certainly can be a strong indicator in

1. This list is adapted from Estes, *Questions*, 37–38.

modern texts; see §2.B.4). It is also not an actual factor in question formation in the GNT.

When it comes to Koine Greek, the only three tells that are in play for the sake of our discussion here are the first three: interrogative force (§2.C.1), interrogative adverbs (§2.B.10), and discourse particles (§2.B.7). The second and third of these are challenges, but they have parameters to guide the exegete. Of the three, the first is by far the most difficult to come to terms with, as interrogative force gets to the heart of the contextual meaning and use of questions as we find them in play in the GNT.

A. The Parts of Language

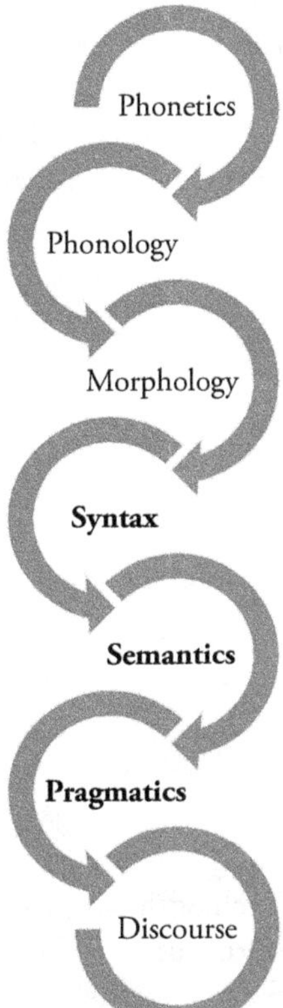

Human communication is incredibly complex, and the study of language recognizes the complexity of it. In recognition of this, the study of language is often broken down into more manageable parts. This was true in the ancient Greek-speaking world, and it is (even more) true today. When we break language down into smaller parts, we can achieve better comprehension of the use of language, though there is always a small price to pay as we are eliminating some parts out of the study. The modern study of languages (linguistics) recognizes at least eight major parts to the comprehensive study of language:

> Starting from the bottom, [we ground] language first in the physical world of sound (phonetics) and moving up through the organization of sound in language (phonology), to the combination of sounds into words (morphology), and the combination of words into sentences (syntax). Meaning (semantics) usually comes next, on the grounds that it operates on words and sentences. These areas are traditionally said to form the core of linguistics, because they deal with the most formally structured aspects of language. Within the last few decades, however, linguists have come to realize that we cannot understand the most formally structured aspects of language without also understanding the way language is used to convey information (pragmatics) in conversation (discourse) and in literature, and the way language interacts with other aspects of society (sociolinguistics).[2]

These eight parts are not always dealt with equally, and linguists strongly debate how each of these intersect with each other. In this book, we will focus our

2. Aronoff and Rees-Miller, *Handbook of Linguistics*, xv.

attention on the *syntax*, *semantics*, and *pragmatics* of the questions in the GNT. Each of these parts of language are important for the study of language, and each play a role in the determination of interrogative force in natural-language situations. However, given that our interest is in the GNT, several other of these parts of language are beyond the scope of our work. For example, if modern readers better understood the phonetics and phonology of Koine Greek, we could interpret the questions in the GNT much more accurately. Likewise, the value of questions in the GNT in light of their function in discourse and sociolinguistic situations is important but would move us beyond our primary goal.

By focusing on the syntax, semantics, and pragmatics of questions, what we are saying in a simple way is that we are focusing on the *form*, the *meaning*, and the *use* of questions in the GNT. Therefore, our concerns will be on how the writers of the GNT created their questions, what they were trying to ask—not say —by way of their questions, and how their questions affected the remainder of the discourse around them. We illustrate our focus:

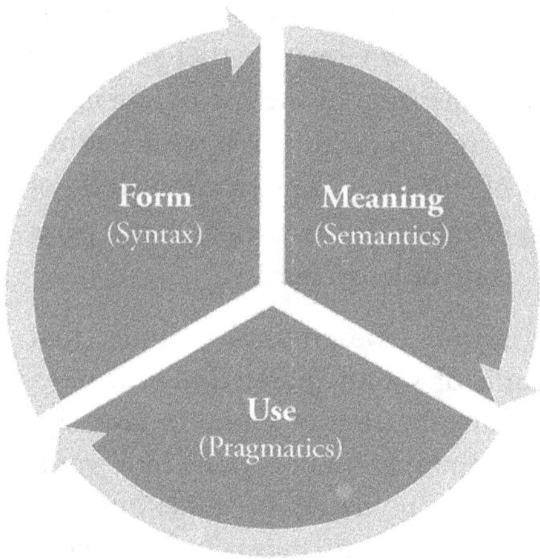

Each of these three areas represent large fields of study and are beyond the scope of this book. What we will do in the next section is survey a number of features from these fields that directly impact the study of questions. We cannot cover everything in detail and will out of necessity omit many smaller topics, such as interrogative pressure and question absorption in hearers/learners.

Key Bibliography

Aronoff and Rees-Miller, *Handbook of Linguistics*, xiv–xv; Baker and Hengeveld, *Linguistics*, 22–24; Finch, *Linguistics*, 166–67; Pavlidou, "Units-Levels"; Szabó, *Semantics versus Pragmatics*, 1–8.

B. Questions and Syntax

The first part of language wherein we will survey the way questions work is in the area of syntax. *Syntax* is "the analysis of the arrangements of words in phrases, phrases in clauses and clauses in sentences and the grammatical relations between them" (*CDL* 431). The syntax of questions concerns itself with how these questions are formed. Syntax is the most straightforward part of question interpretation, partly because it tends to be more concrete and partly because Greek grammarians have spent more time studying it in relation to the GNT than the other areas. Another positive for approaching the syntax of questions in the GNT first is that most syntactical ideas are nearly universal across human languages.[3] Therefore, while we cannot confuse English with Greek, there is nothing in our discussion of Greek questions that will be completely alien to English syntax (different, yes; alien, no). Below we consider several of the most important factors that shape the syntax of questions.

Key Bibliography
Boas and Huitink, "Syntax," 134–50; Estes, *Questions*, 43–45; Robertson, *Grammar*, 379–89; Tallerman, *Understanding Syntax*, 1–24; Wackernagel, *Lectures*, 7–33.

---

1. Sentence Formation

A *sentence* (λόγος) is a syntactical construction of one or more clauses and either represents the highest form of grammatical concern or the lowest form of discourse interest (*CDL* 400).[4] A sentence can be as small as one word or as great as one can imagine (assuming the increasing complexity of multiple clauses makes sense—and in Paul's writing, it certainly seems to). Sentences are constructed of words, and whenever two or more words are put together to form a sentence there is always the question of how well that sentence is formed. To communicate well, a writer must use *well-formed* sentences. However, a well-formed sentence is language dependent—meaning that the formation of a sentence in one language may be well formed but when transferred into another language is no longer considered well formed. This situation can easily be seen in the difference between Greek and English questions. For example, the question the Pharisees ask in Matthew 12:10 is well formed in the Greek:

(1) καὶ ἐπηρώτησαν αὐτὸν λέγοντες. Εἰ ἔξεστιν τοῖς σάββασιν θεραπεῦσαι;

---

3. Fromkin, Rodman, and Hyams, *Introduction to Language*, 77.
4. Prior to the writing of the GNT, λόγος was also the grammatical term for "sentence"; cf. Dionysius Thrax, *Ars Grammatica* 634.1–5; Apollonius Dyscolus, *Syntax* 3–4; cf. Plato, *Sophist* 262c.

Putting this literally into English gives us:

(2) And they asked him, "If it is lawful to heal on the Sabbath?"

Here the Greek question is well formed, but the literal English translation is not well formed. In modern English translations, this question is usually reformed by the translator to communicate in better English. However, in doing so, the logic of the conditional is dropped, and the erotetic logic of the sentence is changed to a simple polar question.

The reason for pointing this out is that a number of questions in the GNT are not well formed *based upon English expectations* (for example, request questions [§4.S]). As a result, it is especially important to work through the logic of these particular sentences in Greek only, without relying on the English equivalent. Of course, this is true with any sentence in Greek, but it is most felt when working with sentences that would not be considered well formed in English.

Key Bibliography

BDF §458; McKay, *New Syntax*, §1.6; Murphy and Koskela, *Key Terms*, 152.

---

2. Sentence Function

When is a sentence a question and not a proposition or exclamation? This is a major challenge for interpreters of the GNT. The first place to start will be to consider the syntax of the sentence. While we want to be careful not to create a "naked question" (a natural-language question divorced of its context) nor to disregard semantic or pragmatic indicators of interrogativity, the simple truth is that syntax gives—by far—the most powerful indications of whether or not a particular sentence is a question. What kind of question, though, is often driven as much by semantics and pragmatics.

Since every sentence in natural language is delimited by a certain number of words, phrases, and clauses, every sentence has a purpose and a function. Actually, every sentence in natural language will have multiple functions, but the traditional approach relies on understanding the primary function. Sentences are often thought of and spoken of in terms of their function. Traditionally, there are four primary functions for sentences: declarative, interrogative (πευστικός), exclamative, imperative.[5] A *declarative* sentence functions to say, tell, and assert. An *interrogative* sentence functions to ask, request, and deliberate. An *exclamative* sentence functions to call, shout, and emote. An *imperative* sentence functions to order, suggest, and demand.

The philosopher John Stuart Mill is noted for remarking, "The structure of

5. Modern-language studies often speak of just three: declarative, interrogative, and imperative; see König and Siemund, "Speech Act Distinctions," 277.

every sentence is a lesson in logic."[6] Mill's observation will prove to be true as we discover the meaning(s) of the questions in the GNT. Every sentence (whether a question or not) has a logic that is associated with its form, meaning, and context. This logic differs in every sentence, and every time we approach a new sentence armed to understand its logic, we get a new lesson on the subject. As we interpret sentences, we also need to remember that form does not always dictate function.[7] As a result, it is artificial to categorize sentences only by their primary function because each sentence has its own distinct logic and its own distinct set of functions. However, we will retain the traditional (and artificial) nomenclature of sentential function, as it is useful for informal categorization.

Finally, there is a strong relationship between the function of a sentence and the illocutionary force of a sentence (§2.C.1). In fact, in most cases it is the force that defines the function of the sentence. When it comes to the function of sentences, there is no final, simple differentiation into neat, traditional categories because any category created to describe function (which includes the logic and illocutionary force) can always be further subdivided.[8]

Key Bibliography

Givón, "Speech-Act Continuum," 248–51; König and Siemund, "Speech Act Distinctions," 276–84.

---

3. *Word Order*

When a writer constructs phrases, clauses, and sentences, the words in these constructions follow a pattern or order in most languages. In some languages, like English, word order is important and tends to be a major feature of acceptable language acquisition. However, in other languages, like Koine Greek, word order is not as strict. "Not as strict" does not mean free or no order; rather, it means that the way writers create order allows for more flexibility than some modern languages, such as English, tend to allow. In some places, Greek word order is as strict as English (cf. §2.B.3). In modern linguistics, the study of *information structure* has often superseded the study of word order in helping to clarify complex organizational relationships in syntax. Since scholars sorely debate the overall word order of the ancient Greek language with no concise resolution, we will skip that discussion and focus on the relationship between word order and interrogativity.[9]

---

6. Mill, *Inaugural Address*, 30.
7. Levinson, *Pragmatics*, 265.
8. Fiengo, *Asking Questions*, 170.
9. Further, I view the word order of GNT interrogatives as largely unaffected by Semitic influence; for more discussion, see Porter, *Verbal Aspect*, 145; and contra Niccacci, "Marked Syntactical Structures."

Word order plays an important syntactic role in the identification of some formations of questions in the GNT. In languages such as English, word order is overall a strong indicator of interrogativity; in Koine Greek, it is overall only a weak indicator. More specifically, word order in the Greek of the NT is a nonindicator of interrogativity in polar questions (§3.A), a strong indicator of interrogativity in variable questions (§3.B), a weak indicator of interrogativity in alternative questions (§3.C), and a strong indicator of interrogativity in set questions (§3.D). Additionally, word order is a weak indicator of interrogativity in most composite questions (§3.E). Of these, the most challenging is the polar question. In English, the polar question has a clear indicator in word order, but in Koine Greek not only is there no indicator, but the polar question maintains the same word order as the corresponding proposition. For example, if in English we wanted to ask if someone understood everything, we would ask:

(1) Have you understood everything? (QUESTION)

The word order of this question (1) is distinct from the word order of the corresponding proposition (2):

(2) You have understood everything. (PROPOSITION)

As a result of English's strict word order, we would not consider either of the following sentences (3) or (4) well formed in English:

(3) You have understood everything? (QUESTION)
(4) Have you understood everything. (PROPOSITION)

Note that word order drives the meaning coming from the syntax, not the punctuation; if you were to read (5) in English:

(5) Have you understood everything...

You would naturally read it with interrogative force due to word-order constraints on well-formed polar questions in English.

Turning to Koine Greek, we do not have the same word-order indicators. Matthew 13:51 (6) asks a similar question as above:

(6) Συνήκατε ταῦτα πάντα; (QUESTION)

However, if we were to write the sentence in Greek as the corresponding proposition, the sentence (7) would read:

(7) Συνήκατε ταῦτα πάντα. (PROPOSITION)

Again, note that punctuation plays no role in the determination of sentential function or illocutionary force as there is no punctuation in the earliest manuscripts (§2.B.4). Thus, word order is a nonindicator for identifying polar questions in the GNT. In contrast, word order is a strong indicator of variable questions in the GNT (cf. §2.B.11). Word order is a syntactic feature that can (in some situations) indicate interrogativity, but it should not be the deciding factor for identifying questions in the GNT.

Key Bibliography
Boas and Huitink, "Syntax," 148–49; McKay, *New Syntax*, §1.7; Pitts, "Greek Word Order," 311–46.

---

4. Punctuation

Punctuation (στιγμή) is a standardized and convenient feature of modern languages, but it was also a feature largely absent from languages before the invention of printing. As a result, modern readers are at a disadvantage when reading ancient languages, because modern readers are so accustomed to receiving syntactic, semantic, and pragmatic clues from punctuation marks included in modern texts. In fact, modern texts' use of punctuation becomes almost a canonical issue in the sense that once a modern text is created and punctuated, a later editor, publisher, or reader cannot simply alter the punctuation as they see fit, no more than they could alter the words. Thus, one of the great challenges for the modern reader of the GNT is to come to terms with the *psychology* of punctuation.

Ancient Greek, from its first articulation as a written language up until its form in late antiquity, followed the practice of *scriptio continua*, a letter-by-letter writing style without distinction between words or sentences. Punctuation in Greek language occurs as early as the eighth-century BC, but this initial punctuation was purely to clarify the beginning and ending of words, and with later texts, phrases (a system replaced in late antiquity by the *space*).[10] As frustrating as it can seem to a modern reader to decipher *scriptio continua*, the lack of clarification on wording was also at times frustrating to educated ancients as well.[11] The earliest literary text with punctuation is probably the Derveni Papyrus (ca. fourth-century BC). Tradition holds that Aristophanes of Byzantium (ca. 257–180 BC) created a system of punctuation, which is certainly possible, and Nicanor of Alexandria (ca. second-century AD) almost certainly did, though neither system appears to have taken hold in any significant way. Dionysius Thrax (ca. 170–90 BC) knew of punctuation, but later editing of his work is possible.[12] From the eighth century up until late antiquity, punctuation of any sort was always an on-again, off-again feature. By the time of the writing of the

10. Tsantsanoglou, "Punctuation," 1327; and Coakley, "Early Syriac Question Mark," 211.
11. Aristotle, *Rhetoric* 1407b11–19.
12. Dionysius names the three puncuation types as τελεία, μέση, and ὑποστιγμή; see Dionysius Thrax, *Ars Grammatica* 630.6–15.

New Testament, some minimal punctuation was applied at times to older literary works to aid contemporary readers. For example, in the Greek of 7Q1 (ca. 100 BC), the LXX of Exodus 28:4–6, the roll includes what appears to be a couple ὑποστιγμή, or lowstop, which has a pause value similar to a comma today. As a result, we can be certain that the writers of the GNT understood punctuation (in at least some rudimentary manner), though they were unlikely to have used any in the original editions. Modern readers who have seen ancient Greek papyri following the practice of *scriptio continua* may incorrectly assume that the earliest New Testament manuscripts never had punctuation. They did, but it was sporadic and nonstandardized. For example 𝔓46 (ca. AD 200) makes use of spaces in some places plus the occasional diaresis and breathing marks. Punctuation also occurs in early manuscripts such as 𝔓45, 𝔓66, S, and B. The first question marks (ἐρωτηματικόν) in Greek texts did not appear until the ninth-century AD and took a form similar to the English semicolon (;). It is likely that an early Syriac New Testament (the Peshitta) included a type of punctuation mark to note polar questions.[13]

When a modern reader of the GNT sees punctuation in a modern English version, it can be difficult to recognize it as a form of interpretation, much like chapterification and versification is. This is part of the challenge of the psychology of punctuation—overcoming our modern tendency to see punctuation as authoritative (when reading ancient texts). What is more, when we turn to modern editions of the GNT, the punctuation there is also a modern form of interpretation applied to an ancient text; yet this punctuation is neither canonical nor authoritative. (This is not to disparage the work of modern GNT editions!) This is true even of any ancient attempts at punctuation that we find in early manuscripts.[14] However, the *punctuation of questions is the most tenuous of all punctuation in the GNT.*[15] Therefore, all the questions of the GNT are subject to discussion; in such a large body of literature there are certainly sentences punctuated today as statements that are really questions (and vice versa). The good news, though, is that we can distinguish questions from propositions in the GNT with a high degree of certainty, based first on grammar and second on linguistic features.

Finally, punctuation is not the final answer for determining sentential function. Its primary purpose is to create divisions of different degree among the various units of a text.[16] A further reason for this is that punctuation is akin to words. It has a "semantic" range, so to speak, which allows some question marks to be used in modern literature for deeply thoughtful questions and in other places in the same text for much more shallow questions that border on

13. Coakley, "Early Syriac Question Mark," 201–3.
14. Metzger, *Manuscripts*, §19; Moulton, *Grammar*, 2:48.
15. BDF §16.
16. *CDL* 366; Crystal, *How Language Works*, 118–20.

assertions. Even with modern texts, linguists should not base sentential differentiation solely on punctuation.[17] Punctuation is not, by definition, a definitive indicator, and whether in ancient or modern texts is best understood as a hint or clue for the reader rather than an answer to the purpose of the sentence.

Key Bibliography

BDF §16; Blass, *Grammar*, 17; Coakley, "Early Syriac Question Mark"; Colvin, *Brief History*, 84–85; Estes, *Questions*, 8–9; Metzger, *Manuscripts*, §19; Moulton, *Grammar*, 2:46–49; Nunberg, *Linguistics of Punctuation*; Randolph, "Sign of Interrogation"; Tsantsanoglou, "Punctuation"; West, *Textual Criticism*, 54–55.

---

5. Mood

Mood has two different meanings in modern language studies, and we can distinguish these two meanings as *verbal* (or traditional) *mood* and *sentential mood*. Throughout this book, we will use the simple term *mood* to refer only to verbal mood, or mood as it has traditionally been understood throughout grammatical history. In contrast to the traditional view, sentential mood differentiates sentences based on their communicative potential or their semantic properties.[18] Redeploying the word *mood* this way for English-language study can work, since English has mostly lost its original verbal moods, but it does not work for Koine Greek. Especially when studying ancient languages, this confuses (semantic) force with (syntactic) mood. We point this out this way as the relationship between mood and force is not always obvious for English speakers, and there are at least two major erotetic theories that argue that questions are indeed a subset of mood.[19]

Mood (ἔγκλῖσις) is the morphological feature of a verb that specifies the quality or degree of its potentiality.[20] For most modern interpreters, the four moods of Koine Greek are indicative (ὁριστική), subjunctive (ὑποτακτική), imperative (προστακτική), and optative (εὐκτική). The ancient grammarians did not always agree with this assessment; Dionysius Thrax believed there to be five different moods (the standard four plus infinitive [ἀπαρέμφατος]), and Apollonius Dyscolus (ca. second-century AD) held to six different moods (the standard four plus infinitive and adhortative [ὑποθετική]).[21]

---

17. Han, "Interpreting Interrogatives," 216.
18. Akmajian et al., *Linguistics*, 246; Kroeger, *Analyzing Grammar*, 163.
19. For example, Wilson and Sperber, *Meaning and Relevance*, 211, 221–27; plus Bell, "Questioning," 193; Dickman, "Dialogue and Divinity."
20. Wallace, *Greek Grammar*, 443–45.
21. See Dionysius Thrax, *Ars Grammatica* 638.7–8; Apollonius Dyscolus, *Syntax* 361.7–11; 364.8–365.4.

There is no interrogative mood in ancient Greek, nor is interrogativity expressed by way of mood. In fact, interrogativity is not expressed as a verbal mood in any IE language.[22] However, mood *does* affect the erotetic logic of a question. A classic example of this impact is in the deliberative question, which frequently uses a verb in the subjunctive mood to indicate uncertainty and facilitate deliberation (§4.D). Koine Greek can allow for well-formed questions in all four moods, but writers of the GNT tended to form direct questions in the indicative and subjunctive moods and only very rarely in the imperative (e.g., John 4:7) or optative (e.g., Acts 8:31).[23] While the exact relationship between interrogative use and mood is not well established, it is probable that Greek is close to many other IE languages in that interrogative force trumps mood.[24] This allows greatest flexibility in the asking of questions, with many options for shaping their meaning and with little difference from propositions in this regard.

Key Bibliography

Akmajian et al., *Linguistics*, 246–50; Blass, *Grammar*, §63; Boas and Huitink, "Syntax," 138–39; Burton, *Syntax*, 5; Hahn, "Apollonius Dyscolus," 29–48; Lyons, *Theoretical Linguistics*, 307–9; McKay, *New Syntax*, §5; Moulton, *Grammar*, 1:164–201; Wallace, *Greek Grammar*, 442–93; Wilson and Sperber, *Meaning and Relevance*, 210–29.

6. Reducibility of Questions

One issue that sometimes arises in the study of questions is their *reducibility*. What this usually means in everyday language is, "Can a question be reduced to a statement, so that there is no need to deal with it as a question with erotetic logic?" Linguists have heavily debated this issue, and in the past the argument for the reducibility of questions was more popular than it is today. The simple explanation for this is that if a question can be reduced to a proposition, it makes for a neater logic for the linguist to work with. However, mounting evidence from natural-language use makes a strong case against reduction.

One reason we do not want to interpret the questions in the GNT by reducing them to some form of propositional thought is that we lose the *original intent* of them as questions.[25] In other words, linguists can try to reduce simple sample questions that they create themselves to propositions all day long without violating the implications of interpreting historical (and meaningful) texts. For our

22. Szemerényi, *Indo-European Linguistics*, 230–31.
23. The optative occurs in indirect questions (e.g., Luke 1:62; 3:15; 8:9; 15:26; 18:36; 22:23; John 13:24; Acts 10:17).
24. Cf. Wallace, *Greek Grammar*, 447.
25. I use the term original intent here loosely. I am not arguing for any one interpretive theory but rather just noting their historical position.

purpose, though, the questions in the GNT were voiced as questions and read as questions for nearly two millennia, and therefore we not only do not want to reduce them to propositions (it is probably not the best linguistic strategy) but also *should* not want to reduce them to propositions. Of course, one challenge for the modern interpretation of the GNT is that interpreters *do* (perhaps unwittingly) reduce the questions of the GNT to propositions all the time in commentaries, articles, sermons, and Bible studies. We want to be consciously aware at this point that this is not a sound grammatical or linguistic interpretive strategy for the GNT.

Key Bibliography

Estes, *Questions*, 39–40; Harrah, "Logic of Questions and Answers," 40–46.

7. *Particles*

A *particle* is a part of speech that adds expression to discourse. Generally speaking, particles usually have a small range of meaning and are neither inflected nor syntactically necessary (though omission may produce a poorly formed utterance). Particles do contribute to the semantic and especially pragmatic effect of the utterance (*CDL* 136–37; 332). Particles are often classified according to their function; three are noted here. A *discourse particle* adds flavor to the utterance and provides additional pragmatic information. They are sometimes referred to as *discourse markers*. An *interrogative particle* indicates the clause is interrogative in force. Here interrogative particles do not refer to interrogative adverbs such as *when* or *how*. A *negative particle* changes polarity (most commonly in negated sentences; cf. §2.B.8). In ancient Greek, discourse particles can often indicate interrogativity or polarity; therefore, strict lines should not be drawn around any of these terms.

In Classical Greek, writers could use a number of different particles to emphasize or shape interrogative force, including ἆρα, δαί, δή, δήπου, δῆτα, ἦ, μήν, as well as ἀλλά and possibly γάρ. By the time of the GNT, many of these particles fell out of use and do not directly contribute to interrogativity. While these particles often appeared in questions in Classical Greek, even then they were more discourse particles than true interrogative particles.[26] This includes ἆρα, whose role in the GNT is to mark an expression within discourse and not to mark sentential force.[27] As a result, particles like ἆρα are *interrogative-oriented discourse particles*, and in the GNT they function as bias words or negative polarity items.[28] This is why the use of ἆρα is at times similar to the use of οὐχί in

26. Though on Classical Greek, cf. Philippaki-Warburton, "Syntax," 597–98.

27. Robertson, *Grammar*, 1176.

28. Cf. L&N 69.14; and by way of comparison, Holmes, "Interrogative *Nam*."

direct questions in the GNT—οὐχί is a negative particle, not an interrogative particle, but it is still interrogatively oriented in its use (cf. §2.B.11). Ancient writers in a predominantly oral culture used discourse particles (since there was no punctuation) to mimic verbal expression.[29] Similar interrogative-oriented discourse particles still exist in *spoken* English; some writers do capture these in order to better convey the spirit of the utterance:

(1) *Well*, where is the lantern?
(2) *Oh* . . ., do you know where the lantern is?
(3) *Hey*, where are you going?

These examples show common particles in English that convey expression, not interrogativity. However, when these particles (especially [3]) occur at the front of a written sentence in modern American English, readers can expect the possibility of a direct question. However, discourse particles such as these more likely create cohesion with the previous utterance than predict the forthcoming utterance.[30] These particles do not convey interrogativity but color the semantics and pragmatics of the utterance.

Key Bibliography
Blass, *Grammar*, §77.2; BDF §440; Boas and Huitink, "Syntax," 138–39; Caragounis, *Development of Greek*, 205–6; Denniston, *Particles*; Drummen, "Discourse Cohesion"; König and Siemund, "Speech Act Distinctions," 294–96; Sicking, "Particles"; Thrall, *Particles*.

---

8. *Polarity*

(Logical) *polarity* is a syntactical property of clause structure that is best defined by the semantic opposition it creates. In the study of questions, polarity is generally used as a way to describe the impact of negation (or nonnegation) on the logic of a particular question. In the most simple terms, a sentence with some type of negation is said to possess a negative polarity, and a sentence with either no negation or, in rarer cases, self-cancelling double negation is said to possess a positive polarity. These terms, *positive polarity* and *negative polarity*, describe situations that are created through syntax, but they are not syntactical values; they reflect the semantic effect of certain words or syntax on erotetic logic. Every clause possesses either a positive or negative polarity, and complex sentences (such as composite questions, §3.E) can possess different polarities in different clauses.

---

29. For example, Dionysius Thrax lists ἆρα as a conjunction that suggests hesitation or doubt; see Dionysius Thrax, *Ars Grammatica* 643.9; cf. Robins, *Byzantine Grammarians*, 85.

Indo-European languages tend to have a natural state for polarity—positive polarity—and this is true for Greek as well. The most common way for a sentence to switch polarities is for it to include a polarity item (often a particle or adverb). A *positive polarity item* (PPI) has the ability to hold a sentence to a positive polarity, or to switch a sentence with a negative polarity into a sentence with a positive polarity. In Greek, PPIs are rare, and there are no obvious examples in the GNT. However, a *negative polarity item* (NPI) is quite common.[31] A negative polarity item has the ability to switch a positive polarity sentence into a negative polarity sentence. In the GNT, the most common NPIs are negative particles. Thus, GNT NPIs include μή, μήποτε, μήτι, οὐ, οὐδέ, οὐδείς, οὐδέν, οὐδέποτε, οὐκ, οὐκοῦν, οὔπω, οὐχ, and οὐχί. An abundance of NPIs seems to be common in IE languages.[32] For the sake of discussion here, these NPIs do not vary in degree; in other words, one NPI is not stronger than another, making a question "more negative," though some particles may be more emphatic (most obvious example being οὐ μή).[33] Further, a question may be more or less biased, even while maintaining its positive or negative polarity. Because of the importance of NPIs for discovering the logic of a question, they are one of the most important syntactical elements of erotetic logic for the identification of question meaning.

Since polarity is a universal property, it will affect every form and type of question that we will encounter. However, the simplest form of question where polarity plays a big part in determining the erotetic logic is the polar question. (We should not confuse polarity, in the sense of a syntactic-semantic property of a clause, with a polar question, a form of question, though the ideas are closely related.) Perhaps the greatest impact polarity has on the logic of questions is in its rhetorical force. While questions with positive polarity tend to have a small amount of rhetorical force, negative polarity tends to greatly increase the rhetorical force of a question. As a result, some types of questions are incompatible with some polarities. For example, a *negative polar question* (NPQ) cannot possess a positive polarity, because it by definition must be constructed with negative polarity; and open questions cannot possess a negative polarity, because they cannot by definition include any (noticeable) rhetorical force. Finally, polarity creates a preferred response to a question. What this means is that polarity limits the acceptable range of answers, making some possible answers problematic or

30. Drummen, "Discourse Cohesion," 136.

31. We should not confuse a negative polarity item (NPI) with what linguists sometimes call a *negative polar interrogative* (also shortened to NPI). These items are related because a negative polarity item is generally what creates a negative polar interrogative, though it also affects all other types of questions as well. In this book, we use the nomenclature *negative polar question* (NPQ) to avoid confusion and for the sake of consistency.

32. Israel, *Grammar of Polarity*, 21.

33. Zwarts (along with other linguists) argues for degrees in polarity, but given the semantic aspects I find his examples better covered under the more general focus on bias; see Zwarts, "Three Types of Polarity."

nonsensical. The preferred response situation is rooted in the syntactical properties of questions, which is what makes polarity such a powerful force in question logic.

Key Bibliography

Cruse, *Lexical Semantics*, 246–55; Krifka, "Semantics and Pragmatics"; May, "Questions as Suggestions," 238–40; van Rooy, "Negative Polarity Items," 239–73; Swart, *Expression*, 12–19.

---

9. Negation

The classical view of *negation* is that it is the contradiction of the truth or meaning of an utterance. Human language has very simple approaches to negation, such that "I am not old" is, for all intents and purposes, the contradiction of the meaning of "I am old." However, negation is far more complicated than this example reveals. Being "not old" could mean things other than a contradiction of old; it could mean "middle-aged, "dead," or "newborn," all of which are something of a contradiction of "old" but not in any way an exact contradiction. Negation is a shifting morass of syntactic structures and semantic/pragmatic values that leads to many different unique situations in natural-language use. Understanding how negation works in natural discourse is anything but simple.[34]

In order for negation to occur in a question, the negative polarity item must negate the verbal phrase carrying the interrogative force of the question. Just because a sentence contains a negative particle or negative polarity item does not mean the question asked is necessarily negative. One feature of negation (of the verbal phrase) that is almost universal is this: If an utterance has a negative polarity item, the utterance will have a negative polarity. However, if an utterance has two negative polarity items, it does not mean the utterance will be positive in polarity (though, in certain situations it could be).[35]

Based on syntax (not semantics and pragmatics), the simple rule of negation for polar questions is: if a polar question is positive, it does not expect an answer of either polarity. It is not uncommon in natural discourse for a speaker to pose positive polar questions while anticipating an answer with negative polarity. The reverse is also true. However, if a polar question is negative, it will expect a positive answer slightly more often than a negative answer. In other words, a negative polar question privileges a positive answer, whereas a positive polar question does

---

34. Israel, *Grammar of Polarity*, 20–26.

35. In English, two negatives often make a positive, so to speak; but ancient Greek is often considered a "negative concord" language, meaning that instead of cancelling, two negatives can amplify the emphasis of the negation. This issue is complex and highly debated.

not privilege an answer with either polarity. Nevertheless, negative polar questions that anticipate negative answers do occur—they are a type of confirmation question (*similar polarity question*, §4.R). For example:

(1) I did go to the store. (POSITIVE POLARITY)
(2) I didn't go to the store. (NEGATIVE POLARITY)
(3) I didn't not go to the store. (AMBIGUOUS/POSITIVE)
(4) Did I go to the store? (POSITIVE POLARITY)
(5) Didn't I go to the store? (NEGATIVE POLARITY)
(6) Didn't I not go to the store? (AMBIGUOUS/POSITIVE)

In this cluster of examples, we see negative polarity items applied to statements and questions. Statement (1) is positive with clear meaning. Statement (2) is negative with clear meaning. However, as with the above example, (2) is not an *exact* contradiction of (1), but it is *understood as* a contradiction of (1). Statement (3) contains two negatives. While one could argue the statement is positive in polarity, what it is heard as in natural discourse is ambiguous (though leaning toward positive). Thus, the more complex the negation, the less obvious the intent of the utterance becomes. Likewise, question (4) is positive polarity and can expect a "yes" or a "no" (if pushed, it leans toward "no"). Question (5) is negative polarity and tends to provoke a "yes" in response (but only a little—semantics and pragmatics play a much greater role in shaping the intent of these kinds of questions). In English, (6) is not particularly well formed, and asking this would be unusual; but if asked, it like (3) is also somewhat ambiguous, though it leans toward seeking a positive answer with a negated complement: "Yes, you didn't go to the store." Though (3) and (6) may not seem simple, these are relatively simple examples based on questions in artificial discourse. When complex questions are employed in representational discourse, such as found in the GNT, the difficulty increases rapidly.

Similar problems arise in the negation of questions in the GNT. For example:

(7) *Οὐχὶ* σὺ εἶ ὁ Χριστός; (LUKE 23:39)
(8) *Οὐδὲ* φοβῇ σὺ τὸν θεόν, ὅτι ἐν τῷ αὐτῷ κρίματι εἶ; (LUKE 23:40)
(9) Ὅτε ἀπέστειλα ὑμᾶς ἄτερ ... *μή* τινος ὑστερήσατε; (LUKE 22:35)

The criminal uses a negative polar question (7) to ask, "Aren't you the Christ?" Based on all factors—syntactic, semantic, and pragmatic—the question clearly anticipates a "yes" answer. The question has informational qualities and slightly stronger rhetorical qualities—the criminal wants to know the answer but still tries to persuade Jesus that the answer is "yes." In contrast, the other criminal also uses an NPQ (8) to ask, "Don't you fear God, since you are under the same sentence?" However, even though both (7) and (8) use similar NPIs (derivative of οὐ), and both front the NPI for effect, question (8) doesn't anticipate a "yes" but is most obviously pushing a "no." Question (9) is even more troubling; in the Koine Greek the literal rendering looks something like, "When I sent you without purse and bag and sandals, [there was] not something you lacked?" In Greek, μή is often considered a negative particle, but if set into modern language grammars it would be closer to a bias word such as "lest" or "even."[36] If we stick with the traditional language for the moment,[37] question (9) carries a negative particle in the Greek as well as in the earliest Latin (*ne*, Codex Bezae), but the particle evolves into a bias word (§2.C.2) in the earliest Syriac (Curetonianus and Sinaiticus) and the later Latin (*numquid*, Clementine Vulgate). It continues the evolution from bias word to interrogative adverb in Wycliffe's early English (*whether*), and it completes the evolution to include no negative, bias, or interrogative word in the modern English (e.g., KJV, ESV, NIV). Thus we have lost the truest sense of negation—and the rhetorical push that comes with it—occurring in (9) over the course of time.[38] In all these cases, when it comes to negation, simple rules based on syntax do not always work well. When it comes to negation, semantics and pragmatics trump syntax when determining the meaning of the utterance.

Key Bibliography
Babbitt, "Use of μή in Questions"; Cruse, *Meaning*, 297–98; Horrocks, "*Ouk Ísmen Oudén*"; Israel, *Grammar of Polarity*; Runge, "Teaching Them What NOT to Do"; Wackernagel, *Lectures*, 712–91.

10. Π-Words

Π-word is a shorthand expression for one of several types of interrogative variable words that serve as strong indicators of interrogativity in clauses. The reason we call them π-words is because almost all of them start with the letter π. Direct questions that start with π-words are called π-questions. Since a π-word functions as a variable in a question, we can also call them variable questions, and the two terms are essentially synonymous. The π-words in use in direct questions in the GNT can be seen in the table below.

Π-Words in Direct Questions in GNT	English Equivalents
τίς	Who? or What? or Why?
ποῦ	Where?

36. The particle μή also fits the broader definition of a negative polarity item that is in use in linguistics.
37. The traditional view is "οὐ simply *denies* the existence or occurrence of something, and so is *direct* or *objective* ... while μή *prohibits* the occurrence of something, and so is *indirect* or *subjective*" (Jannaris, *Grammar*, §1801).
38. Cf. L&N 69.15. A similar type of evolution occurs in John 18:35.

Π-Words in Direct Questions in GNT	English Equivalents
πότε	When?
ποῖος	What kind?
πῶς	How?
πόθεν	Whence?
πόσος	How much?
ποταπός	What sort?
ποσάκις	How often?

Ancient Greek also had ποῖ ("whither?"), πότερος ("whether?"), πηλίκος ("how great?"), and πῇ ("what way?" or "which way?"), but these do not occur in direct questions in the GNT. Τίς doesn't start with π, but it is still considered a π-word. The reason has to do with an interesting coincidence in IE languages. In Greek, all but one of these words start with the letter π.[39] In Latin, almost all these words start with the letter *qu*.[40] In English, all but one of these words start with *wh*, and English linguists refer to them as *wh*-words, and these type of questions as *wh*-questions.[41] In German, almost all these words start with *w*, and German linguists refer to these types of questions as *w-fragen*.[42] In fact, this similarity among variable question words runs throughout IE languages and is not a coincidence.

Π-words have an important function in language, which is why they are treated as a group, even though there are some morphological and usage differences. In Greek, π-words can serve as either interrogative adverbs, interrogative adjectives, or interrogative pronouns. At times, traditional Greek grammars treat interrogative adverbs, adjectives, and pronouns separately, but this distinction can obscure the greater semantic and pragmatic factors that unite π-words. Π-words are a major tell for interrogativity in direct questions and can also be used to identify indirect questions as well (for example, John 7:17).

Key Bibliography

Blass, *Grammar*, §25.2–4; 50.5–7; Hoffmann and von Siebenthal, *Griechische Grammatik*, §60–61; Wallace, *Greek Grammar*, 345–46.

---

39. In Koine and Attic Greek—but in the pre-Classical, East Ionic dialect, the π-words were originally κ-words; see Miller, *Ancient Greek Dialects*, 179–80.
40. Including, for example, *quis*, *quid*, *quando*, *quomodo*, *quot*, and *quantus*. *Cur* and *ubi* are the exceptions to the naming shorthand.
41. Including, for example, *who*, *what*, *when*, *where*, and *why*. *How* is the exception.
42. Including, for example, *wann*, *wie*, *warum*, *wo*, *wer*, and *was*.

11. Fronting

Fronting, or *to front*, describes the movement of one part of syntax in front of another part of syntax (*CDL* 182). Fronting is a type of syntactic displacement where a word or phrase is moved to the beginning of a clause or sentence (usually to comply with a rule of syntax or for rhetorical effect). Linguists also refer to it as *leftward movement*, since the most common examples move from the right-hand side of the clause to the left-hand side. However, the fronted word or phrase will not necessarily be the first word or phrase of the clause, as other words may still occur prior to the fronted word or phrase—a great example of this is a *discourse particle* (§2.B.7). When more than just one word is fronted—or more precisely, when the fronted word carries with it a constituent phrase—linguists call this occurrence *pied-piping*, since the phrase is compelled to follow its lead word (*CDL* 345). Fronting occurs as a part of the structuring of information that occurs in natural language use. Since fronting presupposes the dislocation of syntactical parts from a hypothetical norm, not all linguistic theories agree with the concept. We briefly consider two occurrences of fronting: interrogative variable fronting and negative fronting. This should not be a surprise, as interrogativity and negation are closely related features in IE languages, not just ancient Greek.[43]

Perhaps the most studied kind of fronting in IE languages involves the fronting that occurs in direct questions using π-words (§2.B.10). In ancient Greek, *π-fronting* describes the movement of a π-word to the beginning of a direct question that is not based on a polar formation (§3). In English, linguists call this event *wh-fronting* or *wh-movement*. In this case of fronting, both English and Greek are similar—both languages fully front their variable words in direct questions. Furthermore, both Classical and Koine Greek are π-fronting. This commonality extends to most IE languages as well. We can illustrate this in both English and Greek:

(1) *Where* did Wyatt put the phone? (*WH*-FRONTING)
(2) Wyatt put the phone *where*? (*WH*-IN SITU)
(3) *Why* did Wyatt take the phone? (*WH*-FRONTING)
(4) Wyatt took the phone *why*? (*WH*-IN SITU)

In example (1), the *wh*-word is fronted, and the question is well formed in English, whereas in example (2), the *wh*-word is not fronted, and the question is awkward grammatically. Even though example (2) is not standard English, a speaker may use (2) in uncommon circumstances, most notably as an echo question (§5.B.3). The awkwardness of nonmovement is made even more explicit in examples (3) and (4). In languages where interrogative variable movement is expected,

43. Haegeman, *Syntax of Negation*, 70.

linguists call nonmovement or partial movement—whether for emphasis or due to poor grammar—*in situ* (meaning in its natural place or state).

The same movement is the norm in Koine Greek, as we can illustrate with an example from Matthew 13:54:

(5) *Πόθεν* τούτῳ ἡ σοφία αὕτη καὶ αἱ δυνάμεις; (Π-FRONTING)
(6) Τούτῳ *πόθεν* ἡ σοφία αὕτη καὶ αἱ δυνάμεις; (Π-IN SITU)
(7) Ἡ σοφία αὕτη καὶ αἱ δυνάμεις *πόθεν* τούτῳ; (Π-IN SITU)

Example (5), "From where did this man get this wisdom and these miracles?" is the same wording that Matthew uses and is standard for Koine Greek with the π-word fronted. In contrast, even though πόθεν is near the front in (6), it is still formed as π-*in situ*. While an audience would likely understand (6), it would not sound well formed (as [4] above). Likewise, (7) is also a case of π-*in situ*; if a speaker wanted to create—for rhetorical effect—a π-*in situ* question with the words of Matthew 13:54, this would be the preferred way of forming the question (cf. Luke 9:20; Eph 4:9; 1 Pet 4:18). However, while questions (5) and (7) may have similar meanings, they do *not* ask the same question. This is because the information structure of (7) has been altered from (5) to create new rhetorical effects on the audience.

Why is fronting important? In simplest possible terms, interrogative variable fronting in Koine Greek is important because it (1) creates a standard way for structuring questions so as to show the reader that interrogativity is the prime force of the utterance and (2) creates a standard which allows deviations to be made for additional rhetorical effect. Generally speaking, this fronting makes it easy for a reader or hearer to quickly identify direct questions from indirect questions (with the caveat that this is true only for those people whose language processing is based on IE-language information structure). It is also important linguistically, as it reminds modern readers that (1) Greek is pretty regular in its constructions, and (2) IE languages share a great deal of common ideas about how language works. This is in contrast to non-IE languages, such as Swahili and Japanese, where interrogative variable words and particles do not front (and their information structure for utterances is different).

The second kind of fronting that affects interrogatives in the GNT is negative fronting. Generally speaking, negative fronting in the GNT is primarily associated with questions based on a polar formation. This kind of fronting is less universal in IE languages, and therefore this type of movement has received less study than *wh*-fronting. The reason for this is complex, but one partial explanation is that over time the negative particle drifted from a possible fronted position to an almost always *in situ* position in utterances (cf. 2.B.9).[44] This is especially true of modern English, though linguists speak of *negative inversion* to describe

44. Cf. Jespersen, *Negation*, 4–14.

the movement of negative particles in English. While this type of movement can occur in certain situations in English propositions, it is largely incompatible with *wh*-fronting in English (but not so in Greek).[45] For example:

(8) Is Violet *not* an orangutan? (WELL FORMED)
(9) *Not* Violet is an orangutan? (NOT WELL FORMED)
(10) What *not* is going to work? (NOT WELL FORMED)

In example (8), the negative particle remains *in situ*, but when it fronts in (9), it is not well formed in English. (10) is also not well formed in English. In contrast, in Koine Greek:

(11) *οὐχὶ* τοὺς ἔσω ὑμεῖς κρίνετε; (1 COR 5:12B)
(12) καὶ αἱ ἀδελφαὶ αὐτοῦ *οὐχὶ* πᾶσαι πρὸς ἡμᾶς εἰσιν; (MATT 13:56A)
(13) πῶς *οὐ* νοεῖτε ὅτι οὐ περὶ ἄρτων εἶπον ὑμῖν; (MATT 16:11)

The polar question in (11) fronts the negative οὐχί, which is common in the GNT. Here οὐχί experiences leftward movement to structure the sentence so that the negative becomes highly expressive.[46] Across the GNT, οὐχί consistently fronts polar questions in order to emphasize the questions' negative polarity; however, it is not an indicator of interrogativity as is a π-word. Example (12) reminds us that οὐχί can occur without fronting. In (13), we have both π-fronting and negative fronting. In Koine Greek, as with most IE languages, the movement of the interrogative variable is more potent than the movement of the negative particle; we interpret accordingly by investigating the interrogative logic ahead of the rhetorical effects of negative polarity.

Key Bibliography
Levinsohn, *Discourse Features*, 48–67; López, "Wh-Movement," 311–24; Runge, *Discourse Grammar*, 269–313; Thomson, "Postponement of Interrogatives."

12. Indirect Questions

An *indirect question* is a statement that implies an unasked direct question. Indirect questions are sometimes called *embedded interrogatives* or *constituent interrogatives*, as writers often deploy these unasked questions embedded within a larger (propositional) context. An indirect question does not actually ask, and therefore its primary force is anything other than interrogative.[47] It also does not

45. Haegeman, "Negative Preposing," 26–27; though note, "*Why not* go to the store?"
46. For further discussion, see Runge, *Discourse Grammar*, 269–85.
47. Karttunen and Peters, "Indirect Questions," 352; but also Groenendijk and Stokhof, "Semantic Analysis," 185.

directly seek information, nor does it (typically) have rhetorical strength in the manner of a direct question. Therefore, the primary difference between a direct question and an indirect question is that a direct question *asks* and an indirect question *says* (as part of a larger statement). For example:

(1) What did she want? (DIRECT QUESTION)
(2) Noël knew what she wanted. (INDIRECT QUESTION)

Above, (2) implies the direct question (1), but any interrogative force in (2) is secondary to the assertion. An indirect question is in many ways not a question in that it does not fulfill the basic task of a question, which is to ask. Indirect questions were traditionally known as a form of *oratio obliqua* and a normal part of narrative discourse.

There are syntactic, semantic, and pragmatic differences between direct questions and indirect questions. The simplest to identify is the syntactic. When a sentence is a direct question, the interrogative indicators are in the main clause. When a sentence is an indirect question, any interrogative indicators present are in a subordinate clause. Beyond this, all four formations of direct questions can be restated as indirect questions, but the four formations produce two different forms of indirect questions. For variable questions and set questions, which both rely on π-words, a direct question puts focus on the π-word (and where applicable, its pied-piped clause), whereas an indirect question relegates the π-word clause to the status of a subordinate clause. In contrast, polar and alternative questions are perhaps less frequently restated as indirect questions, but when this happens the indirect polar and alternative questions are reframed as a conditional clause. We can see the way this works in the chart below:

Type of Question	Direct Question	Indirect Question
Variable Question	Main Clause	Subordinate Clause
Set Question		
Polar Question	Main Clause	Conditional Clause
Alternative Question		

As further example, we can illustrate the basic differences between direct and indirect variable questions using Matthew 2:2 and 2:4, both of which use the π-word, ποῦ:

(3) *Ποῦ* ἐστιν ὁ τεχθεὶς βασιλεὺς τῶν Ἰουδαίων; (DIRECT QUESTION)
(4) καὶ ... ἐπυνθάνετο παρ᾽ αὐτῶν *ποῦ* ὁ χριστὸς γεννᾶται. (INDIRECT QUESTION)

In (3), the speaker asks a question of where ("Where is the one born king of the Jews?"), but in (4) the speaker makes a statement ("and ... he asked them where was the Christ born") that implies the question, "Where was the Christ born?" It is not unusual in narrative texts for related direct and indirect questions to work together, as we see in (3) and (4) in Matthew 2:2–4. Similarly, we can show the differences between direct and indirect polar questions using Matthew 9:28 and 27:49:

(5) Πιστεύετε ὅτι δύναμαι τοῦτο ποιῆσαι; (DIRECT QUESTION)
(6) Ἄφες ἴδωμεν *εἰ* ἔρχεται Ἠλίας σώσων αὐτόν. (INDIRECT QUESTION)

In (5), the speaker asks a direct polar question ("Do you believe that I am able to do this?"), but in (6) the statement made ("Enough—let's see if Elijah comes to save him") implies the unasked question, "Will Elijah come to save him?" Example (6) reframes the unasked question within a conditional clause led by εἰ. As with (2), (4), and (6), all these are statements that imply questions never asked.

However, there is another way of looking at indirect questions differently than provided by traditional grammars. When we look closely at indirect questions, some seem to have more interrogative force than others. This is especially true in relation to how certain classes of verbs, such as *epistemic verbs*, handle the subordinate clause of the indirect question. We can see this difference in English:

(7) Noël knew what she wanted (EPISTEMIC VERB)
(8) Noël sang what she wanted (ACTION VERB)

Both (7) and (8) are indirect questions, but their indirect interrogative force is different. Example (7) strongly implies the question, "What did she want?" but (8) only weakly implies the question, "What did she want to sing?" This difference is rooted in the nature of the verbal performance over the indirect question. This difference in impact is not limited to epistemic verbs and action verbs; the division is between verbs that expect an object and those that do not. If the indirect question is needed by the verb, it will carry a stronger indirect interrogative force and form a *complement clause* with the verb, as in (7). If the indirect question is not needed by the verb, it will carry a weaker indirect interrogative force and form an *adjunct clause* with the verb, as in (8). If the verb carries a direct object plus the indirect question, as commonly happens with objectival pronouns and infinitives, then the indirect question is forced into the role of adjunct clause. Thus, the performance of the verb divides indirect questions into two classes, with two different properties: complement and adjunct. How these two properties play out affects the interpretation of the indirect question. Let's look at some examples in English, then in the GNT.

(7) Noël knew what she wanted (*WH*-COMPLEMENT CLAUSE)
(8) Noël sang what she wanted (*WH*-ADJUNCT CLAUSE)
(9) Noël knew whether she wanted (POLAR COMPLEMENT CLAUSE)
(10) Noël sang whether she wanted (POLAR ADJUNCT CLAUSE)

From (7) and (8), we see the force differential between the indirect complement and the indirect adjunct, as above. With (9), the indirect question logically is "Noël knew whether she wanted [to or not]," and the question it strongly implies is, "Did she want to or not?" Example (10), however, is more difficult, as the indirect question logically is "Noël sang whether she wanted [to or not]," which as an adjunct clause is probably the least common form of indirect question.

In the GNT, the difference becomes even more interesting. Rewinding to Classical Greek and starting with the π-words of variable and set questions, Classical Greek differentiates morphologically between π-words in direct questions and π-words in indirect questions. In other words, the *wh*-word "where" is used for both direct questions and indirect questions in English—but not in Classical Greek. Classical Greek uses ποῦ to alert the reader to a direct question and ὅπου to indicate to the reader an indirect question. This morphological approach was true of all interrogative variables in Classical Greek, and the direct and indirect π-words are:

Π-words for Direct Questions	Π-words for Indirect Questions
τίς	ὅστις
ποῦ	ὅπου
πότε	ὁπότε
ποῖος	ὁποῖος
πῶς	ὅπως
πόθεν	ὅθεν
πόσος	ὁπόσος
ποδᾰπός (ποταπός)	ὁποδᾰπός
ποσάκις	ὁποσάκῐς

However, by the time of the composition of the GNT, these indirect interrogative pronouns were falling out of regular use.[48] The result was that in some cases direct interrogative pronouns were used in indirect situations. We also note that by the time of the GNT, some π-words—ποῖ/ὅποι, πότερος/ὁπότερος, πηλίκος/ὁπηλίκος and πῇ/ὅπη—were becoming less popular, more archaic, and therefore were not used by any of the writers in the GNT.[49]

As a test case for this, let's examine the use of the π-words for "where" (ποῦ/ὅπου and πόθεν/ὅθεν) in the GNT. In Matthew 2:2 and 2:4, the writer uses ποῦ for both direct and indirect questions (like English but unlike Classical Greek).

48. Moulton, *Grammar*, 3:48.
49. Though note the use of πηλίκος in an indirect question in Hebrews 7:4.

In the GNT, ποῦ occurs forty-eight times and ὅπου occurs eighty-two times.[50] Πόθεν occurs twenty-nine times and ὅθεν occurs fifteen times. Starting with ὅπου and ὅθεν, the GNT *always* uses both of these terms in indirect questions, never direct questions. What is more, the writers of the GNT use ὅπου and ὅθεν *always* in adjunct indirect question clauses and *never* in complement indirect question clauses. (About a third of the uses of ὅπου and ὅθεν are better classified as correlative clauses, which for our purposes here, carry even less indirect interrogative force than adjunct indirect-question clauses). So ὅπου and ὅθεν are always adjuncts and never complements or directs. If we contrast this with ποῦ and πόθεν, we get a very different situation. Writers in the GNT only use ποῦ and πόθεν in direct questions a little over half the time (~60% for both), and they use ποῦ and πόθεν the rest of the time in indirect questions *almost always* in complement clauses.[51] Combining ποῦ and πόθεν, we can see their usage displayed in the chart below:

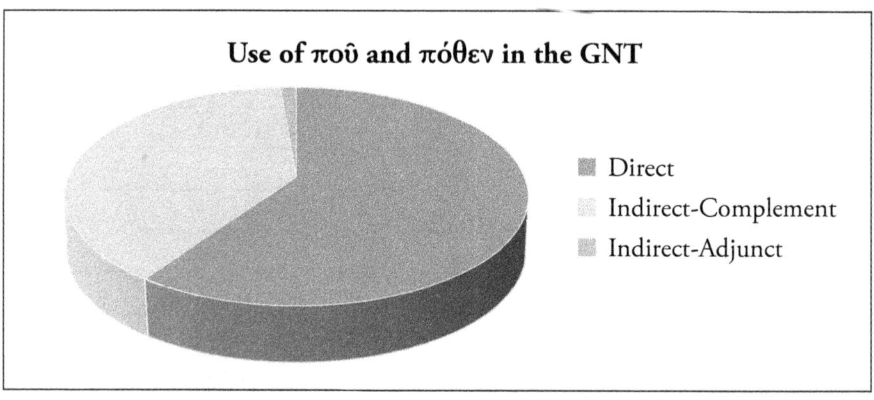

We can see examples of this in the GNT:

(3) *Ποῦ* ἐστιν ὁ τεχθεὶς βασιλεὺς τῶν Ἰουδαίων; (DIRECT QUESTION)
(4) καὶ ... ἐπυνθάνετο παρ᾽ αὐτῶν *ποῦ* ὁ χριστὸς γεννᾶται. (INDIRECT COMPLEMENT)
(11) ... εἰ σὺ ἐβάστασας αὐτόν, εἰπέ μοι *ποῦ* ἔθηκας αὐτόν ... (INDIRECT ADJUNCT)
(12) ... εἶπέν τις πρὸς αὐτόν· ἀκολουθήσω σοι *ὅπου* ἐὰν ἀπέρχῃ. (INDIRECT ADJUNCT)

50. The distinction between ποῦ (interrogative adverb) or πού (enclitic adverb) is not always clear in the GNT; here I have followed the NA[28] and counted forty-eight ποῦ and four πού. However, these numbers are not fixed, as for example, I see no reason why the που in Acts 27:29 cannot be read as ποῦ, the complementizer to the verb ἐκπέσωμεν.

51. The one exception of ποῦ in an adjunct indirect question is in John 20:15c.

(13) *ὅπου* γὰρ ζῆλος καὶ ἐριθεία, ἐκεῖ ἀκαταστασία καὶ πᾶν φαῦλον πρᾶγμα. (CORRELATIVE)

(14) οἶδα *ποῦ* κατοικεῖς, *ὅπου* ὁ θρόνος τοῦ σατανᾶ (COMPLEMENT AND ADJUNCT)

While question (3) from Matthew 2:2 is the preferred use of ποῦ in a direct question, (4) from Matthew 2:4 has ποῦ functioning as the complementizer in the complement clause of the indirect question.[52] Incidentally, (4) from Matthew 2:4 is a classic example of the use of a complement clause, as the verb ἐπυνθάνετο makes little sense without an object (L&N 27.11), with παρ' αὐτῶν being an ancillary part of the verbal phrase. Example (11) from John 20:15c is the only instance of ποῦ in an adjunct clause of an indirect question, but it is an interesting situation (see example below). With (12) from Luke 9:57 ("I will follow you wherever you may go"), Luke uses ὅπου in the standard adjunct role, as ἀκολουθήσω σοι holds the focus as the primary clause. In (13) from James 3:16 ("For where there is envy and selfish ambition, there is disorder and every evil thing"), ὅπου has moved so indirectly interrogative as to form itself as a correlative clause to the main clause that begins with ἐκεῖ. Having said this, make no mistake that ὅπου is still vestigially interrogative, as the sentence ἐκεῖ ἀκαταστασία καὶ πᾶν φαῦλον πρᾶγμα ὅπου ζῆλος καὶ ἐριθεία is a virtual semantic equivalent to the original wording of James 3:16. Stated this way, though, the ὅπου clause is still correlative but now feels closer to an indirect question, leading us to weakly wonder, "Where is jealousy and selfish ambition?" Finally, (14) from Revelation 2:13 ("I know where you dwell—where the throne of Satan is") shows how ποῦ and ὅπου work together to create a complement clause and an adjunct clause. The unasked question is not only, "Where does he dwell?" but also, "Where is Satan's throne?" Here ὅπου is truly an adjunct, as can be seen more clearly if we replace the complement with a simpler semantic equivalent, as in οἶδα τὸν τόπον *ὅπου* ὁ θρόνος τοῦ σατανᾶ ("I know the place where the throne of Satan is").

Of course, the GNT was written by many different writers, and the habits of these writers affect the data. For example, Hebrews uses ὅθεν more than any other text, and it always uses it in more of a correlative clause and not in an adjunct, indirect interrogative clause. As another example, Matthew and Mark always use πόθεν in direct questions, never in indirect, but then Luke and John rarely do this, both choosing instead to use πόθεν three quarters of the time as a complementizer in complement indirect questions. As a result, the trends that we can detect from this is that not only are ποῦ and πόθεν moving away from being exclusively for direct-question use (as grammarians have noted for years),

52. A *complementizer* is the conjunctor that starts the complement clause (*CDL* 91).

but that ὅπου and ὅθεν are not so much falling out of the language at this point in Koine Greek as much as they are moving away from interrogativity.

Indirect questions are a fascinating feature of language, but as they are not direct questions they are largely beyond the scope of the remainder of this book.

Case Study JOHN 20:15C

ἐκείνη δοκοῦσα ὅτι ὁ κηπουρός ἐστιν λέγει αὐτῷ· κύριε, εἰ σὺ ἐβάστασας αὐτόν, εἰπέ μοι ποῦ ἔθηκας αὐτόν, κἀγὼ αὐτὸν ἀρῶ.

[Mary], thinking that he was the gardener, said to him, "Sir, if you have taken him, tell me where you put him, and I will go get him."

John 20:15c is an exceptional situation as it is the only occurrence in the GNT of a writer using ποῦ in an indirect question. John records the indirect question within the larger framework of direct discourse from Mary. Mary's statement is a turn-two response to a double question from Jesus. The response is direct, including both a vocative address κύριε and an imperative εἰπέ. In addition to its mood, εἰπέ is a verb that needs an object: "Sir, tell" leads to the unanswered question, "Tell what?" Typically then, when we see the verb λέγω, we would expect an obvious complement-clause indirect question similar to the use of ἐπυνθάνετο in (4). However, in John 20:15c εἰπέ carries an object in μοι, which has the effect of moving the focus off the ποῦ ἔθηκας αὐτόν clause and onto the object μοι. The standard test for an adjunct clause in this case is, "Does the sentence make sense without the ποῦ clause?" In this case, the answer is yes, making it an adjunct (cf. εἰπέ in Matt 4:3; 20:21). Because the ποῦ clause is an adjunct, the implication for interpretation is that the point of Mary's question is for the groundskeeper to tell *her*, not tell *where*. The *where* is of secondary importance to Mary's involvement. Thus, the emphasis of the verse is on the personal relationship with Jesus that Mary emphasizes.[53]

FURTHER EXAMPLES

ποῦ as direct-question adverb: Matt 26:17; Mark 14:12; John 16:5; Rom 3:27a; 1 Cor 1:20a, 1 Cor 1:20b, 1 Cor 1:20c; Gal 4:15; 2 Pet 3:4

ποῦ as indirect-complement adverb: Matt 8:20; Mark 15:47; Luke 9:58; John 12:35; 1 John 2:11

ὅπου as indirect-adjunct adverb: Matt 6:19; 13:5; Mark 2:4; Luke 22:11; John 12:1; 19:20; Acts 17:1; 20:6; Rom 15:20

ὅπου as correlative adverb: Mark 14:14; 1 Cor 3:3; Col 3:11; Heb 9:16; 2 Pet 2:11; Rev 11:8

53. Note the κἀγὼ in the subsequent clause; see L&N 92.1.

Key Bibliography
Babbitt, *Grammar*, §578–81; Blass, *Grammar*, §65.1; Groenendijk and Stokhof, "Semantic Analysis," 175–233; McKay, *New Syntax*, §13; Moulton, *Grammar*, 3:116–17; Parodi and Quicoli, "Complementation," 325–40.

C. Questions and Semantics

The second part of language where we will survey the way questions work is in the area of semantics. The simplest definition for *semantics* is "meaning"; semantics is interested in what things mean. As a field, semantics "deals with lexical words, the relations between them, and how the meanings of words combine to yield the meaning of phrases, and the meanings of phrases combine to yield the meaning of clauses" (*CDL* 399). Therefore, our goal in studying the semantics of questions is to understand better what they mean. In a way, semantics is more challenging a field than syntax for questions, as it involves not just discovering the interrogative logic but also defining it.

Semantics is an extremely broad field of study. Our approach to semantics is different than what is often meant by the term *semantics* in the study of the GNT. Usually, when the term is used, it refers to *lexical semantics*, or the meaning of words. Our use of the term refers to what can be called *syntactical* or *grammatical semantics*, expressed as the meaning of a grammatical construct (like a clause or a sentence). More accurately, we could call our area of interest *interrogative semantics*, given that we are interested in the meaning of questions (apart from other types of sentences). In all fairness to lexical semantics, grammatical semantics (in this case, interrogative semantics) is much more complex, as we are trying to discover the meaning of sentences rather than words.[54] Below we consider several of the most important factors that shape the semantics of questions.

Key Bibliography
Cruse, *Meaning*, 263–300; Estes, *Questions*, 45–47; Higginbotham, "Semantics of Questions," 361–83; Louw, *Semantics*; Nida and Louw, *Lexical Semantics*, 1–20; Saeed, *Semantics*, 3–19.

1. Force

Force, or *illocutionary force* as it is formally called, is a push found in utterances that is applied toward its audience. To put it another way: If we wanted to move a piece of furniture, we might apply a horizontal-forward force (slide it), a vertical-up force (lift it), or some combination of both forces (shimmy it), but we would

54. Saeed, *Semantics*, 10.

never apply a vertical-down or horizontal-reverse force. To carry the furniture, a force (of some sort) is applied. In the same way, if we wanted to express exasperation to someone, we could apply an exclamative force ("What!"), an interrogative force ("What?"), or both ("What!?"), but not an agreement force ("What," as in "I agree with you"). To carry the point of the sentence, a force (of some sort) is applied. Force comes from both syntax and semantics; it is one of those unique properties that is rooted in the nature of human communication. Force is such an important part of sentence semantics that a sentence cannot have meaning without force.[55]

In natural language, every clause carries at least one force, and almost all will carry more than one force. (The clause is the smallest unit that has force, but since we are focusing on questions we are focusing on force on the sentence level, not the clause level.) Not every force in a sentence is equal; some will be stronger, and some will be weaker; some will be more overt, and some will be more hidden. When it comes to asking questions, besides a basic interrogative force, there are quite a few other types of forces that can be applied to make questions ask what we want them to ask. Our interest will be in the types of *interrogative force* that we find in the questions in the GNT. Among the forces in a sentence, the most powerful or meaningful force is the (illocutionary) *point*.[56] The *point* is the force that carries the primary meaning of the sentence. Because of the diversity of human communication, there are a limitless number of possible forces and also a limitless number of points—though usually points will fit into a relatively small number of possible categories. In many ways, the illocutionary point is similar to the idea of sentence function (§2.B.2).

Key Bibliography

Cruse, *Meaning*, 331–43; Kissine, "Sentences," 169–90; Searle and Vanderveken, *Foundations*, 1–26.

2. Bias

Bias is a semantic property of clause structure that creates a predisposition within the logic of the clause. In the study of questions in the GNT, bias is usually introduced as a way for the writer to prejudice the reader in a certain direction. Bias can be intentional or unintentional, though in natural language it most likely occurs as either consciously intentional or unconsciously intentional and rarely ever unintentional. Unlike polarity, which for the sake of discussion here does not differ in degree, bias is greatly dependent on the semantics of the bias used. Also unlike polarity, bias does not exist oppositionally in well-formed sentences;

55. Searle and Vanderveken, *Foundations*, 7.
56. Ibid., 14; Allan, "Mood," 268.

it only moves along one axis. Thus, bias can vary greatly in degree from mild to extreme bias. Since every clause may possess a different degree of bias, complex questions with multiple clauses may push the receiver in different ways (and perhaps, different directions). Bias must be used with care in questions, as too much or too distinct a bias can quickly render a question nonsensical. Bias is related to *conventional implicature* (§2.D.4), and in some cases there is overlap—the main difference between the two is that bias tends to be less overt and based on the semantics of the words of the utterance, while conventional implicature tends to be more overt and based on the pragmatic use of words in the utterance.

Words with a biased property in narrative come in many different shapes and sizes—really, any type of word can create bias in a question. Identifying bias words in the GNT is more an art than a science, as so much depends on the semantic inferences of possible bias words *in their narrative context.* When it comes to bias words, some word types are more likely to exhibit greater degrees of bias. Typically, stronger bias words tend to fall within the adverbial and particle areas of speech. In the GNT, strong bias words include μόνον ("only") and εὐθέως ("immediately"). Milder bias words include ἄρα ("then") and ἔτι ("still"). These types of bias words are easy to identify as such. On the other hand, verbs are less likely to muster a high degree of bias in natural-language situations. A classic example of verbal bias in the GNT occurs in John 18:4 and 18:7, where Jesus asks a test question using the intentionally thought-provoking verb ζητέω ("seek"). Further, all NPIs create bias in questions as a result of their oppositional polarity. This means all the negative particles in §2.B.8 create bias in a question.[57]

Bias presents an interesting property of question asking because it reveals a great deal of information about the asker. For the asker to ask a question with bias not only indicates that there is a preferred answer; it also indicates that the speaker has some opinion about the question itself (and often, the receiver of the question, as well). Biased questions contain embedded presuppositions that a receiver can or should solve, and this is a big challenge in the interpretation of biased questions in the GNT. Another one of the biggest hurdles for interpreting the erotetic logic of bias in questions is estimating the degree of bias intended. This is where the semantics of bias becomes a challenge—some forms of bias will seem more prejudicial to some readers than other forms of bias. Care must be taken by the interpreter to study the surrounding context for pragmatic clues that will help define the degree of bias intended by the writer.

57. Zwarts (along with other linguists) argues that many bias words are actually (weak) polarity items, but I find this view less effective in natural-language situations; see Zwarts, "Three Types of Polarity."

Key Bibliography
Estes, *Questions*, 157–60; Lawler, "Any Questions?," 163–73; Litwack, "Classification," 182–86; Reese, "Bias in Questions."

3. Asking and Saying

By English conventions, when someone utters a question, the question is *asked*; at the same time, when someone utters a proposition, the proposition is *said*. The same is true of written discourse—writers compose questions that are asked by characters and propositions that are said by characters. In English, it is helpful to differentiate the ideas of asking and saying so that the reader will know when to infer interrogative force and when to infer declarative (or other) force. We use this type of convention regularly in modern language, such as:

(1) "Where is the walnut?" Everett asked.
(2) "There is the walnut," Everett said.

While there is a large number of synonyms in English for say (state, utter, pronounce, verbalize, declare, articulate) and ask (inquire, request, query, question, interrogate, probe), the standardization of "say" and "ask" is pretty high in English, such that one would not find these:

(3) "Where is the walnut?" Everett said.
(4) "There is the walnut," Everett asked.

Actually, one *could* find (3) in certain situations where the author wanted to tone down the interrogativity of the sentence. However, (4) is not well formed. The reason (3) is more acceptable, even in English, is that "said" is close to being a *direct discourse marker*. Modern languages also have other, even more obvious direct discourse markers, such as quotation marks, but these markers are not present as such in the GNT.[58] Therefore, to understand the semantics of written discourse in ancient texts such as the GNT, we must look for other direct discourse markers. If we survey the areas of direct discourse, we note that the vast majority of direct discourse, including direct questions, is introduced by the verb λέγω, often as a participle. Because of the semantic range of λέγω, it is frequently less meant to actually mean "say" and more simply as a way to introduce direct discourse:

(5) Καὶ πάλιν *εἶπεν*, Τίνι ὁμοιώσω τὴν βασιλείαν τοῦ θεοῦ; (VERB)
(6) καὶ ἰδοὺ *ἔκραξαν λέγοντες*, Τί ἡμῖν καὶ σοί, υἱὲ τοῦ θεοῦ; (VERB + MARKER)
(7) καὶ *ἐπηρώτησαν* αὐτὸν *λέγοντες*, Εἰ ἔξεστιν … (VERB + MARKER)

58. Sometimes ὅτι and τό perform a related function.

With (5) from Luke 13:20, Luke use the verb λέγω to introduce a direct question, typical in the GNT. This is not something new introduced into the GNT but was a common occurrence in both Classical and Hellenistic Greek.[59] The construction in (6) from Matthew 8:29a introduces the direct question with both a verb of exclamation and the discourse-marking participle, λέγοντες. Likewise, (7) from Matthew 12:10 actually uses the complex construction of "ask" (ἐπηρώτησαν) and then "say" (λέγοντες). Clearly, from the examples of (6) and (7), Greek direct-discourse construction is different from modern languages such as English, which requires no direct discourse marker in the syntax. Of course, not all the texts in the GNT that have direct questions have placed them within direct discourse. Notably, the letters of Paul contain direct questions that are not in the form of direct discourse and, as such, generally require no introduction in the form of a discourse marker.

The significance of this is in two areas. First, the distinction we make in modern languages (which is helpful in this book) between *ask* and *say* does not hold up in the direct discourse of either Classical or Koine Greek. As a result, we should not undervalue the rhetoric of a question asked in the GNT if it is introduced by a verb form of "say"—especially if the "say" is really more of a direct discourse marker (as is often the case in the use of the Greek participle of λέγω). Second, if verbs semantically expressing *ask* are infrequently used to introduce direct questions, is there a reason that an interpreter should take note in these rare instances? While this question must be answered on a text-by-text basis, here the evidence would indicate that the reason for this is primarily lexical variety. In the end, the verbs that introduce direct questions only rarely provide clues to the interpretation of direct questions in the GNT.

Key Bibliography

Apollonius Dyscolus, *Syntax* 288; BDF §420.

---

4. *Informational Quality*

One of the two most important and fundamental semantic properties of a question is its degree of *informational quality*. This quality of a question measures the degree to which a question seeks information on the part of the asker. Simply put, the greater the degree of informational quality of a question, the more the question *asks*. When we interpret questions in the GNT, we gauge the degree to which a question seeks information. Understanding this semantic feature gives

59. For example, Plato, *Clitophon* 407, uses a similar introduction to a direct question (λέγων· Ποῖ φέρεσθε ὤνθρωποι;), as does Achilles Tatius, *The Adventures of Leucippe and Cleitophon* 2.7.5 (ἔφη, καὶ σὺ κατεπάδεις;); 3.23.2 (Ὁ δὲ Κλεινίας, εἶπον,τί γέγονεν;). For other examples, see Dionysius of Halicarnassus, *Roman Antiquities* 8.39.3; 8.40.1; Herodotus, *Histories* 3.140; 9.109.

us better insight into interpreting what the question asks. The recognition that questions have both informational and rhetorical qualities goes back to at least the time of Quintilian.[60]

As a general rule, all questions accomplish two things to some degree: they gather information and persuade others. As we study the questions in the GNT, we need to remember two semantic principles for the interpretation of questions:

- All questions have at least a minimal degree of informational quality.
- All questions also have at least a minimal degree of rhetorical quality.

In natural-language occurrences, the degree of informational quality may be small in a highly rhetorical question, just as the degree of rhetorical quality may be small in a highly informational question. These two qualities are often divergent. In other words, a question that is maximally informational will often be minimally rhetorical—but not always, as there will be a number of questions in natural-language situations that thoroughly mix the two qualities. Thus, *every question asked, as a minimum, seeks information and tries to persuade*. As a result, while it is popular to speak of *rhetorical questions* and *informational questions*, neither of those two categories actually exists as such (cf. §1.B). For example:

(1) Where do you want to go for lunch? (OPEN QUESTION)
(2) Can you please pass the roast beast? (REQUEST)

Examples (1) and (2) are both maximal-leaning examples of each of these two semantic qualities of questions. Example (1), an open question, is highly focused on gathering information from its hearers (to the point where the question has no apparent pretense of an answer) and seems to make little or no rhetorical point. Yet consider (1), now in the following context:

A: I had such a big breakfast—man, I'm full.
B: Where do you want to go for lunch?

Here (1) moves from highly informational to highly rhetorical, while still retaining much of its informational quality. The question changes from a broad request for information and moves to a push for a specific reaction from *A*. Therefore, as a general rule, *semantics can trump syntax*. Likewise, example (2), a request, is highly focused on persuading action from its hearers (to the point where the question has no apparent pretense of gathering any information) and seems to need no information to be supplied (other than perhaps a reply). Yet consider (2) in the following context:

A: Excuse me, I really need to go to the bathroom.
B: Can you please pass the roast beast?

60. Quintilian, *Institutio oratoria* 9.2.7.

Here (2) moves from highly rhetorical to highly informational, while still retaining much of its rhetorical quality. The question changes from a push for action to a more genuine request for information to intersect the intended action of *A* (which is to leave for the bathroom, and *B*'s question hopes to cause *A* to pause and respond before leaving). Again, a general rule: *pragmatics can trump syntax and semantics.*

Even as pragmatics can force any question to possess any degree of both informational and rhetorical quality, syntactic and semantic qualities of questions also lend themselves well to strongly shaping questions with any degree of these qualities. For example, among the four basic syntactic formations for questions, variable questions and set questions tend to emphasize information, whereas polar questions and alternative questions tend to emphasize persuasion. Yet these tendencies are easily exploited or reversed by overriding semantic and pragmatic effects.

All questions seek information to some degree— no matter how small the degree is and no matter how great the rhetorical quality of the question is.

Key Bibliography

Estes, *Questions*, 49–53; Quintilian, *Institutio oratoria* 9.

5. Rhetorical Quality

One of the two most important and fundamental semantic properties of a question is its degree of *rhetorical quality.* This quality of a question measures the degree to which a question seeks to persuade the hearer in the direction intended by the asker. Simply put, the greater the degree of rhetorical quality of a question, the more the question *pushes.* Not only do questions ask to gain information from the hearers, but they also ask to gain a foothold within the thoughts of the hearer. When we interpret questions in the GNT, we gauge the degree to which a question tries to persuade. Understanding this semantic feature gives us better insight into interpreting what the question tries to achieve. The recognition that questions have both informational and rhetorical qualities goes back to at least the time of Quintilian.[61]

As a general rule, all questions accomplish two things to some degree: they gather information and persuade others. As we study the questions in the GNT, we need to remember two semantic principles for the interpretation of questions:

61. Quintilian, *Institutio oratoria* 9.2.7.

- All questions have at least a minimal degree of rhetorical quality.
- All questions also have at least a minimal degree of informational quality.

In natural-language occurrences, the degree of informational quality may be small in a highly rhetorical question, just as the degree of rhetorical quality may be small in a highly informational question. These two qualities are often divergent. In other words, a question that is maximally rhetorical will often be minimally informational—but not always, as there will be a number of questions in natural-language situations that thoroughly mix the two qualities. Thus, *every question asked, as a minimum, seeks information and tries to persuade.* As a result, while it is popular to speak of *rhetorical questions* and *informational questions*, neither of those two categories actually exists as such (cf. §1.B; for examples, see above §2.C.4).

Why questions are innately rhetorical is one of the mysteries of human communication. Yet on every level of language construction, persuasive techniques are available within question creation. Let's start with the syntax level:

(1) Do you want bacon or mayo? (SYNTACTIC)

Here example (1) is a simple alternative question (§3.C) without much semantic or pragmatic influence at this point. Because syntax is the weakest predictor of rhetorical quality, it is possible to try to read this with minimal rhetorical effect. However, in a natural-language situation, the syntax of the question actually *does* try to persuade the hearer—notably, that the only or preferred option available is bacon or mayo. (Are stewed prunes not an option? The question minimally persuades that they are not.) While syntax is normally overridden by semantics and pragmatics, question syntax does show traces of rhetorical force in their formation.

On the semantics level, we can observe much stronger rhetorical effects:

(2) Don't you even have any driving skills? (SEMANTIC)

Example (2) is a highly biased question ("even" and "any" being key bias words; §4.U), formed as a negative polar question (§4.T). In this case, the semantic bias inserted into the question pushes the hearer to answer the thinly veiled challenge to their driving ability. More so, the hearer of such a question may begin to harbor fears about their driving ability as a result of the strong rhetoric of the question. The question still has an informational quality, though, as the receiver of the question will most likely have to answer in some way so as to defend (what they perceive of) their driving ability.

On the level of pragmatics, the strongest rhetorical effects are in play, to the point that questions may come across almost as assertions:

(3) Hello? Can you take my order now? (PRAGMATIC)

In the case of the double question (§5.D.1) in (3), the asker uses a pragmatic strategy to strongly push the hearer (into taking the asker's order). The use of the first question, "Hello?" is a phatic question (§4.K) meant to "wake up" the hearer—and soften them up for the second part of the double-question combination (most likely a confirmation question [§4.R] or a request question [§4.S]). The question string still has informational qualities, as the asker seeks to know from the hearer if the hearer is awake and able to take the asker's order. The rhetorical expectation placed on the hearer is that they will comply with the asker's aggressive push (or, perhaps, respond negatively). To summarize the general rules from §2.C.4, when it comes to rhetorical quality, *semantics can trump syntax, and pragmatics can trump both.*

> ***The category of*** rhetorical question ***is so broad as to be practically meaningless when it comes to understanding the purpose of a question.***

To bring the conversation back full circle, the concept of the "rhetorical question" is a modern idea that is so broad as to lack any explanatory power. The idea that "rhetorical questions" are simply assertions does not bear out when one considers questions on their own terms in light of their erotetic logic. And yet, the rhetorical force of interrogatives is similar to assertive force in many ways. They are not the same, but they both do rely on a type of rhetorical strategy common to human communication. This rhetorical strategy is what makes questions seem assertive and causes assertions to prompt questions.

Key Bibliography

Estes, *Questions*, 49–56; Jauss, *Question and Answer*, 83–85; Lee-Goldman, "Typology"; May, "Questions as Suggestions"; Quintilian, *Institutio oratoria* 9; Rexach, "Rhetorical Questions," 139–55; Rohde, "Rhetorical Questions," 134–68.

6. EGH Principle

The *EGH Principle* asserts that when analyzing discourse for argumentation, the interpretation of the discourse should follow the path of the "maximally argumentative interpretation."[62] In other words, when we read a text and there are several acceptable options available between weaker and stronger rhetorical intent, we as interpreters are best served to choose the strongest rhetorical intent reasonable for the interpretation of the text. The challenge with understanding the pragmatics of rhetoric and argumentation in texts is that texts do not have

62. Eemeren, Grootendorst, and Snoeck Henkemans, *Argumentation*, 43–44.

clear indicators the way spoken language does. This is especially true of historical texts such as the GNT. Therefore, texts known to be rhetorical or argumentative (such as the GNT) are at a disadvantage contextually, as they are often read and understood without the rhetorical intent that would have occurred in the original creation of the text. Since natural discourse is highly rhetorical, texts (outside of a few types) often are as well, and interpreters must find a way to the strength of rhetorical intent within them. However, the EGH principle should not be used artificially to violate the erotetic logic of a given question, most notably by trying to force a highly informational-driven question into a highly rhetorical-driven one. Here *EGH* stands for the names of the authors of the principle, Eemeren, Grootendorst, and Snoeck Henkemans. The EGH Principle is a principle, not a law, and therefore it is not a rule but a guide for interpretation.

Key Bibliography

Eemeren, Grootendorst, and Snoeck Henkemans, *Argumentation*, 37–45; Estes, *Questions*, 67.

---

7. Predicaments

A *predicament* is a special epistemic situation created by the asking of a question that affects how the question is heard and responded to by hearers. Predicaments are created due to an epistemic imbalance—usually stemming from a lack of knowledge on the part of one participant in the dialogue. The occurrence of a predicament is due to the erotetic logic of a question and is one thing that makes questions inherently different than propositions. Predicaments are not well studied, and while there are many nuanced possibilities, we only include four examples here: *B-events*, *p-predicaments*, *b-predicaments*, and *i-predicaments*.

A *B-event* occurs when a speaker makes an utterance about something that is known to the hearer but not to the speaker, and even though the speaker may form the utterance as a declarative, it is heard by the hearer as a question requesting information (and in most cases, confirmation).[63] The predicament is called a B-event because the speaker (A) does not know about what is being spoken, while the hearer (B) does know about what is being spoken. As a result of the epistemic imbalance, A's utterance carries interrogative force (i.e., it seems to be information seeking) since B knows A does not know what B knows. For example, if speaker A utters, "Tell me about your favorite team," hearer B will receive it with interrogative force (as information seeking) because B knows A does not and cannot know about B's favorite team the way B does.[64]

---

63. Heritage, "Epistemics," 4; Koshik, *Beyond*, 1.

64. Because epistemic imbalance can occur in many directions, there are A-events, AB-events, D-events, O-events, and Type 1/Type 2 knowledge situations. For further study, see Labov and Fanshel, *Therapeutic Discourse*; Pomerantz, "Telling My Side."

A *p-predicament* occurs when an asker asks a legitimate, information-seeking question that the hearer is at a loss to answer because they can imagine what an answer is *not* but not what an answer to it is.[65] This kind of predicament arises when the recipient understands the question but does not understand fully how to give an answer to the question—they are unwittingly ignorant of the answer. This does not mean that an answer cannot be discovered; it is just not currently known—hence the predicament. A p-predicament does not occur just because the hearer does not know an answer to a question; it occurs when the hearer is puzzled by the correct answer.

A *b-predicament* occurs when an asker asks a legitimate, information-seeking question that the hearer has no idea what an answer to it is.[66] In this case, it is not just that an answer is unknown; rather, it is that an answer cannot be imagined—it is "outside their ken of thought." B-predicaments and p-predicaments have a complex logic, overlap in many but not all situations, and are not intended for simple polar or alternative questions. They are common situations in scientific and philosophical inquiry.

An *i-predicament* occurs when an asker asks a (seemingly) legitimate, information-seeking question that the hearer assumes that the asker must know what an answer to it is.[67] Normally, when an asker asks a question, the hearer assumes the asker does not know an answer or is not certain of an answer—this is why the question is asked, and it creates the prototypical question-answer sequence. However, if the hearer believes the asker should know an answer to the question, it alters this normal sequence. Thus, an i-predicament puts a hearer in a similar kind of predicament as b- and p-predicaments.

These are just a few types of predicaments that arise when questions are asked. If a speaker puts a predicament into play in the asking of a question (whether intentional or not), it will subtly affect the rhetorical force of the question. For example:

(1) Ποῦ ἐστιν ἡ ἐπαγγελία τῆς παρουσίας αὐτοῦ; (2 PET 3:4)

Question (1) is a classic example of a p-predicament for both the original readers of 2 Peter and readers of 2 Peter today. Peter explains in his letter that in the last days, scoffers will come scoffing, and the question they will raise is Ποῦ ἐστιν ἡ ἐπαγγελία τῆς παρουσίας αὐτοῦ; ("Where is the promise of his coming?"). This question puts the reader in a p-predicament because the question is legitimate, the reader knows what the answer is *not* (Jesus has not come yet), but the reader is puzzled by what the answer could be. For the reader, the question is not unanswerable, but the reader is unwittingly ignorant of the answer, which

65. Bromberger, *On What We Know*, 4.
66. Ibid., 36.
67. I coin this term while indebted to the earlier work of Bromberger and Heinemann.

creates the rhetorical effect of frustration and agitation in the reader.[68] This is the reason Peter does not (and cannot) give an actual answer to the question; instead, he chooses to soothe his readers in verse 8, Ἓν δὲ τοῦτο μὴ λανθανέτω ὑμᾶς, ἀγαπητοί, ὅτι μία ἡμέρα παρὰ κυρίῳ ὡς χίλια ἔτη ... ("But lest this one thing escape you, beloved—that one day is to the Lord like a thousand years ..."), to mitigate the damage of the successful rhetorical attack and the predicament that scoffers are able to put on believers.

Key Bibliography

Bromberger, *On What We Know*, 26–51; Coulthard, *Introduction*, 9–10; Macaulay, "Asking to Ask"; O'Grady, *Grammar*, 50–52; Stubbs, *Discourse Analysis*, 118–20; Weber, *Varieties of Questions*, 91–121.

D. Questions and Pragmatics

The third part of language where we will survey the way questions work is in the area of pragmatics. A simple definition for *pragmatics* is how language is used in communication. Pragmatics is the cultural and social extension of language use, and it is concerned with how humans shape language use to achieve their communication goals and construct meaning.[69] As a field, pragmatics "covers the acts performed by speakers and writers when they use language, the inferences by which hearers and readers construct a rich interpretation that goes beyond what is actually said or written, the things that speakers and writers presuppose (take for granted), the conventions governing what is appropriate in particular situations" (*CDL* 352). Therefore, our purpose in studying the pragmatics of questions is to understand better how questions are used and what impact they have on their recipients. Of all three parts of language we will consider, pragmatics is the one that most contextualizes questions in the GNT. As a result, there are an enormous number of possible pragmatic features that can affect question use, such as repetition, phatic situations, repair conditions, and many, many more. Thus, pragmatics is the most challenging and open-ended of the three areas of study. Below we consider several of the most important factors that shape the pragmatics of questions.

Key Bibliography

Blakemore, *Understanding Utterances*, 114–19; Estes, *Questions*, 47–49.

68. Note the question is based on the logic of ποῦ, not πότε, which if asked with πότε would *not* put the reader in a p-predicament (see Bromberger, *On What We Know*, 35–36). Hence the devastating rhetorical strategy of this question.

69. Thomas, *Meaning in Interaction*, 183.

1. Intonation

Intonation is the "variation in pitch over a stretch of utterance," and its use in spoken language is useful for differentiating sentence segments, sentence functions, and a variety of pragmatic information such as emotion (*CDL* 239). We distinguish intonation from phonetics (the study of phonemes) in that intonation covers multiple sounds within one or more utterances. When taken together, the individual sounds of an utterance may change from their natural state as they are spoken together. As we analyze intonation over a stretch of language, such as a sentence, we refer to it as an *intonation contour*. Intonation is a useful, basic indicator of sentence function.

Since the GNT is a written, and not spoken, text, one may wonder: What is the purpose of discussing intonation? There are two important reasons for at least mentioning intonation. First, the GNT developed in a far more oral culture than we currently live in, meaning that any written version of these ancient texts was most assuredly created with an oral sense and an oral understanding of how language worked. Second, as the GNT developed in a far more oral culture, it was definitely read aloud (instead of read silently) and most likely read aloud in some type of performative manner (1 Tim 4:13). This is important because, by way of example, an utterance can be written as a declarative even though it is intended to be verbalized with interrogative intonation (this is a common type of hedging device). Thus, the intonation information, while largely inaccessible to us today, played a much greater role in the reception of the GNT than we often assume. Recovering intonation information for any form of ancient Greek language is a nearly impossible task, though a few modern scholars have made attempts.[70] While it is difficult to recover any exact intonation information behind the questions in the GNT, the important thing to remember is that these texts would have had intonational information that was either lost or recorded with imprecision (as there is no way to record intonation), and secondly, that in the reading of these documents, any ancient-world intonational expectations are largely lost today.

The loss of intonational information in written texts is one key fact that spurred the adoption of accentuation (τόνοι) in Greek texts. The origin of accentuation is uncertain, but it was present at least as early as the time of Plato (ca. 427–347 BC). The accent marking of key words in Greek texts for the benefit of the reader started in Alexandria around 200 BC, though for many centuries these marks were infrequent.[71] By the second-century AD, grammarians such as Nicanor of Alexandria began to apply a variety of accent and intonation marks to help the reader better read aloud ancient works (such as Homer).[72] In contrast,

70. Nässelqvist, *Public Reading*.

71. Allen, *Accent and Rhythm*, 244.

72. Devine and Stephens, *Prosody*, 421.

our earliest full example of a copy of the NT with accentuation comes from the fifth-century AD (Vaticanus). These accent markers were important, not just because ancient Greek writers used *scriptio continua* but also because the intonation of the language was changing, and original ideas about intonation (and therefore meaning) were being lost (or in many cases were already far gone). In the Greek of the NT, a great example of the use of accentuation to distinguish interrogative intonation is the fixed acute accent (τόνος ὀξύς) over the interrogative pronoun τίς. While the accent reminds readers that the word is τίς and not τις, it is more than likely a vestigial remnant of an interrogative intonation that helped shape the reading of the word in original Greek discourse.

Key Bibliography

Allen, *Vox Graeca*, 6–9; Allott, *Key Terms*, 104–5; Caragounis, *Development of Greek*, 384–91; Devine and Stephens, *Prosody*; Lee and Scott, *Sound Mapping*, 91–104; Nagy, "Language and Meter," 382–84; Probert, *Ancient Greek Accentuation*, 54–55.

2. Prosody

Prosody (προσῳδία) is the pragmatic feature of language heard in patterns of stress, pitch, tempo, loudness, and rhythm (*CDL* 364). In the study of ancient Greek, intonation is usually limited to differences of pitch, whereas prosody includes intonation as well as the other verbal pragmatic features of an utterance. In modern texts, writers use punctuation to cue the reader into prosodic information about the text. In the ancient world, writers relied on other textual clues to impart prosodic information to their readers. In fact, textual evidence suggests that ancient Greek was intentionally written in a *scriptio continua* in order to facilitate reading aloud (though this is confusing to modern readers).[73] How a text sounded was far more important to Greek speakers than moderns assume—moderns prefer uniqueness and precision, but the Greeks preferred clarity and beauty.[74]

Like intonation, prosody is not truly recoverable, but the vestiges of it are important for discerning the interrogative features of questions in the GNT. The reason is that prosody is one of the major tells for interrogativity in human language. For example, a speaker in English denotes a polar question prosodically by way of an upward intonation at the end of the utterance. The association of higher pitch with polar interrogativity is not limited to English; in fact, it is

73. Lee and Scott, *Sound Mapping*, 70–72.

74. For example, Dionysius of Halicarnassus, *Literary Composition* 11, 15; Aristotle, *Rhetoric* 1408b20–32; Aristotle, *Poetics* 1458a18; Cicero, *De oratore* 3.9.37–38; Horace, *Ars poetica* 40; Quintilian, *Institutio oratoria* 8.1.1.

a common feature of most human languages.[75] Therefore, it is probable that when texts were read aloud in Koine Greek, the reader would heighten the pitch at the end of yes/no questions so that the hearer would know a question was asked. Similarly, languages with *wh*-fronting (ancient Greek, as well as Latin, English, and German) use the interrogative-word fronting to place preliminary stress (of some sort) on the opening sounds which would also alert a hearer that a question is coming.

Key Bibliography

Allen, *Accent and Rhythm*; Allott, *Key Terms*, 160–61; Devine and Stephens, *Prosody*; Estes, *Questions*, 47–49; Lee and Scott, *Sound Mapping*; Wharton, "Pragmatics and Prosody," 567–84.

---

3. Presupposition

The term *presupposition* refers to the occurrence of an unstated belief or argument contained within an utterance (*CDL* 357). Presuppositions are a frequent feature of discourse but are especially important in the study of questions and rhetoric. The primary reason for this is that askers ask questions in light of one of several elementary presuppositions. Askers presuppose that either the audience will know the answer to the question or will be able to be influenced by the question. *Wh*-words in questions automatically act as presupposition triggers for an alert audience. Propositions also contain presuppositional assumptions, but almost always of a far lower level of significance than questions (certainly, in natural-language usage). The use of presuppositions by the speaker can affect the *felicity conditions* of the utterance (*CDL* 169), possibly rendering the utterance disingenuous (*infelicitous*). Beyond this is the actual presuppositional content that speakers include within utterances. Presuppositions are instrumental in rhetoric, as orators build their arguments on what they think their audience knows and can accept. The classic example is the *enthymeme* (ἐνθύμημα), a rhetorical argument with a presumed premise. Thus, the importance of presupposition in creating questions and rhetorical content cannot be overstated.

Presuppositional content within utterances occurs in essentially two different degrees; low-level presuppositional content and high-level presuppositional content. Low-level presuppositional content in natural language is content that expects a minimal degree of prior knowledge; for example:

(1) Where is a restaurant?

This question presupposes there is a restaurant, and that it is locatable by the hearer. In the GNT, a similar example might be:

---

75. Devine and Stephens, *Prosody*, 454.

(2) Τίς ὁ ἁψάμενός μου; (LUKE 8:45)

Here Jesus's question ("Who is the one who touched me?") presupposes that someone touched him (or Jesus believed someone touched him, or perhaps somewhat more infelicitous, Jesus is falsely accusing someone of touching him). Typically, the existence of such presuppositions are a normal feature of language, and are not worthy of comment.

In contrast, there are many situations in natural language where high-level presuppositions come into play; these are presuppositions that assume some sort of important knowledge or action. We can amend (1) by changing the article, for example:

(3) Where is the restaurant?

Question (3) contains a higher level of presupposition in that the asker does not appear to be asking about *any* restaurant but rather about a specific restaurant that the asker assumes the hearer knows (or should know). In this case, the asker uses the definite article indexically to presuppose prior knowledge important in the asking of the question.[76] Let's look at a more significant example:

(4) Τί σοι ὄνομά ἐστιν; (LUKE 8:30)

In (4), Jesus's question ("What is your name?") presupposes that the demon has a name (and that it is capable of uttering it). This presupposition raises many additional questions: How did Jesus know demons can have names? Why did Jesus think the demon would give him his name? Do all demons have names? Are the names of demons personal or generic (as with "Legion")? Can a regular person ask a demon its name and expect an answer?

High-level presuppositions, especially as they relate to questions, are an important point of study as they relate to fields such as rhetoric, politics, and logic. Below is a simple example of the use of high-level presuppositions in rhetoric:

(5) Ἀρχόμεθα πάλιν ἑαυτοὺς συνιστάνειν; (2 COR 3:1A)

In 2 Corinthians 2:14–15, Paul reminds his audience that those in Christ are captives of Christ's triumph, the pleasing aroma of Christ's sacrifice. It is only then that Paul questions the role of self-commendation in example (5) at 3:1 ("Again we begin to commend ourselves?"). Not only does this question carry with it the presupposition of a discussion of commendation but also that this is not the first time this issue was at the forefront (note πάλιν as a common presuppositional-content indicator). In fact, it is the presuppositional content in

76. In narrative, indexicals serve as important indicators of both reference and presupposition; see Estes, *Temporal Mechanics*, 246–48.

(5) that at once makes Paul's argumentation powerful but not easy to follow for later readers.

Key Bibliography

Allott, *Key Terms*, 148–53; Austin, "Performative-Constative," 17–18; Dekker, "Presupposition," 42–52; Gazdar, *Pragmatics*, 89–128; Sandt, "Presupposition," 329–50.

---

4. Implicature

Implicature is the intentional communication of more than the stated meaning of an utterance. To *implicate* is similar to the more general idea of to *imply*, with the difference being that to implicate is always a conscious and intentional act on the part of the speaker. It is not a presupposition, nor is it an inference. Implicature happens outside of the overt syntax and semantics of a question,[77] but the speaker uses the syntax and semantics of the question as a stepping-off point to create it pragmatically in the asking of the question. Implicature helps us to "go beyond what speakers say to what speakers actually mean" (*CDL* 222). It is a universal feature of human communication that is not language dependent. Some types of language use, such as phatic language, depend heavily on implicature to carry their meaning. The antonym of implicature is *explicature*—the overt meaning of a sentence driven by its syntax and semantics.

Generally speaking, there are two types of implicature: *conventional implicature* and *conversational implicature*. Following linguistic tradition, when we use the word implicature, we are referring to conversational implicature. It occurs when the speaker creates a sentence with additional meaning beyond the explicated meaning. More specifically, implicature from a question is distinct from the basic interrogative content of a question (which a reader ascertains primarily from its syntax and its base semantics). A question with an implicative meaning is a question that asks something outside of the summation of the literal meaning of its parts. Let's consider the implicature of the following two questions:

(1) What do you want out of the box of chicken? (NONIMPLICATIVE)
(2) What do you want out of life? (IMPLICATIVE)

Both of these questions (1) and (2) are asked as variable questions (§3.B), and based on their syntax, we could expect them to be strong information-seeking questions. In (1), there is no significant implicature from the speaker; the speaker seems to want to know what kind of chicken the audience desires. But in (2), the speaker is not asking the question so as to get a simple answer but implicates a

77. Bach, "Top 10," 23.

desire to know what the audience is going to do in the future (and to persuade the audience to think about this). We can see the same in the GNT:

(3) τί πάλιν θέλετε ἀκούειν; (JOHN 9:27A)
(4) μὴ καὶ ὑμεῖς θέλετε αὐτοῦ μαθηταὶ γενέσθαι; (JOHN 9:27B)

In (3) and (4), the double questions asked by the man born blind from John 9:27, we see two adjacent questions where the first (3) is not implicative and the second (4) is implicative (for rhetorical effect). In (3), "Why do you want to hear it again?" the man does not implicate much above the already-present interrogative force encoded in τί (plus note the focus on πάλιν to make the point). By (4), "Do even you want to become his disciples?" the man amplifies his position by asking a polar question calling for a decision. Yet reading the narrative account, we know that the man is implicating something very different than simply asking the Judaean religious leaders whether they would like to decide to become disciples of Jesus. The response of these leaders in v. 28 (καὶ ἐλοιδόρησαν αὐτὸν; "and they abused him") gives credence to this assessment.

In contrast, *conventional implicature* is more limited and specific. It is related to, but not the same as, presupposition.[78] It occurs when, in the course of creating a sentence, a speaker uses a word or phrase that does not seem to alter the basic meaning of the sentence syntactically or semantically but still has the effect of creating additional meaning for the sentence. It is related to *bias* (§2.C.2). For example:

(5) ἐπεὶ πῶς κρινεῖ ὁ θεὸς τὸν κόσμον; (ROM 3:6)
(6) Τί οὖν ἐροῦμεν εὑρηκέναι Ἀβραὰμ τὸν προπάτορα ἡμῶν κατὰ σάρκα; (ROM 4:1)

Question (5) ("Otherwise, how will God judge the world?") is along the lines of classic implicature, as ἐπεί does not affect the interrogative content of the question—from a semantic perspective, ἐπεὶ πῶς κρινεῖ ὁ θεὸς τὸν κόσμον asks the same question as πῶς κρινεῖ ὁ θεὸς τὸν κόσμον. However, without even looking yet at context, intuitively we understand that the ἐπεί adds *something* to the meaning. Once we look at context, we see that Paul uses ἐπεί to show causality beyond (and with a different sense than) the actual question asked. In (6) ("Then what will we say that Abraham—our forefather according to human nature—has found?"), we have an example of τὸν προπάτορα ἡμῶν κατὰ σάρκα serving as a nominal appositive to Ἀβραάμ, creating a supplemental type of conventional implicature.[79] As with (5), semantically τί οὖν ἐροῦμεν εὑρηκέναι Ἀβραὰμ τὸν προπάτορα ἡμῶν κατὰ σάρκα is the same as τί οὖν ἐροῦμεν εὑρηκέναι Ἀβραάμ. The significance of this supplement added by Paul is that it implicates that Paul

78. Sauerland and Stateva, *Presupposition and Implicature*, 1–3.
79. Potts, *Logic*, 89–93.

is related to his audience, so the question is as relevant to him as his readers. Linguists debate the consequence of conventional implicature, so care is warranted in using it in interpretation.[80]

Implicature is particularly difficult in historical linguistics (such as our study in the GNT) because we later readers are unfamiliar with Koine-Greek conventions and conversational assumptions. With each question we encounter we ask: What is explicatively being asked? And is there something implicatively being asked? At the same time, as interpreters, our goal is to avoid inferring what a writer may have said; rather, we are trying to understand what the writer is implicating to the reader. A challenge with implicature is that it creates indeterminacy in interpretation, as many times there are several implications possible. This is because the implicated meaning of a sentence is not entailed within the explicated meaning of the sentence—which also means that the implicated meaning may not be rationally deducible from the sentence itself. While the answers given to questions may be helpful at times in identifying implicature, they are not the solution, as the recorded response can be based on misunderstanding or inferring the wrong idea. Several types of questions naturally tend to be implicative: request (§4.S) and retort questions (§5.B), for example. Figurative language is often a sign of implicature. Questions with implicature are common in the GNT, especially in the Gospels, where Jesus, his opponents, and minor characters tend to use their questions implicatively. As a theory, implicature started with Paul Grice, but later followers of the theory proposed other pragmatic situations, such as when a speaker asks a question, seeking not a literal answer but rather a culturally-dependent response (*CDL* 306).

Key Bibliography

Allott, *Key Terms*, 91–97; Bach, "Top 10," 21–30; Chapman and Routledge, *Key Ideas*, 86–92; Davis, *Implicature*, 1–32; Gazdar, *Pragmatics*, 37–62; Grice, *Studies in the Way of Words*; Horn, "Implicature," 3–28; Potts, *Logic*.

---

5. Genre

Genre, as we most often use the word, refers to a type or kind of something created. In order to better understand a text, when we read a text we consciously or subconsciously try to identify what kind of text it is. Identifying the kind of a text is identifying its genre. The idea of genre is a broad one, and for the sake of our discussion here we will only consider two subfields with genre research:

80. It is useful for raising questions in translation. For example, Acts 7:52 in the GNT reads, τίνα τῶν προφητῶν οὐκ ἐδίωξαν οἱ πατέρες ὑμῶν; but the NIV not only alters the interrogative logic (switching a set question to a polar question) but adds the word *ever*, a word well known for creating bias in questions and opening up implicative implications.

traditional genre theory and *rhetorical genre studies*. Both of these outlooks on genre affect the way we interpret the pragmatic features of questions in the GNT.

Traditional genre theory goes back to at least Plato, who distinguished between different kinds of literary works.[81] This traditional approach is best described as taxonomic, as it tries to classify created works by formal characteristics into recognizable categories usually based around an ideal example. In traditional literary theory, readers use genre to differentiate between different kinds of literary texts (such as epic, tragedy, comedy and parody, or biography, for example). In a similar manner, traditional biblical criticism sees evidence of various genres, such as gospels, prophecies, histories, apocalypses, law collections, wisdom sayings and testaments. Genre may also describe simple-language use in created works, such as speech acts like exclamations or questions, and it also may describe complex-language use in created works, such as the nineteenth-century English romantic novel or the medieval chronicle. Traditional genre theory affects question interpretation in the GNT. For example:

(1) Τίς ἀποκυλίσει ἡμῖν τὸν λίθον ἐκ τῆς θύρας τοῦ μνημείου; (MARK 16:3)
(2) τίς με ῥύσεται ἐκ τοῦ σώματος τοῦ θανάτου τούτου; (ROM 7:24)

Both questions (1) and (2) are syntactically similar, but their genres are different. Question (1) appears as part of reported speech within a narrative genre, a generic situation that encourages—but not mandates—the reading of the question to have a stronger informational quality and a weaker rhetorical quality. The reverse is true of (2), where the rhetorical nature of the genre encourages a strong rhetorical quality. This use of genre satisfies a basic hermeneutical principle common in biblical interpretation.

In contrast, rhetorical genre studies are a modern take on an ancient idea. In large part it launched with the work of Carolyn Miller, who argued that genre "must be centered not on the substance or the form of discourse but on the action it is used to accomplish."[82] Thus, the genre of a creative work is not based on the form of that work as much as it is based on the rhetorical situation in which that work appears. In many ways, this approach to genre is more useful than the traditional approach when applied to distinct speech acts. We can then apply rhetorical genre studies to the same two questions from the GNT, (1) and (2). Rather than asking what form of text the question is embedded in, we ask what way each question is used within the discourse, and to accomplish what purpose. In (1), the question is used by Mark to create reported dialogue between characters in the story. Thus, its purpose is to show interaction and character attitudes on a topic more than to state anything to the reader of the text. This type of characterization reveals the question to be about openness of dialogue, and there-

81. Plato, *Republic* 394c.
82. Miller, "Genre," 151.

fore it is a classic open-question type. Even though (2) carries a similar syntax to (1), its social action is very different. Paul writes (2) in the midst of a personal reflection contained within a highly rhetorical letter intended for a general audience. Thus, Paul's use of τίς points to the reflective power of "Who?" which is both informational ("I'd like to know") and rhetorical ("Only God knows"). In conclusion, modern approaches to genre (such as rhetorical genre studies) offer a potent method to better understand specific speech acts and their pragmatic effects that make up the various texts in the GNT.

Key Bibliography

Bakhtin, *Speech Genres*, 60–102; Devitt, *Writing Genres*, 1–32; Frow, *Genre*; Miller, "Genre," 151–67.

---

6. Discourse

Discourse refers to "any coherent sequence of sentences with a structure, typically marked by cohesive devices" (*CDL* 136). Thus, anytime a speaker or writer strings several complete utterances together that fit together in some way, they are engaging in the creation of discourse. Discourse is often classified in the modern West as within four different forms or modes: *description*, *narration*, *exposition*, and *persuasion*.[83] Each of these forms, or modes, of discourse is the raw stuff from which writers compose their texts—their large structures of coherent sequence of utterances. While there are a variety of competing lists of forms and different definitions for the modes, the most important differentiation of quality that occurs between modes of discourse is *temporal*.[84] For example, within the GNT, the Gospels primarily use the narration mode of discourse, with events and a progression through time; but the letters primarily use the persuasion mode of discourse, with a defined state and a development of thought. These four forms of discourse (and their variations) evolved from exercises in discourse creation in classical rhetoric and composition. The student handbooks of ancient Greek rhetoric, called *progymnasmata*, contain exercises to help students create different forms of discourse, such as narrative.

Within the modes of discourse, there are three primary ways to represent speech. Confusingly, each of these ways is also typically referred to as a form of discourse. They are *direct discourse*, *indirect discourse*, and *free (indirect) discourse*. (Herein I will refer to these three as *direct speech*, *indirect speech*, and *free indirect speech*, to avoid confusion.) These three ways of representing speech are most prominent in the narrative mode of discourse, but they are found in all the other modes as well. For the purpose of familiarizing ourselves with questions

83. Devitt, *Writing Genres*, 99.

84. Smith, *Modes of Discourse*, 22–38; cf. Estes, *Temporal Mechanics*, 8–10.

and rhetoric in the GNT, we will focus our attention in this section on (a) *direct speech* and (b) the *persuasive mode.*

First, *direct speech* is the recorded speech of a character within a larger narrative text or literary work. Direct speech is sometimes referred to as *reported speech* or *oratio recta* (*CDL* 135). Direct speech is easily identified in modern languages such as English:

(1) His daughter asked, "What if there are dolphins that are also like unicorns?"

In (1), the direct speech is identified by prominent indicators such as quotation marks and a change in tense.[85] Unlike modern languages, which clearly distinguish direct speech through one or more indicators, ancient languages such as Koine Greek did not possess clear ways to distinguish direct speech from indirect speech or nonspeech parts of the text. To detect direct speech in the GNT, the interpreter must decode the text based on circumstantial indicators provided by the writer. For example (with NA[28] formatting and punctuation removed in both cases, but emphasis mine):

(2) *Καὶ ἐπηρώτησαν αὐτὸν οἱ μαθηταὶ* λέγοντες τί οὖν οἱ γραμματεῖς λέγουσιν ὅτι Ἠλίαν δεῖ ἐλθεῖν πρῶτον (DIRECT SPEECH)

(3) *Καὶ* προσελθόντες οἱ *Φαρισαῖοι καὶ Σαδδουκαῖοι* πειράζοντες *ἐπηρώτησαν αὐτὸν* σημεῖον ἐκ τοῦ οὐρανοῦ ἐπιδεῖξαι αὐτοῖς (INDIRECT SPEECH)

At first glance, both utterances (2) and (3) reveal almost identical syntax in their opening clauses. However, question (2) from Matthew 17:10 ("Then why do the scribes say that Elijah must come first?") possesses only one indicator that it may be reporting direct speech, the duplicative participle λέγοντες with the clause-fronted τί. In this case, both elements together are needed to indicate direct speech. Conversely, question (3) from Matthew 16:1 ("They asked him to show them a sign from heaven") is most likely indirect speech, also possessing only one indicator, the infinitive ἐπιδεῖξαι in the speech clause. The use of the infinitive to indicate indirect speech (and therefore, not direct speech), is quite common in the GNT.[86] When a question is formed using indirect speech, it is essentially synonymous with an indirect question (§2.B.12). In final analysis, in some cases in the GNT it is impossible to know for certain whether the author intended the utterance as direct or indirect speech.

Second, the *persuasive mode* is a form of discourse where the author creates structure from a series of utterances in order to help the reader move through a metaphorical situation.[87] The persuasive mode is a common form of discourse

85. Jacobson, *'Many Are Saying,'* 20.
86. Wallace, *Greek Grammar*, 603–5.
87. Smith, *Modes of Discourse*, 20.

within the GNT, and writers use it to directly engage the reader. Since forms of discourse are derived from a sequence of sentences, it is not possible to identify the form of discourse a question falls within based on the question alone. However, educated guesses can be made based on questions found in the narrative and persuasive modes. For example:

(4) I asked, "When did you become such a Francophile?" (NARRATIVE MODE)
(5) That is the truth. After all, who can argue against it? (PERSUASIVE MODE)

In (4), the direct speech is a likely indicator that the utterance belongs to the narrative mode of a larger text. In (5), the appeal to the thought process is a likely indicator that the utterance belongs to the persuasive mode of a larger text. It is interesting to note that the question from the narrative mode, (4), naturally leans toward information seeking, whereas the question in the persuasive mode, (5), naturally leans toward rhetorical seeking.

One way to use discourse features to better interpret questions in the GNT is to evaluate where questions occur within the movement of individual discourses. For the sake of simplicity, there are four positions that a question may occupy in a discourse form: *opening*, *closing*, *standalone*, and *middle*. Each of these positions affects the pragmatic qualities of the question asked. For example, a question asked in the opening position of a discourse tends to overshadow the rest of the discourse, whereas a question asked in the closing position of a discourse tends to provoke a response from the audience as well as overshadow whatever form of discourse follows. In the GNT, a question in the opening and closing movement of a discourse is common and to be expected. What is more uncommon and more unexpected is when a question occurs in the middle of a discourse; this type of occurrence reveals that the asker intends the question to be more highly rhetorical than if used in either of the other positions.

Key Bibliography
Maier, "Switches," 118–39; Smith, *Modes of Discourse*, 1–48.

---

7. *Turn-Taking*

Turn-taking is the interplay in narrative discourse between the two different roles of speaker and hearer. Turn-taking is sometimes called an *exchange* (*CDL* 160) or *adjacency pair*. When two or more people engage in dialogue, there is a natural human affinity toward the taking of turns between roles. First, one person or group is the speaker, and second, another person or group is the speaker. Dialogue exchanges, however, need not be limited to two speakers or groups. Each speaking part counts as a turn for that speaker (*CDL* 453). The speaker's turn can count as any communicative attempt: it can be short or long; it can be a speech or merely a nod or other gesture. However, sometimes these turns can be broken up if too much occurs between turns. Because of human nature, turn-taking is not always neat or organized, though often discourse does follow turns closely. Turn-taking appears to be a universal feature of language, regardless of the specific language or culture. In ancient written texts, it is not always easy to delimit turns within recorded dialogue; recourse must be made to various tells, such as discourse markers. Discourse markers often appear at the beginning of a turn and are useful in interpreting the turn-taking.[88] Within discourse, questions have a unique ability to shape turns, probably more than almost any other sentence function.

Turn-taking also provides an indicator for interrogative force within a question. For example, a first-turn question is well known for being both highly information seeking as well as discourse controlling (§5.A). Turn-taking is genre dependent; it occurs frequently in the Gospels but infrequently in the rest of the GNT. Some examples of turn-taking in English:

(1) Excuse me, do you know where I can buy milk? (SPEAKER 1)
(2) No, sorry, I'm not from around here. (SPEAKER 2)
(3) Oh, OK, sorry about that, never mind then. (SPEAKER 1)
(4) OK, sorry, bye. (SPEAKER 2)

In examples (1)–(4), discourse markers such as "excuse me" and "OK" are helpful in delimiting conversational turns. We can observe clear turns in the GNT, for example from John 1:19–20:

(5) *ἱερεῖς καὶ Λευίτας*: Σὺ τίς εἶ; (SPEAKER 1)
(6) *Ἰωάννης*: Ἐγὼ οὐκ εἰμὶ ὁ Χριστός. (SPEAKER 2)
(7) *ἱερεῖς καὶ Λευίτας*: Τί οὖν; Σὺ Ἠλίας εἶ; (SPEAKER 1)
(8) *Ἰωάννης*: Οὐκ εἰμί. (SPEAKER 2)
(9) *ἱερεῖς καὶ Λευίτας*: Ὁ προφήτης εἶ σύ; (SPEAKER 1)
(10) *Ἰωάννης*: Οὔ. (SPEAKER 2)

Utterances (5) through (10) above represent direct discourse between John the Baptist and the priests and Levites. In each case, the speakers follow a rather typical conversation pattern.

Areas of language study such as discourse analysis and conversation analysis focus a great deal of attention on turn-taking in a more nuanced manner. In analyzing the pragmatics of questions via turn-taking, there are two major items to determine: (a) in what turn is the question asked, and (b) where in the turn is the question asked. For (a), the interpreter must evaluate the dialogue to discover the turn in which a speaker asks a question. This evaluation is not always easy

88. Drummen, "Discourse Cohesion," 136.

within ancient narratives; many textbooks that discuss turn-taking use artificial dialogues that are simplistic when compared to representational dialogue found in ancient historiographical texts (§2.D.8). As a result, when evaluating turn-taking in narrative discourses within the GNT, interpreters should not sketch turn-taking with absolute numbers but should understand turns relative to the other explicit or implicit turns in the dialogue.[89] Besides keeping track of speakers, a reader must consider how temporal or spatial markers segment the narrative and whether there are any subject (scene) changes in the course of the discussion.[90] For the purpose of our study, we limit our attention to *first-turn* and *second-turn* questions. Questions that appear in more nuanced positions (such as third turn, and beyond) can still be profitably analyzed by the interpreter using principles herein as a starting point. The same is true for questions that exist in a diegetic level above the level of the primary discourse (e.g., Luke 19:31; Rom 11:34a, 34b; Rev 18:18).[91]

For (b), the interpreter must evaluate the dialogue to discover where in the turn a speaker asks a question. For the purpose of our study, we limit our attention to the *opening*, *middle*, *closing*, and *standalone* positions within direct speech. Each of these positions describes the position of the question within one dialogue turn *only*. The positions are distinguishable as follows:

Opening: Question occurs at the beginning of the dialogue turn; additional utterance(s) by the same speaker follow the question (E.G., REV 17:7).

Middle: Question occurs in the middle of the dialogue turn; additional utterances by the same speaker precede and follow the question (E.G., ROM 11:1).

Closing: Question occurs at the end of the dialogue turn; additional utterance(s) by the same speaker precede the question (E.G., JOHN 5:47).

Standalone: The only utterance in the dialogue turn is the question; no other utterances are made by the speaker (E.G., ACTS 23:19).

There are several general rules that apply to question asking in each position. Questions in the opening position tend to shift focus and allow narrow dialogue to develop (the subsequent utterances by the speaker often sharpen or modify the original question, if not answer it outright). Or they allow monologues to develop. They can possess both informational and rhetorical qualities. With

89. An implicit turn occurs when dialogue is described, not represented (e.g., Luke 20:1; John 3:25).

90. On markers and the segmentation of ancient narrative, see Estes, *Temporal Mechanics*, 131–64.

91. On diegetic levels in narrative discourse, see Estes, *Temporal Mechanics*, 173–75, 234–38.

questions in the middle position, the more embedded (toward the middle) the question is in a turn, the more highly rhetorical it is. If the question falls in the middle, it is more likely than not meant to be rhetorical. (This does not mean a middle question cannot be information seeking, as the semantics of the question still play an important role [§2.C.4]). Questions in the closing position tend to "hang" after the buildup from the initial utterances, and they are great dialogue starters. Standalone questions do not have the weight of closing questions and are used in more open and general information-request situations. If the question closes a turn or is a standalone question, then it has a much greater likelihood of being an information-seeking question.

Key Bibliography

Allott, *Key Terms*, 189–90; Estes, *Questions*, 128–44; Haugh, "Conversational Interaction," 251–73; Sacks, "Initial Characterization," 35–42; Sacks, *Lectures*, 1:624–32; 2:32–43; Sidnell, *Conversation Analysis*, 36–58; Tottie, "Turn Management," 382–84.

8. Dialogue

Dialogue, in the most general sense, is simply communication between two parties (*CDL* 133). In everyday speech, dialogue usually refers to a type of oral communication, but dialogue is equally important in the study of written texts as well. Within texts, two of the most prominent types of dialogues occur (a) between characters and other characters or the narrator (think *narrative discourse* and *turn-taking*) and (b) between the author and the reader (think *persuasive discourse*) (§2.D.6–7). In texts containing the narrative mode of discourse, dialogue always involves *representation*, with the most common types broadly considered to be either historical or fictional. In texts comprised of the persuasive mode of discourse, dialogue always involves *demonstration* (ἀπόδειξις), of which there are many strategies such as *ethos* (ἦθος) and *pathos* (πάθη).[92]

These issues touch on extensive matters in many fields of study; yet one important factor that every interpreter of the GNT must recognize when evaluating the pragmatics of their texts is the distinction between *natural dialogue*, *artificial dialogue*, and *representational dialogue*.[93] Here I develop these terms in such a way as to bridge the gap between the many theoretical and philosophical attempts to understand discourse and the practical needs of biblical interpretation and exegesis. *Natural dialogue* is any discourse that takes place and is observed or participated in within the normal progression of the world. An obvious example of this would be a conversation between two people. *Artificial*

92. Aristotle, *Rhetoric* 1354a1–14; 1356a1–4.
93. Cf. Aristotle, *Rhetoric* 1355b41–46.

dialogue is any discourse that does not arise naturally but is created or invented. Books on language study and linguistics (including this one) are full of artificial dialogue. *Representational dialogue* is any discourse that tries to represent a natural dialogue. Representational dialogue strives to be like natural dialogue, but it is never actually natural dialogue. For this reason, sometimes representational dialogue is included as a subset of artificial dialogue (though I do not see it that way). At first glance, a person may put works of fiction in with artificial dialogue, but fiction is a special form of artificial dialogue in that it is artificial dialogue that is acting as representational dialogue. Literary critics treat it as representational dialogue. Likewise, historiographical texts (such as the Gospels) may seem to contain natural dialogue, but these discourses are comprised of representational dialogue.

The reason this is important is that neither artificial dialogue nor representational dialogue are natural dialogue. In studying texts, we are studying representational dialogue by way of artificial dialogue—neither of which are actual natural dialogue. Thus, our attempts to understand the pragmatics of a text will always be severely limited. For example, unlike in natural dialogue (which never actually has a beginning and end, except ones that we create to make sense of our world), historiographical narratives must truncate all recorded discourse (regardless of how and what is recorded), thereby creating a representation of the natural dialogue. This makes distinguishing original pragmatics nearly impossible, but it does give a clue to what the writer believed the original pragmatics to represent. A great example of this occurs with turn-taking. In the Gospels, Jesus regularly opens a conversation with a question (e.g., Matt 16:13, with a first-turn, opening-position question); but because this is representational discourse, there is no way to know how this representation of the events fits into any natural dialogue. However, Matthew writes the narrative in such a way as to indicate that the question in Matthew 16:13 functioned as a first-turn, opening-position question. And any responses recorded in the representational dialogue will be built around author-created pragmatic expectation. Nonetheless, pragmatic features within the representational dialogue of historiographical texts are truly useful in unlocking a better understanding of the rhetorical values of ancient texts.

Key Bibliography

White, *Content of the Form*.

---

9. Rhetorical-Shift Principle

Pragmatics shape the rhetorical qualities of an utterance, much the same way syntax and semantics do. To understand the informational and rhetorical qualities of a question, the reader must include all indicators available. When a question appears in artificial discourse (as is often the case in linguistic studies), the question can only be interpreted by looking at syntax and semantics; but when a question appears in natural or representational discourse, pragmatics come in to play (§2.D.8). In written texts, the pragmatic factors come in to play when reading a question that is embedded within a discourse. The written utterances all around the question represent pragmatic vectors that shape the qualities and meaning of the question. Generally speaking, the more rhetorical of a discourse situation that a question is included in, the more the question will likely undergo a rhetorical shift. For example, a question that looks strongly informational based on syntax and semantics will, when placed in a highly charged rhetorical environment, no longer be primarily informational but instead be far more rhetorical in its quality. Thus, the pragmatics twist the original nature for a new rhetorical purpose. This is part of the power of the so-called "rhetorical question."

The *rhetorical-shift principle* states that the more informational in nature a question is, the greater the possible rhetorical shift will be when pragmatics are applied. Let's break this principle down using simple examples:

(1) Can't you go pick up lunch for me? (LEANS RHETORICAL)
(2) Who can go pick up lunch for me? (LEANS INFORMATIONAL)

First, we observe that questions (1) and (2) are in artificial discourse, without any surrounding text. Based on syntax and semantics, question (1) leans rhetorical, and question (2) leans informational. Using the rhetorical-shift principle, if (1) and (2) were used in a highly rhetorical environment—say a letter of Paul or Cicero—then the rhetorical-quality shift that (2) undergoes will be significantly greater than the rhetorical shift that (1) undergoes. Because (1) already has a strong rhetorical quality, highly rhetorical pragmatic factors will have little effect on the reading of this question. In contrast, because (2) has a strong informational bent, if it is placed in a rhetorical situation its shift in rhetorical quality is much, much greater. Questions with strong rhetorical qualities undergo little or no shift when put into a discourse or dialogue that has a strong rhetoric. However, even with the shift, information-leaning questions will still hold onto many of their information-leaning qualities. Persuasion is a force that taints—not transmutes—utterances.[94] For example:

(1) τίς στρατεύεται ἰδίοις ὀψωνίοις ποτέ; (1 COR 9:7A)

Here in (1) Paul asks, "Who would serve as a soldier—ever—using his own wages?" Based on syntax and semantics, Paul uses τίς to form a variable question, using a speculative question type with a bias word (ποτέ)—surely more informational than rhetorical (§4.B). Then Paul puts the question in a string, which amplifies its qualities (1 Cor 9:7b–c; see §5.D). When this question is put into a discourse pragmatically oriented toward stronger rhetoric and persuasion,

94. Cf. Maneli, *Perelman's New Rhetoric*, 38.

such as 1 Corinthians, the pragmatics of the text shift this question toward a stronger rhetorical orientation. This is what causes readers to read the question as a "rhetorical question" and commentators to note what the question "says." However, 1 Cor 9:7a is not intended by Paul to simply say something; it still raises a question with both strong informational and rhetorical qualities. For example, some readers will simply pass over this question or see it as an assertion, but many will think, "Do I know anyone who has done this?" and others will think, "This is not likely except there was a story on this last week in the paper," and still others will think, "Actually, I do know someone who has done this." In fact, the remaining informational quality even causes a commentator to think of occurrences of this![95] No matter how the reader receives the question, they will get the gist of what Paul is trying to say, but they will usually get to the gist by consciously or unconsciously going through the required interrogative logic of the question. This is what makes Paul's use of a question so much more important than making an assertion. That is the power of the so-called "rhetorical question" and the importance of the rhetorical-shift principle.

E. Answers

In erotetics, or the study of questions and their logic, there are two important ways to think about what questions mean: (a) what questions ask or (b) how questions are answered. For the purpose of our study, we will be focusing almost exclusively on what questions ask. However, a number of prevalent erotetic theories do define questions in light of their answers.[96] For them, the answer to a question is as important as the question itself. I disagree for the simple fact that an answer represents an independent (though related) speech act, and while answers may be entailed by a question, they are not required in any way in order to ask the question. In fact, in natural-language situations the answers given may not relate at all to the questions asked. The possible exception to that in this book are dilemma questions (§4.O). There are two possible scenarios for answers to questions: a *reply* and the *set of answers*.

The first scenario for understanding the answers to questions is their *reply*. The reply is also called their *possible answers*. A reply is any utterance, sign, or action that is given in response to a question asked. It does not need to be related to, or linked logically to, the question that came before. In fact, in many natural-language situations like everyday discourse, replies to questions may be very erratic if one were to write them out to be read. In written discourse, the same is not usually true, but this does not mean that replies in texts will necessarily be

95. For example, Conzelmann, *1 Corinthians*, 154.

96. For example, Groenendijk and Stokhof, "Questions," 1079; Stahl, "Effectivity," 211; Fales, "Phenomenology," 60.

logically consistent (or even answer the original question). Greek, as with most IE languages, does not have a required answer pattern[97]; replies must be evaluated on a case-by-case basis.

In natural-language situations, possible replies to questions generally fall into one of six categories. We can see these six categories in the narrative sections of the GNT:

Confirmation: Yes-or-no, positive-or-negative replies (E.G., MATT 13:51; JOHN 1:21b, 21c; ACTS 22:27).
Informational: Any reply that seeks to fill in the question with missing information (E.G., JOHN 18:5).
Rhetorical: Any reply that seeks to persuade the asker or turn the dialogue (E.G., JOHN 18:23).
Undetermined: "Maybe," "I don't know," or some other indefinite, nonanswer reply (E.G., JOHN 8:6).
Phatic: Replies that fulfill social expectations more than given a logical answer (E.G., MATT 27:11).[98]
None: When no reply of any kind is made (E.G., JOHN 18:24).

In any of the six categories of replies, the asker may feel that the question was sufficiently answered or addressed by these replies in natural-language situations.

The second scenario to understand how answers relate to questions is determining a question's *set of answers*. When a question is asked, it *always* seeks an answer no matter the degree of rhetorical effects that are applied. As noted above, this desire for an answer is what fundamentally differentiates a question from a proposition or any other kind of sentential force. A question's *set of answers* are the sum and total of possible answers that will logically satisfy what the question is asking. As we break down questions by their syntactic, semantic, and pragmatic features, we will see that different kinds of questions have different kinds of set of answers. For now, the simplest way to see how this plays out is to look at the four primary syntactic formations for questions: polar, variable, alternative, and set questions.

Polar questions have the most limited set of answers: yes (positive) and no (negative) are the only two answers that comprise a polar question's set of answers. For example:

(1) Do you like Tolkien's works? (POLAR QUESTION)

---

97. Usually found in relation to polar questions; although cf. Apollonius Dyscolus, *Syntax* 247.

98. Given the culture gap between ourselves and the events of the GNT, it is hard to know for certain which answers are definitively phatic. One of the telltale signs is an idiomatic expression. In Matthew 27:11, Jesus's short response may be somewhat phatic, as a perfunctory response to Pilate more than an affirmation.

In example (1), "Yes" or "Yes, I do" or "Uh huh" or a nonverbal head nod or any similar positive expression is within the appropriate set of answers as a positive response; likewise, the same is true of any negative response. However, saying "I like pizza" or "Do you like Tolkien's works?" or smiling or saying nothing at all are not within the set of answers for polar questions. The exception to this for polar questions is an indication of indecision, such as "maybe." An indecisive answer does not actually fulfill the question's set of answers but is socially acceptable (and therefore confused with what is logically acceptable). Thus, while a polar question may generate lots of replies in natural discourse, only a positive or negative response can be within the actual set of answers for the question. In Koine Greek, the commonly used positive answer is ναί and the negative answer is οὐ.

In contrast to polar questions, *variable questions* have the most open set of answers of any question formation. Their set of answers can be nearly limitless and are constrained only by the semantic range of the interrogative variable and the logic of the question itself. For example:

(2) What should I do? (VARIABLE QUESTION)
(3) Where did you buy this book? (VARIABLE QUESTION)

The interrogative variables *what* in (2) and *where* in (3) are the primary limiters to the openness of the set of answers of these questions. Question (2) is an extremely open question, and its set of answers would include any logical response: "Run a marathon," "Move to Fiji," "Do nothing," or even "Build a house on Mars" would all fit within the set, but "Yesterday" or "Blue," would not. In contrast, while (3) tilts toward openness in what it asks, its set of answers is actually much more limited: "A bookstore" or "A garage sale" would work, but "Yesterday," "Blue" or even "On the moon" would not. Note that the set of answers does not conform to the truth conditions of a question-answer pair; within the set of answers for (3) there is only one answer that would fulfill the truth conditions of the pair. The openness of (2), based on its erotetic logic, is also the reason why an answer of "I don't know" seems more acceptable as an answer to (2) than for (3).

Alternative questions possess a limited set of answers. The set of answers of an alternative question is always explicitly or implicitly contained in the question itself. For example:

(4) Do you want chocolate cheesecake or rhubarb pie? (ALTERNATIVE QUESTION)
(5) So, is it this, that, or the other? (ALTERNATIVE QUESTION)

The set of answers in both (4) and (5) are found within the question itself. In (4), the set of answers includes "Chocolate cheesecake, please!" or "I'll take rhubarb pie" but not "Yesterday" or "Blue." Likewise, the set of answers in (5) includes "This," "That," or "The other" (where these three pronouns index something in the mind of the asker), but nothing else. The only exceptions to this are "Neither" or "Both," which are generally accepted to be a part of the set of answers for alternative questions.

Set questions actually derive their name from the fact that they have a limited set of answers. When a speaker asks a set question, they ask for an answer that comes from that set. Set questions are more open than polar questions or alternative questions, but less open than variable questions. For example:

(6) Which of these candies do you want? (SET QUESTION)
(7) Which do you want—the sofa, the chair, or the futon? (SET QUESTION)

While both (6) and (7) are set questions, the set of answers for question (6) is implicit in the question, and the set of answers for (7) is explicit in the set of answers. This scenario is almost the same as alternative questions (4) and (5), with their implicit and explicit delimitation of a set of answers. In (6), the question is not open because there is a set of candies in the mind of the asker that the hearer is supposed to choose from. "That one" or "All three" or "The licorice" would be answers within the set of answers, but "Yesterday" would not—though "Blue" could be if one of the candies was blue (and the asker could interpret the poorly-formed reply). Unlike alternative questions, set questions are more open to more than one answer. With (7), the asker delimits the set of answers to three possibilities: "The sofa," "The chair," or "The futon."

What happens when any of these four question formations receive no reply or answer to the asking? In the case when no answer is given to any question, it is never a part of any set of answers, even though it may be a logical response to the question and a socially acceptable reply. However, the hearer who gives no answer may end up communicating more—by staying silent—than they may realize or intend.[99]

Key Bibliography

Estes, *Questions*, 28–30; Harrah, "Logic," 40–46; Quintilian, *Institutio oratoria* 9.2.12.

99. Cf. Perelman and Olbrechts-Tyteca, *New Rhetoric*, 108–9.

Chapter 3

Questions Driven by Syntax

The base upon which all question formation occurs is their syntactical construction. There are essentially four formations of questions in natural language: *variable questions*, *polar questions*, *alternative questions*, and *set questions*. These types of question formation are nearly universal in human languages. Each of these four question formations are formed differently from each other in both English and Koine Greek. In English, word order plays a large role in the shaping of all four basic formations—but it only plays a small role in shaping two of the basic formations in Koine Greek. Let's look at several examples:

A *polar question* is one that contains a binary opposition in its formation:

"Do you like pizza?" (POLAR QUESTION)

A *variable question* is one that contains a variable, *x*, in its formation:

"What color is your car?" (VARIABLE QUESTION)

An *alternative question* is one that imposes a preselected number of options:

"Do you want a new book or a used book?" (ALTERNATIVE QUESTION)

A *set question* is one that imposes a limited set of possible answers:

"Which of those books will you buy?" (SET QUESTION)

Eroteticians, or scholars who study question asking, debate the number of questions that can be distinguished by syntax. The number generally ranges from zero to four, with many preferring two or three. One reason why some theories argue for less than four question formations is that two of these four formations seem to be partly related to the other two. Alternative questions sometimes seem related to polar questions, and set questions sometimes seem related to variable questions. We can see the relationship between set questions and variable questions more easily in Koine Greek than modern English, since the Koine Greek of the GNT does not employ a special *wh*-word to designate a set question (as English does).

The easiest way to understand the differences between these forms of questions is to differentiate them based on their expected answers—but this approach to interpreting questions is inaccurate. It is an inaccurate method since we define a question by *what it asks* rather than *how it is answered.* If an interpreter tries to start with the answer and work backward, they will commit an exegetical fallacy by reading the answer back into the question, missing the interrogative logic of the question under consideration (cf. §2.E). Thus, it is important for the interpreter to discover the interrogative logic built into the question first, without resorting to evaluating the response. Once the interpreter gets a handle on the logic of the question, then this logic can be double-checked alongside any responses given or other auxiliary information provided nearby in the text.

In the chart below, we can see several key differences between polar and alternative questions (which lean toward being closed), and variable and set questions (which lean toward being open):

Key Distinctions Between Open and Closed Question Types

	Open	Closed
Particle	Yes	No
Verb Required	Usually	No
Answer Range	Unlimited to Limited	Binary
Prone to Bias	Less	More
How Bias Enters	Via Set of Answers	Via Word Choice
Rhetorical Base	Leans Informational	Leans Rhetorical

Beyond these four major formations, there is an unofficial fifth formation, which we will call a *composite question*. A composite question is not actually a different formation than the first four but is formed when one of the basic four formations is modified with an additional clause that effects the erotetic logic of the question.

Key Bibliography

Chisholm, Milic, and Greppin, *Interrogativity*, 255–69.

A. Polar Questions

Polar questions ask for a positive or negative answer. In the secondary literature, they are often referred to as *yes/no questions*, *choice questions*, or *confirmation questions*. Based upon an elementary syntax, they are the most basic type of question that occurs in natural language. Polar questions get their name from their bent toward asking for an answer that is either positive or negative. They are considered a closed question type in that the set of answers for polar questions is extremely limited (§2.E), and the question is highly directed by the asker. For example:

(1) Do you have time to read this? (POLAR QUESTION)

This sample polar question (1) is closed as it directs the audience to respond positively or negatively to the asker's wishes. This is in contrast to *variable questions*, which are a highly open question type. Polar questions are an extremely common form of question and make up about 39% of the questions asked in the GNT.

Formation

Polar questions can be difficult to identify via syntax. Their formation is the most varied among question types within IE languages. In many languages, including both Koine Greek and English, polar questions do not require any one definitive formation or element of syntax. Of the four types of questions driven by syntax, polar questions are unique in this regard—all the other types possess easily identifiable syntactical elements. This does not mean that polar questions do not contain syntactical elements identifiable by careful readers. However, polar questions do possess different syntactical clues in Koine Greek and English. As a basic formation of questions, polar questions can occur in any turn, in any dialogue position, with any degree of informational and rhetorical qualities, and with virtually any semantic and pragmatic features not exclusive to one of the other three question formations.

Several factors in the formation and identification of polar questions include:

1) Polar Questions Do Not Use an Interrogative Variable Word

In Koine Greek, as in English and other IE languages, polar questions do not use interrogative variable words (π-words) in order to create their erotetic logic. Interrogative variable words are highlighted in the examples below:

(2) *Where* are you going? (VARIABLE QUESTION)
(3) *Which* way are you going? (SET QUESTION)
(4) Are you going or not? (ALTERNATIVE QUESTION)
(5) Are you going? (POLAR QUESTION)

As a general rule of thumb, if an utterance is interrogative, and it does not have a fronted interrogative variable word, it is most likely a polar question. (Alternative questions also do not have fronted interrogative variable words, but they are far less common than polar questions, and they are marked by their alternating conjunction.) The key to this rule of thumb is "fronted," because polar questions may still contain relative pronouns or adverbs:

(6) Are you going to the place *where* we met? (POLAR QUESTION)
(7) *Where* we met—are you going? (POLAR QUESTION)
(8) Γινώσκετε *τί* πεποίηκα ὑμῖν; (POLAR QUESTION)

Examples (6) and (7) are both polar questions (as they both seek a confirmation or a positive/negative response), yet both of them contain an adverb that can be used as an interrogative variable word in different contexts. The same situation happens in the GNT, as we see in example (8) from John 13:12 ("Do you understand what I have done to you?"). In (8), it is tempting for the interpreter to focus on the nearly fronted τί to reflect on what Jesus has done for the disciples—but this misses the point of the interrogative logic, which is solely focused on γινώσκετε ("do you understand").

At the same time, if a question fronts its interrogative variable word (§2.B.11), it cannot be a polar question. This is true in almost all IE languages.

2) Polar Questions Do Not Require Any Type of Interrogative Marker

Polar questions do not require any type of interrogative marker. In IE languages, interrogative markers can take one of several forms; usually they are either fronted interrogative variable words or interrogative particles. Whereas well-formed variable questions and set questions require a fronted interrogative variable word, polar questions do not require anything. Thus, a polar question is often indistinguishable from a proposition. This is especially true in the GNT, where punctuation is not available as a clue.

The lack of any interrogative indicators in polar questions has not always been the case in the history of the Greek language. One of the linguistic evolutions from Classical Greek to Koine Greek was the near loss of interrogative-oriented discourse particles (for example, ἦ and ἆρα) that a speaker could use to differentiate a polar question from a declaration. For example:

(9) ἆρα ἐρωτᾷς ἥντινα τέχνην φημὶ εἶναι;
"Then you ask what art I say it to be?" (PLATO, *GORGIAS* 462B)

In this question (9) from a dialogue of Plato, Socrates uses the particle ἆρα to help alert his audience that he is probably asking a question. However, the use of a discourse particle to denote a polar question was not universal in Classical Greek; in fact, based on existing evidence, it was just as likely not to be used as it was to be used. For example:

(10) καὶ ἀγνοεῖτε οὐδὲν τῶν δεόντων πράττοντες;
"And don't you know your accomplishments account for nothing?" (PLATO, *CLITOPHON* 407)

Example (10) is one of many, many cases in both Classical and Koine Greek where the audience must determine whether the utterance is a question or a proposition (cf. Isocrates, *Nicocles* 26). Discourse particles fronting polar questions occur only a few times in the GNT, most notably:

(11) Ἆρά γε γινώσκεις ἃ ἀναγινώσκεις; (ACTS 8:30)

Here ἆρα signals hesitancy and introduces an audible pause, followed by the emphatic and ornamental γε, which suggests a question: "So ... *do you* know what you are reading?"[1] The earliest readers would have performed this when reading aloud, but that pragmatic knowledge would have dried up during late antiquity.

3) Polar Questions Do Not Require a Verb

Technically, none of the four basic types of questions require a verb in the utterance to make the utterance a question; all are guided by their erotetic logic, their pragmatics, and the presence or absence of an interrogative marker. However, since polar questions do not usually possess an interrogative-oriented discourse particle in NT Greek, if the reader encounters an utterance in the text that seems like a question yet lacks a verb, the general rule of thumb is that it is more likely a polar question than any of the other question formations. For example, note these three polar questions without verbs:

(12) Ready? (POLAR QUESTION)
(13) Lunch? (POLAR QUESTION)
(14) προφήτην; (POLAR QUESTION)

In cases (12) and (13), each of these questions are well formed in English but contain no verb. They are asked to find out (or confirm) whether the hearer is ready (or not) and whether they have or want lunch (or not). Question (14) from Matthew 11:9b ("A prophet?") accomplishes the same thing, and we see an example of this phenomenon in the GNT. Thus, polar questions in natural-language situations can be formed with just one word.

4) Polar Questions Are Syntactically Similar to Statements in Koine Greek

For English readers, the biggest challenge in identifying and interpreting polar questions is the lack of distinct word order in Koine Greek. As English is an SVO language, there are strict rules of word ordering within sentences that make identifying well-formed polar questions relatively easy:

(15) I am the good shepherd. (STATEMENT)
(16) Am I the good shepherd? (POLAR QUESTION)

---

1. On γε, cf. Dionysius Thrax, *Ars Grammatica* 643.14; note the Vulgate renders ἆρα γε as *putasne*.

As the examples of (15) and (16) show, English readers can spot a polar question through the syntactical tell of *subject-verb inversion*. Since Koine Greek does not share this strict word order, it is often impossible to know for certain from syntax whether some sentences in the GNT are statements of fact or polar questions.[2] For example:

(17) βλέπεις ὅτι ἡ πίστις συνήργει τοῖς ἔργοις αὐτοῦ (JAS 2:22)
(18) βλέπεις ταύτας τὰς μεγάλας οἰκοδομάς (MARK 13:2)

The utterances in (17) and (18) may look similar, but their sentential force is not: (17) is a proposition while (18) is a polar question. The difficulty in determining the difference between the two is significant. However, if interpreters cannot accurately identify the force of an utterance, they will misunderstand the purpose of the passage being read. This is true not just of obvious examples but also of more nuanced examples that rely on highly complex forms of interrogative logic.

5) Polar Questions Are Often Negative in Polarity

Of the four basic formations of questions, polar questions are most likely to be negative in polarity. This holds true in the GNT where more than 56% of polar questions are negative polar questions. Since confirmation is a strong effect of polar questions, the bias that comes with negative polarity further encourages askers to ask negative polar questions. For example,

(19) *Οὐχὶ* υἱός ἐστιν Ἰωσὴφ οὗτος; (LUKE 4:22)

Example (19), "Isn't he Joseph's son?" is a classic case of a negative polar question. While the asker (the crowds) could have asked the same question as a positive polar question and received the same degree of confirmation from their audience, the use of the negative stresses the need for confirmation greater than a positive polar question would.

Rhetorical Effects

Polar questions tend to have three primary rhetorical effects, and because of their fundamental nature, can be modified so as to have a limitless number of secondary rhetorical effects. Their primary effects include the following three items.

1) Polar Questions Are Asked to Get a Decision

The most elemental rhetorical effect generated by a speaker asking a polar question is the prompting for a decision from the audience. When a polar question is asked, the natural language places an expectation on the responder to make a choice, yes or no. If a polar question is left unanswered, the violation of

2. For greater discussion, see Estes, *Questions*, 6–9.

the *question-answer pair* will arouse suspicion in the audience toward the target of the question and may engender sympathy for the asker.

In interrogative logic, the standard approach to polar questions is that they have two possible answers: positive (yes) and negative (no). However, this is where linguistics and natural-language samples collide head on. In the real world, polar questions have at least five possible answers: yes, no, maybe, no answer, or an indeterminate answer. Thus, a great deal of caution must be taken when evaluating a polar question by its answer (§2.E).

2) Polar Questions Are Asked as a Confirmation

Another base effect of the polar question is its use to confirm or deny a supposition.[3] This is especially helpful in areas of rhetoric or argumentation, where a speaker is trying to build a case, or in *institutional discourse*, where an asker is trying to follow a process. More than a yes or no answer, the speaker wants to know whether a presupposition is true or false:

(20) Do you have my car keys? (POLAR QUESTION)
(21) βλέπεις ταύτην τὴν γυναῖκα; (POLAR QUESTION; LUKE 7:44)
(22) You see this woman? (POLAR QUESTION)

3) Polar Questions Are Prone to Bias

Due to the basic nature of polar questions, they are more prone to *bias* than the other three types of questions. Bias is a critically important issue in the interpretation of all question types (§2.C.2). On the one hand, a polar question can be asked so simply so as to appear to be the most neutral of questions:

(23) Do you like it? (POLAR QUESTION)

On the other hand, given the right semantic or pragmatic factors, this simple question in (23) may betray a great deal of bias within context:

(24) Hudson gave his baby sister a slug to eat.
"Do you like it?" (POLAR QUESTION)

In this example (24), there is no way to hide the semantic bias of the verb. Hidden within average polar questions is a great deal of bias that can be difficult for the reader to interpret correctly. The reason is that natural language is especially adept at imbuing polar questions with bias in less obvious situations than the previous example. When bias is present in polar questions, it telegraphs the answer to perceptive listeners and readers.

As a result of the specific characteristics of polar questions, they are often heavily used in a variety of specialized settings; for example, medical diagnosis, legal argumentation, political debating, and institutional discourse.[4]

3. Fiengo, *Asking Questions*, 10.
4. This was the case even in the ancient world; Aristotle, *Posterior Analytics* 77a28–32.

Case Studies

MATTHEW 18:21B

ἕως ἑπτάκις

PETER: Until seven [times]?

Peter asks the most basic of questions when he asks Jesus, "Until seven?" This is syntactically an elementary polar question, lacking even a verb. The key to interpreting this question is based in understanding its interrogative logic: Peter is not asking for Jesus to reveal to him a number (of times of forgiveness). It is not asked to garner new information. In asking this question, Peter is looking for Jesus to either confirm or deny his supposition (that is, that the number of times for forgiveness is quite large).

(Interpreters should note the larger discourse context; this question is also the second half of a *double question* [§5.D.1], so care must be taken to interpret remaining rhetorical effects in light of this.)

MARK 7:18

οὕτως καὶ ὑμεῖς ἀσύνετοί ἐστε;

JESUS: So, are you also senseless?

Jesus's question in Mark 7:18 is also indicative of a basic polar question. He asks the question, phrased simply, but it is easy to see the bias enter into the question through ἀσύνετοί ("senseless"). Jesus wants to know whether his disciples are without any sense. The presence of the semantic bias will tempt many readers untrained in interrogative logic to read the question merely as a "rhetorical question." Yet while polar questions lean rhetorical, and the bias word pushes it much further toward the rhetorical, there is still an informational aspect to the question that must be addressed in interpretation—notably the opportunity for the disciples (and readers) to choose for themselves whether they have the sense to understand Jesus's parable. As such, the question is rhetorical due to the presence of bias, but not so far from its informational roots as to not call for a decision from its audience.

Key Bibliography

Estes, *Questions*, 111–18; Fiengo, *Asking Questions*, 7–16; Higginbotham, "Interrogatives," 214; Pavey, *Structure of Language*, 290; van Rooy and Šafářová, "On Polar Questions," 292–309; Walton, *Dialog Theory*, 22.

B. Variable Questions

Variable questions ask for their variable, *x*, to be solved. They get their name from the presence of an interrogative variable word. In the secondary literature, they are most often referred to as *wh-questions* (and rarely *x-questions*), as they are created syntactically on a *wh*-fronted clause form. Since our study goes far beyond just their form and into their meaning and use, we refer to them as variable questions, since this term more accurately addresses their primary role in discourse. In IE languages such as Koine Greek, the variable occurs in the form of a π-word (§2.B.10) that we can describe as being either an interrogative pronoun or an interrogative adverb. Of all four syntactical formations of questions, variable questions are the easiest to identify. They also are the most broad and indefinite of the four basic formations of questions, as they are the most open in what they ask. For example:

(1) Where should we go to lunch? (VARIABLE QUESTION)

In this sample variable question, the asker asks a question that can legitimately be answered in a variety of ways. Even more so, the question is—depending on context—most likely seeking information from those who hear it. Thus, variable questions stand in contrast to *polar questions* as well as *alternative questions*. This also means that variable questions skew toward a higher degree of informational quality than any of the other four basic formations. Variable questions are the most common form of question in the GNT and make up almost 55% of the questions asked.

Formation

Variable questions are relatively easy to spot via syntax since Greek as a rule fronts its interrogative variables, or π-words (§2.B.10). Thus, with few exceptions the interpreter can simply look at the beginning of the clause or sentence carrying the interrogative force to see if there is π-fronting. In this regard, Koine Greek follows many other IE languages. Sometimes the reader of the GNT will come across a π-word that appears in the middle of a sentence or clause; in this case, the text is using the π-word as a relative pronoun or a relative adverb. (This is in contrast to Classical Greek, where the tendency was marked by the use of ὁπ-words as relative pronouns and relative adverbs.) As a basic formation of questions, variable questions can occur in any turn, in any dialogue position, with any degree of informational and rhetorical qualities, and with virtually any semantic and pragmatic features not exclusive to one of the other three question formations.

Several factors in the formation and identification of variable questions include:

1) Variable Questions Do Require an Interrogative Variable Word

Unlike polar questions, variable questions always require a distinct marker of interrogativity, which in this case is an interrogative variable word such as τίς or πῶς. This requirement makes the Greek language very similar to other languages in its family tree. For example:

(2) *τί* γάρ μοι τοὺς ἔξω κρίνειν; (1 COR 5:12A)
(3) *Ποῦ* ἐστιν ἡ ἐπαγγελία τῆς παρουσίας αὐτοῦ; (2 PET 3:4)
(4) Διδάσκαλε, *ποία* ἐντολὴ μεγάλη ἐν τῷ νόμῳ; (MATT 22:36)

In these examples, both (2) and (3) are variable questions that employ fronted interrogative variable words which both indicate the interrogative force of the sentence as well as restructure the sentence to signal information gathering. In both (2) and (3), the interrogative variables introduce "What?" and "Where?" respectively. *However, not all sentences that use interrogative variable words are variable questions.* An example of this scenario is (4), where the reader may first assume ποία acts as an interrogative variable word—it does, but it does so to introduce a set question, not a variable question. Set questions are rare, and they can be recognized by the interrogative variable word plus additional tells (§3.D). Still, a careful reader identifies the semantic force of the interrogative variable word to positively rule out the chance of a set question.

2) Variable Questions Front Their Interrogative Variable Words

Variable questions as a rule front their interrogative variable words. This reorganization of information structure makes fronting in languages significant for interpretation and causes the interrogative force of the question to come to the fore for the hearer (§2.B.11). While fronting is the rule in the Greek of the NT, as well as in the larger Koine- and Classical-Greek language, readers still must examine each sentence to determine if and how fronting occurs. For example:

(5) Διδάσκαλε, *τί* ἀγαθὸν ποιήσω ἵνα σχῶ ζωὴν αἰώνιον; (MATT 19:16)
(6) ἕως *πότε* ἀνέξομαι ὑμῶν; (MARK 9:19B)
(7) Γινώσκετε τί πεποίηκα ὑμῖν; (JOHN 13:12)

At first glance, each of these three examples appear to have "nearly-fronted" interrogative variable words, and on the surface they seem to have similar syntactical structure. Upon closer inspection, one of these is not a variable question at all. In example (5), the interrogative variable word τί fronts the main clause, and the word in front of it in the sentence, Διδάσκαλε ("teacher"), is simply a vocative for the purpose of address. (We can see how information structure works even here, with the addressee first and the request for information second, followed next by the limiters to the request for information.) In example (6), the conjunction ἕως ("until") opens the question clause followed by the fronted πότε. Yet in both (5) and (6), the interrogative variable fronts even though it is not the first word of the sentence, making both questions variable questions. In contrast is example (7), which does not have π-fronting and is not a variable question at all—it is a polar question with a π-word *in situ* introducing the relative clause. Thus, the proximity to the front can be misleading, especially in Greek.

3) Variable Questions Do Not Require a Verb

Technically, none of the four basic types of questions require a verb in the utterance to make the utterance a question; all are guided by their erotetic logic, their pragmatics, and the presence or absence of an interrogative marker. The absence of a verb in a variable question is uncommon, but it occurs in at least two situations in natural language, as we see for example in the GNT:

(8) *Τί* ἡμῖν καὶ σοί, υἱὲ τοῦ θεοῦ; (MATT 8:29A)
(9) *Ποῖα*; (LUKE 24:19)
(10) διὰ *τί*; (ROM 9:32)

Example (8), "What do you want with us, Son of God?" is an instance where an asker asks a variable question without a verb, using what is most likely a phatic expression (such as the current American English, "What up?"—a further contraction of "What's up?"). With examples (9) and (10), both of these are examples of variable questions where the speaker does not feel the need to limit the variable in any way. (In fact, [9] is a sluice; see §3.E.4). These two examples demonstrate an extremely open sense for information gathering (§4.A).

4) Variable Questions with Negative Polarity Are Uncommon

Variable questions with negative polarity are uncommon, and this is true not just in the GNT but in many IE languages, such as modern English. In fact, in the GNT less than 4% of variable questions are negative (and less than 2% of all questions in the GNT are negative variable questions). This is in sharp contrast to polar questions, of which more than 56% are negative in the GNT. The reason for this is that the inherently open, information-seeking qualities of variable questions are usually at odds with the closed and strongly persuasive qualities that often accompanies negative polarity. For example:

(11) πῶς *οὐχὶ* μᾶλλον ἡ διακονία τοῦ πνεύματος ἔσται ἐν δόξῃ; (2 COR 3:8)

Here (11) is a variable question with negative polarity. It is unusual enough that a literal translation is not well formed in English, which is why the NIV omits the interrogative variable altogether ("will not the ministry of the Spirit be even more glorious?") and the NRSV omits the negative particle ("how much more will the ministry of the Spirit come in glory?").

Negative polarity affects the interrogative logic of variable questions in a different way than it does for polar questions. With negative variable questions, not only is bias and rhetorical effect greatly enhanced, closing the sense of the question, but the role of the variable is affected. For example:

(12) Who is the king of France?
(13) Who isn't the king of France?

Question (12) is a clear and obvious open question (assuming a context-neutral environment), but question (13) subverts the variable *who* in favor of a strong rhetorical push to raise a question about people, or the king of France, or other characters in the discourse. In fact, trying to interpret (13) without contextual clues—because of its strong rhetorical nature—is impossible.

5) Variable Questions in the GNT Are More Likely to Be Formed with τίς

Variable questions formed in the Koine Greek of the GNT differ from variable questions formed in modern IE languages such as English and German in one important way: the Koine Greek of the GNT possesses an indefinite variable word, τίς. In English and German, each of the *wh*-words/*w*-fragen has a definite meaning that helps limit the set of answers expected from the variable question asked. The same is true for all the Greek variable words except τίς, which does not have a clear limit. We can see this in the multiple applications of τίς in a short span of dialogue in Luke 18:

(14) Διδάσκαλε ἀγαθέ, *τί* ποιήσας ζωὴν αἰώνιον κληρονομήσω; (V. 18)
(15) *Τί* με λέγεις ἀγαθόν; (V. 19)
(16) Καὶ *τίς* δύναται σωθῆναι; (V. 26)

Even in a short span, questions (14), (15), and (16) are each asking three different questions: (14) asks, "What?" (15) asks, "Why?" and (16) asks, "Who?" Yet to better understand the semantic array of τίς, we can substitute the English "what" into each of these questions: (14) becomes "What?" (15) becomes "For what reason?" and (16) becomes "What person?" Of course, this is a semantic game between languages; for the average Koine-Greek speaker, τίς is just the indefinite interrogative variable word alongside of definite interrogative variable words such as ποῦ and πότε. We also see this effect played out in the GNT based on the frequency of use of the interrogative variable words, displayed in the chart below:

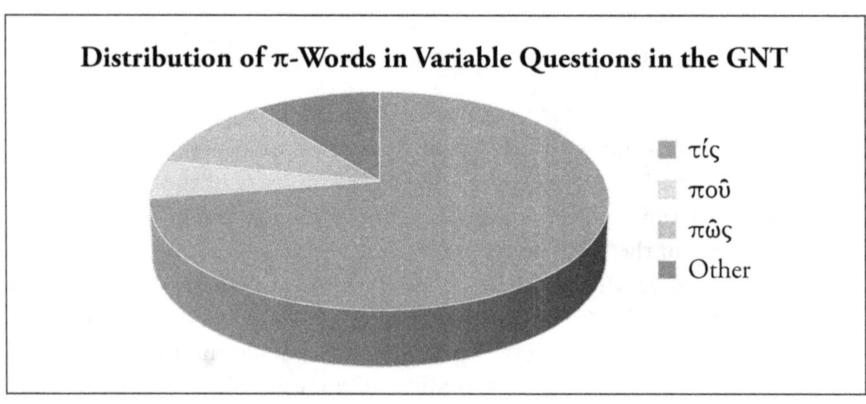

Rhetorical Effects

Due to their syntactical nature, variable questions start out with the least degree of inherent rhetorical effects of any of the four formations of questions. When an asker applies rhetorical effect to a variable question, it also produces the widest range of possibilities among question formations. The four most important rhetorical effects of variable questions are:

1) Variable Questions Are Asked to Gather Information

The primary pragmatic purpose of variable questions is to gather information for the asker based on the missing variable in the question asked. When a variable question is asked, its base nature seeks to discover information for the asker. For example:

(17) Ἴδε *τί* ποιοῦσιν τοῖς σάββασιν ὃ οὐκ ἔξεστιν; (MARK 2:24)

The primary purpose of question (17), "Look, why are they doing on the Sabbath what is not allowed?" is to discover something that is unknown. In this case, the Pharisees seek to find out why the disciples of Jesus are behaving in a certain manner. The Pharisees do not know the answer (even if they may have opinions or suspicions), and thus they want to know the why, the *x* variable in the question.

2) Variable Questions Can Indicate Ignorance

When an asker asks a variable question, the result of the asking indicates some degree of ignorance on the part of the asker. This ignorance can be mitigated by any rhetorical force placed on the question by the asker. In many cases, this ignorance is benign and a part of the normal ebb and flow of information exchange. However, the hearer of the question is still aware of the lack of information—or perceived lack of information—on the part of the asker, something that can be exploited in natural-language situations. For example:

(18) *Ποῦ* ἐστιν ὁ τεχθεὶς βασιλεὺς τῶν Ἰουδαίων; (MATT 2:2)

Question (18), "Where is the one who was born king of the Jews?" is a classic example of this ignorance, as the magi do not know where the one born king of the Jews is. And to find out this information, the magi are forced to admit their ignorance on this issue. In the previous example (17), the Pharisees do not appear to know the answer, though they may be able to guess. Either way, by asking they admit they are uncertain.[5]

In some cases, the asker may ask a variable question to feign ignorance in order to elicit a number of different responses from his audience. John 6:5 is a classic example of this in the GNT:

5. As Nigel Turner correctly points out, "It was not so much a concern to them *who* he was as *where* he was"; see Turner, *Grammatical Insights*, 26.

(19) Πόθεν ἀγοράσωμεν ἄρτους ἵνα φάγωσιν οὗτοι; (JOHN 6:5)

Here Jesus asks a question, "Where might we buy bread so that these people might eat?" to which he feigns ignorance to see how Philip would respond (see §4.L). Without pragmatics (or an intrusive narrator) and without some guessing on the part of the hearer, it can be difficult to tell when a variable question is actually feigning ignorance in representational discourse. Further, when there is a strong rhetorical push, or when the variable question is within a highly rhetorical text (such as Paul's letters), the feigned variable question does not indicate ignorance in the asker as much as an implication that the asker is wondering if the ignorance applies to the intended audience. As an example:

(20) *Τί* οὖν ὁ νόμος; (GAL 3:19)

Question (20), "Why, then, the law?" is part of a rhetorical discourse, and in asking this question Paul is not indicating his ignorance of the answer but rather implying that the reader may in fact be ignorant of the answer. The result of this produces a rhetorical effect that causes the reader to think, "Do I know why the law was given?" It is the existence of the variable that causes the implication of ignorance in the asking of variable questions.

3) Variable Questions Are Open Questions

The syntax of variable questions creates an openness on the part of their logic. This openness results in both a broad range of possibilities for the variable to be solved and gives variable questions an unlimited feel. This is in contrast to the other three formations of questions, all of which are more closed than open. The distinction between an open and closed question comes through the implication of its range of possibilities. Variable questions are not actually unlimited, and some eroteticians are quick to point out that variable questions can be as limiting as other forms of questions.[6] Nonetheless, an undefined variable without significant semantic constraints will always lean open. For example:

(21) Διὰ *τί* ἐν παραβολαῖς λαλεῖς αὐτοῖς; (MATT 13:10)
(22) *Τίς* σοφὸς καὶ ἐπιστήμων ἐν ὑμῖν; (JAS 3:13)

Here (21), "Why do you speak to them in parables?" reveals that the range of possibilities for the "Why?" is quite large. A legitimate answer could really be anything—"To see who the smartest is," "To confuse folks," "Parables are actually my native language," or even "I like to trick people," and the hearers may have no way of knowing either way. (Fortunately, Jesus gives a helpful answer that Matthew records in 13:11.) Even in written discourse with a moderate degree of rhetorical emphasis, (22) still manages to come off as open: "Who is wise and

6. Cf. Karttunen, "Syntax and Semantics," 20.

knowledgable among you?" In thinking through James's question of "who," the reader could undoubtedly consider many people (including the reader themselves!). In fact, every reader will have a similarly open experience based on a completely different range of possibilities.

When an asker subjects a variable question to a stronger rhetorical force, the openness is subverted and the question can come across as highly accusatory or condescending on the part of the asker.

4) Variable Questions with τίς Are Indefinite Variable Questions

To a large extent, Koine Greek forms variable questions in much the same way as other IE languages (such as English) do. One of the primary differences between variable questions in English and Koine Greek is that Koine Greek possesses an *indefinite interrogative variable*, τίς. (Note: this is an interpretive rule for English readers, not an actual function of Koine Greek as such.) The simplest way to explain this is that the interrogative variable words in Koine Greek do not match up with the interrogative variable words of modern IE languages, such as English or German (see the chart in §2.B.10). In fact, Classical Greek has several π-words that English does not have (and thus, English usage in these areas would be indefinite compared to the Greek), and English has several *wh*-words that are indefinite in Koine Greek.

For interpretation of variable questions in the GNT, the challenge is the indefinite τίς. We can understand this variable in English as either "Who?" or "What?" or "Why?" However, the indefinite nature of τίς causes problems for the thoughtful interpreter. We can see this problem in Jesus's famous question of Matthew 14:31:

(23) Ὀλιγόπιστε, εἰς *τί* ἐδίστασας; (MATT 14:31)

English translations almost always render (23) as "O you of little faith, why did you doubt?" However, this makes the reader wonder, did Matthew really intend to ask (what we would say in English), "Why?" Or, is Matthew really asking, "What?" In English, we interpret as "Why?" due to seeing faith as a process more than an object. We can illustrate this part of the problem better in English:

(24) Why do you fear?
(25) What do you fear?
(26) Whom do you fear?

In English, we would natively see that all three of these questions have a different range of possibilities for answers. "Why do you fear?" could be "Because I am weak." "What do you fear?" could be "A stock market crash." And "Whom do you fear?" could be "The boogey monster." Again, English readers see these as three distinct questions, *but native readers of the GNT did not.*

Returning to the problem of (23), Jesus may be asking Peter *why* he has doubts, but he may also be asking Peter *in what* his doubts are. Even more dramatically, Jesus could also be asking *in whom* does Peter's doubts arise. Clearly, these three questions are quite different (in English) and have different meanings (in English). Even more problematic, the indefinite nature of τίς means that to a Koine-Greek reader, Jesus's question may reflect *all three* of these ideas equally. For Matthew 14:31, the "best answer" may not be "too little faith," but rather "in you, Jesus." The same is true in (20), where Paul may be equally asking, "Why then the law?" as "What then the law?" Context is critical to help limit the range of possibilities for interpretation into English.

As a result, τίς leans even more toward an open characterization when we render it into English. Care should be taken in analyzing the erotetic logic of τίς so as not to overly limit the variable range that a native Koine-Greek speaker may imply in its usage.

Case Study — MARK 14:12

Ποῦ θέλεις ἀπελθόντες ἑτοιμάσωμεν ἵνα φάγῃς τὸ πάσχα;

JESUS'S DISCIPLES: Where do you want us to go, that we might prepare, so that you can eat the Passover?

On the first day of the Festival of Unleavened Bread, Jesus's disciples come to Jesus with a question. Among commentators, there is some debate as to whether the question comes after, or in anticipation of, the slaughter of the lamb.[7] The question is an ordinary variable question, which the disciples use to ask to gain information from Jesus. The question is highly informational with almost no rhetorical force at all. By asking such an information-seeking variable question, the disciples betray that they do not know where Jesus wants (or plans) for them to go. By asking the question this way, the disciples truly are asking for Jesus to supply them with the needed information, and this has the effect of putting his answer at the center of their concerns.[8] Even though this is an open question, where the *x* variable can be solved by the hearer from a wide range of possibilities, it does not mean that the disciples do not understand that there are limits to the question or that they may have opinions on the issue (in this case, perhaps remaining within the city limits, as was expected).[9] Pragmatically, the question in Mark 14:12 also functions as a governing question (§5.A.1). As such, it guides the rest of the dialogue and the subsequent story (Mark 14:12–16).

7. See France, *Mark*, 564.
8. Cf. Hooker, *Mark*, 334.
9. Cf. France, *Mark*, 564.

Key Bibliography
Estes, *Questions*, 71–76; Wang, "Questions," 543–45.

C. Alternative Questions

Alternative questions ask for the hearer to select one alternative from the multiple options provided by the asker. They get their name from the group of alternatives within the question. They may also be referred to as *disjunctive questions* (though see §3.E.2) or *whether questions*. While alternative questions constitute one of the four major formations of questions, its syntactic structure and internal erotetic logic are related to polar questions. Speakers rarely use alternative questions in natural language—they are the least used of the basic formations and comprise only 2% of all questions in the GNT. Generally speaking, alternative questions can appear in two distinct forms:

(1) Do you know *whether* Jason *or* Ken have the car keys? (ALTERNATIVE QUESTION)
(2) Should Eric cook spaghetti, lasagna, *or* manicotti? (ALTERNATIVE QUESTION)

In the above examples, both questions (1) and (2) are alternative questions. Syntactically, (1) and (2) appear different. An asker can pose an alternative question in two distinct ways, using either an alternating conjunction (sometimes called a disjunctive word or particle), which in English is *or* and in Koine Greek is ἤ, as in (2), or the alternating *wh*-word, which in English is *whether* and in Koine Greek is πότερος, as in (1). The structural difference between these examples is that (1) uses the *wh*-word *in situ* (§2.B.10). However, both questions ask essentially the same thing, namely, for the hearer to (1) choose between the alternatives of Jason or Ken, and (2) to choose between the alternatives of spaghetti, lasagna, or manicotti.

Formation

Most alternative questions are based on a simple syntactical form, akin to polar questions. This is less true when the disjunctive *wh*-word is present. Either way, they are often easy to identify in discourse. As a general rule of thumb, if an utterance is an interrogative and it has a disjunctive word, it is most likely an alternative question. Alternative questions hold to the same formation style in many IE languages, including English and Koine Greek. As a basic formation of questions, alternative questions can occur in any turn, in any dialogue position, with any degree of informational and rhetorical qualities, and with virtually any semantic and pragmatic features not exclusive to one of the other three question formations.

Four factors in the formation and identification of alternative questions are listed below.

1) Alternative Questions Require a Disjunctive Word

Alternative questions—as well as any other kind of alternative or disjunctive utterance—require an alternating conjunction or disjunctive word to set up the alternative logic. This is true in many IE languages, not just English and Greek. This conjunction is *not* in itself an indicator of interrogativity. While not a tell for interrogativity, it is a sign that the utterance could be an alternative question. Furthermore, the disjunctive word is usually explicit, but it also may be implicit within the question asked rather than explicit. In the GNT, the alternating conjunction is ἤ. Below is an example of this:

(3) Ἄρτι γὰρ ἀνθρώπους πείθω ἢ τὸν θεόν; (GAL 1:10A)
(4) ἢ ζητῶ ἀνθρώποις ἀρέσκειν; (GAL 1:10B)

In Galatians, Paul asks a double question of his readers ("For do I now strive to win the approval of men or God? Or do I seek to please people?"), and both of them possess a disjunctive word. However, while question (3) is an alternative question, question (4) is not. There is an indication of this in that the conjunction ἤ in (3) is used within a clause to present two phrasal alternatives, whereas the conjunction ἤ in (4) is used to join two different thoughts, two different questions, in a disjunctive rather than conjunctive union.

In some instances, set questions may also employ a disjunctive word to help establish their set of possibilities. As a rule of thumb, the best way to distinguish between a set question with a disjunctive word and an alternative question is to look for a fronted interrogative variable word. If the interrogative variable word is there, it is likely a set question, not an alternative question. We can see examples of this in the GNT:

(5) τίς γὰρ μείζων ἐστίν, ὁ χρυσὸς ἢ ὁ ναὸς ὁ ἁγιάσας τὸν χρυσόν; (MATT 23:17)

A first glance at (5) may tempt the interpreter to assume that this question is an alternative question ("For which is greater—the gold *or* the temple that sanctifies the gold?"). However, the presence of the τίς + options marks the question as a set question. What then is the difference in the erotetic logic of a set question with a disjunctive scheme and an alternative question? Not much—usually the distinction is made between selection and comparison. The set question (being based on an interrogative variable) invites comparison, whereas the alternative question asks for confirmation (see also §3.D).

In ancient Greek, πότερος functions as a disjunctive word, though it is rooted in the π-word scheme. Unfortunately, there are no direct questions in the GNT that make use of πότερος.[10]

10. Though, for example, see Job 7:12 LXX and Plato, *Euthydemus* 295e.

2) Alternative Questions Do Not Require Any Type of Interrogative Marker

Similar to polar questions, but dissimilar to variable and set questions, alternative questions do not require any type of interrogative marker. This includes either interrogative variable words or interrogative-oriented discourse particles. The result is that it can be difficult at times to distinguish an alternative question from an alternative statement on syntax alone. However, well-formed alternative questions do require a disjunctive word and will at times use an interrogative marker *in-situ* (πότερος). In Classical Greek, such as example (6), a speaker could also introduce alternative questions with an interrogative-oriented discourse particle such as ἆρα:

(6) *ἆρα* ἄλλως ἢ οὕτως ἔχει, ὦ Καλλίκλεις; (PLATO, *GORGIAS* 509C)

By the time of the GNT, this use fell out of favor—none of the alternative questions in the GNT carry any overt syntactical tells for interrogativity.

3) Alternative Questions Do Not Require a Verb

As with all major question formations based on syntax, alternative questions do not require a verb in order to be asked. They are guided by their internal logic and pragmatic use. Since alternative questions do not require an interrogative marker, the presence of a disjunctive word plus a careful reading of the text will be the only signs to differentiate the alternative question from an alternative assertion. Fortunately, this distinction is usually quite clear in natural-language discourse. For example:

(7) Chicken or fish? (ALTERNATIVE QUESTION)
I'll have the chicken.

(8) And what would you like for dinner?
The chicken or the fish. (ALTERNATIVE ASSERTION)

(9) ἐξ οὐρανοῦ ἢ ἐξ ἀνθρώπων; (MATT 21:25B)

We see in examples (7) and (8) that alternative questions and alternative assertions can appear almost identical when only considered via syntax. At the same time, when we consider the pragmatics of natural language in context, the interrogative and assertive forces become much more obvious (than, for example, a polar question without a verb). In example (9), we see this phenomenon in the GNT, where Jesus asks the chief priests and elders an alternative question without a verb. As the second half of a double question, Jesus's alternative question intends to limit his first question and steer the answer toward a confirmation (or even decision) rather than leave it entirely open.

4) Alternative Questions Are Syntactically Similar to Alternative Statements in Koine Greek

Alternative questions run up against the same challenge that polar questions do—namely, identifying an alternative question from an alternative proposition. Fortunately, pragmatic factors usually make this clear, but not always, as we see in this example:

(10) Ἄρτι γὰρ ἀνθρώπους πείθω ἢ τὸν θεόν; (GAL 1:10A)

In example (10), this alternative question could also be read as a proposition with an alternating conjunction: "For now I strive to win the approval of people or God." In this sense, Paul could be suggesting that he is open to approval by God or people. However, when we consider the circumstances of the utterance—its context, the subsequent, closely related utterance joined by disjunction (1:10b), and the concluding utterance (1:10c)—we come away with a stronger sense that (10) is an alternative question (part of a common double question, see §5.D.1), not an alternative proposition.

Rhetorical Effects

At first hearing, alternative questions seem tailored more to gain information rather than to act persuasively, but that view is quickly dispelled when they are used in natural language. In their most basic usage, alternative questions have two primary rhetorical effects, but with any extra force or bias a third primary rhetorical effect surfaces. Beyond these three are other possibilities with additional rhetorical force. The three most important rhetorical effects of alternative questions are listed below.

1) Alternative Questions Are Asked to Confirm a Selection

The primary rhetorical effect of an alternative question is to confirm a selection between two or more alternatives. This aspect of the alternative question is what gives the alternative question its seemingly open features, more like a set question than a polar question. In asking, the speaker expects the hearer to select one of the alternatives. In the absence of any other rhetorical effects, alternative questions are useful for askers to provide several options to their audience so as to elicit a confirmation on one (or more) of these alternatives.

2) Alternative Questions Are Asked to Limit Choices

Alternative questions intentionally limit the choices that a speaker asks a hearer to make—often severely. In this way, alternative questions are somewhat similar to set questions in that both seek to limit an audience's options, which makes them highly contrastive with variable questions. By asking an alternative question, the asker is also signaling to the speaker that they believe only a limited number of alternatives exist or are acceptable. As a result, alternative questions are actually more of a closed question, as the asker's goal is to coax the hearer to choose between several options. Hidden within the asking is the intent of the asker to *not* include other options, for example:

(11) Do you want tea or coffee? (ALTERNATIVE QUESTION)

With question (11), it is possible that the asker only can provide tea or coffee (or both). It is also possible, however, that the asker could provide other options to drink, such as water, but does not offer them for one of several reasons, including: (a) water is always a possibility, (b) water won't go with the meal, or (c) the asker doesn't want the hearer to have water. Thus, alternative questions are not actually neutral, though they usually hide overt bias.

Limiting choices in alternative questions can work both ways. In some situations, a speaker will ask an alternative question to overturn one of the alternatives or will use a rhetorical strategy to subvert the possible range of choices. Here are two great examples of this rhetorical push from the GNT:

(12) ἀπὸ τῶν υἱῶν αὐτῶν ἢ ἀπὸ τῶν ἀλλοτρίων; (MATT 17:25C)
(13) θλῖψις ἢ στενοχωρία ἢ διωγμὸς ἢ λιμὸς ἢ γυμνότης . . . ; (ROM 8:35B)

In example (12), "From their own sons or from others?" Jesus asks Peter an alternative question that uses semantics to embed bias. Peter is given the choice of either "from their own sons" or "from others." Here the possessive αὐτῶν coupled with the open-ended ἀλλοτρίων skews the expected answer. What is more, this question sets up two unequal alternatives—such as in the more obvious alternative question, "Do you want tea or a million dollars?" In example (13), Paul rhetorically subverts the erotetic logic of alternative questions by asking his readers to consider whether *x* or *y* or *z*—whether anything that could be considered—could separate us from the love of Christ. In asking this, Paul is not merely adding a rhetorical flourish (as he might with a negative polar question) but is using each alternative example to push the reader to realize that none of these alternatives (or any others) could possibly separate them from the love of Christ.[11]

3) Alternative Questions Are Asked to Force a Decision

Even though alternative questions can seem open, in many cases they are not; they are a little too close to their syntactic partner, the polar question. As a result, askers often use alternative questions not just to confirm or limit a selection but to force a decision between one or more options. If asked with negative polarity, an alternative question even more so takes on this rhetorical force. In fact, it is possible in natural language to create alternative questions with an unstated

11. Cf. Porter, *Verbal Aspect*, 423.

disjunctive word through a heavy-handed use of pragmatics. This pragmatic use verges on the decisive force of a polar question:

(14) So ... coffee ... tea ...? (ALTERNATIVE QUESTION)

Question (14) carries the formation of an alternative question, but when asked within natural language situations, it comes close to the rhetorical force of a polar question. We can see a similar situation in the GNT:

(15) ἔξεστιν δοῦναι κῆνσον Καίσαρι ἢ οὔ; (MATT 22:17)

Here in (15), "Is it right to pay the tax to Caesar or not?" the Pharisees ask an alternative question that is constructed so close in form to a polar question that it really is a push for a decision. This is because the question resembles what English speakers would consider a tag question (strong pragmatic push for a reply, usually positive in nature). Semantically, this question is a dilemma question (§4.O).

The lack of any interrogative marker sometimes allows alternative questions to drift toward the erotetic logic of polar questions, as we see in (15).[12] One way to help determine which way the question leans is to look carefully at the set of answers; if the best set of answers is "yes" or "no," then the question leans far toward being a polar question. If the best set of answers is one of the alternatives given, then the question still leans enough toward working as an alternative question. In some cases, as in (15), both set of answers can seem appropriate—which is why interpreters must keep returning to the logic of the question rather than relying too much on the answers.

Finally, in the presence of strong rhetorical force, alternative questions can seem pushy, rigid, and demanding. In those situations, they are frequently off-putting to an audience, who may feel they are highly limited in what they can actually decide based on the question of the asker.

Case Study — GALATIANS 3:2

ἐξ ἔργων νόμου τὸ πνεῦμα ἐλάβετε ἢ ἐξ ἀκοῆς πίστεως;

PAUL: Did you receive the Spirit by works of the law or by hearing in faith?

In his letter to the Galatians, Paul asks a straightforward alternative question of his readership: "Did the Spirit come from works by law (ἐξ ἔργων νόμου) or hearing by faith (ἐξ ἀκοῆς πίστεως)?" This is not simply a "rhetorical question." The key to interpreting this question hinges on understanding the alternatives

12. Han and Romero, "Disjunction, Focus, and Scope," 180.

provided by the asker; here Paul provides only two. In looking at Paul's erotetic logic, we can see that Paul seeks to discount all other options; for example, being Jewish, being Greek, loving others, or many other "legitimate" options that a reader may wonder about. Instead, Paul alerts his readers that he believes there really is only two (real) options by which one can receive the Spirit—works or faith. As this question is embedded in a rhetorical monologue with other questions, Paul continues this line of reasoning by chiding the reader away from any belief that the Spirit could come through works of the law. Thus, the purpose of Paul's question is to ask the reader to confirm for themselves: Was the Spirit a result of works under the law? If not, then it must be only by hearing the gospel in faith that the Spirit can be received.

Key Bibliography

Aloni and Égré, "Alternative Questions," 1–27; Estes, *Questions*, 118–23; Hagstrom, "Questions," 484.

D. Set Questions

Set questions ask for the hearer to select an answer from within a limited set of possibilities. In English, we often refer to set questions as *which questions*. Like variable questions, set questions ask for a variable, *x*, to be solved. Unlike variable questions, set questions solve for the variable within a closed, not open, set. Set questions get their name from their focus on a particular set of possibilities defined by the asker (whether implicitly or explicitly). Or to put it another way, since we evaluate questions based on the asking and not on the replies or answers, the set that is limited by the erotetic logic of set questions is the set that is in the range of possibilities in the mind of the asker and *not* the range of possible answers in the mind of the hearer. The reason for this is that the hearer will always construe that set inexactly from the ideal set in the mind of the asker. For example:

(1) Which book do you want to read?

In this sample set question, the asker asks a question that can only be answered from within the possible set intended by the asker. In this case, the asker presumes that there is a set of books that are known to both the asker and the hearer, and the asker wants the hearer to select one book out of the set. This set can be broad (which book of all books ever written) or narrow (which book of the three books sitting on the table); for textual-interpretation scenarios like the GNT, context is key to interpretation of most set questions.

One challenge occurs when an asker asks a set question, and the set is unknown or not fully known to the hearer. If I were to ask you, the reader of this book, "Which key is yours?" you would not know to what set of keys I was referring. Thus, askers of set questions must be careful to ensure that the audience can reference the most likely set of possibilities before making their selection. Set questions are relatively uncommon; less than 4% of questions in the GNT are set questions.

Formation

Set questions are most often formed with a specific variable world (such as "which" or "who" or "what") plus a corresponding genitive phrase (such as "of these"). However, set questions are not always easy to identify via syntax. The primary reason for this is that set questions do not have as standardized a format as the other three primary question formations. Also, set questions do not require any certain marker of interrogativity, as askers can use several different markers, each with many variations. As set questions in Koine Greek do front their π-word, the biggest challenge is differentiating set questions from variable questions. As a basic formation of questions, set questions can occur in any turn, in any dialogue position, with any degree of informational and rhetorical qualities, and with virtually any semantic and pragmatic features not exclusive to one of the other three question formations.

Several factors in the formation and identification of variable questions are listed below.

1) Set Questions Do Require an Interrogative Variable Word

Set questions, like variable questions, make use of interrogative variable words in their formation. Because of this, set questions take on an open, informational quality based on what is asked, modified by the remainder of the clause as well as the possible set of possibilities specified. For example:

(2) διὰ *ποῖον* αὐτῶν ἔργον ἐμὲ λιθάζετε; (JOHN 10:32)

In this set question (2), Jesus asks his antagonists to identify the works of his for which they think they have a right to stone him. The question identifies a range of possibilities ("all the works of Jesus") with the purpose of isolating one or more within that set.

Also like variable questions, set questions have more than one possible interrogative variable word in the GNT. In the GNT, there are only two interrogative variable words used to ask set questions: ποῖος and τίς. The usage distribution of these two words is depicted in the following chart on page 117. Interestingly, the writers of the GNT all seem to prefer the more indefinite τίς over the more precise ποῖος (which only occurs in the Gospels in recorded speech).

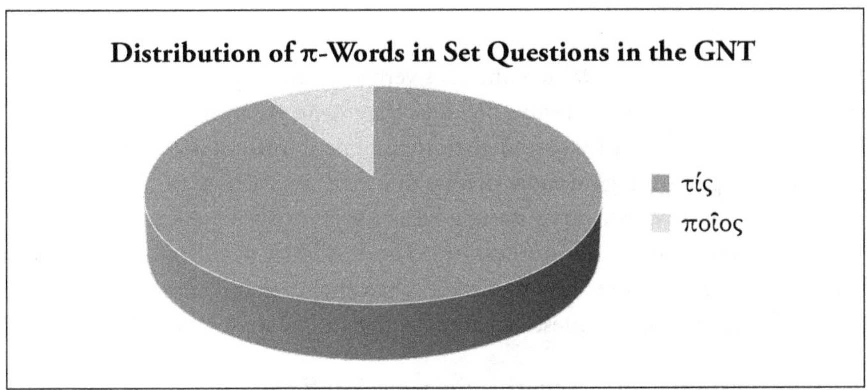

2) Set Questions Front Their Interrogative Variable Words

As the structure of set questions are akin to variable questions, set questions also front their interrogative variable word as a rule, just as variable questions do. The π-fronting organizes the informational structure of the question so that the interrogative intent is given primary focus. While fronting is the rule in ancient Greek, interpreters must still examine each sentence to determine the primary sentential force as well as whether fronting occurs.

Exceptions to this rule are rare, but they do exist. Equally important for set questions is the careful reading of the text for pragmatic features. For example:

(3) ἐν τῇ ἀναστάσει οὖν *τίνος* τῶν ἑπτὰ ἔσται γυνή; (MATT 22:28)

Example (3), a set question, does not front its π-word, τίνος, which normally indicates that this word would function as a relative pronoun. At the same time, the context of example (3) suggests its primary force is interrogative. In this situation, the Sadducees ask Jesus a type of composite utterance, with an assertion prefacing a question. Thus, we would understand the meaning of the utterance as "Now in the resurrection—who of the seven's wife will she be?"

3) Set Questions Do Not Require a Verb

As with all of the four basic formations of questions based on syntax, set questions do not require a verb to be asked in natural-discourse situations (see §3.E.4). However, set questions are different than the other three formations in that when an asker asks a set question without a verb, it always takes on the same basic role in meaning: "Which of these?" or "Which ones?" As a result, speakers frequently use verbless set questions in a different manner than typical set questions: they are used for repair, as a noncommittal response, or as a rejoinder (to name but a few examples). This also means that set questions are best formed with a verbal clause, unlike the other three formations. Below is an example in the GNT:

(4) *Ποίας;* (MATT 19:18)

The set question in (4), "Which ones?" is verbless, asked by the rich young man as a way to bring clarity to Jesus's previous statement. As a verbless set question, it carries both informational and rhetorical effects. Informationally, it allows the rich young man to gain more precise information; rhetorically, it allows the rich young man to create conversational space so as to evaluate Jesus's assertion. Since it is one of the few occurrences of ποῖος, it is likely to be slightly idiomatic and possibly a little more "distinguished" than the more common use of τίς. In natural-language use, set questions are effective in this rhetorical role.

4) Set Questions with Negative Polarity Are Rare

Set questions with a negative polarity are rare in natural-language situations. This is why in the GNT less than 1% of all questions are negative-set questions (and all these are in Matthew and Luke–Acts). Instead of limiting the hearer to a set of possibilities, the negative set questions turn this on its ear by limiting the hearer to anything but a reasonable set of possibilities. For example:

(5) *τίνα* τῶν προφητῶν *οὐκ* ἐδίωξαν οἱ πατέρες ὑμῶν; (ACTS 7:52)

The negative set question (5), "Which of the prophets didn't your fathers persecute?" is a classic use of negative set questions in dialogue. By adding the negative particle οὐκ, Stephen adds bias to the question that pushes the hearer away from selecting one within a set to forcing all of the set on the hearer. As a result, negative polar-set questions are often used by a speaker to pigeonhole, mock, or be condescending to their audience (cf. Acts 7:54).

5) Set Questions May Have a Genitive or Disjunctive Phrase(s)

The flexibility of forming set questions in Koine Greek leads to several distinctive syntactical possibilities. The most obvious is either the inclusion of a genitive phrase or more than one phrase joined disjunctively, both intended to support the interrogative variable and create a limited range of possibilities in the asking. Two examples:

(6) *τίς* οὖν *αὐτῶν* πλεῖον ἀγαπήσει αὐτόν; (LUKE 7:42)
(7) *τίς* γὰρ μείζων ἐστίν, ὁ χρυσὸς *ἢ* ὁ ναὸς ὁ ἁγιάσας τὸν χρυσόν; (MATT 23:17)

Example (6) uses a clear genitive phrase to set up the set question by severely limiting the range of possibilities. Without αὐτῶν, the sense of the question would be much more open ("Then who will love . . . ?"), but with the pronoun the goal of Jesus's question is more exactly identified by the reader. In example (7), the disjunctive word may at first point to an alternative question, but the presence of the π-word τίς is the best indicator that it is not (see also §3.C).

Rhetorical Effects

Due to their syntactic similarities with variable questions, set questions also have less inherent rhetorical effects than either polar or alternative questions. Askers ask set questions primarily to limit a range of possibilities for the hearer, with the hearer further limiting the range with their answers. The range of possibilities is more limited than variable questions but greater than polar or alternative questions. The unique characteristics of set questions make them useful for dialogue.[13] Notice the distribution of set questions in the GNT:

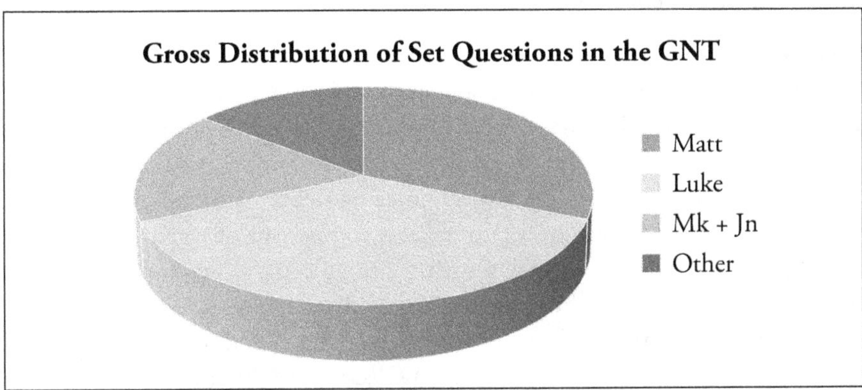

The three most important rhetorical effects of set questions are listed below.

1) Set Questions Are Asked to Gather Select Information

The primary pragmatic use of set questions is to gather select information from within a range of possibilities. This is primarily a result of their use of an interrogative variable word. By limiting the variable, set questions can hone in on a determined, limited set while remaining open as a question in their natural state. For example:

(8) ἢ *τίς* ἐστιν ἐξ *ὑμῶν* ἄνθρωπος, ὃν αἰτήσει ὁ υἱὸς αὐτοῦ ἄρτον ...; (MATT 7:9)

In question (8), Jesus, while teaching, asks the gathered crowd to consider which of them would give their son a stone. If Jesus had asked with a variable question, the audience would be free to consider anyone they knew that happened to pop into their mind. By using a set question, Jesus limits the range of possibilities to the gathered audience and makes the question more closed and therefore more personal.

13. For example, Comorovski, *Interrogative Phrases*, 11.

2) Set Questions Are Asked to Confirm a Selection (Through Comparison)

Another major use of set questions is to confirm a selection that is identified in the question asked. This use of set questions (and their embedded interrogative variable) is what distinguishes them from variable questions. Set questions become helpful in leading an audience toward a selection without forcing them into one choice (polar questions) or making them choose between the selections (alternative questions). For example:

(9) *τίς ἐκ τῶν δύο* ἐποίησεν τὸ θέλημα τοῦ πατρός; (MATT 21:31)

Here, Jesus tells a story which culminates in a question (9) for his audience to answer ("Which of the two did the will of his father?"). Jesus starts the story by identifying two sons that make decisions during the course of the narrative. In order to lead his audience to best understand the story, Jesus asks a set question designed to help them confirm a selection ἐκ τῶν δύο. As the asker, Jesus is as much asking them to think (i.e., to make a comparison) before a selection is made. (Alternative questions may cause the hearer to make a comparison before choosing their alternative, but it is not implied in the erotetic logic in the same way as with set questions.) Thus, the hearer now has to compare from a limited range of possibilities in order to confirm a selection for the asker.

3) Set Questions Are Asked to Limit Choices

One of the most significant rhetorical effects of set questions is in their ability to limit choices. By taking an interrogative variable and severely limiting it, a set question quickly constrains the options of the audience as put forward by the asker. In many situations, this limitation is of a positive or helpful nature. When this happens, the asker is often making a suggestion of sorts to the audience whether they realize it or not. This is certainly the case in (1), (4), and (9), examples above. For example:

(10) *Τίνα* θέλετε *ἀπὸ τῶν δύο* ἀπολύσω ὑμῖν; (MATT 27:21)

In asking (10), Pilate asks the crowd about a prisoner release: "Which of the two should I release to you?" Yet Pilate doesn't ask the crowd—who are neither his friends nor peers—as if any prisoner they thought of could be released. Rather, by limiting the interrogative variable and asking a set question, Pilate wants to make sure that other prisoners are not options. (Pilate, whom we know from the NT as a wily debater, may devilishly have wanted to set up a comparison between Jesus and Barabbas as well). The crowd was all too willing to follow Pilate's lead and ask for the release of Barabbas.

In more negative situations with stronger rhetorical force, a hearer may be aware that the asker is trying to limit their choices by asking the set question.

With strong rhetorical force, a set question can be quite demanding or even condemnatory.

Case Study MATTHEW 6:27

τίς δὲ ἐξ ὑμῶν μεριμνῶν δύναται προσθεῖναι ἐπὶ τὴν ἡλικίαν αὐτοῦ πῆχυν ἕνα;

JESUS: But *who of you* by being anxious is able to add a single unit of time to your life?

In the middle of his Sermon on the Mount, Jesus engages his audience over the issue of anxiety in life, encouraging them not to be apprehensive. In making this argument, Jesus caps his first point by asking the crowd a set question: τίς δὲ ἐξ ὑμῶν ("But who of you . . . ?"). The two ways this question is often handled in the secondary literature misses the point of the erotetic logic of the question, not to mention the particulars of what Jesus is asking.

First, the question is often treated simply as a "rhetorical question," where Jesus "says" to his audience that worry cannot add to their lives or make their lives better.[14] While it is true that Jesus uses the question in the midst of persuasive discourse, and that his goal is more to persuade than to dialogue, Jesus still asks the question as a question for a reason. Second, Jesus's question in 6:27 is often translated as a polar question in modern translations instead of a set question (for example, the NIV, NLT, NRSV, and HCSB). This is the way it is often colloquialized for the modern English reader. Yet the logic of a polar question—the point of its asking—is quite different than the logic of a set question. What Jesus is *not* asking is: "Can you do this? Yes or no? Then if not. . . ." Jesus is not calling the crowd to a decision about their worry. Rather, the emphasis (as Jesus addresses a crowd of people who apparently are listening intently to his message) is on the comparison to be made in the minds of the listener at this point, as in "Who of you. . . ?"

Here Jesus's question is quite a bit more sophisticated than a straightforward assertion or a rudimentary polar question. Set questions push the hearer toward comparison, and this is exactly what Jesus seems to intend.[15] By asking a set question, Jesus wants each hearer to consider whether they—or anyone around them, or anyone they know—have the ability to add a block of time to their life through worry. The audience, by looking around and thinking, "Who can do this?" comes to the realization that *no one* can add time to their life. Only God can accomplish that. Thus, Jesus's argument structure in Matthew 6:25–27 works like this:

14. For example, Newman and Stine, *Handbook*, 187.
15. Cf. Luther, *Luther's Works*, 21:196; Nolland, *Matthew*, 311.

- Assertion—v. 25a (PROPOSITION)
- Negative Polar Question—v. 25b (CONFIRMATION FOR PROPOSITION)
- Analogy—v. 26a (ANALOGY OF PROPOSITION)
- Negative Polar Question—v. 26b (CONFIRMATION FOR ANALOGY OF PROPOSITION)
- Set question—v. 27 (CONCLUSIVE COMPARISON FOR PROPOSITION)

Jesus concludes with the set question after two call-and-response refrains of argumentation, leading the hearer to understand the initial proposition that no matter who you think you are or your situation in life, no one can change the parameters of life except God. The set question also leads into the variable question opening his second point (v. 28), where Jesus broadens the argument again before returning finally to a similar, concluding proposition (v. 34).

Key Bibliography
Comorovski, *Interrogative Phrases*, 11–13; Estes, *Questions*, 76–80.

E. Composite Questions

The fifth (and unofficial) formation of questions based on syntax are *composites*. This form of question is a catchall grouping that represents any question shaped by syntactically modifying one of the four standard formations. An asker can modify any of the four primary formations to create a composite question. Composite questions are also known as *compound questions* or *modified questions*. They are most often formed by affixing together two independent question formations, although they also include questions that are either overly complex or poorly formed in their original language. These types of questions are found frequently in sample questions in linguistic studies, partly because they are a peculiar feature of natural-language use. For example:

(1) Where will you go and what will you do? (COMPOSITE)
(2) If I leave, will you stay? (COMPOSITE)

Here both questions (1) and (2) are examples of composite questions in that their interrogative logic is fundamentally affected by a composite construction. In (1), two different clauses are affixed conjunctively, which ties together their interrogative logic and meaning for the utterance (especially as it affects the pragmatics of the larger discourse). In (2), a conditional clause is affixed to a clause formed as a polar question, coloring the overall question. Beyond these examples and the types studied below, other types of composite questions are possible. One example that is much discussed in modern IE-language study is the *multiple* wh-*question* (for example, "Which kid gets which book?" and "Who wants what assignment?"). By their nature, composite questions are much more difficult for the reader to process, and interpretation should proceed accordingly.[16]

A composite is a form of question that is either (a) comprised of two or more of the four major formations of questions, (b) comprised of one of the major formations of questions plus makes use of some type of conditional logic, or (c) comprised of one or more modifications to one of the four major formations (that alters the syntactical form of the question).[17] In this section, we'll consider two examples of (a), *conjunctive questions* and *disjunctive questions*, one example of (b), *conditional questions*, and one example of (c), *sluices*.

Of the four considered below, conjunctive questions and disjunctive questions are related syntactically as compound utterances with two (or more) clauses affixed by a conjunction.[18] In language, there are four primary, logical paths to affixing clauses: conjunctive (such as with the conjunction *and*), disjunctive (such as with the conjunction *or*), adversative (such as with the conjunction *but*), and causal (such as with the conjunction *because*).[19] These types of questions create their interrogative force by affixing two related clauses; we can see their interaction occurring on the clause level. This is in contrast to phrase-level and sentence- or discourse-level interaction. However, the logic of compound propositions is more clear cut than the logic of compound questions.[20] Let's use a disjunctive situation as an example to show these differences:

Example	Disjunction Level	Question Form/Type
Do you want coffee or tea?	Phrase	Alternative (§3.C)
Will you go *or* will you stay?	Clause	Disjunctive (§3.E.2)
When are we going? Or are we even going at all?	Sentence/Discourse	Double (§5.D.1)

While these artificial examples are relatively clear, the same cannot always be said for natural-language situations.[21] In modern languages, conjunction usage in written discourse is typically more precise than in spoken discourse. Of special concern is the common use of the disjunctive question in Koine Greek—these

16. For example, see Pratarelli and Lawson, "Conjunctive Forms," 415–28.
17. Cf. Aristotle, *Interpretation* 17a21–23.
18. Traditionally called a *compound sentence*; see *CDL* 93; Bussmann, *Routledge Dictionary of Language and Linguistics*, 223.
19. Bussmann, *Routledge Dictionary of Language and Linguistics*, 231.
20. Peetz, "Disjunctions and Questions," 264–65.
21. Some grammars treat the sentence, "Do you want coffee or tea?" as a reduction of "Do you want coffee or do you want tea?" (appearing to be clausal), but the disjunction occurs between coffee and tea. The true distinction occurs in the semantics of the verb phrase for each clause.

questions carry shades of nuances that are not easy to translate into the more streamlined use of disjunction in English (for example, Heb 2:6). Likewise, Koine Greek (as it has come to us in its written examples in the GNT) is a naturally syndetic language (intersentence and intrasentence); many questions start with conjunctions in Greek that would not start that way in modern English. Technical treatises in Classical Greek followed strict usage patterns for syndesis, akin to the aforementioned modern logical paths for affixing clauses. At the same time, Aristotle pointed out that compound questions (if not carefully observed by the audience) can make for fallacious arguments.[22]

1. Conjunctive Questions

Conjunctive questions are formed with two (or more) questions added together within the utterance. In the secondary literature, these types of questions are sometimes called *multiple questions* (though this term can refer to other question types as well). An asker makes use of a conjunctive question to yoke together two related questions that—in some cases—may anticipate one reply synthesized from both set of answers. Due to the prevalence of conjunctions in language and the inherent ambiguity that can be introduced through conjunctions, conjunctive questions are at times easily confused with other forms of questions. This is especially true in the GNT, which features a large number of double questions (§5.D.1) joined with the conjunctive καί in *scriptio continua*. The difference between conjunctive questions and other question formations and types comes down to the relationship between the number of thoughts expressed. For example:

(1) Where did you move my towel *and* why did you move it? (CONJUNCTIVE)
(2) Where *and* why did you move my towel? (CONJUNCTIVE)
(3) Do you have a camera *and* a computer? (POLAR QUESTION)
(4) Where are you going? And what are you doing? (DOUBLE QUESTION)

Here (1) is a conjunctive question formed from the conjunction of two variable questions. Note that the question is conjunctive because (a) the artificial example is phrased in this way and (b) it expresses one related thought. Likewise, (2) is a conjunctive question that relies on a sluice (§3.E.4) in the first clause to create a conjunctive question with an implicit complement (in other words, "Where [did you move my towel] *and* why did you move my towel?") With question (3), it is tempting to view it conjunctively, as a hearer may have a camera but not have a computer (or vice versa). However, this question is actually a complex polar question, as the basis of the interrogative logic here is the polar "Do you have?" which

22. Aristotle, *Sophistical Refutations* 167b38–169a23.

still seeks a positive or negative answer about both objects (together, as a set). The reason this is complex is that if a hearer possessed a camera but not a computer, the answer to the question is therefore "No," but in natural-language situations the hearer would probably give a broken reply to (3) such as "Well, I have a camera, but I don't have a computer." Finally, (4) is asked as a double question, and contra (1), the indicator that it is a double question, not a conjunctive question, is because (a) the artificial example is asked in this way and (b) it expresses two somewhat distinct thoughts. With these English examples, we must remember that the conjunction καί in Greek is not the exact same as "and" in English; "and" and καί have variant semantic ranges and roles, as do "love" and ἀγάπη.[23]

Conjunctive questions are not uncommon in representational discourse such as the GNT; nearly 9% of all questions in the GNT possess some degree of conjunctive formation. At the same time, only half of those are probably truly conjunctive questions; most of the other half of these questions follow the logic of double questions more closely than a true conjunctive question. When interpreting conjunctive questions, one question that arises is: "For an ancient language without punctuation, how do we tell if an utterance is a true conjunctive question or simply two individual questions loosely linked by καί?" In the GNT, reason (a) in example (1) and (4) is undetermined, and so it can be difficult for the interpreter to know for certain whether an utterance is a conjunctive question or a double question. In fact, as a general principle, in natural language it is more difficult to discern whether a question is a conjunctive question or another kind of question than these simple, artificial examples indicate.

Formation

Conjunctive questions require a copulative conjunction (συμπλεκτῖκός σύνδεσμος).[24] Potential conjunctive questions are relatively easy to spot by the presence of a conjunction such as καί. At the same time, a question with a conjunctive word is *not* necessarily a conjunctive question; in fact, it more often is not. In other words, the presence of καί in a question does not make it conjunctive. For a question to potentially be a conjunctive question, the conjunction must occur either in the primary clause (the one with the interrogative force) when coupled with an implicit clause (e.g., a sluice; see §3.E.4), or it must occur between two (or more) independent clauses, each with distinct interrogative force but related semantic interest. The latter of these two options is more prevalent. Conjunctive questions are the easiest form of composite question to understand—their logic derives from the combination of two sentential forces working together (to some degree). Conjunctive questions are most normally formed from two variable-question clauses or two polar-question clauses. An

23. See for example, Titrud, "Function of Καί," 241–42.

24. Cf. Dionysius Thrax, *Ars Grammatica* 642.27.

example of more than two clauses is rare, as are conjunctive questions formed with alternative-question clauses, set-question clauses, or a mixture of two different forms of question clauses (though see the unusual construction of 2 Cor 11:29a, 11:29b). In some cases, the order of the conjunction will play a critical role in interpretation.[25]

The primary factor in the formation and identification of a conjunctive question is discussed immediately below.

1) Conjunctive Questions Are Two or More Related Interrogative Clauses Joined Conjunctively

Conjunctive questions are a composite-question formation that ask two related questions in one utterance. As such, they require two distinct conjunctive clauses that have some degree of semantic compatibility. The relationship is generally more equal than the second building on the first. Without punctuation, this relationship is what we must rely on to distinguish conjunctive questions from double questions in ancient Greek literature. For example:

(5) *Τίς* ἐστιν ἡ μήτηρ μου, *καὶ τίνες* εἰσὶν οἱ ἀδελφοί μου; (MATT 12:48)

Matthew records that in one situation where Jesus was informed that his mother and brothers were outside waiting for him, he asked (5), "Who is my mother and who are my brothers?" In some ways, Jesus's question is oddly worded; he could have simply asked, "Τίς ἐστιν ἡ μήτηρ μου καὶ οἱ ἀδελφοί μου;" (as in Mark 3:33).[26] In fact, these two variations are somewhat equitable in meaning.[27] However, based on the context, it may mean that Matthew did not want Jesus to ask merely about who his family is (in the nonconjunctive variable question above), but he wants to single out his mother from his brothers and ask about both of them. In doing so, Matthew's Jesus asks who is his mother and who are his brothers without conflating the two categories, yet connecting them as two distinct parts of a related issue. Using a conjunctive question constructed with two interrogative variable words, Matthew's Jesus intends his audience to reflect on the distinction between the two categories. It suggests there is not a familial relationship that is not subject to Jesus's mission for the kingdom.

25. Noveck, "Pragmatic Inferences," 309.

26. It is not just the wording of Matthew 12:48 and Mark 3:33 that is different—it is the interrogative logic of the question as well. Mark conflates the two categories into a variable question which brings out a different nuance. It is possible that Mark is "correcting" Matthew, but more likely Mark is simply telling his version of the events.

27. The difficulty in reducing one to the other is borne by the use of the "to be" verb, which clouds the semantic issues much more than semantically simple verbs like "walk."

Rhetorical Effects

Conjunctive questions have a broad range of rhetorical usage in representational and natural-language situations. Generally speaking, conjunctive questions tend to be more strongly informational and more weakly rhetorical. This is a result of their composite syntax, and does not take into account any semantic or pragmatic influences. Thus, conjunctive questions are on average far less rhetorical than double questions. Also, unlike double questions, the first question clause typically carries the same degree of informational quality as the second (and subsequent) clauses—any amplification is mild. When amplification does occur, conjunctive questions create a mild rhetorical effect from the repetition of the two or more interrogative forces in succession. Thus, conjunctive questions are great for provoking thoughts from an audience on complex issues.

Two of the most significant rhetorical effects of conjunctive questions are discussed immediately below.

1) Conjunctive Questions Are Asked to Link Two or More Closely Related Concerns

Since conjunctive questions are one utterance that asks two (or more) questions, they are intended by the asker to tie together two (or more) closely related questions. This begs the question as to why the asker forms the question as a conjunctive question rather than two separate questions. Often, it is because the asker hopes to expose a relationship between the two questions for the audience—such as hinting that the answer to one is tied to the answer to the other. In other cases, it is because the asker hopes a hearer will synthesize the two pieces of information into one composite answer. For example:

(6) εἰπὲ ἡμῖν, *πότε* ταῦτα ἔσται *καὶ τί* τὸ σημεῖον
τῆς σῆς παρουσίας καὶ συντελείας τοῦ αἰῶνος; (MATT 24:3)

In (6), the disciples asked Jesus, "Tell us, when will these things happen, and what will be the sign of your coming and the total completion of the age?" The issues that the disciples wonder about is complex, and it is not unusual for them to use a composite question to ask for several pieces of information (two interrogative clauses, one of which is composed of two parts). These question clauses are closely related, and by asking this way the disciples are indicating they want a lot of answers. In responding to their question, Jesus takes note of the composite question and answers the question by synthesizing the answers into one long reply (Matt 24:4–25:46).

2) Conjunctive Questions Mildly Amplify Their Individual Informational Qualities

As with most complex questions, the repetition of interrogative clauses tends to amplify the total interrogative force of composite questions and question strings (§5.D). Since conjunctive questions tend toward stronger informational qualities and weaker rhetorical qualities, the amplification that occurs within conjunctive clauses works differently than the amplification that occurs within a question string. With question strings, the amplification tends to build forward such that by the end the rhetorical effect is like an avalanche or a crescendo; with conjunctive questions, the amplification tends to build across the question, putting equal focus on both clauses or, in some cases, putting a little extra focus on the first clause. For example:

(7) οὐχ οἱ πλούσιοι καταδυναστεύουσιν ὑμῶν,
καὶ αὐτοὶ ἕλκουσιν ὑμᾶς εἰς κριτήρια; (JAS 2:6)

In (7), James asks, "Isn't it the rich who exploit you, and those who drag you into court?" One tell that this question is more probably a conjunctive question than a double question is the implicit οὐχ οἱ πλούσιοι construction in the second clause; while this is not in any way definitive, the implicit construction plus the nondramatic καὶ αὐτοὶ creates the feel of a conjunctive question. In asking this conjunctive question, James asks his readers to consider and answer this question, but by forming it as a conjunct, James amplifies how important it is that his readers recognize that it is the rich who are doing these things to them. In fact, the amplification creates a light backward focus, as it amplifies the intensity of the asking about those who exploit them, since these are also the ones who drag them into court.

Case Study — 2 CORINTHIANS 11:29A

τίς ἀσθενεῖ, καὶ οὐκ ἀσθενῶ;

PAUL: Who is weak, and I am not weak?

In developing his argument in 2 Corinthians, Paul begins to boast as if a fool in what he has personally endured for Jesus (11:16). After detailing what he has endured, Paul begins to list his constant work for the kingdom and reminds his readers that he has a daily burden for the churches (v. 28). It is at this point Paul raises the first part of a double question, "Who is weak, and I am not weak?" Paul's question here is a challenge for the reader both syntactically and pragmatically. Paul forms his question as a conjunctive question, yet uses two different syntactic constructions (a variable question followed by a polar question). Paul's first clause carries a positive polarity, but the second clause carries a negative polarity with οὐκ. The question also contains semantic bias in the repetitious use of ἀσθενέω. Though it is a conjunctive question, it occurs in the middle of rhetorical (and not narrative) discourse. The conjunctive question raises two important and related questions for the reader to consider: "Who is weak?" and "Isn't Paul weak?" Though the questions use different constructions, Paul has an ear to synthesizing the questions raised in the minds of his readers.

There is a missing piece to this puzzle, and most likely it is in the pragmatics to the question. As we read Paul's argument, we see that this conjunctive question is the first part of a double question (§5.D.1). It is a common argument technique to introduce a double question with first an open question and then a negative polar question. Instead of taking the classic approach, Paul rearticulates his argument by creating two conjunctive questions that play between the different tensions of conjunction and doubling. Paul wants his readers to consider who are those who are weak and to confirm that Paul experiences their same weakness. He wants them to synthesize this truth and then amplify and apply it to not just weaknesses but to struggles with sin (v. 29b). Instead of what at first appears to be awkward syntax, these questions form an interlaced rhetorical figure. This is perhaps even more true if we treat καί as a "consecutive" καί; "Who is weak, and *then* I am not weak?"[28] Paul's argumentation strategy here is of the highest sophistication found in any of the world's rhetorical literature.

FURTHER EXAMPLES

Matt 3:14; 6:25; 7:22; 25:44; Luke 13:18; John 3:10; 14:10; Acts 21:13; 1 Cor 3:16; 9:7b, 7c; 2 Cor 11:29b; Rev 5:2; 7:13.

Key Bibliography

Peetz, "Disjunctions and Questions"; Wiśniewski, *Posing of Questions*, 91–94.

2. Disjunctive Questions

Disjunctive questions are formed with two (or more) questions joined disjunctively within the utterance. An asker makes use of a disjunctive question to juxtapose two related questions that—in some cases—may anticipate one reply synthesized from both sets of answers. As with conjunctive questions, the common use of disjunction in the *scriptio continua* of the GNT means that it is difficult to differentiate alternative questions (§3.C), disjunctive questions, and double questions (§5.D.1) joined with a disjunctive conjunction. Whereas the more common alternative question typically uses the disjunct to force a choice between two nouns or phrases (and is built upon the logic of a polar question), the disjunctive question typically uses the disjunct to join two different clauses that may or may not be related syntactically. Yet, these clauses will be closely

28. Cf. Martin, *2 Corinthians*, 570–71, though Martin's deemphasis of the interrogative force is unnecessary.

related semantically (cf. the table in §3.E). This is in contrast to the double question joined by a disjunctive conjunction, which needs to be only loosely related semantically. For example:

(1) Do you want bread or soup? (ALTERNATIVE QUESTION)
(2) Do you want lunch or do you want to lie down? (DISJUNCTIVE)
(3) Where are you going, or do you even know? (DISJUNCTIVE)
(4) Is there a way in? Or is there a way over? (DOUBLE QUESTION)
(5) Where can I get a mocha, or who drove the bus? (NONSENSICAL)

Example (1) is a common alternative question where the audience is prompted to choose between two possibilities. In (2), a disjunctive question, the logical difference between (1) and (2) is not large. Instead of being given an alternative between two things, the hearer is prompted to choose between two actions or events in close association. By question (3), the logic becomes a little more complex than (2) due to the looser association. Conversely, there is even less association in (4), as the two questions are not asked with the same intent as (2) or (3). Question (5) is nonsensical, demonstrating the necessity of relationship for meaningful disjunction to occur in discourse. As a general principle, distinguishing between the types of questions that use disjunction is difficult in natural-language situations (e.g., 2 Cor 6:14a, 14b, 15), but the differences between the syntactic formations of each create shades of semantic and pragmatic meaning in order to better persuade their hearers. With these English examples, we must remember that disjunction in Greek is not the exact same as "or" in English; "or" and ἤ have variant semantic ranges and roles, as do "hope" and ἐλπίς.

Formation

Disjunctive questions require a disjunctive conjunction (διαζευκτικός σύνδεσμος).[29] Like conjunctive questions, disjunctive questions are relatively easy to spot by the presence of a disjunctive conjunction. In the GNT, the chief disjunctive word is ἤ. At the same time, a question with a disjunctive word is *not* necessarily a disjunctive question; disjunctive questions are uncommon, and what matters is how the disjunction occurs within the utterance. For a question to be a disjunctive question, the disjunct word must occur either in the primary clause (the one with the interrogative force) when juxtaposed with an implicit clause (e.g., a sluice; see §3.E.4), or it must occur between two (or more) independent clauses, each with distinct interrogative force but related semantic interest. Disjunctive questions are mentally taxing on the reader and are hard to get a handle on.[30] Their logic is moored in the realm of alternatives, but the alternatives may be juxtaposed to each other along many different tangents.

29. Cf. Dionysius Thrax, *Ars Grammatica* 642.30.
30. For example, see Pratarelli and Lawson, "Conjunctive Forms," 415–28.

Typically, askers form disjunctive questions with two variable-question clauses or two polar-question clauses. More than two is rare, as are disjunctive questions formed with alternative-question clauses, set-question clauses, or a mixture of two different forms of questions clauses. In some cases, the order of the conjunction will play a critical role in interpretation.[31]

The primary factor in the formation and identification of a disjunctive question is discussed immediately below.

1) Disjunctive Questions Are Two or More Related Interrogative Clauses Juxtaposed

A disjunctive question is a composite-question formation that creates an alternative between two different question clauses in one utterance. As such, they require two distinct disjunctive clauses that have some degree of semantic compatibility. Unlike double questions, the relationship between the two is generally more equal than the second building on the first. Without punctuation, this relationship is what we must rely on to distinguish disjunctive clauses from double questions in ancient Greek literature.[32] For example:

(6) μὴ δύναται, ἀδελφοί μου, συκῆ ἐλαίας ποιῆσαι ἢ ἄμπελος σῦκα; (JAS 3:12)

James asks, "It's not possible, my brothers [and sisters], for a fig tree to make olives, or a vine, figs?" While (6) carries a disjunctive formation, it is a prime example of the difficulties associated with identifying and interpreting disjunctive questions. At first glance, (6) may look more like an alternative question with the short clauses grouped together; this is due to the polar construction of the question plus the "gapping" (*CDL* 186) with the elided second infinitive (ἢ ἄμπελος σῦκα [ποιῆσαι]). Yet there are two distinct and closely related infinitival clauses that create a mild disjunction in the ears of the hearer. In this case, though, any semantic and pragmatic implications coming from the disjunction are completely overshadowed by the rhetorical force of the negative polar question (§4.T). Thus, when James asks this question of his readers, the disjunction serves to emphasize that no matter how many alternatives he may give, the intended answer will be "No! It is not possible." While James could have asked the question with a conjunctive formation (συκῆ ἐλαίας ποιῆσαι καὶ ἄμπελος σῦκα) or omitted the second example altogether, the disjunctive option creates a stark contrast between impossible alternatives to drive his rhetorical point home.[33]

---

31. Noveck, "Pragmatic Inferences," 309.
32. On ἤ outside the GNT used in a disjunctive question, see Josephus, *Jewish War* 1.626; used as a part of a question string, see Chariton, *Callirhoe* 1.9.
33. In certain cases, disjunctive arguments are equatable to conjunctive arguments; cf. Fălăuş, "Broaden Your Views," 85–86.

Rhetorical Effects

Disjunctive questions have several persuasive strategies in representational and natural-language situations. Because disjunction is rooted in contrastive alternatives, these rhetorical strategies revolve around creating contrasts that are in tension within the utterance or with the larger discourse. They lean more toward having informational qualities than rhetorical qualities. This is a result of their composite syntax, and does not take into account any semantic or pragmatic influences. For example, disjunctive questions are, on average, notably less rhetorical than question strings using disjunctive conjunctions. Also, unlike double questions, the first question clause typically carries the same degree of informational quality as the second and subsequent clauses—any amplification is mild. When amplification does occur, disjunctive questions create a mild rhetorical effect from the repetition of the two or more interrogative forces in succession. Often this effect is dissonant, as the two alternatives are contrastive and competitive. Thus, disjunctive questions are great for provoking thoughts from an audience on complex issues.

Two of the most significant rhetorical effects of disjunctive questions are discussed immediately below.

1) Disjunctive Questions Are Asked to Differentiate Two or More Closely Related Concerns

As the logic of disjunctive questions is rooted in the logic of alternatives, disjunctive questions are often asked to push the audience to distinguish between two related issues or concerns. In fact, as a general rule, the less rhetorical quality the disjunctive question carries, the more of an "alternative question" it becomes. In other words, disjunctive questions with strong informational qualities encourage "the hearer to select one alternative from the multiple options provided by the asker" (from §3.C). This is due to the fact that the speaker places the emphasis on the contrast.[34] For example:

(7) Σὺ εἶ ὁ ἐρχόμενος ἢ ἕτερον προσδοκῶμεν; (MATT 11:3)

John the Baptist sent his disciples to ask, "Are you the one who is to come, or should we expect some other?" John bases his disjunctive question (7) on a polar formation and intends the question semantically as a type of confirmation question (§4.R). On average, confirmation questions lean toward being informational rather than rhetorical. Rather than ask if Jesus is the "one who is to come" and wait for an answer, John uses a disjunctive-question formation to set up a contrast between two possibilities. By doing so, John emphasizes through contrast the uniqueness and importance of what he asks Jesus. The question calls for

34. The scholia to Dionysius Thrax's *Ars Grammatica* notes the contrast is often oppositional "night or day"; cited in Robins, *Byzantine Grammarians*, 85.

a decision (as confirmation questions do), yet at the same time the more complex interrogative logic discourages a simple response on the part of the hearer (cf. Matt 11:4–6). In this case, a simple "yes" or "no" is nonsensical.

2) Disjunctive Questions Can Create Tension between Two Alternatives

The logical complexity of disjunctive questions allows them to intentionally create tension between two alternatives, usually for rhetorical effect. Often the tension is mild, as well-thought out disjunctive questions will contain two clauses that create a necessary contrast. In highly rhetorical situations, however, a speaker can use disjunctive questions to sow confusion among the audience or stymie attempts at replies. This is because disjunctive questions will slow down dialogue, forcing hearers to weigh their options carefully. In fact, Aristotle singles out disjunctive questions as a prime vehicle for introducing fallacious argumentation and clouding an issue.[35] A speaker may use disjunctive questions in order to be intentionally ambiguous.[36] For example:

(8) Ἄνδρες Ἰσραηλῖται, τί θαυμάζετε ἐπὶ τούτῳ, ἢ ἡμῖν τί ἀτενίζετε ὡς ἰδίᾳ δυνάμει ἢ εὐσεβείᾳ πεποιηκόσιν τοῦ περιπατεῖν αὐτόν; (ACTS 3:12)

With the astonishment of the crowds after a healing, Peter asks them, "People of Israel, why does this surprise you, or why do you stare at us, as if by our own power or godliness we made him walk?" While the preference for disjunction here is difficult, the question's purpose is not. In (8), Peter forms this question with a disjunctive formation, but semantically it is a proof question (§4.G) and pragmatically is used as an expository question (§5.A.2). Thus, Peter uses the question to engage the crowd's concerns and to launch into a longer monologue. Yet Peter's preference for a disjunctive question does introduce a bit of persuasive rhetoric on his part—by casting the question disjunctively, he creates "false" tension that is both serious and mocking. If "Why does this surprise you?" is a legitimate question, then the tangential "Why do you stare at us?" is not; if the audience decides that Peter's actions are surprising, then they would stare for that very reason. Yet if they deny (or find no reason) for the first question, then the alternative is even worse (and would make his fellow Israelites seem foolish). The rhetorical goal is to tie up the thoughts of his audience, thereby giving Peter an edge to engage his hearers in greater detail through his sermon.

35. Aristotle, *Sophistical Refutations* 168a4; 176a7–9.

36. Peetz, "Disjunctions and Questions," 265–67.

Case Study 1 CORINTHIANS 9:8

Μὴ κατὰ ἄνθρωπον ταῦτα λαλῶ, ἢ καὶ ὁ νόμος ταῦτα οὐ λέγει;

PAUL: Even by human standards, can I say these things, or doesn't the law say these things also?

After his counsel to the Corinthian church about eating food sacrificed to idols, Paul ends with an explanation of what he would be willing to do in regard to helping his fellow believer not to stumble (8:13). At this point, Paul turns to the issue of his role in ministry, especially as it relates to any expectations that others may place on him. Here he leads off with a multiple-question string (§5.D.2) of four negative polar questions (§4.T), badgering his reader to acknowledge Paul's role in their ministry (9:1–2). Following this, Paul keeps raising questions related to his authority to conduct his business as an apostle, again using negative polar questions to badger his Corinthian audience into recognizing his perspective on these matters (9:3–6). Next, Paul asks a multiple question comprised of three speculative questions (§4.B), all designed to amplify Paul's challenge to the Corinthians to think deeply about the role of the laborer in relation to their pay. Paul's rhetorical goal is to help them see for themselves that laborers for the kingdom should have a share in the kingdom. Paul concludes this multiple-question string with a composite question, based on a disjunctive polar formation: "Even by human standards, can I say these things, or doesn't the law say these things also?"

Paul's badgering—perhaps prosecution—of the actions of the leaders of the Corinthian church over their expectations for his life and role in their ministry is well-encapsulated here by the many questions Paul uses. In this section, most of the questions are raised by Paul as part of a question string, and most of the question strings employ the same formation and type of question—the repetition helps to amplify Paul's concerns. The notable exception to this is 9:8, a disjunctive question that serves as the hook in the *one-one-one-two combination* following the jab-jab-jab of the three previous speculative questions (§4.B). Normally the hook would carry a much stronger rhetorical quality than the jabs, but in this case, Paul rather unusually chooses a question form that is more complicated than straightforwardly persuasive.

Paul's question is a disjunctive composite, comprised of two related question clauses. Both of these question clauses carry bias; the first clause carries the negative polarity item μή, and the second clause is a standard negative polar question that is probably the most common type of hook in a rhetorical combination. This begs the question: Why did Paul not raise his three jabs (1 Cor 9:7a, 7b, 7c) and then simply ask, καὶ ὁ νόμος ταῦτα οὐ λέγει; This would have made for a common (and proven) use of a multiple-question rhetorical argument. However,

Paul does not ask this; instead, he adds in the first clause. Our understanding of the role of the first clause hinges on Paul's use of μή. While the grammars present several options for μή with the indicative in a question (cf. §2.B.9), μή is perhaps best summarized in these situations as a bias word that introduces a note of unenthusiastic suspicion (best exemplified in the archaic English word "lest" and sometimes "even"). As a result, while it is often suggested that Paul expects a strong "no" to the first clause,[37] the question logic suggests that Paul is being more ambiguous than this. Paul asks this question expecting the possibility of both a "yes" and a "no"—in that Paul is not suggesting that he bases his argument on human perspective *even though such a view would be acceptable by human standards*. Paul intentionally couples this slightly ambiguous decision question (§4.Q) to an unambiguous NPQ (§4.T) that results in an encouragement for the hearer to respond with a strong "yes!" In the end, Paul employs this complex question to challenge the Corinthians—while it is possible for them to quibble over whether Paul's needs are covered under human standards, Paul pushes them to accept that they cannot quibble over the alternative, which is that his needs are covered clearly under God's law.

FURTHER EXAMPLES

Mark 4:30; Acts 7:49; Rom 3:1; 1 Cor 1:13b; 14:36; 2 Cor 6:14a, 14b; 6:15; Heb 2:6.

Key Bibliography

Peetz, "Disjunctions and Questions"; Pratarelli and Lawson, "Conjunctive Forms"; Walton, *Informal Logic*, 50–55; Wiśniewski, *Posing of Questions*, 91–94; Woods, *Aristotle's Earlier Logic*, 186–91.

3. Conditional Questions

Conditional questions ask for an answer if and only if the stated condition of the question is valid. If the conditional is not valid, it is *inoperative*, and thus the question does not have a real set of answers (though the rhetorical force of the utterance is still in effect, and legitimate replies may be made to the question based on grounds other than a real set of answers).[38] Conditional questions are formed with the addition of a conditional phrase or clause onto an interrogative utterance. They are composite questions in that they are composed of a conditional phrase or clause (often called a *protasis*) affixed to the main clause which carries the inter-

37. For example, Thiselton, *First Epistle to the Corinthians*, 684; Collins, *First Corinthians*, 338.

38. Leonardi and Santambrogio, "Pragmatics, Language Games, Questions and Answers," 457.

rogative force of the utterance (often called the *apodosis*). The primary role of the conditional is to limit the question asked, which in turn sets up a more complex logic than if the question was asked without the limiting conditional.[39] To understand the logic and rhetoric of a conditional question, the hearer must understand both the question itself and then the conditional limiter. The challenge to interpretation, however, is not only the differing erotetic logic that can make up the interrogative force of the main clause but also the variety of conditionals that can limit the question.[40] For example:

(1) If I order a steak, will you pay for it? (CONDITIONAL)
(2) Were the sign to be stolen, would the police surely come? (CONDITIONAL)
(3) If you could pass the salt, please? (REQUEST QUESTION)

Example (1) is a conditional question that uses a polar-question formation to raise the question of the hearer paying for the speaker's steak. However, the speaker only asks the hearer to pay for the steak if the speaker orders a steak. (Rhetorically, this could be used by the speaker to set up the expectation that the hearer will pay for the speaker's food, regardless of what is ordered.) In English, the use of the particle *if* + a common clause is referred to as the *canonical* form of a conditional; it is the standard by which all other conditionals are measured. Example (2) is a conditional question similar to (1), but it does not use the particle *if*, which makes it a *noncanonical* form of a conditional. For the sake of these simple, artificial examples, the limitation introduced by *were* is logically close to (1) but not as close rhetorically. Even though (3) contains an *if* particle, the question is not a conditional question as it is not a composite that sets up a limiter for an affixed question (cf. request questions, §4.S).

Relative to the overall study of Koine Greek, many traditional reference grammars cover conditional utterances in no small extent. However, these grammars do not distinguish the logic and effects of conditionals attached to propositions from conditionals attached to questions. With the limits of this book, we will primarily focus on the interrogative aspects of conditional questions, and not on the conditionals themselves (the subject of another book). As almost 10% of the direct questions in the GNT contain conditions, this form of question is important for NT interpretation.[41] Some GNT texts especially favor conditional questions. For example, the most statistically significant book that employs conditional questions is 1 Corinthians, wherein almost 22% of the questions are conditional questions. Also of interest are the books of Ephesians, Colossians,

39. Isaacs and Rawlins, "Conditional Questions," 269.
40. Cf. Dancygier, *Conditionals and Prediction*, 124.
41. Aristotle held it to be one of the four fundamental questions; Aristotle, *Posterior Analytics* 89b25.

1 Timothy, and 1 Peter: these four books *only* contain conditional questions. For 1 Peter, four out of the four questions are conditional. 1 John contains two conditional questions out of four questions total. In contrast, none of the questions in Revelation are conditional (in the spirit of the purpose of that text).

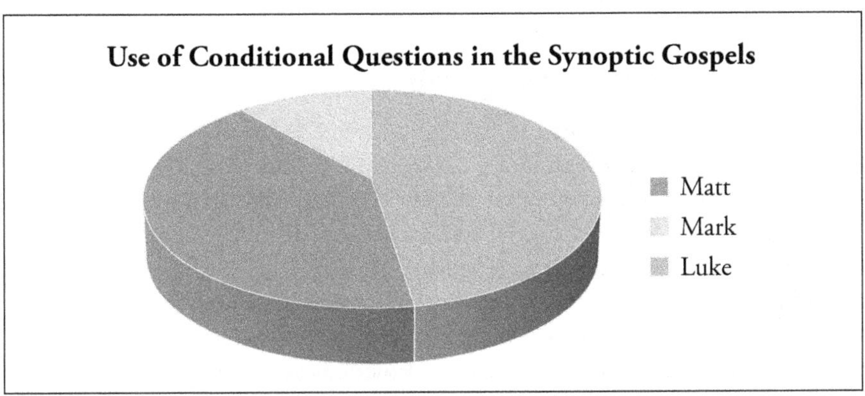

Formation

Conditional questions are relatively easy to spot in language, as they require a conditional phrase or clause for the question to be formed as a conditional question. Typically, the conditional clause will front a conditional conjunction, and this conditional conjunction is the best tell for identifying a conditional question.[42] The standard conditional question will often appear as "cond conj + cond complement, normal interrogative clause. . . ." As a result, speakers will form conditional questions as composite questions (at least one phrase and one clause or more). In English, the canonical conditional particle is limited to *if*, but in Koine Greek there are at least two canonical conditional particles, εἰ and ἐάν, plus a few noncanonical particles such as ὅταν (e.g., see John 7:31; 1 Cor 3:4).[43] Noncanonical conditional questions are harder to identify, as they tend toward weaker or less certain conditions. However, it should be noted that even the presence of canonical particles such as εἰ and ἐάν in questions are not always indicators of conditional questions. When it comes to the syntax of the main clause, this clause may take the form of any question clause.

The primary factor in the formation and identification of a conditional question is discussed immediately below.

42. Normally, a συναπτικός σύνδεσμος; see Dionysius Thrax, *Ars Grammatica* 642.32.

43. Other noncanonical conditional particles in Koine Greek include εἴπερ, used in a conditional question in Susanna 54 (Theodotion). Noncanonical constructions in the GNT include the use of the crastic κἄν (in Luke 6:34 of Codex Bezae) and κἀγώ in the likely conditional question in Matthew 26:15 (cf. Robertson, *Grammar*, 951).

1) Conditional Questions Must Include a Conditional Phrase or Clause

Conditional questions are a composite-question formation that limits the question asked by way of a conditional phrase or clause. To qualify as a conditional question, the question must (at minimum) contain a conditional phrase or clause affixed to a second clause with interrogative force. For example:

(4) εἰ ὁ θεὸς ὑπὲρ ἡμῶν, τίς καθ' ἡμῶν; (ROM 8:31B)

In (4), Paul asks the famous conditional question, "If God is for us, who can be against us?" What is fascinating about Paul's question is that it is in fact a conditional question. Paul does not ask, ἐπεί ὁ θεὸς ὑπὲρ ἡμῶν, τίς καθ' ἡμῶν; ("Since God is for us, who can be against us?"). If Paul had used ἐπεί instead of εἰ, the question would still be powerful. Yet Paul does form this question as a conditional question—the reader cannot simply gloss over the conditional. Breaking the question down, we see that Paul forms the interrogative clause using a variable form, and semantically it functions as an open question (§4.A). Thus, the interrogative logic points to the fact that Paul does not have anyone (or anything) in mind with τίς—the "who" is wide open for anyone to suggest someone or something that might be against those whom God has called (Rom 8:28–30). Paul's rhetorical point is that there is no limit to the audience's consideration—he is challenging the audience to find anyone or anything who could be against God's people. This much is often understood. Yet the conditional must still be factored in to our reading. Paul's argument only becomes operative if the conditional is valid—that God is for those whom he has called. Here we see that Paul's argument is actually circular and rests on the nature of God himself: Paul challenges the reader to find anyone who can be against God's people in the situation where God is for them. Because God was the one who called them, in all the world the reader will not be able to find anyone or anything that can be against them.

Rhetorical Effects

As a relatively common form of question, conditional questions possess a variety of rhetorical effects that a speaker may exploit. Most of the rhetorical effects engage a tension between what is asked and the condition that must be valid for the question to work. In argumentation, audiences need to listen carefully for the conditional part of conditional questions—these questions are often "skipped over" by their audiences, to the point that the condition is assumed and the audience only responds to the main interrogative clause. (A classic and ironic example of this occurs in John 21:22–23.) The temptation is for hearers to not take the rhetorical effects of the conditional seriously.

Three of the most notable rhetorical effects of conditional questions are discussed immediately below.

1) Conditional Questions Can Redirect Hearers to Specific Options and Possibilities

A speaker may use conditional questions to test the water or to speculate about a possibility. In doing so, the speaker raises the question with a specific, limiting conditional designed to push the audience toward options or possibilities raised by the conditional (usually those that would not be raised as clearly without the conditional). Conditional questions can seem hypothetical, and this is related to their push for the audience to consider less likely scenarios within a set of answers. For example:

(5) εἰ δέ τις τοῦ ἰδίου οἴκου προστῆναι οὐκ οἶδεν,
πῶς ἐκκλησίας θεοῦ ἐπιμελήσεται; (1 TIM 3:5)

The question in (5) is a conditional question asked in the midst of rhetorical discourse: "For if someone does not know how to manage his own family, how will he care for God's church?" More than just an aside, the question is asked to redirect its readers to consider certain options. To understand the role of the conditional, let's ask the same question without the conditional, based on the context of the argument of 1 Timothy 3. In this case, the question asked is a variable question with the semantics of a means question (§4.H); it is also an informational-leaning question embedded in rhetorical discourse. Prior to the question, the qualifications of an overseer are discussed (vv. 1–4), and so the point of the nonconditional question here would be to encourage the reader to think through the means by which the overseer can complete the task of taking care of God's church. The reader may quickly draw up a list of possibilities as the rhetorical effect of an informational question in rhetorical discourse. Now we contrast this with the actual conditional question. The interrogative clause is still the same; the question asked is a means for the reader to identify how they will care for God's church. However, the conditional clause limits the question to "if someone does not know how to manage his own family." Given the type of discourse, the intent is not for the reader to say, "I know how to manage my family; hence, I do not need to consider how I will care for God's church." Instead, the conditional limits and redirects the focus away from the broader question to the situation wherein a person does not know how to manage his family and how that lack of knowledge affects his caring for God's church. As a result, the conditional creates a limiter that pushes the reader to consider the ways in which they may not be able to know how to manage their family, and how those ways may not equip them to take care of the church. The difficulty with this question is that since no overseer is perfect, there are always real worlds where this conditional is true to some degree. This rhetorical effect is what allows these types of conditional questions to "haunt" the reader long after the text is read.

2) Conditional Questions Allow Speakers to Bait Their Audiences

A speaker may use a conditional question when the speaker has no intention of the condition being fulfilled or realized. This can bait the hearer into trying to reply as if the conditional is or will be true (the challenge with too quickly "skipping over" the conditional). For example, I may say, "If I go to the store, do you want a snack?" I may not go to the store, but I may ask the question to bait the hearer into answering a question that I can deny that I have intended to do. I may just want to find out if the hearer wants a snack. If the reply to the conditional question is not what the asker hoped for, the asker can back out by ensuring the condition is never met.[44] This rhetorical effect can be particularly effective in the work of argumentation. For example:

(6) εἰ δὲ τοῖς ἐκείνου γράμμασιν οὐ πιστεύετε,
πῶς τοῖς ἐμοῖς ῥήμασιν πιστεύσετε; (JOHN 5:47)

The conditional question in (6) is set up not only by the previous monologue but especially by the previous conditional assertion. In John 5:46, Jesus states, "For if you had faith in Moses, then you would have faith in me (for he wrote about me)." Here the conditional is actually a counterfactual (firmly held from the speaker's perspective; cf. §4.P), making it a second-class conditional proposition in traditional grammars.[45] With the counterfactual, the proposition is in essence a contingent denial of both clauses, with a line of causality drawn between the two (exemplified in the use of the imperfect tense). Then Jesus next asks the conditional question, "But if you don't have faith in what he wrote, how will you have faith in my words?" As with (5), we could break the question down in such a way as to see in which direction the limiting conditional is pushing the audience. First, the question comes in the closing position (§2.D.7). Second, given the topic, οὐ πιστεύετε adds bias to the question, which increases the tension past the normal use of the conditional (the EGH Principle; §2.C.6). Both of these factors make the question more strongly rhetorical than informational. Since Jesus has just implied that the conditional of the question is met in the previous utterance, he intends to bait his hearers more through bias than through waiting to see how the hearers will respond. What is unstated here is that any reply that Jesus goads the Judaeans to make to his question will actually *not* satisfy the condition. By employing this type of conditional, the rhetoric of the question is so forceful as to almost act as an assertion.

44. Cf. Belnap and Steel, *Logic of Questions and Answers*, 103–5; Bell, "Questioning," 210.
45. Wallace, *Greek Grammar*, 663, 695.

3) Conditional Questions May Contain a Variety of More Complex Conditions

As conditional logic is almost as complex as interrogative logic, there are many kinds of conditions that a speaker may use in natural language. Usually a speaker develops these conditions to exploit their rhetorical effects upon an audience, though occasionally a speaker seeks a rather precise answer. One noteworthy type of condition is the counterfactual condition (which we consider at length in §4.P). Other types of conditional clauses include the *speculative* (1 Pet 4:18), *hypothetical* (1 Cor 15:32), *exceptive* (1 John 5:5), and *causal* (Luke 6:32, 33; 1 Pet 3:13).[46] The combination of conditional-clause types and question forms results in a near-limitless range of logical and rhetorical interrogative possibilities.

Case Study — MATTHEW 12:27

καὶ εἰ ἐγὼ ἐν Βεελζεβοὺλ ἐκβάλλω τὰ δαιμόνια, οἱ υἱοὶ ὑμῶν ἐν τίνι ἐκβάλλουσιν;

JESUS: And if I cast out demons by Beelzebul, by whom do your sons cast them out?

Part of Jesus's public ministry is healing those possessed by demons, and Matthew records Jesus's discussion during one such healing. The crowd brings forth a demon-possessed man who was both blind and mute, with the expectation that Jesus will heal him. Jesus does heal him, not just of possession, but also so that the man could both talk and see (12:22). The crowd is astonished and begins to ask among themselves if Jesus could possibly be the son of David. On hearing this, the Pharisees state their case that they believe that Jesus only has the power to cast out demons by Beelzebul, the prince of demons. Jesus responds to this charge by saying that a kingdom divided cannot stand. Then he asks them, "If Satan casts out Satan, he has divided himself; then how will his kingdom stand?" followed by, "And if I cast out demons by Beelzebul, by whom do your sons cast them out?" With no response recorded, Jesus continues: "So then they will be your judges." Jesus then moves on in his response, suggesting that it might be the Spirit of God that allows him to cast out demons, and if so, they should decide whose side they are on.

In Matthew's Gospel, Jesus's question that challenges the Pharisees on who uses what power to cast out demons is a conditional question with a variable formation asking about the means of action (§4.H). It is in the middle position

46. Ancient grammarians also made similar distinctions, such as Dionysius's note about συναπτικός versus παρασυναπτικὸς σύνδεσμος; see Dionysius Thrax, *Ars Grammatica* 642.32–643.3.

(§5.C) in a narrative discourse. Of all these factors, the fact that the question is asked in the middle position—amidst the multiple lines of thought in this short monologue—is a strong indicator that the question leans more rhetorical than informational. This is because in most cases the rhetorical placement (pragmatics) trumps the composite form (syntax) and the means goals (semantics). This does not mean Jesus does not seek a reply; instead, he is slightly more interested in pushing them to respond in the way that he wants them to respond (or not to respond at all, realizing they are incorrect).

If we take the question without the pragmatic factors and the conditional clause, the question clause is strongly informational; it acts as a means question that encourages the audience to think on how it is possible that the "sons" of the Pharisees can cast out demons. Yet the conditional in the question is troublesome; to understand the logic of the full question, we must determine whether the conditional is operative or inoperative (and under what conditions). While the conditional may be operative in the story world of the narrative, we the readers know that the conditional is actually inoperative. This creates a certain dissonance for us today, as we are tempted to read over the conditional since there is no question in our mind that it is inoperative. However, in the story world the conditional is possibly operative, and to many members of the audience the conditional *is* operative (as many believe Jesus does cast out demons by Beelzebul). Therefore, Jesus's question is fully operative in the ears of his audience in the story world (again, even though we know it is not). Following the logic of the question, if Jesus casts out demons by something other than Beelzebul, the means of the "sons" of the Pharisees to cast out demons is a moot point. But because many in the audience do believe Jesus casts out demons by Beelzebul, the means by which the "sons" of the Pharisees cast out demons becomes a live issue. Of course, Jesus himself knows the question is inoperative, which brings us back to the fact that the question is strongly rhetorical before pragmatics are applied. Jesus intentionally asks an inoperative conditional question, and he asks an open question with a strongly limiting (either/or) conditional. The rhetorical effect of this is to persuade the hearer into considering the conditional for themselves. A simple example: "If I go to the store by train, how do you go to the store?" (*by train* or *not by train* is suggested, though the former is usually stronger).[47] The way in which Jesus asks the question reveals a great deal about his rhetorical strategy: he strongly suggests the Pharisees break in either direction, as almost any answer the Pharisees give to the question could be countered by Jesus. Placed in the middle of the monologue as it is, Jesus pushes his question constrained by the conditional onto the Pharisees without giving them a chance

47. If Jesus asked the reverse, καὶ εἰ ἐγὼ ἐν πνεύματι θεοῦ ἐκβάλλω τὰ δαιμόνια, οἱ υἱοὶ ὑμῶν ἐν τίνι ἐκβάλλουσιν; ("And if I cast out demons by the Spirit of God, by whom do your sons cast them out?"), he has not cornered them in exactly the same way; it is a weaker argument.

to respond. Either way the Pharisees try to go in mustering a response, Jesus's statement is true: their "sons" will be their judges.[48]

FURTHER EXAMPLES

Matt 6:30; 12:11; Luke 6:32; John 21:22; Acts 11:17; Rom 2:26; 11:15; 1 Cor 10:30; 15:12; Gal 2:14, 17; Col 2:20; Heb 2:2; Jas 2:14a, 15–16; 1 Pet 2:20; 3:13; 4:17.

Key Bibliography

Estes, *Questions*, 91–97; Evans and Over, *If*; Isaacs and Rawlins, "Conditional Questions," 269–319; McKay, *New Syntax*, §21; Rawlins, "(UN)Conditionals"; Velissaratou, "Conditional Questions"; Wallace, *Greek Grammar*, 688–89.

4. Sluices

A *sluice* is a form of question that elides the explanatory part of the question.[49] In asking a sluice, the part of the question that carries the interrogative force is articulated, but the complementary part of the question that carries the limiting information is deleted. Sluices are a feature of interrogative language that handles ellipsis, which is "the omission of words, phrases or clauses that are recoverable from the context" of the utterance (*CDL* 150). Sluices are a common feature of most IE languages. This form of question was a common feature of discourse and argumentation in the ancient world.[50] They are useful for keeping the flow of dialogue moving. For example:

(1) *A*: I want to get something for lunch.
(You want to get what [for lunch]?)

(2) *A*: I think I'm going to the store later.
B: When? (SLUICE)
(When [are you going to the store]?)

(3) *A*: I don't want to go to the store.
B: You don't? (SLUICE)
(You don't [want to go to the store]?)

Examples (1) through (3) are sluices as uttered by asker B. In each example, below the sluice, we can see what the original question would be (with the elided part of the question in brackets). Sluices can be elided in several different ways,

48. Cf. Morris, *Matthew*, 316.
49. Merchant, "Sluicing," 271.
50. *Rhetorica ad Herennium* 4.16.23.

as examples (1) through (3) illustrate. What makes a sluice so effective is that the first speaker *A* will fully understand the sluice of *B* even though *B* omits most of the information in the question.

Formation

In the secondary literature, the predominant discussion of sluices is most often limited to *wh*-questions (variable and set questions). In these cases, the sluice is often just a *wh*-word plus any introductory utterances. In this case, the variable word will often appear to be *in situ*—but it is not, because the explanatory clause was omitted in the asking (cf. Luke 17:17b). Movement actually occurs past the deleted phrase or clause. However, recent turns of study in linguistics have broadened what constitutes a sluice, and if we accept the more sweeping definition, then it is possible to construct a sluice based on a polar- or alternative-question formation. In natural-language situations, sluices will always occur as a second-turn (or comparable) utterance. They cannot appear in the first turn as there would be nothing meaningful to elide.

The primary factor in the formation and identification of a sluice is discussed below.

1) Sluices Require an Elided Complement from within the Question Asked

Sluices are questions with elisions, and as such, what is being asked must be placed in abeyance. The result is that the question takes an abbreviated form. To work, a sluice must be intelligible as such; the elision must be understood by the audience. If it is not understood, there is a danger of confusion or the sluice will be taken as an attempt at repair. For example:

(4) Ποῖα; (LUKE 24:19)

While on the road to Emmaus, Cleopas asks the unrecognized Jesus, "Are you the only one visiting Jerusalem who does not know the happenings of the last few days?" To this, Jesus replies with (4), "What kinds?" Jesus's response is a sluice, as it is missing the complement to what we could expect the intended question to be: "What kinds of happenings of the last few days?" (perhaps "Ποῖα τὰ γενόμενα ἐν αὐτῇ ἐν ταῖς ἡμέραις ταύταις;").[51] By asking his question as a sluice, Jesus comes across as informal and conversational, which helps to create a sense that he is uninformed about what kinds of things were occurring in Jerusalem. In this situation, Jesus's rhetorical goal is to try to quickly indicate an ignorance about what the two of them were talking about.

51. Cf. Parsons, Culy, and Stigall, *Luke*, 744.

Rhetorical Effects

The rhetorical effects of sluices are not well understood or well studied. Potentially, a sluice can appropriate the effects of whatever semantic and pragmatic type of question it represents. However, it is easier for a sluice (formed with an interrogative variable word) to function as an open question than as a lyric question (for example; see §4.C). Pragmatically, sluices are often employed as elided echo questions (§5.B.3) or repair questions (§5.B.4). With their short, incomplete syntactic formation, sluices contain several built-in rhetorical effects that interact with the sense of brevity and incompleteness. For example, one rhetorical effect of the sluice in representational discourse is to move the conversation along by quickening the pace of speakers. The goal is to keep the audience interested. Another rhetorical effect is a feeling of understatement, where a sluice might be used to introduce ambiguity as a strategy against the previous speaker.

One of the more notable rhetorical effects of sluices is discussed below.

1) Sluices Are a Pointed Response toward the Previous Utterance

Though they may help to speed up discourse, sluices also can come across abruptly or with a pointed expectation of a clear, fast answer. This abruptness can sometimes help refocus the audience on the previous issue raised. As a result of them occurring as a question in turn two, their abruptness can be seen as a type of pushback against the first-turn speaker. Rather than as an objection, the ambiguous nature of the sluice can cause the first-turn speaker to rethink their original utterance. In rhetorical discourse, sluices can heighten tension in regard to the earlier utterance. For example:

(5) διὰ τί; (2 COR 11:11A)

In the midst of his discourse on his public ministry, Paul suggests that no one in Achaia can keep him from boasting (2 Cor 11:10). As soon as he suggests this, he writes, "Why? Because I don't love you? God knows I do." The first question is (5), a sluice that is the first half of a double question (that follows the classical combination; §5.D.1). Paul could easily have written a complete question, such as "Why will I not stop this boasting?," but it would not have the same rhetorical effect. By using a sluice, the reader is almost too quick to read over the question; a pause must occur. By asking "Why?" the question semantically is either a speculative question (§4.B) or a proof question (§4.G). Here the openness of the question makes it feel more speculative. At the same time, the question is abrupt. When coupled with the second question in the combination, the sluice actually has the effect of pointing backward and forward at the same time. This is what causes the mild sense of uneasiness about what Paul means when this question is encountered by a reader.

Case Study — LUKE 17:17B

οἱ δὲ ἐννέα ποῦ;

JESUS: But the nine—Where?

In a village on the border between Samaria and Galilee, Jesus encounters ten lepers who call out to him in the hopes of being healed (vv. 11–13). Jesus sends them to the priests, and as they go their faith heals them on the way (v. 14). Out of the ten, one came back to Jesus when he saw that he was healed (and he was a Samaritan, too!; vv. 15–16). Seeing this, Jesus asks the one man, "Weren't ten cleansed? But the other nine—Where? Aren't any of them going to return to give glory to God except this foreigner?" (vv. 17–18).

In asking the second question, Jesus uses a sluice to pointedly show his frustration at those other nine. At first glance, it is tempting for the reader to want to translate this question as "Where are the other nine?" In Koine Greek, syntax demands a fronted π-word unless there is some desire on the part of the speaker for greater stylistic focus (as can occur rarely in English). In this case, Jesus moves οἱ δὲ ἐννέα to the front of the sentence to put full focus on those words, even as he breaks the standard rule of π-fronting in Koine Greek. This creates an artificial or partial sluice, in that part of the complement of the question precedes the actual question asking. Forming the question this way grants the question a noticeable, abrupt feeling even as it is asked from a middle dialogue position within a multiple-question string (which creates a *two-one-two combination*; §5.D.2).

FURTHER EXAMPLES

Matt 7:10; 11:9b; 19:18; Phil 1:18.

Key Bibliography

Merchant, "Sluicing," 271–91; Merchant and Simpson, *Sluicing*; Ross, "Guess Who?" 252–86; Toosarvandani, "*Wh*-movement," 677–722.

Chapter 4

Questions Driven by Semantics

Once an interpreter has come to terms with the syntax of a question, it is time to determine how much the question is also driven by semantics. Questions that are driven by semantics make up most of the questions that we encounter in natural discourse. Part of the reason is the very wide range of possibilities in the semantics of questions in discourse. The semantics of a question is related to the interrogative force of the question, in that the force is the first step in determining the goal of the utterance, and the semantics is the broadening of the question as the next step. Determining the semantic goals of a question cuts to the heart of what the question is trying to ask (about). With questions driven by semantics in narrative discourse, it is tempting for the reader to evaluate the semantic qualities of these questions based primarily on their replies. This, however, is an interpretive fallacy, since there is no way to know what kind of reply is actually being offered (§2.E). Within narrative discourse it is useful to consider replies made, as they can be clues, but they are not answers. Thus, the reader must carefully interpret the question itself to discover its semantic attitudes and goals. Just as all questions will have a syntactical structure, all questions will also have semantic meaning.

One way to decide whether a question is strongly driven by semantics is to ask: Is the question more meaningful than the sum of its parts? Are there parts of the question that color or change the entire question? If so, the question is probably driven by semantics at least as much as syntax or pragmatics. A more direct approach to the semantic force of questions is to look for a number of preestablished *tells* that tend to crop up frequently in natural language. In interpreting questions, a *tell* is an indicator or tip-off that lets the reader know something more is being asked by this question than first meets the eye. Once an interpreter of the GNT has developed an eye for interrogative tells, they will become quite proficient at understanding the rhetorical role groups of questions play within NT texts. A simple example of this is an asker's use of semantic bias

(§4.U). For example, in 1 Corinthians 9:4 Paul asks, μὴ οὐκ ἔχομεν ἐξουσίαν φαγεῖν καὶ πεῖν; ("Don't we even have the right to eat and to drink?"). Here Paul intentionally uses both strong (μή) and weak (ἐξουσίαν) intentional bias to help shape his question. Paul could have asked, οὐκ ἔχομεν εὐλογίαν ὑμῶν φαγεῖν καὶ πεῖν; ("Don't we have your blessing to eat and to drink?"). If he had, the question would not have had the same pointedness as his original question. Or even Paul could have reversed the polarity to ἔχομεν εὐλογίαν ὑμῶν φαγεῖν καὶ πεῖν; ("Do we have your blessing to eat and to drink?"); with this option, the attitude and intent of the question is radically altered. These kinds of radical alterations do not occur only in the meaning of the individual words but in the meaning of the utterance in its fullness—what it asks and how it helps shape the overall discourse. Thus, Paul's inclusion of semantic bias in 1 Corinthians 9:4 is for the intentional coloring of his argument.

There are an unlimited number of possible semantic overtones in the asking of questions. In what follows, we look at many examples of the most clear and well established. When it comes to the semantics of questions in natural language, there is no parity between any of these types driven by semantics. An asker may ask any of these questions with more or less force and for more or less rhetorical effect. Further, there is always the possibility of significant overlap between semantic types. A particular question could easily share semantic values of several different semantic types. While it may seem imprecise to modern readers to focus on semantics, as this is often equated with interpretation, the ancients did not feel the same way, and often approached grammar more semantically (and rhetorically) than we do today.[1] Interpreting questions is an imprecise business—a little bit of science and a whole lot of art.

While this list of question types driven by semantics is far from exhaustive, these represent some of the most prominent types in natural discourse. As other semantic influences in questions come to light, interpreters can identify new types. Further, there are a number of types of which identification in the GNT is more problematic than those listed below. Of those listed below, it can be helpful to see the interrelationships that exist between many of these types; it is quite possible to speak of semantic effects as "categories" or "families" of questions. For example, §4.A through §4.E are representative of questions formed from open variable questions and that are colored to introduce a sense of thoughtfulness or reflection in the audience. §4.F through §4.H are questions conditioned by the speaker to engage the audience in thinking about numbers and process. §4.J through §4.K are questions that require the audience to engage society and culture in some way in order to understand what the asker is asking. §4.L through

1. For example, Dionysius Thrax, *Ars Grammatica* 629.1–10; Quintilian, *Institutio oratoria* 1.45.54; cf. Robins, *Byzantine Grammarians*, 32, 34; Coakley, "Early Syriac Question Mark," 205–10.

§4.O are questions that attempt to test or trick the audience. §4.Q through §4.S are questions that call a hearer to respond and decide. Finally, §4.T through §4.W are strongly coercive questions, meant to compel the audience to agree and comply. These categories are broad, exceptions abound, and they do not take the pragmatics of a question into consideration.

A. Open Questions

Open questions are asked without any push toward or expectation of a possible answer. They get their name from the fact that they are "open-ended" questions, as they have an unbounded or unclear set of answers.[2] In many cases, they are so open as to not elicit any definitive replies from the audience. Open questions are asked to gather information in a situation where the range of possibilities (and usually, the set of answers) is so broad as to seem almost limitless. In order to be an open question, the question under consideration must be asked without any rhetorical pretense on the part of the asker. Open questions are closely related to variable questions (§3.B). For example:

(1) Where are my keys? (OPEN QUESTION)
(2) What is similar to a car? (OPEN QUESTION)
(3) Who taught you how to write? (OPEN QUESTION)

Example (1) is an open question as it does not prejudge the audience toward the location of the keys. In fact, based on the logic of the question, the keys could be anywhere. Similarly, questions (2) and (3) both are open in their feel and expectations. Open questions are the most "true-neutral" questions available to a speaker.

Formation

Open questions are bound by strict limitations in the areas of syntax, semantics, *and* pragmatics. With syntax, an asker can only form an open question with a variable question or a set question. When forming an open question, certain variable words such as "who" and "where" lean more toward openness than other variable words, such as "how" and "why." This does not mean that an asker cannot employ "how" and "why" in open questions; it means that when a speaker turns to "how" and "why" they more often than not have some rhetorical strategy in mind. Thus, an open question cannot (for our purpose here) be based on a polar- or alternative-question syntax.[3] While an asker can form an

2. Wiśniewski, "Erotetic Search Scenarios," 423.

3. Some eroteticians do not agree, arguing polar-formed questions may indeed be a type of open question (e.g., Fiengo, *Asking Questions*, 44–52; Davies, "Speaking, Telling and Assertion," 172–76). In artificial-language situations, some polar questions may indeed

open question with a set question, it is more difficult to do so than with a variable question and is by its nature less open than a variable question. Questions formed with set, polar, and alternative formations that seem open are normally more of a decisive semantic type (see §4.Q). To be truly open, an asker should only use the variable-question formation. One way to look at open questions is to see them as vanilla variable questions. Whereas variable questions can include bias, possess a negative polarity, and have semantic and/or pragmatic spin, open questions contain none of these rhetorical effects as they are the most plain of all variable questions. Open questions must not contain any bias words, and they must always be positive in polarity. The reason for this is that positive polarity is strongly indicative of impartiality—which is the demand of open questions.[4] Open questions cannot include any indication of the asker's point of view in asking the question.[5] An asker can only ask an open question when there are not any notable semantic or pragmatic influences shaping the question. For example, while an open question could occur in any turn or position within discourse, open questions generally cannot be asked as middle-position questions; the pragmatic influence on those types of questions is too rhetorical for the open question. In some cases, open questions may have a phatic function as well (§4.K).

Two factors in the formation and identification of open questions are discussed below.

1) Open Questions Cannot Contain Any Semantic Spin

For a speaker to ask an open question, the question asked may not contain any semantic spin that closes the question for the audience. One of the most common ways of closing the audience is to put semantic limiters that bias or lead the hearer toward or away from some desired reply (or lack of reply) from the asker. For example:

(2) τίνα οὖν καρπὸν εἴχετε τότε ἐφ' οἷς νῦν ἐπαισχύνεσθε; (ROM 6:21)

Example (2) from Romans 6:21 is *not* an open question. At first glance, this question may appear to be rather open-ended ("Therefore what profit did you earn at the time on which you all are now ashamed?"), but the semantic spin coming at the end of the question creates too much discord for the audience. There are two problems with considering this an open question: first, the multiple adverbs (τότε and νῦν) lead the audience too much toward a predrawn

---

seem to be semantically open (and probably are, taken without any context). However, in natural-language situations—where there are more utterances than just the question itself—the weight of the semantic and pragmatic effects placed on these forms of questions do not really permit them to be truly open.

4. Cruse, *Lexical Semantics*, 247.
5. Fiengo, *Asking Questions*, 58.

conclusion; and second, the use of the bias word ἐπαισχύνομαι creates too much of an emotional response that will condition any reply to the question. It also occurs within rhetorical discourse, which typically prohibits a variable question from being considered open. Under different circumstances, such as change to the type of discourse and the removal of the bias words, this question could be an open question.[6]

2) Open Questions Cannot Contain Any Pragmatic Spin

Likewise, in order for a speaker to ask an open question, the question asked may not contain any pragmatic spin that closes the question for the audience. One of the most common ways of closing the audience is to put pragmatic limiters that push or condition the hearer toward or away from some desired reply (or lack of reply) from the asker. For example:

(3) Τίς ὁμοία τῇ πόλει τῇ μεγάλῃ; (REV 18:18)

Example (3) from Revelation 18:18 is *not* an open question. At first glance, it may appear to be open-ended ("What [city] is like the great city?"), and it is true that if it occurred with different pragmatic qualities it could function as an open question (though the semantics of the metaphor pushes it away from openness also). In this situation, however, there are two strikes against considering it open: first, the question is asked in a higher diegesis than the narrative discourse, adding a rhetorical quality to the question; second, the question is asked as an expository question (§5.A.2) in that the asker asks the question, intending to self-answer the question (Rev 18:19–20).

To avoid pragmatic spin, open questions need to be asked in situations that will not limit their replies or answers, or lead or condition the audience. Open questions typically occur in the first turn, or in third or later turns; it would be unusual to ask them in the second turn. As a result, open questions often make good governing questions (§5.A.1). Open questions are best suited for standalone or closing position in narrative discourse. While not impossible, it is hard to find truly open questions in rhetorical discourse.

Rhetorical Effects

Informational
Rhetorical

Open questions have little rhetorical effect on the audience. They are information seeking and asked simply to receive a reply that may work as an answer. Therefore, open questions possess strong informational qualities and very weak rhetorical qualities. Open questions have almost no persuasive power and are not

6. The NA[28] and UBS[5] both render the question as "τίνα οὖν καρπὸν εἴχετε τότε;" moving the second clause to the next sentence. In this case, the question becomes *more* open, but is still not truly open, mostly as a result of its occurrence in rhetorical discourse.

formed to assert any influence over hearers. In order to remain rhetorically weak, shorter questions tend to make better open questions.

Two mild rhetorical effects of open questions are discussed below.

1) Open Questions Admit Ignorance on the Part of the Asker

While all questions (even test questions) admit some degree of ignorance on the part of the asker, open questions are one of the strongest question types that signal that the asker does not know the answer to the question. The fact that an open question is a genuine request for information, without any bias or push from the asker, is what creates the semantic force of openness in these kinds of questions. For example:

(4) τίς ἡ αἰτία δι᾽ ἣν πάρεστε; (ACTS 10:21)

Peter asks question (4), "What is the reason for your being here?" as an open question because he does not know the answer to the question—it is a genuine inquiry without any pretense on Peter's part. In a sense, there is no "wrong answer" to the question because it is entirely open. Because the question is open, and Peter does not know the answer to the question, the question has a mild governing effect on the rest of the dialogue sequence.

2) Open Questions Expand the Horizons of the Audience

An open question seeks information that, by its interrogative nature, is broad and undefined. In doing so, the question has the mild rhetorical effect of opening up the topic in the minds of hearers. For example:

(5) Κύριοι, τί με δεῖ ποιεῖν ἵνα σωθῶ; (ACTS 16:30)

The open question (5), "Sirs, what must I do to be saved?" is asked by the jailer with little pretense on what the question intends and what the answer might be. By asking the question as an open question, the mild rhetorical effect on the hearer is that it may cause them to raise the same question or at least in their mind suggest possible answers to the question. As an open question, it is not rhetorically provocative, but because all questions (no matter how information seeking) have some degree of rhetorical quality, the open question is still mildly suggestive of the opening up of possibilities.

Case Study REVELATION 5:2

Τίς ἄξιος ἀνοῖξαι τὸ βιβλίον καὶ λῦσαι τὰς σφραγῖδας αὐτοῦ;

MIGHTY ANGEL: Who is worthy to open the scroll and break its seals?

At the beginning of John's vision, John ἐγενόμην ἐν πνεύματι ("was in the Spirit") when he sees a throne in heaven with someone seated on it (4:2). John describes his vision of the throne and its events for his readers (4:3–11). Then John sees that there is a two-sided scroll with seven seals in the right hand of the one seated on the throne (5:1). A mighty angel announces in a mighty voice, "Who is worthy to open the scroll and break its seals?" John weeps because no one is found who was worthy—until one of the elders points out to John that the Lion of the tribe of Judah is able to open the scroll and break its seals.

The question asked by the mighty angel is a great example of a question in the GNT whose meaning greatly impacts the interpretation of the larger passage. Is this question rhetorical? Or informational? What role does it play? John's inclusion of this question reveals something important in the asking.

The question in 5:2 is asked by the mighty angel based on a variable-question formation. Based on the setting and context, the question might appear speculative (§4.B), aporetic (§4.E), or even lyric (§4.C) in semantic quality. But we have a pragmatic clue—John records his response to the question (i.e., he wept; 5:4). Since speculative questions often focus on hypotheticals, and since John hears the question as being imminently possible, it is not a speculative question. David Aune argues this question is an aporia, but the semantics of the question plus the seeking for an answer (see 5:3–5) indicates it only has a feel of aporia for creating dramatic flavor.[7] Since lyric questions focus on wonderment, John's response would be unusual, and so we rule out the possibility of a lyric question. We see in the response of John and then the elder that the question was heard as highly information seeking, and so we can conclude the question is an open question (and pragmatically, with a governing function; §5.A.1). With the semantic quality of openness, the question of the mighty angel is announced for any possible answer to be given. The angel asks the question to all who can hear; it is universal in nature.[8] Because it is an open question, it is not prejudging the answer—anyone could try their worth to break the seal and open the scroll. While John does not record any attempt to open the scroll other than by the Lion, there is no reason to assume that someone else could not have had the opportunity to try, at least in the sense that the interrogative logic suggests the question is asked without pretense. Thus, we can have confidence that the only

7. Aune, *Dictionary*, 54.
8. Osborne, *Revelation*, 251.

one in creation who can approach the throne of God and take the scroll from his hand and open it is the Lion of the tribe of Judah (and not the dragon).

When open questions—with their very weak rhetorical effects—occur in texts with strong rhetorical agendas (such as in the GNT), it is tempting for the reader to overlook their importance or to pass them by as narrative filler. Instead, open questions such as Revelation 5:2 serve an important information-seeking role even within persuasive texts, creating space for the audience without prejudging any immediate replies.

FURTHER EXAMPLES

Matt 2:2; 8:29a; 13:54; Mark 5:9, 30, 31; 6:24; 10:36; 16:3; Luke 17:37; John 4:11, 27a; 7:20; Acts 9:5; 10:21; 16:30; 1 Cor 5:12a; 9:18; 1 Pet 2:20.

Key Bibliography

Dickman, "Dialogue and Divinity"; Dickson and Hargie, "Questioning," 127–31; Estes, *Questions*, 69–71; Fiengo, *Asking Questions*, 44–53; Groenendijk and Stokhof, "Questions," 1118–9; Wang, "Questions," 543–45.

B. Speculative Questions

Speculative questions are asked to prompt deep thinking about a subject. The semantic focus of speculative questions is usually profound, hypothetical, or addresses some kind of universal. As a result, this type of question overlaps with what we would in English call a *hypothetical question*.[9] These types of questions encourage replies but are by their nature difficult for a hearer to offer a concrete answer. Speculative questions take their name from the fact that their asking usually causes a hearer to engage in speculation to make a reply. These questions emphasize the possible and encourage the audience to engage in thoughtful reflection on possibilities. They are often associated with the philosophical. For example:

(1) Why did God create life? (SPECULATIVE QUESTION)
(2) What good does good do? (SPECULATIVE QUESTION)
(3) Who is the greatest third baseman in baseball? (SPECULATIVE QUESTION)
(4) If aliens exist, can they be saved? (CONDITIONAL SPECULATIVE)

Though using different interrogative variable words, (1), (2), and (3) are all spec-

9. With this question type, we use *speculative question* instead of the more common *hypothetical question* in part because in ancient Greek thought ὑπόθεσις was often a concrete point of departure for disputation, and not at all speculative; see for example, Kennedy, *Classical Rhetoric*, 80, 99, 202.

ulative questions. Note that while it is possible for someone to try to reply to (1), "God created life because he wanted to glorify himself," thus treating it as a proof question (§4.G; or even a test question in a discipleship class), the hearer's lack of knowledge on this subject—obvious to an audience—makes the question more of a speculative question. Likewise, the archetypal language in (2) could suggest the question is a lyric question (§4.C), but the philosophical bent of the question puts it firmly within the speculative-question type. Question (3) is less theoretical, but the deep thinking and lack of concrete answer (to most people) makes this another example of a speculative question. Example (4) is another common form of the speculative-question type; it uses a conditional clause to create a hypothetical situation. While (4) is technically a conditional question (§3.E.3), the pragmatic overlap in IE languages is too great to ignore in this discussion.

Speculative questions are very much a kind of open question (§4.A); while they can sometimes be shortchanged as a "rhetorical question" that tries to make an assertion, they do possess strong informational qualities. Speculative questions exist on the possible-impossible axis of open questions:

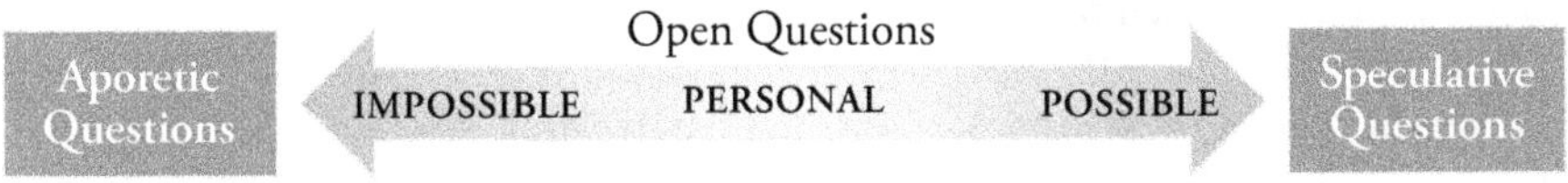

Open Questions

Aporetic Questions | IMPOSSIBLE | PERSONAL | POSSIBLE | Speculative Questions

Speculative questions are—in the general sense of the word—deliberative (§4.D), but what sets them apart from deliberative questions is that speculative questions cause deliberation and reflection about impersonal, large-scope issues in the greater world, whereas deliberative questions cause reflection and deliberation about personal, intimate issues within the life of the asker. In the early period of ancient rhetoric, θέσις was a category of questions that included speculative questions, and later rhetorical handbooks broke this category down into two kinds, with the kind θεωρητικαί coming close to speculative questions.[10] In the Gospels, speculative questions are quite frequently employed as test questions or riddle questions when they occur in the dialogues between Jesus and the Judaean leadership or Jesus's disciples.

Formation

Speculative questions only have semantic requirements in their formation. They are typically formed from variable questions, but it is not impossible to form them from the other major syntactic formations for questions. This is especially true when a conditional clause is involved; conditional clauses often signal that a question leans toward a more speculative nature.[11] Speculative questions are one

10. For example, Cicero, *Partitiones oratoriae* 60; Quintilian, *Institutio oratoria* 3.5.5–18; Kennedy, *Progymnasmata*, 55.
11. E.g., Aristotle, *Topics* 104b8–18.

of the classic extensions of the "why" question. "Why" questions are also commonly formed as open questions (§4.A) and proof questions (§4.G). Whereas speculative questions emphasize uncertainty, proof questions emphasize causal relationships. Speculative questions often start with "why" but are not constrained to only that interrogative variable word. Speculative questions are commonly found with a positive polarity, though negative polarity is possible (cf. Heb 1:14). Speculative questions are like open questions with additional rhetorical effects from pragmatic and semantic influencers. (An open question asked as a middle-position question often is heard as a speculative question). Because speculative questions often seek to open up conversation, they are related to first-turn question types (§5.A). As a result, they are not usually asked in turn two. Speculative questions can occupy any position in dialogue. When they occupy the middle position, they typically are representative of the traditional "rhetorical question." Of all the common extensions of the "why" type of question, speculative questions are the most comfortable in rhetorical discourse.

The two primary factors in the formation and identification of speculative questions are discussed below.

1) Speculative Questions Ask about Possibilities

Speculative questions are constructed around asking about possibilities. At the semantic heart of these types of questions is the implied question, "Is [*the subject*] possible?" Whereas most open questions lean toward asking about a subject (so more essence related), speculative questions take a slightly more limited semantic approach of asking about a subject as it might be (so more potential related). For example:

(5) τίς στρατεύεται ἰδίοις ὀψωνίοις ποτέ; (1 COR 9:7A)

Here in (5) Paul asks, "Whoever would serve as a soldier using his own wages?" This question has a mild speculative quality, as the situation questions whether such a scenario would be possible. Because this question appears in rhetorical discourse as part of a question string, these pragmatics push this particular speculative question into a stronger rhetorical use. Thus, the speculation is supposed to end in the reader's mind with a "probably not very possible" summation, which makes Paul's point (also see §2.C.7).

2) Speculative Questions Create a Wide Epistemic Imbalance between Question and Hearer

The semantic quality that controls the creation of speculative questions is the knowledge differential between what is asked and the audience at hand. To some degree, this is true with all questions, but in the case of speculative questions these types of questions are built on a large gulf between the subject of the question and the knowledge base of the audience. As a result, speculative questions can set up either p-predicaments and/or b-predicaments. Practically speaking, this is the reason why "What is beef jerky?" is not a speculative question but "What is love?" is a speculative question. The latter is not easily answerable. For example:

(6) Ὀλιγόπιστε, εἰς τί ἐδίστασας; (MATT 14:31)

In question (6), Jesus asks Peter, "You of little faith, why did you doubt?" While this question could be read as an open or proof question (Jesus really wants to know the answer from Peter) or as a "rhetorical question" (Jesus really is telling Peter he should not have doubted), it actually leans most heavily in the direction of a speculative question because of the imbalance created by question and hearer. At its root, this question asks something of Peter that Peter must have some sense of because it is internal to his feelings (a p-predicament, of sorts). Yet Peter probably does not know exactly why he doubts, because one minute he is walking on the water and the next he is not. To the audience, this question would come across as speculative because it asks Peter to figure out what it is that is causing him to doubt.

Rhetorical Effects

Informational
Rhetorical

Speculative questions start from a position of openness in their rhetorical effects. They exist because there is a notable epistemic gap between the question asked and replies/possible answers to the question. This gap sets up the predicaments that give speculative questions their rhetorical effects. Because the gap is wide, speculative questions can have a wide range of rhetorical effects and are useful in a great variety of situations (think of how common the "hypothetical" question is today).

Three common rhetorical effects of speculative questions are discussed below.

1) Speculative Questions Often Set Up a Maybe-Could-Know-but-Don't (P-Predicament)

An asker may ask a speculative question to highlight the fact that the hearer could know the answer but probably does not. This situation is a *p-predicament*, and it occurs when an asker asks a legitimate, information-seeking question that the hearer cannot answer because they are unwittingly ignorant of the answer—often the hearer has a sense what the answer is *not*, but not exactly what the answer is (§2.C.7). For example:

(7) Τί τὸ ὄφελος, ἀδελφοί μου, ἐὰν πίστιν λέγῃ τις ἔχειν, ἔργα δὲ μὴ ἔχῃ; (JAS 2:14A)

In example (7) James asks, "What is the benefit, my brothers, if someone might claim to have faith but has no works?" At the base, the question asks τί τὸ ὄφελος, which leads the reader to speculate on what possible value faith without works can have, and not (at first) on whether faith is possible without works. Thus, this question sets up a p-predicament for its readers as they ask themselves this question, because the question is a legitimate question to which a reply would be hard to give. In this case, the hearer of the question can imagine many replies that do *not* fully answer the question. However, to fully answer the question as to what benefit(s), if any, there could be to having faith without works moves the thought process of the audience into the realm of speculating whether such a scenario is ever useful or even possible. Even though James forms the question as an open question (with a causal conditional, §3.E.3), the interrogative logic of the p-predicament is what gives the question the force that it carries. After thinking about it, the hearer is forced to conclude that there is no value in having faith without works.

2) Speculative Questions Sometimes Set Up an Impossible-to-Know (B-Predicament)

An asker may ask a speculative question to highlight the fact that the hearer has no way of knowing the answer. This situation is a *b-predicament*, and it occurs when an asker asks a legitimate, information-seeking question to which the hearer does not and often cannot know the answer—they cannot really even guess (§2.C.7). In these situations, the asker may use speculative questions to point out the futility of trying to answer, the obvious ignorance of an audience, or as an argumentation tool to embarrass a hearer. For example:

(8) τί ἄρα τὸ παιδίον τοῦτο ἔσται; (LUKE 1:66)

In example (8), Luke records the speculative question of those who heard about the impending birth of John the Baptist, "What then will this child be?" In asking this question, the villagers in Judaea asked a legitimate question to which they do not know and could not give an answer. In this example, the unanswerable question becomes almost like a puzzle that leads to guessing (and most likely some wild guessing) on the part of the askers.

3) Speculative Questions Can Push the Audience toward Reflection

Speculative questions are often asked with the intent to challenge hearers to think through the question or the implication of possible answers to the question. Even not-as-serious sounding questions like (3) above can still be used effectively in the right rhetorical strategy. A speaker may ask speculative questions in rhetorical discourse all for the sake of shocking them into thinking more about a particular issue. For example:

(9) τί γὰρ ὠφελεῖ ἄνθρωπον κερδῆσαι τὸν κόσμον ὅλον καὶ ζημιωθῆναι τὴν ψυχὴν αὐτοῦ; (MARK 8:36)

Here (9) is a formidable example of the rhetorical power of speculative questions at work in the GNT. Mark records that Jesus asks, "For what good does it do for someone to gain the whole world and to lose their soul?" As with (7), at the base of the interrogative logic of the question is the clausal τί γὰρ ὠφελεῖ, which speaks not to possibility as much as consequence. In asking this question, Jesus sets up a p-predicament that causes his audience to ask themselves what possible point there could be to gain the world at the loss of their soul. This question is just as information seeking (if not more) as it is rhetorical; Jesus requests a sincere search for an answer. Because of the interrogative logic, the question presumes that the best answer is "it does no good," but not before the hearer speculates on whether there is any point, and if not, what the result of that search must mean for their lives.

Case Study — 1 PETER 4:18

καὶ εἰ ὁ δίκαιος μόλις σῴζεται,
ὁ ἀσεβὴς καὶ ἁμαρτωλὸς ποῦ φανεῖται;

PROVERB OF SOLOMON: If the righteous one is barely rescued,
the godless sinner—where will he appear?

In 1 Peter 4, Peter turns to the issue of suffering that a Christian may face. He notes that Christians should not be surprised by suffering (v. 12) but rather should rejoice because they are blessed to follow in the steps of Christ (vv. 13–16). In fact, Peter warns that a time of judgment will begin with God's house, and he asks his readers that if hardship should start with God's people, what would the result be of such hardship for those who are not God's people (v. 17). Then Peter cites a proverb of Solomon in support of his question, asking, "If the righteous one is barely rescued, the godless sinner—where will he appear?" Peter concludes his argument by challenging any of his audience who suffer for Christ to commit themselves to God and to continue their good works.

Peter puts his question in v. 18 in a noteworthy way by combining together rhetorical artistry and logical argumentation in a complex way. First, the question is a composite question formed with a conditional clause attached to a variable question (§3.E.3). Here the conditional is intended as a hypothetical conditional because of the unspecified subject and a lack of clarity over whether the conditional is operative or not. Second, the semantics of the question (ποῦ + unspecified subject) reveals a bent toward speculation. Normally, a speaker would not form a speculative question with ποῦ, but in this case, asking about "where a godless sinner can appear" shows this to be part of a speculative argument. Third, pragmatically the question functions as the second half of a double question with v. 17 (§5.D.1). Finally, what makes this most noteworthy is Peter's adaption of a proverb from the LXX (Prov 11:31) in a rather skilled bit of rhetorical work. The proverb has several notable semantic features, the most important of which is the fronted hendiadys ὁ ἀσεβὴς καὶ ἁμαρτωλὸς—which focuses the reader on the plight of those who are godless—and the rather curious use of φανεῖται, the verb carrying the interrogative force of the question. With Proverbs 11:31, the protasis of the LXX version is seemingly at odds with the protasis of the original Hebrew version, but Peter stays with the Greek version. The pragmatic use of the inserted quotation compounds the overall rhetorical effect.

Peter asks in v. 17 for his reader to consider what would happen if suffering starts with God's people—what that would mean for those who are not God's people. The rhetorical effect of this conditional question is to push the reader to consider the fate of those who don't obey the gospel, within the limiting condition of this during a time of judgment on God's people. Turning to v. 18 as the second half of a double question, Peter uses this second question to amplify and reinforce the point of the first question, while putting the additional semantic spin of speculation on the argument. However, the reinforcement is interrogative, not propositional; thus the amplification seeks to raise the intensity for reflective thinking among Peter's readers.[12] Thus, Peter's goal is to take what needs to be considered in the first question—what happens to those who don't obey the gospel, specifically in time of persecution—and bump the needle up to raise a higher question: If the righteous barely make it *in general*, what will happen to the godless sinner in general, to say nothing of a time of persecution?[13] Peter uses the proverb to bring home the extreme challenge and difficulty of staying obedient in hard times "so that (ὥστε) those suffering according to the will of God must commit their souls with good works to their faithful Creator" (v. 19).

FURTHER EXAMPLES

Matt 16:26a, 26b; Mark 8:37; 12:28, 35; John 18:38; 1 Cor 7:16a, 16b; 9:7b, 7c; 15:35a, 35b; Heb 1:5a, 5b, 13; 1 Pet 4:17.

Key Bibliography

Blakemore, *Understanding Utterances*, 114; Estes, *Questions*, 97–103; Uygur, "Philosophical Question," 64–83; Wilson and Sperber, *Meaning and Relevance*, 223–27.

12. Contra Achtemeier, *1 Peter*, 316–17, who argues for reinforcement but of a propositional nature.
13. Similarly, Dubis, *1 Peter*, 156–57.

C. Lyric Questions

Lyric questions are asked to push reflection to a higher plane of thought. One of the most notable tells of a lyric question is that they evoke a sense of wonder or greatness. Quite often they deal with emotions and are perceived as highly emotional questions by the audience. They are also often used by speakers as a way to stoke the imagination of the audience. Love is perhaps the most common topic spoken of in lyric questions. Speakers often ask lyric questions to raise an issue with the poetic, the fanciful, or the absurd. They can even be adoring or worshipful. Lyric questions carry a poetic sense about them. For example:

(1) What kind of love can save the world? (LYRIC QUESTION)
(2) "Who could describe that assembly, at which Love was the spokesman?"[14] (LYRIC QUESTION)
(3) How great is our God? (LYRIC QUESTION)

Here (1) and (2) are mild examples of lyric questions. Question (2) comes from an ancient Greek romance novel that was written about the same time as the New Testament. Example (3) could be taken as an aporetic question (§4.E), if we feel overwhelmed at the might of God; but in this case, if we feel wonder at the majesty of God, it becomes a lyric question. Strong examples of lyric questions are often heavily ornamented and can seem extravagant or overblown to a modern audience. Along with aporetic questions, lyric questions are a staple of drama and romance. Recognition of these types of questions goes back to at least the work of Quintilian.[15]

Lyric questions are, at their base, open questions; while they are often categorized as being merely "rhetorical questions" that make broad or fanciful statements, they actually do possess moderately strong informational qualities. At the same time, they resist conceivable answers in a way somewhat similar to speculative questions—they are in many ways unfathomable.[16] Lyric questions exist on the impersonal-personal axis of open questions:

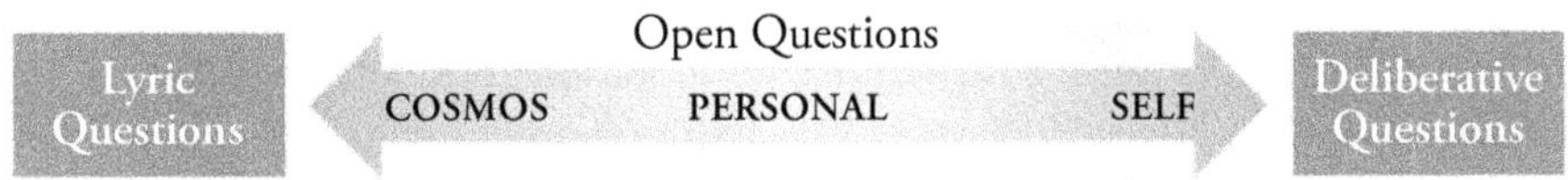

Lyric questions can sometimes come across as aporetic (§4.E), but what sets them apart from aporetic questions is that lyric questions evoke a feeling of wonder about mythic, larger-than-life issues, whereas aporetic questions evoke a feeling of loss at issues that are so great as to be incomprehensible to the asker.

14. Τίς ἂν μηνύσειε τὴν ἐκκλησίαν ἐκείνην, ἧς ὁ Ἔρως ἦν δημαγωγός; Chariton, *Callirhoe* 1.1.12 (Goold, LCL).

15. Quintilian, *Institutio oratoria* 9.2.10.

16. Jauss, *Question and Answer*, 85.

Formation

Lyric questions only have semantic requirements in their formation, though they have strong proclivities in syntax and pragmatics. In general, lyric questions are almost always formed from variable questions. While it is not impossible for an asker to use one of the other major formations for questions, attempts to use these other formations would greatly reduce the lyrical quality of the question. In most cases, lyric questions are asked with a positive polarity. Semantically, lyric questions are frequently ornamented, but this is not an adequate tell; some meaning can be implicative (for example, Heb 13:6). A speaker can employ lyric questions in any turn, though second-turn lyric questions would sound unusual and would most likely be mistaken for some type of retort. Lyric questions are equally comfortable in any of the dialogue positions. Lyric questions occur in narrative dialogue but are especially common in rhetorical and dramatic discourse. When they occur, lyric questions are often asked as part of a question string (§5.D) in order to intensify persuasive power. It is also common for lyric questions to be formed from quotations from other sources, a technique that adds to the poetic-rhetorical power of the question.

One of the most notable factors in the formation and identification of a lyric question is discussed below.

1) Lyric Questions Contain Archetypal or Mythical Language

Lyric questions are semantically conditioned to ask about something larger than life. To do this, they rely on archetypal or mythical language embedded in the question to achieve that goal. Often this results in the use of personification in the question language. This type of poetic language also adds a dramatic effect to the question, which can create a sense of profundity or depth. The use of this type of language leads to a question asked, for which an answer is not truly available. For example:

(4) τί ποιήσει μοι ἄνθρωπος; (HEB 13:6)

In Hebrews 13, the author uses an exact quotation from Psalm 118:6 (117:6 LXX), "What can people do to me?" While this question can be taken literally as an open question based solely upon its syntax, the semantic clue that alters this is ἄνθρωπος, used here not just in the sense of "humanity" but more in the personified sense of "all those others who continue to rebel against God." The author of Hebrews reframes this question in his context but continues with a similar poetic feel as was the case in its original use. Thus, the question persuades the reader to ask themselves this question more than just literally, but in a triumphant way to engender confidence in the greatness and power of God in the reader's life.

Rhetorical Effects

Informational
Rhetorical

Lyric questions are, in one sense of the word, highly rhetorical; yet their rhetorical effects are more aimed at rhapsodizing exalted ideas than persuading others. These questions start from the position of openness in their rhetorical effects, and their primary motivation is to stir deep thoughts and emotions in the audience. Though their themes often cause them to appear to be unanswerable, they are not, but their lack of unanswerability is what makes them cousins to speculative questions. They do not tend toward unanswerability because they are strongly persuasive; rather, they tend toward unanswerability because of the topics they address.

Two of the most significant rhetorical effects of lyric questions are discussed below.

1) Lyric Questions Evoke a Sense of Wonder

Lyric questions use the poetic to heighten their rhetoric. With their focus on the grand and wondrous, lyric questions have the persuasive effect of arousing a sense of wonder and refocusing the imagination of the audience. As the asker accomplishes this through semantic implication, the audience must "get" the sense of wonder that is conveyed in the question. The universals of human communication permit these implications to be understood in most all language environments. For example:

(5) ποῦ σου, θάνατε, τὸ νῖκος; (1 COR 15:55A)

In (5), Paul rewrites Hosea 13:14 and asks the lyric question *par excellence*, "Where, Death, is your victory?" Based upon syntax alone, this question would seem to be a strongly informational question. However, semantically the concept of death is personified (here with the vocative θάνατε), in much the same way as the concept of love is personified in example (2).[17] This personification acts as a tell that the question is likely a lyric question. The wonder that the question evokes is not a wonder at Death, but a wonder that a mortal feels when they realize that even though their physical body is likely dying, Christ's victory turns dying bodies into undying bodies (1 Cor 15:54). Paul puts this question in his argument to acknowledge his own marveling (and to persuade his readers to marvel) at what great transformation and victory God has for his people.

2) Lyric Questions Project a Sense of Deep Unanswerability

More than merely rhetorical, lyric questions contain semantic elements that persuade the audience that the question is deep and unfathomable. Lyric questions are posed within an awe-inspiring situation, which creates an unanswerable

17. Conzelmann, *1 Corinthians*, 293.

condition. In this, lyric questions are akin to aporetic questions (§4.E) in that both are used by speakers to project an air of unanswerability. The difference is that lyric questions project this out of a sense of awe, whereas aporetic questions project this out of a sense of the overwhelming. This rhetorical effect is a large factor in the feeling among hearers that lyric questions are really some type of assertion. For example:

(6) εἰ περισσοτέρως ὑμᾶς ἀγαπῶ, ἧσσον ἀγαπῶμαι; (2 COR 12:15)

In example (6), Paul asks his readers a rather mild lyric question, "If I love you more, am I loved less?" Here, love is not personified, but it is portrayed in idealistic terms, as created by Paul's use of the conditional clause with the comparative περισσοτέρως. Thus Paul's conditional question becomes a lyric question based on its semantics,[18] as Paul asks his readers to consider the might of love in his relationship to them. In a sense, Paul's question as a "frustrated lover" is unanswerable,[19] because there is no end to the love believers are to extend to each other. In the same way, there is no end to the wonder that a reader feels when they understand how much Paul loves and yet how much more Christ loves.

Case Study — ROMANS 10:6

Τίς ἀναβήσεται εἰς τὸν οὐρανόν;

PAUL: Who will ascend into heaven?

In one of the most difficult sections of the NT, Paul expresses his continuing concern for the salvation of those of Israel who possess a zeal for God but not full knowledge of how one obtains righteousness. After expressing his heart's desire (10:1), Paul explains that this faulty reasoning has led much of Israel to create their own standards of righteousness rather than accept God's standard for righteousness (v. 3). In this, Paul contrasts righteousness based on the law with righteousness based on faith (vv. 5–6).[20] To explain the mind-set and attitude of the person who accepts that righteousness is based on faith, Paul personifies this righteousness that comes from faith, who then suggests to Paul's readers that they should not ask, "Who will ascend into heaven?" or "Who will descend into the abyss?" Before allowing the reader to respond, the personified "righteousness by faith" continues the argument by asking what the Law itself says and supplying an answer (v. 8; cf. Deut 30:14; Isa 28:16; Joel 2:32).

18. Perhaps the reason for scribal alterations of εἰ (omission or modification with καί) and uncertainty between ἀγαπῶ and ἀγαπῶν in this verse are created by the tension between a conditional and lyric reading of this verse; cf. Metzger, *Textual Commentary*, 517–18.
19. Harris, *Second Epistle to the Corinthians*, 885.
20. For discussion on the nature and extent of the contrast, see Schreiner, *Romans*, 551–56.

If we take Paul's question here in a literal manner, it would seem to suggest that he is saying that with faith no one can or should go up into heaven (or likewise go down into the abyss). However, the questions posed by the personified "righteousness by faith" introduce a complex interrogative logic into Paul's writing. Before tackling that logic, we need to outline what is at play in Paul's writing. First, Paul writes in a form of highly persuasive rhetorical discourse. Second, in making his argument, Paul personifies a theological viewpoint in order for it to speak for itself.[21] Thus, Paul implies that he does not need to speak for this idea; this idea can fully speak for itself (and has, throughout Scripture). Third, not only does the personified "righteousness by faith" speak for itself, its spoken discourse moves the reader from one diegetic level to a second.[22] Thus, it is not the personified "righteousness by faith" who asks the question, "Who will ascend into heaven?"; rather, it is the reader of Paul's letter who is the intended asker of this question. To understand these questions, we must understand what it is that the personified "righteousness by faith" does not want us (i.e., the implied readers of Paul's letters) to ask.

Returning to the literal level of the question, the personified "righteousness by faith" forms this question as an open question. From this perspective, the question is made to feel as if the hearer is to seek out the answer to the question, to ask who can or by whom it is possible to ascend into heaven. However, there are a number of clues that the question is not meant in this literal way—the most important being that it is rare for an open question to exist as such in rhetorical discourse (§4.A). Therefore, the question in v. 6 is likely to be speculative, aporetic, or lyric. While a case can be made for each option, this question is likely more lyrical than aporetic or speculative for several reasons. First, the question is part of a personified discourse. Second, the question is the rhetorical transformation of a quotation (Deut 30:12). Third, the question is followed by an aside that clarifies that the question is not meant to be a reflection on possibilities (speculative) or a contrast between the immense and the small (aporetic). Thus, while the interrogative logic of this question has several shades, the most pronounced is the lyrical.

In his rhetorical discourse, Paul creates a personified character, "righteousness by faith," who can speak for itself as to what righteousness is. When it speaks, it transforms Scripture to make an argument about how righteousness comes by faith. When it speaks, it speaks to Paul's readers to tell them what *not* to ask: do not ask, "Who will ascend into heaven?" as if this is some wondrous thing to do. The personified "righteousness by faith" warns Paul's readers that their imagining of such a fanciful journey—one that would bring Christ down from heaven—is unnecessary. There is no need to get caught up in any romantic

21. Dodson, *'Powers' of Personification*, 161; Moo, *Epistle to the Romans*, 650–51; Jewett, *Romans*, 625.
22. For diegesis and diegetic levels, see above (§2.D.7).

ideal when the truth is both accessible and close at hand (Deut 30:11). Intended as a grand argument, Paul exploits the lyrical patterns of a personified "righteousness by faith" to encourage his readers that "the word is near you — it is in your mouth and it is in your heart" (Rom 10:8).

FURTHER EXAMPLES
Matt 11:23; Mark 4:30; Rom 10:7; 11:34a, 34b, 35; 1 Cor 15:55b; 2 Cor 6:14a, 14b.

Key Bibliography
Jauss, *Question and Answer*, 85–94.

D. Deliberative Questions

Deliberative questions are asked of oneself in order to reflect on a topic. With deliberative questions, the asker and the audience are the same — the audience is the asker. While the semantic context of deliberative questions can be either thoughtful or confrontational, the pragmatic context of these questions must always be internal to the asker. This internal-oriented context of deliberative questions does not mean they must be asked silently; one of the hallmarks of drama is that deliberative questions are asked aloud so that the narrator may give the implied readers/hearers insight into the character. This explicit, internal dialogue occurs in the space of "actual physical solitude or temporary withdrawal from contact or merely the mild distance created by self-conscious rhetoric."[23] The classic deliberative question occurs when the asker asks themselves using the first person. Questions with deliberative qualities are those which the asker asks themselves, but they do not contain a first-person struggle and are more general in nature. While deliberative questions are a fairly common question type in ancient literature, their use has fallen out of favor in modern literature.[24] This is due to the perception that they are clichéd and unrealistic, as the narrator cannot know the inner thought patterns of the narrative's characters. They are also uncommon in modern dialogue. Nonetheless, if internal dialogue is counted, deliberative questions could be one of the most common types of questions asked in natural-language situations — most people ask themselves questions quite regularly, with most not spoken aloud. For example:

(1) How can I be a better father? (DELIBERATIVE QUESTION)
(2) Who am I to live forever? (DELIBERATIVE QUESTION)

23. Mastronarde, *Contact*, 10.
24. The study of deliberative questions is at least as early as Quintilian; see Quintilian, *Institutio oratoria* 9.2.11–12.

(3) τί κομπέω παρὰ καιρόν;[25] (DELIBERATIVE QUESTION)
(4) Who do people say that I am? (NOT DELIBERATIVE)

Examples (1), (2), and (3) all exhibit the classic tell of deliberative questions—the speaker's use of "I" as the subject of the complement to the question. In (1), the question may be answerable by the asker in some way, but in (2) the question is less informational and more rhetorical. In (3), from the works of Pindar, the narrator questions himself as to whether it is the best time for boastful speech. Example (4) is not strictly a deliberative question in that "people" is the subject to the complement of the question, even though the question contains an "I." However, context of the question does play a significant role in identifying the deliberative type. For example, if (1) were asked at a parenting conference, it would not be received as a deliberative question. Similarly, if (4) were asked to oneself, it would become quasi-deliberative.

Deliberative questions are very much a kind of open question; while they are often dismissed as a "rhetorical question" or misunderstood as an assertion about the speaker, they do possess strong informational qualities. Deliberative questions exist on the impersonal-personal axis of open questions:

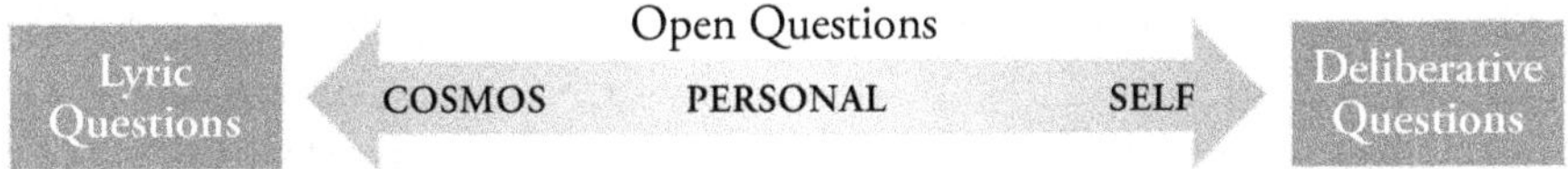

Deliberative questions are—quite often—speculative (§4.B), but what sets them apart from speculative questions is that deliberative questions cause reflection and deliberation about personal, intimate issues within the life of the asker, whereas speculative questions cause deliberation and reflection about impersonal, large-scope issues in the greater world. Unlike speculative questions, a deliberative question must (a) focus on the asker and (b) ask a question that can be sufficiently answered by the asker. Deliberative questions can also overlap with aporetic questions (§4.E) when the question is put to oneself to question one's self-worth. Pragmatically, deliberative questions can function as expository questions in that both can shape subsequent discussion, with one major difference: An expository question is asked outward, with the asker answering the question immediately, and a deliberative question is asked inward, and no answer need be given by the speaker.

Formation

The most critical formation factor in deliberative questions is the self-reference to the asker in the complement clause of the question. Typically, the asker of a deliberative question will appear as the subject/predicate nominative of the

25. Pindar, *Pythian Odes* 10.4.

complement clause. Conversely, however, a question may contain an overt use of the first person but not be deliberative. To be a deliberative question, the asker must ask the question to themselves and ask the question about themselves. For example, (4) is not a deliberative question even if the asker asks the question toward themselves, because the question is not about themselves—it is about people. Deliberative questions are not limited by syntax and can be asked using any of the major question forms. They are most frequently phrased as variable questions. Deliberative questions will almost always employ an overt use of the first person as the subject of the complement clause. Unlike most other questions that are based on the open-question type, deliberative questions are comfortable being asked with either positive or negative polarity. In ancient Greek, an asker could use the interjection ὦ to signal a deliberative question (e.g., Matt 17:17a// Mark 9:19a//Luke 9:41), especially in a situation where heightened drama and tension is required. Likewise, deliberative questions in the GNT primarily use an *aorist, active, subjunctive* formation for the main verb of the question complement, though the presence of this formation does not necessarily indicate a deliberative question (e.g., Mark 8:37). The use of the subjunctive to indicate internal possibilities is exactly the reason deliberative questions are, in fact, questions and not merely statements.[26] The subjunctive was historically associated with the emotion of doubt, and this emotion is a powerful part of deliberation.[27] The semantics and pragmatics of deliberative questions must be asker focused. Deliberative questions can occupy most positions in dialogue, but by their nature are typically excluded from anything other than the first turn of dialogue (or equivalent) since the question is not put to anyone other than the asker. An exception to this is Luke 9:41, where Jesus asks an unconventional deliberative question as part of an ongoing discussion. Similarly, a number of Jesus's questions in John's Gospel are quasi-deliberative.

Two factors in the formation and identification of deliberative questions are discussed below.

1) Deliberative Questions Contain Deeply Personal, First-Person Language

At the semantic root of deliberative questions is an appeal to the speaker's own self, the *ego* of the asker. The intent of the question is to petition the asker to answer their own question. As a result, the language and focus of the question is often deeply personal and frequently reveals (to external readers and hearers) a profound struggle within the inner soul of the asker. To be a deliberative

26. Contra Wallace, *Greek Grammar*, 467.

27. Though Apollonius Dyscolus believed the subjunctive had no inherent meaning, being conditioned by its coordinating conjunction; see Apollonius Dyscolus, *Syntax* 264–66.

question, the asker must ask a question meaningful enough to engender self-examination and introspection. For example:

(5) Νῦν ἡ ψυχή μου τετάρακται, καὶ τί εἴπω; (JOHN 12:27A)

In (5), Jesus asks, "Now my soul has been troubled, and what can I say?" as the first part of a double deliberative question. Even though Jesus asks this question when he is in the presence of others, he uses this deliberative question to transition from the pronouncement that his hour has come (vv. 23–26) to deliberating over the difficulty of his coming task. In the first clause, Jesus uses deeply personal language to describe his internal emotional and spiritual condition, followed in the second clause (carrying the interrogative logic) by a variable question with first-person language as the subject coupled to an aorist, active, subjunctive verb. Even though Jesus does not ask the question silently or at a distance, he does ask this question for the same reason the crowd hears a voice from heaven—"not for my sake, but for your sake" (John 12:30).

2) Deliberative Questions Imply That an Internal Resolution Is Needed

Deliberative questions use semantics to create a situation where the asker implies that some kind of resolution is needed to answer the question. This resolution is always based on an internal conflict within the asker. While a reply can always be made, any viable answer will resolve the tension that the asker expresses either explicitly or implicitly within the question. For example:

(6) Τί ποιήσω; (LUKE 20:13)

Example (6), "What shall I do?" is a question asked by one of the characters in one of Jesus's parables. In the parable, a man plants a vineyard, turns it over to tenants, and goes away. When harvest time arrives, the man successively sends three servants to gather some fruit, but each one is treated poorly and runs off. As the man becomes aware of the predicament, he asks the deliberative question in (6). Jesus uses the question in the story to alert his hearers that the character asking the question is a character at a crossroads and is in search of a resolution. The question also helps the hearers of the parable empathize with the plight of the asker.

Rhetorical Effects

Informational
Rhetorical

Deliberative questions start from a position of openness for the asker—there should be a genuine need or concern that causes the question to arise. The sought-after information typically derives from internal reflection rather than external suggestion. At the same time, deliberative questions carry important, but mild, rhetorical effects meant to persuade the hearer (i.e., the asker) as well as any eavesdropping audiences. Because of the unique semantic effects of deliberative questions, negative or biased deliberative questions tend to possess stronger rhetorical effects that heighten drama as much as persuasion. In narrative discourse, a character may ask a deliberative question, or the narrator may reveal the question from the thoughts of a character; in rhetorical discourse, the orator must verbalize the deliberative question for persuasive effect. If the rhetorical effect of a deliberative question is strong enough, it can indicate dismay (and approach the feel of an aporetic question).

Three common rhetorical effects of deliberative questions are discussed below.

1) Deliberative Questions Set Up an Intentional Uncertainty

An asker may ask a deliberative question to highlight the fact that the asker—*who in the case of a deliberative question is also the hearer*—should know the answer but does not. This situation is a kind of *p-predicament*, and it occurs when an asker asks a deliberative question that the hearer cannot answer because they are unwittingly ignorant of the answer—often the hearer has a sense what the answer is *not*, but not exactly what the answer is (§2.C.7). With deliberative questions, the p-predicament creates a puzzle for the asker. For example:

(7) Ὦ γενεὰ ἄπιστος καὶ διεστραμμένη, ἕως πότε μεθ' ὑμῶν ἔσομαι; (MATT 17:17A)

Example (7) creates an intentional uncertainty for the asker/hearer as well as for the crowd gathered around. Here Jesus asks, "O unfaithful and perverse generation, how long will I be with you?" This question takes the form of the classic deliberative question, with the introductory ὦ "woe" phrase and the use of the first person in the subject of the complement clause, even though Jesus asks the question amongst a crowd of people. Laying aside Jesus's epistemic supremacy for a moment, this question creates a p-predicament—Jesus asks a question that the recipient of his question (i.e., himself) should know the answer to but does not seem to know. Yet Jesus clearly seems to know what the answer is *not* (i.e., that he will be with them for a long time). For the crowd and the extended audience (the reader), the rhetorical effect of the question is to create the perception that Jesus is deliberating about how long he should exist among these people, when in fact Jesus may very well not know how much longer his Father's mission for him will last. Commentators often describe this as a complaint,[28] but it is better understood as a legitimate question by Jesus. It reveals to the reader Jesus's uncertainty about the faith of his followers and offers a glimpse of the anguish that faithlessness and perversity cause in Jesus's life.

28. For example, Luz, *Matthew 8–20*, 408; Nolland, *Matthew*, 713; Smith, *Matthew*, 212.

2) Deliberative Questions Can Add a Dramatic Element to the Discourse

Readers have long associated deliberative questions with their use as a dramatic device. Deliberative questions can add tension to a scene where a character needs to express an emotional response (and having the narrator simply state the emotions of the character is insufficient). When performed, deliberative questions can add multiple layers of angst to a character's predicament without pausing the action. This allows the asker to persuade the audience without engaging in an overt argument. For example:

(8) Τίνι δὲ ὁμοιώσω τὴν γενεὰν ταύτην; (MATT 11:16)

In example (8), Jesus asks, "But to what can I liken this generation?" Here Jesus employs a deliberative question in the midst of a longer monologue to the crowd. Although it contains the typical, standard formation of a deliberative question in the GNT (variable formation; first-person subject of the complement clause), it is asked in the middle of a longer discourse and in public before a crowd. Semantically it is deliberative, but pragmatically it is expository (§5.A.2). Yet Jesus's question is a rhetorical (and dramatic) peak in the monologue, raising tension among the audience. Jesus asks the question to himself, as if he is torn by the issue, but the rhetorical effect is troubling to the audience (to whom he is referring). By deliberating this issue in public, it allows Jesus's hearers to begin to ask their own questions about τὴν γενεὰν ταύτην without being overtly told to do so by Jesus. As the question lingers, Jesus uses the simile ὁμοία ... παιδίοις ("like children") to label τὴν γενεὰν ταύτην, thus confirming the fears of the audience that Jesus's deliberation has sided against them.

3) Deliberative Questions Admit to a Weakness or Conflict in the Life of the Asker

When an asker asks a deliberative question, the question reveals the conflicted emotional state of the asker. In dramatic dialogue, the deliberative question allows the audience to perceive the internal thoughts of the speaker. As a result, when an asker uses a deliberative question, they reveal internal conflicts, thoughts, and feelings to the audience (which, if the audience is antagonistic, it can exploit). Either way, hearers of deliberative questions are privy to personal information about the asker. For example:

(9) Ἄρτι γὰρ ἀνθρώπους πείθω ἢ τὸν θεόν; (GAL 1:10A)

In (9), Paul asks of himself, "Now, do I want the approval of people or of God?" In a typical letter, the writer would ask a question of his readers and not of himself. However, Paul's letters are not typical and are strongly rhetorical. In this situation Paul asks a question of himself, setting up a dramatic sense of personal conflict to which the reader is exposed. Syntactically, Paul forms the question as an alternative question, setting up a stark contrast between his apparent appealing to either people or God. Semantically, Paul asks his question as a deliberative question, which reveals to the reader that Paul is wrestling with an issue that is much bigger than himself or even his readers. In doing so, Paul's readers become aware that Paul has taken to heart criticisms of his position on these issues.[29] However, the question for the interpreter is this: Do we read Paul's question with sincerity in that he is truly troubled that he may be accused of appealing to people, or do we read Paul's question merely as a rhetorical flourish, meant to flush out and criticize those with whom he disagrees? Given the alternative construction, the bias word (ἄρτι), and the rhetorical context of the question, it would be too easy to suggest the latter. In this case, the question does have strong rhetorical effects, but we cannot discount the larger purpose of Paul's asking. To complicate matters further, Paul asks this question as part of a double question (§5.D.1) where the first opens the case—in a very narrow way—and the second tries to push it closed with a biased, polar question (Gal 1:10b). Therefore, for the interrogative logic to work there must be some truth to Paul's deliberation. In this case, Paul's deliberation seems to be less about an internal conflict in his own heart and more about the presumption of a conflict that impacts his readers—a conflict that Paul takes very personally. Paul deliberates this presumption of conflict as a way to push his readers to see that there really is no conflict, as both need to be about the gospel.

Case Study — LUKE 1:43

καὶ πόθεν μοι τοῦτο ἵνα ἔλθῃ ἡ μήτηρ τοῦ κυρίου μου πρὸς ἐμέ;

ELIZABETH: But why is this for me, that the mother of my Lord should come to me?

In the days after the angelic announcement of the birth of Jesus, Mary prepares for a journey and goes swiftly to the hill country of Judaea and to the home of Zechariah and Elizabeth, her relative (Luke 1:39–40). Entering into Elizabeth's home, Mary greets her relative. When Elizabeth hears her words, Elizabeth's baby leaps in her womb, and Elizabeth becomes filled with the Holy Spirit (v. 41). As a result of the infilling, Elizabeth pronounces a blessing on Mary (v. 42). After the blessing, Elizabeth is too excited to stop talking and asks aloud, "But why is this for me, that the mother of my Lord should come to me?" Elizabeth continues to talk by explaining why she speaks up (v. 44), followed by another word of blessing (v. 45).

29. Cf. Bruce, *Galatians*, 84.

The deliberative question in v. 43 is a real puzzle of interrogative language and logic. First, the question is not asked out of contact with others but in the midst of a short monologue, and the subject of the complement is τοῦτο, not the asker. As a result, the question is more quasi-deliberative than a true deliberative. Second, the clause carrying the interrogative force of the utterance takes the form of a phatic expression (§4.K), similar to John 2:4. Thus, the clause containing the interrogative force of Elizabeth's question takes on a type of discourse strategy that is not easily conveyed in English ("But why me?" may be closer).[30] Elizabeth forms the question as a variable question, using πόθεν, and includes an explanatory ἵνα clause, which increases the speculative and deliberative emphasis of the question. As with most deliberative questions, the question is both moderately informational (Elizabeth really does want to know) and moderately rhetorical (Elizabeth persuades the audience of an intentional uncertainty, while adding some drama to the blessing pronouncement).

It is commonly suggested Elizabeth uses the question to state her unworthiness.[31] Rather, Elizabeth asks an important question because she does not know the answer—or fears what the answer could be. What she does not fear is a difference of honor between her baby and Mary's baby. Elizabeth asks her question to herself and to Mary and to her "audience" at large. Her question raises an important question that must be thought about and reflected on: Why would a person such as her receive such a great blessing? The use of a phatic expression carries the importance of this question far better than a longer, formal interrogative form would, as it expresses better the emotional rush that Elizabeth feels by the sudden appearance of her relative Mary and the infilling of the Holy Spirit. In reporting this question, Luke conveys the very real emotional situation felt and pondered by Elizabeth at this momentous event.

FURTHER EXAMPLES

Matt 17:17b; Mark 9:19a–b; John 11:40; 12:27b; 18:11; Gal 1:10b.

Key Bibliography

Burton, *Syntax*, 76–78; Estes, *Questions*, 123–27; Mastronarde, *Contact*, 9–11; Mayo, "Deliberative Questions," 58–63; McKay, *New Syntax*, §11.4; Wheatley, "Deliberative Questions," 49–60.

30. Cf. Zerwick and Grosvenor, *Grammatical Analysis*, 173.
31. E.g., Marshall, *Gospel of Luke*, 81; Bovon, *Luke 1*, 59.

E. Aporetic Questions

Aporetic questions are asked to question the loss the speaker feels over the magnitude of the issue raised by the question. In ancient rhetoric and dialectic, an aporetic question was simply known as a kind of ἀπορία.[32] The term ἀπορία carried several different meanings, but in the broadest sense it was an expression. These questions emphasize the impossible; they try to imply that the speaker is at a loss about something which is greater than the asker. Since aporetic questions can give the impression that the speaker is doubtful of themselves, they are akin to the *dubitatio*.[33] As a result, aporetic questions tend to express doubt in the face of impossible-to-reconcile greatness. They also can express an inability to know what to say or do when faced with this greatness. For example:

(1) Who is like you, O God? (APORETIC QUESTION)
(2) What is the life of a person in the sands of time? (APORETIC QUESTION)

Here questions (1) and (2) form standard aporetic questions. In (1), the asker asks if it is possible to compare anything to God. In (2), the asker asks how the lifetime of a person may compare to the vastness of time. In both cases, questions are raised that seek answers but that also seem to be asserting something about these grand concepts.

Aporetic questions are fundamentally open questions; while they are often written off as being merely "rhetorical questions" that make assertions, they actually do possess strong informational qualities. Aporetic questions exist on the possible-impossible axis of open questions:

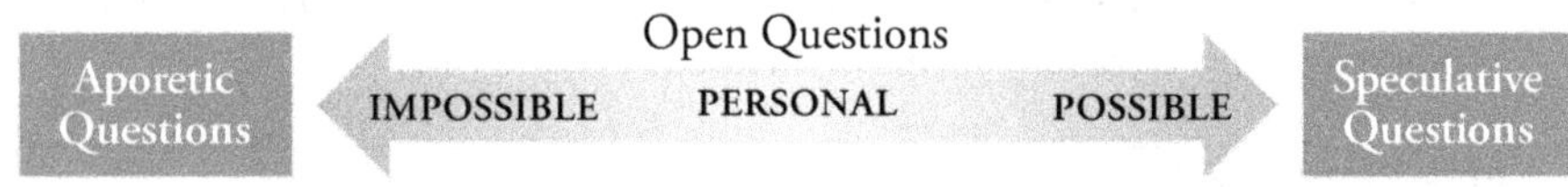

Aporetic questions can sometimes come across as having lyric qualities (§4.C), but what sets these two question types apart is that aporetic questions evoke a feeling of loss at issues that are so great as to be incomprehensible to the asker, whereas lyric questions evoke a feeling of wonder about mythic, larger-than-life issues.

Formation

Aporetic questions only have semantic requirements in their formation, though they have strong proclivities in syntax and pragmatics. In general, aporetic questions are almost always formed from variable questions. The writers of the GNT were fond of the Τίς ὅμοιος... ("What is like...") fronted phrase to indicate the

32. For one of the earliest general uses, see Plato, *Protagoras* 321c.
33. Quintilian, *Institutio oratoria* 9.2.19.

question would have aporetic quality. Sometimes the interjection ὦ will signal an aporetic question (for example, Rom 9:20a), though this is less true in the GNT than in other forms of dramatic literature. While a speaker can form aporetic questions from one of the other formations for questions, usually this creates more a hybrid question type and reduces the aporetic quality of the question. Though not technically impossible, it is quite unusual to see an aporetic question employ a negative polarity. A speaker can employ aporetic questions in any turn, though second-turn aporetic questions would sound unusual and would most likely be mistaken for some type of sarcastic reply or even a retort question. Aporetic questions are equally comfortable in any of the dialogue positions. They occur in narrative dialogue but are especially common in rhetorical and dramatic discourse.

Two factors in the formation and identification of aporetic questions are listed below.

1) Aporetic Questions Create a Semantic Contrast between Small and Immense

One indicator of an aporetic question is the contrast made in the question between something small and mundane and something immense and beyond understanding. This contrast can be explicit (as in (2), where the asker contrasts people's lives against the axis of time) or implicit (as in (1), where the asker implicitly contrasts all of creation with God). This contrast is what creates much of the rhetorical effect for which aporetic questions are known. For example:

(3) ὦ ἄνθρωπε, μενοῦνγε σὺ τίς εἶ ὁ ἀνταποκρινόμενος τῷ θεῷ; (ROM 9:20A)

This example sets up the classic contrast of something small and finite (a person) with something great and immense (God). In (3), Paul asks, "O man, indeed who are you to sass God?" which persuades the reader to recognize the vast difference between people and God. Readers may wonder whether this question is more of a lyric question (given the poetic use of ὦ ἄνθρωπε), but the ornamental construction of the question cannot hide the doubt driven by the idea of back-talking a God who is so very much greater than σύ.

2) Aporetic Questions Raise the Issue of Impossibility

Another key characteristic of aporetic questions is that they intentionally develop a sense of impossibility within the audience. Because the contrast between the small and the immense is so great, whatever gap the speaker asks about between the two seems impossible to bridge. A tell of aporetic questions is that the contrast created often follows a "I am at a loss to compare the small with the great."[34] For example:

34. Mastronarde, *Contact*, 9.

(4) τίς ἡμᾶς χωρίσει ἀπὸ τῆς ἀγάπης τοῦ Χριστοῦ; (ROM 8:35A)

Example (4), where Paul asks as part of a question string, "Who will separate us from the love of Christ?" is an aporetic question that implies that the love of Christ is so great that it is impossible for anything or anyone to separate believers from it. While this is a common understanding, what is sometimes not emphasized enough is that the love of Christ is so many degrees of magnitude greater than the powers of our world as to make it practically *impossible* for any earthly power to cut the love of Christ from the believer's life. Paul amplifies this argument in the second part of his question string by pointing out that common earthly powers simply cannot separate believers from the love of Christ (Rom 8:35b).

Rhetorical Effects

Informational
Rhetorical

Aporetic questions start from the position of openness in their rhetorical effects. This is what gives aporetic questions their potency—they are based on a sincere asking that leads to the recognition of the magnitude of the subject. Aporetic questions tend toward strong rhetorical qualities, and attempts at direct replies are difficult (and usually not attempted).

Three of the most significant rhetorical effects of aporetic questions are listed below.

1) Aporetic Questions Project an Air of Unanswerability

With a great contrast embedded in the question, aporetic questions project to the audience that the question is not answerable. Even a reply is rhetorically dissuaded when an aporetic question is asked. This rhetorical effect is a large factor in the feeling among hearers that aporetic questions are really just assertions. Aporetic questions are akin to lyric questions (§4.C) in that both are used by speakers to project an air of unanswerability. The difference is that aporetic questions project this out of a sense of being overwhelmed whereas lyric questions project this out of a sense of awe. Because of their air of unanswerability, aporetic questions can come across as a challenge to an audience in that whatever great idea is being expressed cannot be answered or compared to anything the audience may suggest. For example:

(5) Τίς ἄξιος ἀνοῖξαι τὸ βιβλίον καὶ λῦσαι τὰς σφραγῖδας αὐτοῦ; (REV 5:2)

Technically, question (5) from Revelation 5:2 is an open question with aporetic tendencies, but it demonstrates the point here quite well. The angel asks "Who is worthy to open the scroll and break its seals?" in such a way that the rhetorical effect persuades the reader that the worthiness needed to open the scroll and break the seals is so great that there is no answer to the question—no one is worthy. In fact, the reader learns that John wept because the question had no answer (Rev 5:4), but only to learn soon after that there was one who was worthy (Rev 5:5).

2) Aporetic Questions Admit Limitation or Uncertainty on the Part of the Asker

Most questions give away insight about the asker, but aporetic questions admit limitation and uncertainty about the asker in only a shallow way. This is because aporetic questions draw a contrast between the small and the great, with the great being so many magnitudes greater than the small that this contrast is usually self-evident. Thus, an asker is usually safe by admitting their weaknesses next to the impossible concept raised by the question. For example:

(6) Τίς γὰρ ἔγνω νοῦν κυρίου; (ROM 11:34A)

Here in (6), Paul quotes Isaiah to challenge the reader with the question, "For who has known the mind of the Lord?" As an aporetic question, this question persuades the reader to ask whether it is possible to know the mind of God. The reasonable conclusion is "no, it is impossible" and then to experience a sense of loss or doubt that a person could know the mind of God. At the same time, the admission is small; most people would readily assume that a person cannot know the mind of God. God's mind is so much greater as to be incomparable to a person's mind. Because this question occurs as a quotation, we may also interpret it as a lyric question (§4.C)—it is used lyrically but its subject matter is more suited for aporia.

3) Aporetic Questions Stress the Greatness of the Immense

The contrast between small and immense placed within aporetic questions has the side rhetorical effect of stressing the magnitude of greatness of the immense (especially in comparison to the small). In many, if not most, cases, the audience will need little convincing that the immense object is really so great. A classic example of this occurs when the very great object is God, as in examples (1), (3), and (6). However, in other situations such as (4) and (5), the use of a question with aporetic quality has the rhetorical effect of persuading hearers that the object of the question really is so great. In (4), where the object is the love of Christ, the question not only persuades the audience that the love of Christ is so great that it trumps any earthly power, but that the love of Christ is already as great as anything that we can imagine. Perhaps (5) is a better example, where a reader may not understand the importance of opening the scroll and breaking its seals, but the rhetorical effect of the question pushes the reader to accept that for some reason this act of opening the scroll and breaking its seals is *so great* as to not compare to any similar earthly act. Though only partly aporetic, question (5) is more strongly persuasive than any similar proposition for the reader to understand the immense worth needed to open the scroll and break the seal.

Case Study — REVELATION 13:4

Τίς ὅμοιος τῷ θηρίῳ, καὶ τίς δύναται πολεμῆσαι μετ' αὐτοῦ;

THE WORLD: Who is like the beast and who is able to war against him?

During the vision God gave John, there comes a point when John sees a beast arise out of the sea (Rev 13:1). After giving a cryptic description of the beast, John tells his readers that the dragon gave the beast his power, throne, and authority (v. 2). The people of the world become entranced by the wonder of the beast and begin to worship the dragon and then the beast, asking, "Who is like the beast and who is able to war against him?" John suggests that the world worshipped the beast by raising a question indicative of the type of worship that ensued.

It is noteworthy that the worship of the beast is expressed as a question rather than an assertion. Often people express worship with assertions—statements or affirmations to a deity. As a result, it is tempting to see the utterance of the world toward the beast as simply a "rhetorical question" that poetically asserts the greatness of the beast through a hymn of praise.[35] Yet here the world is not making an assertion and simply stating with flourish "the beast is great."[36] Instead, this is an aporetic question asked to cause a strong rhetorical effect in the reader—revulsion and anger. Because the question is also either conjunctive or a double question, it carries the added capacity to amplify this rhetorical effect.

After the epistolary opening, Revelation is a type of narrative with a low level of direct discourse. Therefore, the direct discourse that John does include is of special importance to the reader. Scholars have long recognized that the use of a question here is meant to parody the worship of God's incomparable and inexhaustible nature by his people (e.g., Exod 15:11; Ps 35:10, also aporetic questions).[37] Thus, the world uses an aporetic question to describe their worship of the beast in the same way that the worshippers of God use aporetic questions to describe God. The world ascribes the kind of worship language to the beast—and thus that they are at a loss to compare themselves to the beast—that according to the Bible is due only to God. When a speaker raises an aporetic question, the audience is rhetorically oriented toward everyone and anyone (cf. Rev 5:2). Thus, when worshippers of God ask, "Who is like our God?" they are not simply saying "God is greater than anything else"; they are asking, "Who can tell us of anyone greater than God?" Worshippers of God are, in a sense, daring hearers

35. For example, Krodel, *Revelation*, 251; Reddish, *Revelation*, 253.
36. Here I avoid language such as "how great is the beast!" which is an indirect question that raises interrogative as well as assertive force to make its point.
37. Aune, *Revelation 6–16*, 741; Beale, *Revelation*, 694.

to answer their question—if they can. As Exodus 15:11 suggests, worshippers of God dare others to proclaim if any among the gods are greater than YHWH. The worshippers of the beast are doing the same—they are not just saying the beast is great but are daring anyone in the world to bring evidence contrary to the incomparability of the beast.[38] This is the power of the aporetic question; it magnifies the greatness of its object. In this case, the world is not content just to speak well of the beast or to lift the beast up but to magnify the beast *as if a greater god* than YHWH in a shocking act of worship.

FURTHER EXAMPLES

Mark 8:37; 15:34; John 6:60; Rom 8:35b; 11:34b; 1 Cor 1:20a, 20b, 20c; Rev 15:4; 18:18.

Key Bibliography

Aune, *Dictionary*, 54; Cain, *Socratic Method*, 16–18; Mastronarde, *Contact*, 9, 17; Quintilian, *Institutio oratoria* 9.2.19.

F. Sequence Questions

Sequence questions are asked to ascertain a course of action or a series of steps. Sequence questions can also be called *method questions* since their most common use is to ask for details about a method or process.[39] Quite frequently they are simple-sounding questions that entail a complex or multipart answer. A sequence question is a real nuts-and-bolts type of question. When an asker asks a sequence question, the logic of the question implies that there are steps needed to satisfactorily provide an answer to the question. Along with open questions (§4.A) and means questions (§4.H), sequence questions are one of the types of questions that are formed with the interrogative variable word *how*. The request for details in sequence questions comes from the semantics of *how* plus the verb and the object of the question. For this to work, sequence questions expect that the implicative request for complexity in the reply be understood by both the asker and the hearer. For example:

(1) How do you build a computer? (SEQUENCE QUESTION)
(2) What are the steps to building a computer? (SEQUENCE QUESTION)
(3) How do I get to Bubba's house? (SEQUENCE QUESTION)

Question (1) asks for more than a simple answer to the question. While a hearer could reply to the question with "one piece at a time" or "by following the

38. Cf. Bengel, *Gnomon*, 5:306.
39. Jaworski, "Logic," 134.

instructions," this is not the real intent of the question, and the answer would feel unsatisfactory. Of course, the asker is probably not looking for an explanation that takes six hours to deliver either. Sequence questions rely on implicature within the question to request a complex answer from the hearer. As a result, they seek a Goldilocks reply—one that is not too short and one that is not too long, but one that is just right. Though (2) does not use *how* as the interrogative word, its logic is nearly identical to (1). Example (3) is a sequence question where an expected answer will give sufficient details to allow the asker to travel to the destination. Due to their practical nature, sequence questions are quite common in natural language situations but are rare in the GNT.

Formation

Sequence questions can only be formed as a variable question, since polar, alternative, and set formations do not provoke a complex response. They are most commonly positive in polarity; it is rare to see a sequence question that is negative in polarity in natural-language situations. Sequence questions will almost always use *how* to construct their question; in the GNT, speakers employ πῶς to ask sequence questions. Certain verbs of "doing" (that involve actions) with *how* questions are more likely to indicate a sequence question (e.g., ἀνοίγω in the GNT) whereas verbs of "thinking" and "feeling" found in *how* questions are rarely implicative of a sequence question. Unlike means questions, which often rely on *how* plus modal possibilities, sequence questions prefer practical realities. This interest in details is the semantic focus of sequence questions. An asker can employ a sequence question in any turn of dialogue. With their strong informational qualities and request for a detailed answer, it would be unusual to ask a sequence question in the opening or middle dialogue position; closing and standalone dialogue positions work best.

The two main factors in the formation and identification of sequence questions are listed below.

1) Sequence Questions Ask for Details on a Process or Method

Sequence questions use *how* to gather greater details about a process or a method. Even though the question may seem elementary or answerable in a brief manner, usually the asker's intent is to receive a complex answer from the audience. With their focus on details, sequence questions are a common part of hearings and inquisitions. For example:

(4) Πῶς [οὖν] ἠνεῴχθησάν σου οἱ ὀφθαλμοί; (JOHN 9:10)

In (4), the neighbors and observers of the man born blind ask him, "Then how were your eyes opened?" They are curious as to the events that led to a man whom they knew to be born blind to now be able to see. In all probability, these askers will not be satisfied with a simple reply such as Ἰησοῦς ἐθεράπευσεν με. They want more details. In light of John's text, we see that the man born blind also understands this as a sequence question (based upon his detailed answer in v. 11). Unfortunately, his rough sketch of the details of the healing does not seem to fully satisfy his inquisitors.

2) Sequence Questions Usually Contain a Complex Idea or Object

In order for the sequence question to develop semantically, it will usually contain a complex idea or item that is the object of the request for explaining its sequence. Complexity will be in the ears of the hearer. For example, while walking could be considered a complex activity biologically, asking someone "how do you walk?" would in most situations not be heard as a sequence question (though "how do you walk to the bus station?" would). Conversely, example (1) would probably be heard as a sequence question in most situations. In (4), the process by which Jesus opened the eyes of the man born blind would presumably be complex—therefore the neighbors and watchers want to know all the details of exactly how Jesus pulled off such a complicated and wondrous feat. In this case, they want to know how the trick was engineered.

Rhetorical Effects

Informational
Rhetorical

Sequence questions lean toward openness as a question type. They typically have a strong informational and a weak rhetorical quality. As a result of their informational and rhetorical mix, sequence questions are rarely heard as a trick or as a test (unless pragmatics compel context to dictate otherwise). However, when rhetorical effects are added, sequence questions can then take on a testing quality. Sometimes a speaker can apply enough rhetorical effects to cause the sequence question to be forceful or menacing and the hearer to be put on the defensive.

The most notable rhetorical effect of sequence questions is described below.

1) Sequence Questions Can Be Used to Reveal or Confirm Intimate Details

A speaker may use a sequence question not just to learn a method but to see how much detail the audience may know about a specific process. Sometimes the speaker may hope that the audience will reveal too much detail. At the same time, inaccurate or misleading details included in an answer can tip off the speaker to what the audience does or does not know. Under these circumstances, sequence questions can make for useful test questions since a hearer who attempts an answer will reveal a certain amount of detail about the question.

(5) πῶς ἤνοιξέν σου τοὺς ὀφθαλμούς; (JOHN 9:26B)

In example (5) the Pharisees ask, "How did he open your eyes?" This question is similar to (4) except with more rhetorical force. While the neighbors and watchers may ask (4) out of curiosity, the Pharisees have different motives for their inquiry (v. 14). The Pharisees ratchet up the emotion over the course of this questioning scene in John, first asking polar questions to establish facts (v. 19a) and then switching to more substantial variable questions such as the sequence question (5). The Pharisees' goal is to use the sequence question to dig into the details to see if there were any infractions against the law.

Case Study — LUKE 1:34

Πῶς ἔσται τοῦτο, ἐπεὶ ἄνδρα οὐ γινώσκω;

MARY: How will this be, since I am a virgin?

During Elizabeth's pregnancy, God sends the angel Gabriel to visit Mary in Nazareth (Luke 1:26–28). Luke informs his readers that Mary is a virgin who is pledged in marriage to Joseph, a descendant of David. When the angel greets Mary, the greeting troubles her. The angel encourages Mary to hold back her fears because she has found grace with God. Then the angel tells Mary she will bear a son named Jesus, and her son will be a great king as his father David was—except that her son's kingdom will never end (vv. 30–33). Upon hearing this weighty pronouncement, Mary raises a practical question: "How will this be, since I am a virgin?"

Mary's question turns the dialogue away from the epic toward the need for a simple explanation to a complex question. Mary forms her question as a variable question, using πῶς, and she asks about something not yet arrived (ἔσται τοῦτο). She qualifies her question with the literal ἐπεὶ ἄνδρα οὐ γινώσκω. At first glance, this question could be considered a speculative question (because of its topic) or a means question (because Mary is asking about something that seems impossible). It is not primarily speculative because the question is concrete and deals with a very real issue at hand. It also is not primarily a means question; while there is concern over whether this is even possible, Mary does not actually ask how *this is possible* but how *this will proceed*.[40] Thus, the question is primarily a sequence question. Certainly, Mary is not likely asking for great details or to know the entire process, but the sincerity of her question makes the rhetorical effect present but mild so as to place it within the realm of a sequence question. Mary's goal is to elicit whatever information she can of a practical nature. Any information that the angel would be willing to provide would be well received by Mary. In fact, Luke records that the angel does receive the question to some degree as a sequence question—the angel informs Mary that (a) the Holy Spirit

40. Cf. Parsons, Culy, and Stigall, *Luke*, 32.

will come upon her, (b) the power of God will overshadow her, (c) this will make the child holy and will cause him to be called the Son of God, (d) God showed he could do this with her cousin Elizabeth, even in her old age, and (e) nothing is impossible with God (vv. 1:35–37).

Key Bibliography
Estes, *Questions*, 103–7; Jaworski, "Logic."

G. Proof Questions

Proof questions are asked to establish the reason behind the complement of the question. They are questions that ask about the causal relationships between things and events. Proof questions are also called *causal questions* and *rationale questions*. The semantic qualities of proof questions are rooted in the interrogative logic of causality, which goes back to at least the works of Aristotle.[41] Proof questions are one of the classic extensions of the *why* question. *Why* questions are also commonly formed as open questions (§4.A) and speculative questions (§4.B). Whereas speculative questions emphasize uncertainty, proof questions emphasize causal relationships. For example:

(1) Why do you want to go to the moon? (PROOF QUESTION)
(2) Why are you so blue? (PROOF QUESTION)
(3) Why can't you do anything right? (PROOF QUESTION)

Example (1) takes the standard form of a proof question. The asker of (1) seeks information on the cause of the hearer wanting to go to the moon. There is an easy tell for proof questions: A proof question seeks an answer that a hearer can usually form as "subject + question complement + *because* + proof." In this case, a reply might be something along the lines of "I + want to go to the moon + *because* + I love cottage cheese."[42] By asking (1), the asker hopes to ascertain the rationale behind the subject's involvement with the complement. The same is true in (2), where a hearer can offer an answer such as "I + am so blue + *because* + today is Monday." Because of its negative polarity and its bias word, question (3) has much greater rhetorical force than questions (1) and (2), such that a reply to (3) is much harder to muster. Natural-language occurrences will not always be as tidy as these examples, but naturally occurring proof questions will try to ascertain reasons so as to allow the hearer the chance to prove the causal relationship.

41. For example, book two of his *Posterior Analytics*.
42. Cf. Aristotle, *Posterior Analytics* 94a4–5.

Formation

Proof questions are formed from variable-question formations, and they cannot be formed from polar-, alternative-, or set-question formations. ("Can you prove that aliens exist?" is not a proof question; it is a polar question asking whether you *will* or *are able to* prove something or not). Proof questions are a little more difficult to distinguish in ancient Greek than in English. One tell for proof questions is the fronted διὰ τί. In English, most proof questions will use the interrogative variable word *why*; but in Greek, the speaker would use τίς, an interrogative variable word with a broader semantic range. Thus, the semantics of a proof question is the most important quality of this type of question. Proof questions have a unique logic wherein they expect a reply that is an informal proof of the complement. Like sequence questions, proof questions seek a Goldilocks reply—one that is not too short and one that is not too long but one that is just right. In the case of proof questions, they seek answers that complete the causal relationship in question between the subject and the complement. Proof questions can be equally positive or negative polarity, and bias can be added by the speaker to effect replies. Too much bias will alter the rhetorical effects of the question to the point where it would no longer be a proof question.

The primary factor in the formation and identification of a proof question is described below.

1) Proof Questions Require a Semantic Focus on Causality

A speaker uses a proof question to try to establish the rationale or the cause behind an event or an action. To establish the basis of a proof question, the asker must recognize there is a rationale that is unknown (unless the proof question is also a test question; §4.L). Much of their interrogative logic is based on the semantic property of *why* in establishing causal relationships. For example:

(4) Διὰ τί οἱ μαθηταί σου παραβαίνουσιν τὴν παράδοσιν τῶν πρεσβυτέρων; (MATT 15:2)

Some Pharisees and scribes ask (4) of Jesus, "Why do your disciples break the tradition of the elders?" Formed as a variable question, it is asked with notable informational qualities so that the Pharisees and scribes can establish a causal reason for the disciples' act of breaking the tradition of the elders. In asking this, the Pharisees and the scribes are hoping for a reply along the lines of "My disciples + break the tradition of the elders + *because* + . . ." The main rhetorical effect on the question is that it is asked in an opening, and not standalone or closing, dialogue position; thus, the utterance οὐ γὰρ νίπτονται τὰς χεῖρας [αὐτῶν] ὅταν ἄρτον ἐσθίωσιν ("for they don't wash their hands when they eat!") becomes a jab at Jesus that undermines the informational focus of the question. Unfortunately for the Pharisees and scribes, Jesus is not interested in giving a reason; instead, he responds with his own proof question employed as an opposing-turn question (§5.B.1) to show reproof.

Rhetorical Effects

Informational
Rhetorical

Proof questions are akin to test questions in their rhetorical effects, and test questions are often formed as proof questions. The rhetorical application and epistemic balance are what distinguish the two; proof questions do not have as strong a "testing" effect and are not always asked by an asker who knows the (correct) answer. Even though they are an open type of question, they can put people on the defensive with their request for establishing causality. Proof questions use the strongest rhetorical force among the *why* question types included here:

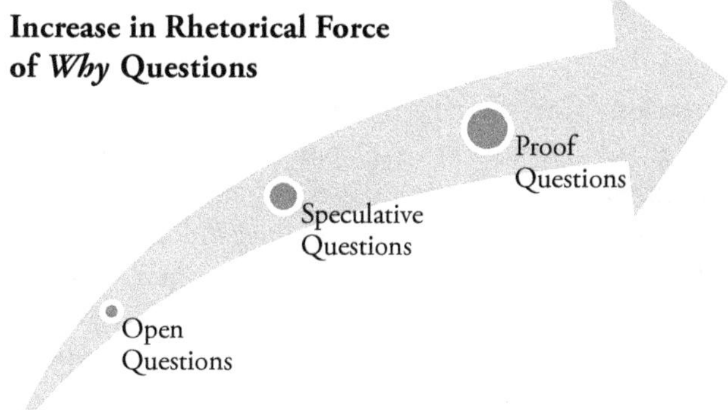

Proof questions are common in rhetorical discourse when there is a need to challenge the audience on the rationale of an issue.

Three common rhetorical effects of proof questions are listed below.

1) Proof Questions Cause Reflection in the Minds of the Hearers

Determining causality and explaining rationale are complicated intellectual processes. As these are the goals anticipated by the asking of a proof question, hearers must devote significant mental energy before they can attempt a meaningful reply. Proof questions stimulate the audience's thinking on the reason behind an event or action. For example:

(5) Τί με ἐρωτᾷς περὶ τοῦ ἀγαθοῦ; (MATT 19:17)

Example (5), "Why do you ask me about the good?" is the interrogative response Jesus gives to the opening question of a wealthy young man. As such, first and foremost (5) functions pragmatically as an opposing-turn question (§5.B.1) with the goal of pushing back against the previous question. This pragmatic factor makes the question have a stronger rhetorical effect. Yet there is something else occurring within the interrogative logic of the question. Popular interpretation tends to focus on the issue of goodness, but this does not exactly match the interrogative logic of the question. As a proof question, Jesus asks the question, hoping to push the addressee to think about the causality behind the object of the question. Because the question carries strong rhetorical effects as an opposing-turn question, Jesus is even more so pushing for reflection than he is seeking a verbal answer (though the question retains informational qualities). If the rich young man were to try to articulate an answer, the answer would be formed as "I + asked you about good + *because* + . . ." This should give us pause—why does the rich young man ask about goodness? In other words, the question Jesus raises is *not* what good is for the rich young man but why the rich young man focuses on good in his question. Therefore, Jesus wants the rich young man to reflect on the reason why he would ask this question about goodness. What is missing in this man's life that goodness is the focal point? What goodness is missing from him?

2) Proof Questions Can Clarify the Thoughts of Askers and Hearers

Since proof questions ask for an explanation, an asker can use them to gain assistance from the audience in refining their thoughts on a subject. Proof questions can also persuade an audience to clarify their thoughts before attempting a reply. Both askers and hearers of a proof question may never have thought before on how to explain the issue asked about, and therefore asking or hearing a proof question often has the effect of bringing clarity to an issue simply by attempting the question or the reply. This is the reason that proof questions are so commonly used as test questions and in learning environments. For example:

(6) Διὰ τί ἡμεῖς οὐκ ἠδυνήθημεν ἐκβαλεῖν αὐτό; (MATT 17:19)

In (6), the disciples do not understand their previous failure at exorcism, and so they ask, "Why did we not have power enough to cast it out?" The disciples' question is strongly informational, asked with a real desire to have an answer given to them. In asking the question, the disciples are making a conscious realization that there is a cause or reason why their attempt at exorcism was unsuccessful. They are admitting they do not know the reason, and they are hoping that Jesus will give an answer so that the reason can be made clear to them. As evidence that the disciples' question is a proof question, Jesus literally answers "because + . . ." with διὰ τὴν ὀλιγοπιστίαν ὑμῶν (v. 20).

3) Proof Questions Can Be an Effective Form of Skepticism

Proof questions with strong rhetorical force can evoke skepticism or even dismay in an audience. Part of dialogue and persuasion is the asking of questions that run counter to a speaker's proposition. In its most basic form, asking "why" in response to a speaker's proposition is a form of skepticism (generally defined). When a hearer is skeptical of a previous utterance or wants a better explanation, they can use proof questions as a way to resolve their concerns. Greater rhetorical effects can create antagonism or feelings of guilt (e.g., "Why did you do this?"). For example:

(7) τί ἔτι σκύλλεις τὸν διδάσκαλον; (MARK 5:35)

Question (7) is an example of a proof question with stronger than usual rhetorical effects applied. Coming from the house of Jairus, they inform Jesus and Jairus that Jairus's daughter has died and ask, "Why are you still bothering the Teacher?" By stating ἡ θυγάτηρ σου ἀπέθανεν ("Your daughter is dead") as a premise and then asking the question, the context indicates the goal of the question is to be persuasive. Yet the question falls in the closing dialogue position, which means that the speakers anticipate some response (note that the two clauses could easily be reversed, with the question in the opening position and the premise following—which would indicate that the speaker feels no reply is needed or warranted). To add to this, the question has a number of other rhetorical effects; most notable is the strong bias word ἔτι ("still") and the mild bias that comes with the verb σκύλλεις. Thus, the speakers use the question to express skepticism at the *reason* or *cause* for Jairus to remain with Jesus, pushing him with strong bias to reconsider his current course of action. With the question hanging as it does in the closing position, the speakers may anticipate a mild objection from Jairus. In fact, Jesus senses this, which is the reason why he interjects with μὴ φοβοῦ, μόνον πίστευε ("Do not fear, only have faith") and shuts down the rhetoric of skepticism espoused in the speakers' question.

Case Study — MARK 4:40A

Τί δειλοί ἐστε;

JESUS: Why are you so afraid?

One day after teaching the crowds by a lake, Jesus goes to his disciples and tells them he would like to go over to the other side of the lake (Mark 4:35). The disciples help Jesus into the boat and they set sail, with other boats also crossing over. During the crossing, a fast-moving storm appeared, and the waves began to break over the boat. While the disciples worried, Jesus slept soundly in the stern. Out of their concern, the disciples wake Jesus, asking him if he cares if they drown. Jesus rises, rebukes the winds and waves, and suddenly the storm ceased and everything became calm. Then Jesus turns to the disciples and asks them, "Why are you so afraid? Don't you have faith yet?"

Jesus asks his question to the disciples as the first half of a double question (§5.D.1). Semantically, δειλοί introduces a mild bias. Aside from these, the question is short and free from any other notable rhetorical effects. Thus the question leans toward a more informational than rhetorical bent, with the second question of the double question amplifying the moderate degree of persuasion. This is in sharp contrast to popular readings of Mark 4:40 where the interpreter often describes Jesus using "rhetorical questions" to make an assertion about the disciples' lack of faith.[43] Unfortunately, this kind of reading ruins the nuances of what Jesus asks. In fact, Jesus is very much asking the disciples a question that they need to answer. Jesus employs a proof question so that the cause and rationale for the disciples' fear can identified. In stilling the storm, Jesus has just shown unalterable proof that anyone with him has no reason to fear. Yet the disciples are still afraid. Why? Have the disciples given thought to the cause of their fear? Jesus asks this question to push them toward considering that "they are afraid *because*..." For them to be free from their fear, they must find the root cause.

Jesus's second question in the double question further pushes the disciples to explore whether they have a lack of faith, and if so, is their lack of faith the cause behind their fear. This question is a negative polar question, so it is much more pointed and rhetorical and much less informational. What is remarkable about this exchange is that Mark describes the disciples as ἐφοβήθησαν φόβον μέγαν even on hearing Jesus's question, and instead of answering Jesus's question they respond with an opposing-turn question—but instead of toward the speaker as an attack, toward themselves as a defense. By asking the question τίς ἄρα οὗτός ἐστιν ("Who is this!?"), the disciples unwittingly *do* reveal their reason for being afraid—they are afraid because they do not know who Jesus really is.[44]

FURTHER EXAMPLES

Matt 17:10; 19:7; 20:6; 21:25c; John 4:27b; 8:43; Acts 9:4; Gal 3:19; Rev 17:7.

Key Bibliography

Hintikka and Halonen, "Semantics and Pragmatics," 636–57; Koura, "Approach"; Kubiński, *Outline*, 42–44; Reese, "Meaning and Use," 331–54; Sintonen, "Why-Questions," 168–76; Teller, "On Why-Questions," 371–80; Temple, "Contrast Theory," 141–51.

43. For example, Brooks, *Mark*, 88.

44. Cf. Thurston, *Preaching Mark*, 60.

H. Means Questions

Means questions are asked to learn about the way in which something can be made possible. This question type gets its name because it inquires as to the means by which something may happen or be accomplished. Means questions are one of the primary question types most often formed with the interrogative variable word *how*. Like all *how* questions, means questions tend to focus on details more than the bigger picture. *How* questions are also commonly formed as open questions (§4.A) and sequence questions (§4.F). Whereas means questions emphasize the possibility of occurrence, sequence questions emphasize the steps to realizing the occurrence. Means questions ask "how" without asking for the steps. Along with speculative questions (§4.B), means questions are one of the types of questions that ask about possibilities—speculative questions ask *if* or *why* something is possible, whereas means questions ask *how* something is possible. For example:

(1) How can I get to Seattle asap? (MEANS QUESTION)
(2) How do you know it is love? (MEANS QUESTION)
(3) How can you not see your own weaknesses? (MEANS QUESTION)

Example (1) is a rudimentary means question, using the interrogative variable word *how* to ask the means to accomplish the complement of the question. There is an easy tell for means questions: A means question seeks an answer that a hearer can often form as "*it is possible to* + question complement + *by means of* + evidence." In this case, a reply might be something along the lines of "*it is possible to* get to Seattle asap *by means of* catching the next flight." Likewise in (2), the question seeks the means by which the hearer "knows that it is love." A satisfactory answer could be "it is possible to know that it is love by means of a sickness in the pit of your stomach." These answers are of course wooden, but they do reveal the basic erotetic logic of the question. Example (3) is both negative in polarity and includes a bias word, so the rhetorical effects are greatly increased. Nonetheless, at its semantic heart (3) still pushes the audience toward reflecting how it is possible for the hearer to not see their own weaknesses. Means questions are a widely used question type.

Formation

Means questions are formed with a variable-question formation and cannot be formed from polar-, alternative-, or set-question formations. Thus, "Is it possible to fly to Seattle?" is not a means question (though it could be a confirmation or a speculative question; cf. John 7:41). Means questions will almost always use *how* to construct their question; in the GNT, speakers employ πῶς to ask means questions. Rarely, a speaker will use τίς plus a preposition (for example, κατὰ τί in Luke 1:18). As a result, the biggest tell for means questions is usually syntactic. Means questions also favor certain modal verbs of possibility; this is not pronounced in Koine Greek (though cf. Rom 10:14a–15; 1 John 3:17), but the common, modern-English translation of this mode is to supplement the translation with the word *can* (for example (5), below). When it comes to semantics, the means question is strongly influenced by the unique interrogative forces generated from the innate meaning of πῶς. When it comes to pragmatics, a means question does not have strong preferences toward any dialogue position; they are found comfortably in any dialogue turn and in any dialogue position.

The primary factor in the formation and identification of means questions is described below.

1) Means Questions Ask about the Explanation to a Possibility

Means questions ask the audience to explain the way in which something is possible. Their semantics are based on the question, "How is it possible to..." Unlike speculative or open questions that also ask about possibilities, means questions often push for an answer in concrete situations or details. For example:

(4) ὃς δ' ἂν ἔχῃ τὸν βίον τοῦ κόσμου ... πῶς ἡ ἀγάπη τοῦ θεοῦ μένει ἐν αὐτῷ; (1 JOHN 3:17)

In (4), John asks, "Who can have a full worldly life and can look at his brother in need and can close his heart to him—how does the love of God stay in him?" In this question, ὅς plus the subjunctive verb in the first three clauses indicates a weak conditional premise; this premise must be met for the interrogative force of the final clause to be in effect. Assuming this condition to be true, John asks a means question to push his readers to consider under what means it would be possible for the love of God to stay in this person. Because this is a means question used with strong rhetorical qualities, John is not asking his audience to simply agree with him ("it is not possible"); rather, John desires his audience to try to work through the avenues of possibility before coming to a conclusion. We know this because John could have more simply phrased this as a polar question, ὃς δ' ἂν ἔχῃ τὸν βίον τοῦ κόσμου ... ἡ ἀγάπη τοῦ θεοῦ μένει ἐν αὐτῷ; ("Who can have a full worldly life and can look at his brother in need and can close his heart to him—does the love of God stay in him?") if he simply wanted the audience to confirm that this was not possible. John's push for an answer is that the means for the love of God to stay in a person like this is surely weak and fleeting.

Rhetorical Effects

Informational
Rhetorical

Means questions may appear to have strong informational qualities, but they are also effective when used with strong rhetorical qualities. It often represents the strongest rhetorical use of πῶς questions, and thus πῶς questions found in rhetorical discourse are quite often means questions.

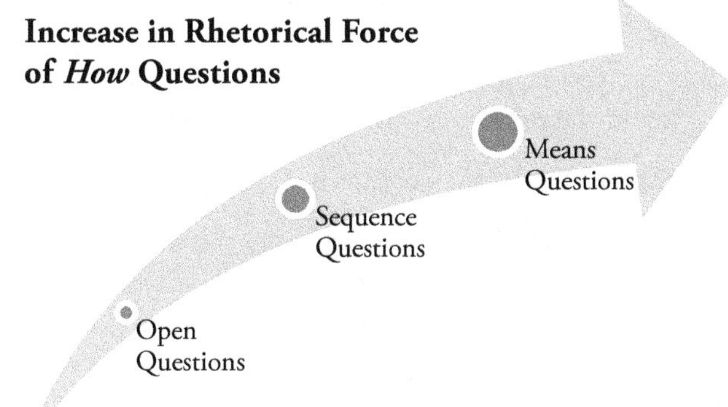

Means questions are common in rhetorical discourse when there is a need to ask whether something can be made possible (and often with the asker revealing whether the asker believes there is a means possible or not). Rhetorically, means questions can run tangential to deliberative questions (when the means question becomes self-focused and introspective) and speculative questions (when the means question becomes philosophical and unanswerable).

The two most significant rhetorical effects of means questions are described below.

1) Means Questions Encourage Hearers to Consider How Something Is Possible

When a speaker applies mild rhetorical effects to means questions, their intent shifts a few degrees away from asking how something is possible to asking the audience to consider how something could be possible. In these situations, means questions are quite good at inducing reflection, and they are often part of healthy dialogue and discussion. This use of the means question is quite common in representational and rhetorical discourse. For example:

(5) καὶ πῶς ἡμεῖς ἀκούομεν ἕκαστος τῇ ἰδίᾳ διαλέκτῳ ἡμῶν ἐν ᾗ ἐγεννήθημεν; (ACTS 2:8)

Question (5) is one voiced by the Jerusalem crowd: "How can we hear, each in our own native dialect?" As a result of the bewildering events described in Acts 2, the crowd in Jerusalem encountered the earliest believers speaking in foreign languages under the influence of the Holy Spirit. The natural response by the crowd is to wonder how this is possible, which leads them to ask (5). The crowd asks the question with mild rhetorical effect, as they are both seeking an answer but also reflecting out loud how unlikely this occurrence seems to them. Thus, this means question has a dual effect on the hearer.

2) Means Questions Can Create a Sense of Exasperation

In strongly rhetorical situations, a speaker can ask a means question to show frustration, exasperation, or incredulity at an idea or assertion of another speaker. When used this way, a means question can be a mild form of pushback, along the lines of "how can you say that?" This rhetorical use of the means question is also quite common in rhetorical discourse. For example:

(6) ἐπεὶ πῶς κρινεῖ ὁ θεὸς τὸν κόσμον; (ROM 3:6)

In (6) Paul asks, "Otherwise, how will God judge the world?" Given that (6) is asked within rhetorical discourse, if we consider context we see that Paul argues God is true and valid in his application of justice (Rom 3:4–5). After expressing μὴ γένοιτο at the thought of an unrighteous God, Paul asks his readers ἐπεὶ πῶς will God judge. As a means question, Paul uses this question to further press his reader to ask themselves, "How else would God judge the world?" The question challenges the reader to go back to the premise of the argument and realize that it is the righteousness of God that makes it possible for God to judge. In fact, it is the *possibility* of righteousness that makes God able to judge (in comparison to the world), and it is the *impossibility* of justice (without righteousness) that makes God needed to judge the world.

Case Study ACTS 8:31

Πῶς γὰρ ἂν δυναίμην ἐὰν μή τις ὁδηγήσει με;

ETHIOPIAN EUNUCH: How should I be able if no one will teach me?

In the early days of the church, Philip is preaching the gospel in Samaria (Acts 8:5). At the end of this journey, an angel of the Lord speaks to Philip and encourages him to take a different route (a desert route) back to Jerusalem. Along this route Philip encounters a eunuch from Ethiopia, who happened to be a royal official of the Ethiopian queen Candace leaving Jerusalem after spending time there in worship (vv. 27–28). As the royal official passed by, reading Isaiah in his chariot, the Spirit tells Philip to approach. When Philip hears him reading Isaiah, Philip asks, "Do you understand what you are reading?" At this the royal official responds, "How should I be able if no one will teach me?" Then the official invites Philip to join him to read further.

The question of the Ethiopian eunuch occurs within representational dialogue indicative of everyday speech. The ἂν δυναίμην ἐὰν construction is unusual.[45] The use of ἄν plus the optative indicates uncertain (possibly pessimis-

45. Conzelmann, *Acts of the Apostles*, 68.

tic) future possibility.[46] Pragmatically, it is first and foremost an opposing-turn question (§5.B.1)—the Ethiopian responds to Philip's opening question with an objection that serves as a violation of the question-answer pair. At the same time, the semantics of the question plays a crucial role. In creating an oppositional utterance, the Ethiopian is layering the opposition with a request. Often readers interpret the question as a proposition, wherein the Ethiopian says "it's not possible" without help, but instead the Ethiopian asks a legitimate question that challenges Philip to respond and make it possible.[47] The legitimacy of the challenge is tied to Philip's assistance; the Ethiopian knows it is possible to understand Isaiah but is asking and challenging Philip to be the one to provide the means for him to understand.

FURTHER EXAMPLES
Matt 7:4; 16:11; 22:12; Mark 3:23; John 6:52; 7:15; 8:33; 9:19b; Rom 6:2; 10:14a, 14b, 14c, 15; Gal 2:14.

Key Bibliography
Jaworski, "Logic," 133–55.

I. Indexical Questions

Indexical questions are asked to introduce a degree of uncertainty or ambiguity in the asking process. In many cases, the introduction of uncertainty or ambiguity is not intentional on the part of the asker, but is instead an (usually) unintentional rhetorical effect of the question asking. An indexical is "a word that has a pointing function" (*CDL* 125). In IE languages, the most common indexicals are pronouns (such as *it*, *this*, *that* in English) or adverbs (such as *here*, *there*, *when* in English). Linguists refer to an indexical by several different terms such as *deictic* and *anaphora*. Indexicals are a common IE-language phenomenon, and they occur regularly in every kind of utterance including questions. However, indexical questions are *not* merely questions with an indexical. Instead, indexical questions are those questions that contain an indexical on which a great deal of semantic focus is placed. Often this focus will occur because the reference drawn by the indexical is ambiguous or because the speaker wants the audience to guess at the reference to be drawn. For example:

(1) What do you want to do with that? (INDEXICAL QUESTION)
(2) If you hold on to the money, what will you do with it? (QUESTION WITH INDEXICAL)

46. Cf. Beck, Malamud, and Osadcha, "Semantics," 56.
47. On the hypothetical possibility, see Zerwick and Grosvenor, *Grammatical Analysis*, 377.

Questions (1) and (2) set up a contrast between an indexical question and a question with an indexical. In (1), the indexical "that" is used as the object of the question, "What do you want to do with..." For a hearer to be able to answer the question—a relatively open, information-seeking type of question—the hearer must make the reference to what "that" is. In some cases, "that" is a clear reference, and the indexical question has a weak rhetorical effect. In other cases, "that" may be an oblique reference, in which case the indexical question will have a stronger rhetorical effect. In contrast, (2) contains the indexical "it," but a hearer will easily make the reference to "money" in the earlier clause. Since there is little or no chance for ambiguity, we consider (2) a question with an indexical rather than an indexical question. Because indexicals are a common language phenomenon, questions with indexicals are very common; actual indexical questions are less common (but not rare).

Because of their pointing, indexical questions are similar to what is sometimes called *forward-pointing questions* or *backward-pointing questions*.[48] The difference between a forward-pointing question and an indexical question is that forward-pointing questions only address the indexical possibilities in the interrogative variable word, and only if the indexical points forward to subsequent utterances. Indexical questions do address forward-pointing and backward-pointing references, but they do so through the indexical, not the interrogative variable word. Indexical questions are a type of question in the GNT where the English rendering can be misleading; modern English translations will occasionally attempt to clarify the indexical for the reader instead of allowing ambiguity to remain. Of course, the ambiguity of an indexical is often greater in English than in Greek, given the differences in language agreement (such as the declension of substantives in Greek, which does not occur in English). As a result, determining the intended ambiguity in indexical questions can be quite challenging.

Formation

A speaker may form an indexical question from any syntactic formation for question asking. Indexical questions have one syntactic requirement—the presence of an indexical in the object position of the question. For a question with an indexical to be an indexical question, the indexical must refer to something outside the bounds of the question. Even though this is a syntactic requirement, it is also a semantic requirement. A speaker may ask an indexical question in any turn or position; thus, they are without pragmatic constraint. The formation of an indexical question is dependent on the syntactic and semantic reference of the indexical. It is unnecessary for the thing to which the indexical refers to be known by either the asker or the audience.

48. Runge, *Discourse Grammar*, 64–66.

The sole factor in the formation and identification of an indexical question is described below.

1) Indexical Questions Use an Indexical as Object of the Interrogative clause

To be an indexical question, the indexical must appear in the interrogative clause and contribute in some way to the question asking. Again, this differentiates an indexical question from a question with an indexical in it. For example:

(3) Ποῦ ἐστιν ἐκεῖνος; (JOHN 7:11)

Example (3)—"Where is he?"—is an indexical question because the question (and its interrogativity) hinges on the identification of the indexical ἐκεῖνος by the audience. If no identification can be made by a hearer, the question results in confusion and a search for the indexical's referent. In the case of (3), the indexical is well formed and the reference is obvious: ἐκεῖνος refers to Jesus. However, as below, not all indexicals make for a clear and obvious reference.

Rhetorical Effects

Informational
Rhetorical

When a speaker asks an indexical question, the reference made by the indexical can add a rhetorical effect to the question. Indexicals, as a natural feature of language, allow utterances to be made faster by standing in as a substitute for longer, more complex words and phrases. At the same time, speakers may use the referential features of indexicals to bring ambiguity or imprecision into their language use. In most cases, this ambiguity is weak, and the rhetorical effect is weak when it occurs in questions. Since indexical questions have weak rhetorical effects, they are easily trumped by the rhetorical effects of other types of questions. This is the reason why many speakers form indexical questions on variable-question forms and open-question types—the mild rhetorical effects of these two kinds of questions do not trump the almost-as-mild rhetorical effect of indexical questions.

1) Indexical Questions Have Stronger Rhetorical Effect with Weaker Indexicals

When an indexical is weak, this weakness adds strength to the rhetorical effect of the indexical question. As a general rule, the rhetorical strength of indexical questions is inversely proportional to the clarity of the indexical: the more obvious the indexical reference is, the weaker the rhetorical force; the less obvious the indexical reference is, the stronger the rhetorical force. Thus a speaker may intentionally ask a question with a weak or vague indexical reference to add a greater rhetorical effect. For example:

(4) τί ἐστιν τοῦτο; (MARK 1:27)

Question (4), "What is this?" is an example of the use of a weak indexical within a question to produce a rhetorical effect. In Mark 1, Jesus is in Capernaum and teaching in the synagogue when a man with an unclean spirit cries out to him. When Jesus exorcizes the unclean spirit, observers in the synagogue are so amazed that they ask, *τί ἐστιν τοῦτο;* Understandably, they use an indexical to express what just happened — the indexical makes a vague reference that the people use to indicate confusion or a lack of understanding about what occurred. As a result, when the audience (and readers) hear τοῦτο, they are forced to think about what τοῦτο is and what τοῦτο means. The less clear the indexical, the stronger the rhetorical effect. Question (4) also has expository qualities; the speakers then answer their own question, creating a new reference to διδαχὴ καινή ("new teaching").

2) Indexical Questions with Weak References Can Pique Interest

The study of indexicals in natural-language use reveals that sometimes indexicals do not hit their target — they do not make adequate reference to their referent, and so the hearer of the utterance containing the indexical cannot make any useful association. When this happens, confusion ensues at least for the audience and perhaps for the speaker. In dialogue, this event typically triggers a repair question (§5.B.4). But in a written text where the reader cannot ask for and receive a repair, the reader may not make the association or may remain confused about the association. For example:

(5) Οὐ μνημονεύετε ὅτι ἔτι ὢν πρὸς ὑμᾶς *ταῦτα* ἔλεγον ὑμῖν; (2 THESS 2:5)

Paul raises question (5) in the midst of his encouragement about the return of Jesus: "Don't you remember that even when I was with you, I was telling *these things* to you?" For some original readers of the text, it is possible that ταῦτα would trigger past conversations they had held with Paul or past sermons they had heard from him. But what about other readers? Other original readers who may not have been present in the church at Thessalonica would not remember what ταῦτα referred to and would not be able to make a complete association. For readers after Thessalonica, including readers today, the ambiguity introduced by ταῦτα creates a mild rhetorical effect of interest in what ταῦτα refers to. Does ταῦτα simply refer to what is covered in 2 Thessalonians 2:1–4? Or does ταῦτα reference something much more, some knowledge to which we are not privy? If so, how would the additional knowledge of ταῦτα add to the briefer information that Paul provides in 2 Thessalonians 2:1–4? Here the indexical has the mild rhetorical effect of making the reader wish they could know ταῦτα as the Thessalonian church once did.

When the use of a weak indexical in a question goes too far and the indexical reference is not just weak but unclear or misunderstood, confusion can occur. It is possible that some readers who read (5) may ask, "What things?"

out of confusion instead of having their interests piqued. While there is not an obvious case of this in the GNT, this does happen frequently in natural-language situations.

Case Study MATTHEW 21:23A

ἐν ποίᾳ ἐξουσίᾳ *ταῦτα* ποιεῖς;

CHIEF PRIESTS/ELDERS OF THE PEOPLE: By what authority do you do *these things*?

After the temple clearing, the chief priests and the scribes are outraged because people are praising Jesus (Matt 21:15). Jesus decides to lay low that evening, so he leaves the city and spends the night in Bethany. The next morning, Jesus gets up, makes an example of a fig tree, and returns to the temple. As Jesus enters the temple again and begins to teach, the chief priests and elders approach Jesus and demand to know, "By what authority do you do these things?" Jesus does not take their question well and starts to dispute their question.

The chief priests and the elders of the people open up a line of questioning against Jesus with a double question (§5.D.1), the first half of which is an indexical question.[49] To start their argument, the chief priests and elders ask Jesus what authority he has to do ταῦτα ("these things"). This indexical seems a reference of some sort to his public ministry. But because the dialogue begins with the chief priests and elders' question, and the setting is minimal, the reader is left with an incomplete reference. Does ταῦτα refer to Jesus's presence in the temple courts, including his teaching activity (v. 23)? Or does ταῦτα refer to his previous ministry activity in general? Or does it refer to something else? For the reader, it is hard to know exactly to what ταῦτα refers. Their question is simple, but their logic is cunning. While it may seem that the chief priests and elders use an indexical for expediency, this is not the whole story. A classic trick of interrogation is to use broad generalities in the hopes that the accused will slip up and add more exact details (cf. Luke 16:2). In this case, ταῦτα is broad enough that Jesus would need to be careful how to respond if he were to give a defense. (Perhaps this is one reason Jesus does not give a defense; he goes on the offense with a delayed opposing-turn dilemmaton in Matt 21:25a–b). For the reader, we perceive that the Pharisees are reaching, and the inclusion of the indexical means they do not have a strong case against Jesus.

49. Following NA[28]; though if we compare their question in Matthew to Luke's version of events (Luke 20:2), it is probable that Matthew's question was originally read as a conjunctive question. Either way, this does not have a major effect on our study of the indexical.

FURTHER EXAMPLES

Matt 8:27; 9:28; 13:51, 56b; Mark 2:7a, 8; 11:3, 28a; Luke 16:2; John 6:61; 11:26; 1 John 3:12.

Key Bibliography

Estes, *Questions*, 83–87; Runge, *Discourse Grammar*, 61–71.

J. Endoxical Questions

Endoxical questions are asked with an appeal by the asker to some kind of common or accepted knowledge. Endoxical questions get their name from ἔνδοξα, meaning "generally accepted opinions ... which commend themselves to all or to the majority or to the wise."[50] These opinions were generally considered reliable or truthful, at least as a starting point for discussion. Endoxical questions are questions with an embedded premise based on an opinion held by most people or cultural consensus or expert knowledge. Ἔνδοξα were an important feature of ancient Greek dialectic, and Aristotle used the term *dialectical protasis* to describe a type of endoxical question.[51] For our purposes, we deal with endoxical questions more broadly defined than ancient Greek dialectic.[52] When employing an endoxical question, the asker usually phrases the question with one of three premises: (a) a premise that the asker believes the hearer(s) should know, (b) a premise based on an established consensus, or (c) a premise on which the asker appeals to expert opinion or worldly wisdom. For example:

(1) Don't you believe like most people that the sky is blue? (ENDOXICAL QUESTION)

Embedded in (1) is the general premise that most people believe the sky is blue (and is overtly stated as such). While we may be able to accept that premise, other premises are more tricky and less overt. For example:

(2) Did you know that orange is the new black? (ENDOXICAL QUESTION)
(3) Can you be as good as Jesus? (ENDOXICAL QUESTION)
(4) Can you ride your bike as fast as Jason can? (LOADED QUESTION)

The speaker in (2) asks this question in light of an appeal to an expert knowledge base (in this case, fashion culture), and a reasonable answer to this question

50. Aristotle, *Topics* 100b21–23 (Forster).
51. Ibid., 104a8.
52. Partly this is due to the evolution of thought in these areas, notably toward a less rule-bound approach, as is evidenced even in the changes in Aristotle's own thought over the course of his writing lifetime.

will include some interaction with that knowledge base. Without some expert knowledge (in this case the role of black), the question cannot be appreciated or answered. The speaker in (3) asks a less simplistic endoxical question. Here the question contains the premise that Jesus is good. The ἔνδοξα is based on common culture in the West that Jesus was a good person. In asking the question, the asker not only presumes that Jesus is good and that the audience accepts that Jesus is good, but also that the audience understands and agrees with what it means that Jesus is a higher form of good. Furthermore, using *good* to describe Jesus is not likely to be challenged in many audiences because *good* is an emotionally positive word that *most* people in the West feel toward Jesus.[53]

Endoxical questions can be a part of a powerful argument structure built on established knowledge. They must include a premise based on an ἔνδοξον, or reference to an accepted knowledge base. In the ancient world, speakers used established ἔνδοξα to build a bridge to an audience and to augment their arguments. However, just because an ἔνδοξον is generally accepted does not mean that it (a) is necessarily true or (b) will be accepted by all parties in the audience.[54] Some parties may disagree with the premise. Endoxical questions can be tricky, and a skilled questioner can use them to fool an audience to agree with something they otherwise would not agree with. Endoxical questions are one of two question types that contain an implicit premise; the other type is the loaded question (§4.V). The difference between an endoxical question and a loaded question is that an endoxical question builds its premise on common knowledge or worldly wisdom while a loaded question builds its premise on implicit knowledge (that may be inaccurate). Endoxical questions also are similar to indexical questions in that both appeal to information outside the question in order for the question to make sense. The difference is that indexical questions make an appeal via syntax, and endoxical questions make an appeal via semantics.

Formation

A speaker can form an endoxical question from any syntactic formation possible. This is broader than Aristotle, who originally held that endoxical questions should be formed as polar questions.[55] Since the interests of the writers of the GNT were not as focused and limited as Aristotle's interests, we will treat endoxical questions more broadly than Aristotle. At the same time, the most powerful and notable endoxical questions tend to be formed with either a polar formation or as a tag question (cf. §4.W). In essence, though, the only requirement for a question to be an endoxical question is semantic. Endoxical questions must contain a reference, implicit or explicit, to some prevailing ἔνδοξα and

---

53. Macagno and Walton, "Argumentative Structure," 535.
54. Aristotle himself was known to refute ἔνδοξα; see Rubinelli, *Ars Topica*, 46.
55. Aristotle, *Topics*.

in such a way that it affects the asking of the question. One possible tell that a question is an endoxical question is if the question is a polar question that uses the verb "know," though this is by no means a guarantee.[56] In some cases, the ἔνδοξον will appear in a conditional clause. Finally, a speaker can use endoxical questions in almost any pragmatic situation, although they tend to be slightly more common in first-turn, standalone (highly answerable) situations.

The sole factor in the formation and identification of an endoxical question is described below.

1) Endoxical Questions Contain a Semantic Appeal to a Common Knowledge Base

Endoxical questions must contain ἔνδοξα, generally accepted opinions that form part of the point of the question or serve the larger argument scheme. To be considered an endoxical question, the ἔνδοξον must be integral to the point of the question. For example:

(5) οὐκ ᾔδειτε ὅτι ἐν τοῖς τοῦ πατρός μου δεῖ εἶναί με; (LUKE 2:49B)

In (5), Jesus asks his parents, "Didn't you know that I must be in my Father's house (or affairs)?" as the second part of a double question (§5.D.1). Pragmatically, Jesus intends the double-question string to work together to argue his point. The first part of the question string, "Why did you look for me?" is a proof question, and thus it is designed to elicit an answer of the "because" kind (§4.G). But Jesus does not allow his parents to respond; he immediately follows the proof question with a negative polar question, which is what gives the second question the strong feeling that Jesus is asserting why his parents did not need to search for him. However, there is something else going on in this question. Jesus does not respond in a simple manner; instead, he asks his parents a question that presupposes a certain accepted truth of common knowledge in the ancient world, namely, that a son should be about his father's business. By appealing ever so slightly to this accepted truth, Jesus links his paternity to God instead of to Joseph, which is why his parents did not understand what he was saying (v. 50).

Rhetorical Effects

Informational
Rhetorical

Endoxical questions possess strong informational qualities and mild to moderate rhetorical qualities. In many cases, they are similar to open and decisive question types, with the little extra rhetorical effect that comes from the appeal to common knowledge outside the question itself. Therefore, in most cases their

56. The verb *know* is part of a class of verbs called *factive verbs* that help convey an asker's presuppositions more than nonfactive verbs (Kartunnen, "Implicative Verbs," 285); thus they naturally make a useful vehicle for endoxical questions.

rhetorical effect on the audience is slight. The exception to this comes when the common knowledge is a little less common, or the expert wisdom is not accepted by the audience. In those cases, the rhetorical effect will be more pronounced (but still subtle).

The two most important rhetorical effects of endoxical questions are described below.

1) Endoxical Questions Can Boost Credibility and Strengthen an Argument

The primary reason ancient Greek speakers used ἔνδοξα was to simplify and strengthen their arguments. They reasoned that if two disputants could start at a common point of departure, resolution could be easier (or the one choosing from ἔνδοξα was more likely to be victorious). For example:

(6) Πῶς δύναται ἄνθρωπος ἁμαρτωλὸς τοιαῦτα σημεῖα ποιεῖν; (JOHN 9:16)

Example (6) occurs when some of the Pharisees asked themselves, "How is it possible that this sinful man can do such signs?" in the face of Jesus healing the man born blind. This question is primarily a means question (§4.H) in that it seeks an answer to explain a possibility, but it has a secondary endoxical quality to it as well. In asking the question, these Pharisees are making an appeal to the commonly held belief that a sinful person cannot participate in divine activities (especially miracles and signs) to suggest that, based on the evidence just observed, Jesus cannot be a sinner. Thus they use the ἔνδοξον cited—not the signs themselves—to show they are at odds with what the others suggest (that Jesus is not from God). Because it was acceptable to use ἔνδοξα as evidence, these Pharisees' argument was as strong as the argument of the first set of Pharisees, creating a σχίσμα ("division") among the Pharisees.

2) Endoxical Questions Can Unfairly Push a Conclusion

While endoxical questions can be a helpful feature of discourse, they have a darker side that emerges when a speaker uses them to argue for a premise that the audience does not agree with or is not well founded. When the endoxical is not agreed upon or is unnoticed by the audience, it can make it more difficult for hearers to attempt replies. For example:

(7) μὴ σὺ μείζων εἶ τοῦ πατρὸς ἡμῶν Ἀβραάμ, ὅστις ἀπέθανεν, καὶ οἱ προφῆται ἀπέθανον; (JOHN 8:53)

Example (7) occurs in a middle dialogue position, and it is a polar question with a negative polarity item; it is mostly meant as a challenge to Jesus, asking (asserting) whether he could be greater than their father Abraham—"You're not greater than our father Abraham—who died, along with the prophets?" However, the question also has a built-in ἔνδοξον based on the Judaean myth of the greatness of Abraham. By appealing to this ἔνδοξον, the question is in a sense unanswerable, as it would be hard to make a comparison between Jesus and Abraham. In fact, it is so hard, the Judaeans do not believe it is possible to answer (John 8:53c). Instead of submitting to the point of the question, Jesus actually challenges it (John 8:56), which continues to amplify the alarm felt by the Judaeans (John 8:57). By citing the conventional wisdom of the greatness of Abraham, the Judaeans hoped to push their conclusion before the crowds about who Jesus really was.

Case Study — 1 CORINTHIANS 3:16

οὐκ οἴδατε ὅτι ναὸς θεοῦ ἐστε καὶ τὸ πνεῦμα τοῦ θεοῦ οἰκεῖ ἐν ὑμῖν;

PAUL: Don't you know that you are the temple of God and the Spirit of God dwells in you?

In his first letter to the Corinthians, Paul reaches a point in the argument where he recognizes that he must address the Corinthians not as spiritual but as worldly people (1 Cor 3:3). This is evidenced in the fact that they are using human slogans (of whom they follow) to define who they are (1 Cor 3:4–8) rather than recognize that they are God's γεώργιον ("farmland") and οἰκοδομή ("building"). Continuing this metaphor, Paul admits that while many can participate in the building of a church, the foundation cannot be anything or anyone other than Jesus (1 Cor 3:11). When people add to this foundation, their works will be tested and the results tallied (1 Cor 3:13–15). Paul then uses the question, "Don't you know that you are the temple of God and the Spirit of God lives in you?" to make what seems to be a rather surprising shift of focus in his argument.

Paul's question is a negative polar question, and given the fact that it appears in rhetorical discourse, both the EGH principle (§2.C.6) and the rhetorical-shift principle (§2.D.9) apply here—it is a strong rhetorical question that asks the reader whether they know what they should know, asserting that they should know they are the temple of God and the house for the Holy Spirit. However, this question does have an endoxical element to it; if nothing else, Paul seems to believe strongly that the Corinthians should know this as a matter of principle. Paul uses this tactic frequently in this letter.[57] This belief is not a new doctrine, as evidenced by Paul's frequent use of this type of question, but a grander view than the Corinthians seem to have of themselves.[58] This creates what Aristotle might call a *dialectical problem*—a situation where people hold a different view than those more studied on an issue.[59] This is the situation that Paul finds

57. For example, 1 Cor 5:6; 6:2, 3, 9, 15, 16, 19; 9:13, 24.

58. Thiselton, *First Epistle to the Corinthians*, 316; Conzelmann, *1 Corinthians*, 77.

59. Aristotle, *Topics* 104b4–5.

himself in—convincing a group of people a truth that should be axiomatic to them.[60] Yet what is often missed in Paul's asking this question is that he uses an appeal to what the Corinthians should know to convince them of what they need to know. By making a mild appeal to wise ἔνδοξα, Paul hopes to persuade the Corinthians to live up to the standard of holiness that God desires of them.

FURTHER EXAMPLES
Luke 5:30; 6:2; John 8:48; 9:2; 1 Cor 5:6; 6:2, 3, 9, 15, 16, 19; 9:13, 24.

Key Bibliography
Anagnostopoulos, "Aristotle's Methods"; Cain, *Socratic Method*, 39–46; Modrak, *Aristotle's Theory*, 132–42; Pritzl, "Opinions as Appearances"; Rubinelli, *Ars Topica*, 33–37; Slomkowski, *Aristotle's* Topics, 19–24.

K. Phatic Questions

A *phatic question* is an interrogative-appearing utterance oriented as much toward social interaction as it is toward informational or rhetorical purposes. In general, *phatic* is the term describing communication (or communion) that fulfills social expectations (*CDL* 338). As a relatively new term in linguistics, phatic communication does not have a strong definition.[61] Phatic questions are those that play some social role in their asking and help to create bonding between the asker and hearers. This does not mean phatic questions do not have both informational and rhetorical purposes; it is that the informational and rhetorical purposes are secondary to the social purposes of the question.

When forming a phatic question, a speaker may ask one of two types. The first is a question that an asker asks solely to conform to social expectations (and thus are not questions by our definition). The second is a question that an asker asks that has become colloquialized due to social uses (and thus may mean something quite different from a literal reading). Especially with the former, phatic questions may not appear to be well formed or follow proper grammatical rules within the language. For example:

(1) What's up? (PHATIC QUESTION)
(2) *Was geht ab*? (PHATIC QUESTION)
(3) *Ça va*? (PHATIC QUESTION)

60. Thiselton, *First Epistle to the Corinthians*, 316.
61. Žegarac, "Phatic Communication," 327–61. Our definition for phatic communication comes through the works of Malinowksi and Jakobson and is not the same as the "phatic act" of Austin; see Senft, "Phatic Communion," 227.

Examples (1), (2), and (3) are all examples of phatic questions—in each case, greetings, in IE languages. Each of these tend to represent the second type of phatic communication; while colloquialized, they nonetheless are used by speakers for informational and rhetorical effect in most situations. Note that more formal greetings are also forms of phatic communication, but their formality can make them less obvious.

Greetings such as these are one type of well-known phatic communication that typically occurs as questions. Since the greatest challenge for identifying phatic communication in ancient texts is our lack of intimate knowledge about cultural practices, greetings and closings make a great place to start in understanding phatic communion in ancient Greek practice. Unfortunately, if recovered letters from the ancient world are any indication, the use of phatic questions in written texts is far less frequent than in modern, everyday oral communication. As a result, there are only a few questions in the GNT that may play a phatic role, and it is to be expected that they will be more formal than their everyday, oral counterparts.

Formation

Phatic questions are formed from the social (semantic and pragmatic) aspects applied to the use and circumstances of the questions. They do not have any syntactic requirements for formation. However, variable-question formations are the most commonly used in phatic questions. Polar phatic questions do exist, whereas some syntactic formations for questions (such as composite formations) are less likely to be used by speakers in phatic communication. Phatic communication tends toward brevity in many IE languages. As a result, phatic questions often stress social interest over grammatical correctness. One tell that a question could be used phatically is poor or irregular grammatical formation that is not easily translated. Another tell is that phatic questions are often highly implicative. Semantically, phatic questions are usually open, vague, or ambiguous in content. Phatic questions can occur in any turn and in any position in dialogue, though it is less common for them to occupy a middle position (outside of rhetorical discourse) or to be a part of a question string.

The primary factor in the formation and identification of phatic questions is described below.

1) Phatic Questions Fulfill a Social Function in an Utterance

The one constant of a phatic question is that it must communicate something social, beyond simply the informational and the rhetorical. We can get a glimpse of this in questions and expressions that have become colloquialized and included in written texts. However, determining the precise meaning of the phatic question is difficult. For example:

(4) τί ἐμοὶ καὶ σοί, γύναι; (JOHN 2:4)

The question in John 2:4, perhaps able to be rendered in English as, "Woman, what do you want with me?" is probably the most famous (and most obvious) phatic question in the GNT. Certainly it is the most studied. Most of the focus is on the perceived rudeness of the expression coming from Jesus, but this simply serves as additional evidence that the question is phatic. The meaning of the question is not based on the literal grammar. To understand what Jesus is asking, the interpreter must consider the context far more than the wording. With (4), Jesus uses a phatic question that is very informal in order to communicate in a brief, conversational way with his mother (who also is very brief and informal with her son; see v. 3). Interpreters miss the most important part of this utterance—that Jesus uses informal slang to ask his mother a question, which in narrative dialogue indicates a close relationship between two characters.

Rhetorical Effects

Informational *Rhetorical*

Phatic questions are more common in oral discourse than written discourse. Much of their rhetorical effects are built on the semantic and pragmatic use of the question in the given social situation. With written texts such as the GNT, phatic questions can occur in both narrative discourse and rhetorical discourse. When phatic questions occur in narrative discourse, one of their most important rhetorical effects is to stress the relationship between the asker and the hearer. When phatic questions occur in rhetorical discourse, one of their most important rhetorical effects is to stress the intended relationship between the orator (or writer) and the audience.

Thus, the most important rhetorical effect of phatic questions is as described below.

1) Phatic Questions Create a Social Connection between the Asker and Hearer(s)

When a speaker asks a phatic question, it creates a connection that is based on a social convention or expectation. The speaker can then use this social connection to persuasive effect in the asking of the question. The depth of social connection that a speaker creates with hearers through phatic communication can vary greatly. Using greetings as an example, some greetings are intended to start a conversation without seeming rude while others are genuine greetings of warmth and affection (thus indicating the depth of the bond). In rhetorical discourse, a speaker may use a phatic question to not only persuade the audience (rhetorical) but also to connect with the audience on a social or personal level (phatic). For example:

(5) Τί γάρ; (PHIL 1:18)

Question (5) comes in the midst of an argument by Paul, and at first glance the question seems only to be a typical middle-position question with the typical rhetorical effect that is common in oratory (§5.C). However, Paul's use of a colloquial expression has an additional mild rhetorical effect due to its phatic use. In this passage, Paul talks about good and bad reasons to preach Christ (Phil 1:15–17) and instead of pausing to ask a more formal rhetorical question, drops a τί γάρ ("so what?") on his audience before pointing out that what really matters is that Christ is preached. Why this question works so well in this context is that it is a mildly phatic expression meant to speak to the audience on a deeper level than the literal words. Since the rhetorical effect of (5) remains intact, it carries the peak of the argument for the reader on a persuasive (rhetorical) and connective (phatic) level.

Case Study — 1 CORINTHIANS 14:26

Τί οὖν ἐστιν, ἀδελφοί;

PAUL: So what, brothers??

In 1 Corinthians 14, Paul begins an argument with the Corinthian church that they are to earnestly desire the gifts of the Spirit (especially prophecy). Paul then spends some time contrasting the use of the gift of prophecy with the use of the gift of tongues and explains his preference toward prophecy (vv. 2–5). To do this, he essentially makes two arguments. First, since many people cannot understand the use of foreign tongues, using these tongues with each other creates "foreigners" out of each other (vv. 6–12). Second, if tongues are used, they should be able to be interpreted so that people will be able to understand since "in church five words understood" is much greater than "ten thousand words in a tongue" (vv. 13–19). After referring his readers to the Old Testament (vv. 20–21), Paul explains why prophecy is better for nonbelievers, as the church is to remain outwardly focused in its ministry (vv. 22–25). Reaching the conclusion of his argument on tongues and prophecy, Paul turns the corner in his argument, asking, "So what, brothers??" He then takes his readers toward the practical implications of his arguments.

If we start with the logic and rhetoric of this question, we see Paul forms the question as a variable question that semantically appears to be open. Though it occurs in the middle of rhetorical discourse, Paul appears to use the question as a hinge between two related topics. This may lead us to an expository question (§5.A.2) within rhetorical discourse except that the question does not presuppose or give any indication of the next topic—it is quite short and ambiguous. By way of comparison, the first part of the clause does occur in Luke 20:17 (also 2 Clem. 5.6), though there it is part of a more complete utterance. Further, the same exact wording and similar usage occurs earlier in 1 Corinthians 14:15 and also in Acts 21:22. If we compare with the LXX, τί οὖν ἐστιν; does not occur, but τί ἐστιν; does, asked as a complete thought in dialogue (for example, Gen 21:17; 22:7; 31:11; 46:2; Exod 3:4; Esth 5:1f, 6; Sir 22:10; Zech 5:6; Isa 65:24). Perhaps most interesting is Sirach 22:10 wherein the question is put on the lips of a sleepy person who can't follow the story.[62] Finally, the difficulty in establishing a definitive English translation is telling. Thus, all evidence points to some kind of phatic question.

To interpret 1 Corinthians 14:26, we cannot look at the literal meaning of the words for overall guidance. While the clause is not ungrammatical, it is used throughout the LXX and the GNT to typify a phatic response that is expected within conversation. The meaning of the question is therefore tied to its social function. In narrative dialogue, speakers tend to use the phatic question as a response, to acknowledge hearing the speaker. In rhetorical discourse such as 1 Corinthians, τί οὖν ἐστιν; carries the effect of acknowledgement coupled with exasperation or anxiety about what would come next. Since this is an expressive and pragmatic feature of language written down in the midst of an oral-based culture, we cannot say for certain exactly what spin it would have had when read aloud by the first readers of 1 Corinthians. We can say that Paul uses a colloquial expression to acknowledge for his readers that his point is made and to push them with emotion to engage the next line of his thinking. So what? As a strongly rhetorical type of question, Paul's "so what, brothers??" raises the reader's attention with a needed break and provides a little social glue to help the reader prepare for Paul's next step in his discourse.

FURTHER EXAMPLES

Matt 8:29a; 27:4; Mark 1:24a; 5:7; Luke 4:34a; 8:28; Rom 3:9a; 1 Cor 14:15.

Key Bibliography

Allott, *Key Terms*, 138–39; Finch, *Linguistics*, 22–26; Hultgren and Cameron, "'How May I Help You?'" 330–31; Senft, "Phatic Communion," 226–33; Wilce, *Language and Emotion*, 81–82; Žegarac, "Phatic Communication," 327–61.

L. Test Questions

Test questions are asked so that the speaker may evaluate a response given by the responder. Test questions are also called *exam questions* or *quiz questions*. When

62. In Aristophanes, *Clouds* 82, 825, τί ἐστιν; is translated "what's the matter?" (Rogers, LCL), similar to "what is it?" or "so what?"

an asker asks a test question, they do so to determine whether the audience knows an answer or not. Usually there is some implication implied if an answer is not known. Test questions are a common question type in everyday situations and occur regularly wherever dialogue occurs (for example, historical narrative, modern fiction, and institutional discourse). Since they depend on the goals of the asker, to interpret them requires an accurate understanding of the context in which the question occurs. Test questions have a range of special informational and rhetorical purposes as they are designed to provoke a hearer to respond to the question. However, responses are not good indicators of whether a question is actually a test question or not—poor responses or no response at all to a test question does not make it any less of a test question (cf. §2.E). For example:

(1) What is the largest suburb in the US? (TEST QUESTION)
(2) What color is the sky? (TEST OR INAPPOSITE)

In example (1), we presume that the asker knows the answer to the question, but the audience does not. In this case, the asker asks to see if the audience knows the answer. This type of question could be asked in a classroom discussion, on a test, or as part of a quiz game, for example. In example (2), context greatly shapes whether we interpret the question as a test question or something else. If the asker asks the question under a typical blue sky, it probably would be an inapposite question (§4.M). If the asker asks the question to toddlers during a beautiful sunset, it could be a test question. Because of the contextually based nature of test questions, it is difficult to diagnose them in artificial discourse.

When we encounter potential test questions in representational discourse, there are still challenges in their interpretation. In rhetorical discourse, it is usually not easy to tell when a question is a test question meant for the audience (unless the writer of the discourse makes this plain). In rhetorical discourse, test questions may naturally overlap with a great number of other question types such as open questions (§4.A) or decision questions (§4.Q). In narrative discourse, there can be a great deal of overlap between test questions and riddle questions (§4.N), speculative questions (§4.B), inapposite questions (§4.M) or dilemma questions (§4.O).

This raises a particularly thorny question in reading the Gospels. In most narratives, characters within the narrative typically have a limited knowledge base, and thus their use of test questions is limited to teaching and testing based on that limited knowledge base. The exception to this is the rare instance in Western narratives where the narrator will intervene in an aside and ask a question that blurs the boundaries between what the reader may or may not assume the narrator knows. This is different from the Gospels in which the narratives set up the character Jesus with an atypical knowledge base (what is sometimes called Jesus's *epistemic supremacy*). At times, the reader is left wondering whether Jesus does in fact know the answer to most all of the questions he asks. This is accentuated by the common reference to Jesus as ῥαββί. If so, the cynical interpreter may feel that the Gospel writers do not have Jesus actually ask any questions for purely informational reasons but simply to put his interlocutors to the test. As a whole, this approach seems to be an overreading of the text, and an interpreter should not rush to categorize most or all the questions of Jesus as test questions.

Formation

A test question is driven purely by its semantics and context. A writer or speaker can form a test question from any type of question syntax and with either positive or negative polarity. Semantically, the only requirement for a test question is that it must convey a strong informational quality (so that a hearer will want to respond). The audience does not necessarily have to understand that the question is meant as a test. Normally, a test question will not carry bias; strong bias included in the question will affect the way the question is heard by the audience and potentially become a leading question (§4.W). Pragmatics matter a great deal in the asking of test questions; test questions are not usually asked from the opening or middle position, though they can occur in any turn of dialogue.

The two main factors in the formation and identification of test questions are explained below.

1) Test Questions May Be Noted as Such by the Asker or by the Context

In some cases, the asker is a teacher or functioning in a teaching capacity, and the question will be easily recognized as a test question. Often the asker will admit that the question asked is a test question. Sometimes this admission is explicitly stated, but more often it is recognized by the audience based upon the context of the question. In many cases, the test question is not designed to be tricky (other than it being a test). When the test question is admitted, it is the most obvious way for an interpreter to know whether or not a question functions as a test question. Explicit and implicit identifications of test questions occur in the Gospels. For example:

(3) εἰ ἔξεστιν ἀνθρώπῳ ἀπολῦσαι τὴν γυναῖκα αὐτοῦ
κατὰ πᾶσαν αἰτίαν; (MATT 19:3)

Here Matthew records that the Pharisees came to Jesus πειράζοντες αὐτὸν ("testing him") and asking him, "If [you can tell us whether] it is lawful for a man to divorce his wife for any reason?" The Pharisees form the question as a polar question, implying that a yes or no answer is required. However, they also use εἰ ἔξεστιν to phrase it as a request question (§4.S) as if they simply want Jesus to respond. The goal of the question is to determine whether Jesus can give any reason whereby a person may get a divorce (especially in the light of what Moses seemingly allowed).[63] In this case, the reader is clear that the question is primarily intended as a test question based on the hint of the narrator, how the question is asked, and to a lesser extent by the general context of the question.

2) Test Questions Occur if the Audience Believes the Asker Knows the Answer

If the audience thinks the asker knows the answer to the question and is asking just to see how and whether a hearer will respond, the question will be understood as a test question. In representational discourse, sometimes the reader must read the text for insights into the thoughts of the asker. In those cases, readers will identify test questions based on the probability of the asker knowing the answer and the purpose of the question from the perspective of the asker. For example:

(4) τίνα ζητεῖτε; (JOHN 18:4)

In (4), Jesus asks the group that Judas leads, "Whom do you seek?" The reader is made aware by the narrator of John's Gospel that Jesus was εἰδὼς πάντα τὰ ἐρχόμενα ἐπ' αὐτὸν ("knowing everything that was coming on him"; John 18:4a). Thus the reader knows that Jesus knows the answer to the question and reads it as a test question, though the original audience of characters in the Gospel may or may not have perceived it the same way. In John, the use of ζητέω can indicate the need for reflection (cf. 1:38a), enhancing the purpose of the question for a reply to be thought about and made. In either case, the question comes off as a test question because both hearers and readers expect in general that Jesus knows he is the one being sought—he asks merely to see how Judas and company will respond.

Rhetorical Effects

Informational
Rhetorical

Test questions contain strong informational qualities and milder rhetorical qualities. As a general rule, if a question is not asked to gain a response, it cannot be considered a test question (whether an actual attempt to respond is made or not). Even though test questions cannot have strong rhetorical qualities (without moving into another type of question), they still do have some important rhetorical effects that a speaker can exploit to persuade an audience. Asking a test question creates an *i-predicament* (§2.C.7) since the asker already knows (or is presumed to know) the answer to the question. The i-predicament encourages the hearer to evaluate why the speaker asks a question to which the answer is already known.

63. For further discussion, Turner, *Grammatical Insights*, 61.

Two of the more notable rhetorical effects of test questions are explained below.

1) Test Questions Are Asked to Prod a Hearer to Try to Give a Reply

One way speakers use test questions is to assess the knowledge level of a listener. To do this, the question must prod the hearer into giving a reply. If a question is too vague or too pointed, it will not work well as a test question. Thus, this rhetorical effect must be implicit in what is asked to be most effective (or the context must dictate that a response is mandatory, such as in a classroom). In this case, a question that ordinarily appears to be a rather average question with strong informational value can be altered through the semantics of the interrogative logic or pragmatics of the situation to become a test question. For example:

(5) ὑμεῖς δὲ τίνα με λέγετε εἶναι; (MARK 8:29)

Here Jesus asks the disciples, "Who do you say I am?" Since Jesus presumably knows who he is, the reader may take the question as inapposite (§4.M). However, in the context in which the question occurs there is discussion as to the identity of Jesus (most significant in Mark's Gospel). Since the disciples presume that Jesus knows the answer to the question, they are put in an i-predicament that would make them hesitant to guess incorrectly (lest they fail the test). However, as Jesus asks the disciples directly (following the argumentative warm-up in 8:27), it is hard for them to avoid replying. Mark records only Peter's response; presumably he answers correctly. Peter's response while in an i-predicament implicitly suggests to the reader that Peter's character quality is brave or bold.

2) Test Questions Are Asked to See How a Listener Will Respond

Another rhetorical effect of test questions occurs when they are used by a speaker to see what type of response can be elicited from a listener. When used this way, test questions become provocative. Test questions can be very effective as an information-gathering tool, but with this rhetorical effect the tool is not one that looks to extract a (correct) answer to the question so much as to extract a reply from the listener that the speaker can use to evaluate the responder's position or viewpoint. In such cases, a speaker may even use test questions to try to prove a responder wrong or show the ignorance of the responder.[64] In argumentation, the asker may ask this type of question—knowing the answer—with the purpose of seeing whether or not the audience knows the (correct) answer. For example:

(6) σὺ εἶ ὁ βασιλεὺς τῶν Ἰουδαίων; (MATT 27:11)

Pilate's question to Jesus is a polar question: "Are you the king of the Judaeans?"

64. For example, Aristotle, *Posterior Analytics* 71a31–33.

Based on clues in Matthew's Gospel (notably 27:13), the reader knows that Pilate must know something of the accusations against Jesus. Therefore, it is not likely Pilate asks this question without any prior knowledge. It is also clear from the discourse that an exact answer is probably not known to Pilate. Since the question is formed as a polar question in a pointed and decisive manner, it seems probable that Pilate asks this question as a test question to find out just how Jesus will respond. As a test question, it is not that Pilate hopes to gain information *in* the answer (a clear and reasoned *answer* concerning Jesus's royal position) as much as it is that Pilate hopes to gain information *from* the response (in the type of *response* Jesus offers). Finally, we note the phatic response that Jesus makes to the question; while not a tell for a test question, it does alert the reader that Jesus may be aware that Pilate is up to something.

Case Study — JOHN 6:5

πόθεν ἀγοράσωμεν ἄρτους ἵνα φάγωσιν οὗτοι;

JESUS: Where may we buy bread so that these people may eat?

Throughout Jesus's public ministry, large crowds follow him wherever he goes. On one occasion near the festival of Passover, Jesus crosses over to the far side of the sea of Galilee and the crowds follow him there (John 6:1–2). Much of their interest in Jesus is due to his healing of the sick. After crossing over, Jesus goes up on the mountainside and sits down with his disciples. When Jesus sees the large crowd coming, he looks over at Philip and asks, "Where may we buy bread so that these people may eat?" At this point the narrator interjects, telling the reader that Jesus asks this to test Philip, as Jesus is already aware of what he will do.

Jesus's question in John 6:5 may be the test question *par excellence* in the GNT. Jesus forms the question as a variable question using πόθεν, which normally might suggest an open question. Looking at the grammar suggests otherwise; a verbal subjunctive and a causal subjunctive clause is a semantic move that tips the reader off that the question may not be a straightforward informational question. Of course, most explicit is the narrator's intervention in v. 6 where readers are told the question is a test from Jesus to Philip. Even if Philip is unaware that Jesus intends to test him, later readers are made aware by the narrator.

Knowing the question is a test question only gets the interpreter so far. In this situation, what becomes critical is knowing the rhetorical effects placed on the question. Does Jesus ask the question to see if Philip will answer the question correctly? Does Philip "know the answer"? For example, perhaps Philip could have replied, "I believe that you can provide the bread that we could never buy" (cf. v. 27). Or does Jesus ask the question to see what kind of reply Philip will make—perhaps whether the answer leans toward faith or away from faith? For example, Philip could have replied, "I don't know, but I believe you have the answer." As both replies work, it could be either, though most interpreters will opt for the latter. Either way, Philip's answer in 6:7 would fall short of Jesus's expectation of his test for his disciples—Philip would appear to have "failed" the test.

FURTHER EXAMPLES
Matt 16:13, 15; 22:36; Mark 8:27; Luke 10:26a, 26b; John 18:7; 20:15a, 15b; 21:15–17; Heb 3:16a, 17a, 18; Rev 7:13.

Key Bibliography
Blakemore, *Understanding Utterances*, 114; Estes, *Questions*, 87–91; Fiengo, *Asking Questions*, 77–79; Heritage and Clayman, *Talk in Action*, 28; Korta and Perry, *Critical Pragmatics*, 87–88; Searle, *Speech Acts*, 66; Wilson and Sperber, *Meaning and Relevance*, 222–27.

M. Inapposite Questions

Inapposite questions are asked by askers who already know an answer to the question asked, and they know an answer in an obvious or pointed way. The asker may know the answer because the information is known to them or because it is presumed to be known by them.[65] The answer known by the asker need not be the only correct answer or even a correct answer, as long as the answer is believed to be correct by the audience (§2.E.). In a sense, inapposite questions are questions that an audience would feel as not needing to be asked. The fact that an asker does ask an inapposite question points to one of several rhetorical effects of these types of questions. For example:

(1) What is 2 + 2? (INAPPOSITE QUESTION)
(2) A Californian: "What state is the Golden State?" (INAPPOSITE QUESTION)
(3) A seminarian: "How many books are in the Bible?" (INAPPOSITE QUESTION)

Example (1) is an inapposite question since it is generally understood that everyone knows the answer to this question. The purpose of asking (1) is probably to mock the audience in some way. Both (2) and (3) are also examples of inapposite questions because in both situations the audience would naturally presume the asker to know an answer to the question (or should know an answer to the

65. Heinemann, "Inapposite Inquiries," 159–61.

question). Since the audience presumes the asker to know an answer, the audience is now forced to wonder why the asker would ask such a question. With example (2), it could be that the asker is truly unaware that California is the Golden State. With example (3), it could be that the asker intends to test the audience or mock them. However, these scenarios for (2) and (3) are unlikely. Much more likely is that questions (2) and (3) are inapposite, and the effect on the audience will be to cause them to wonder why the asker is asking such a question. Thus, inapposite questions are moderately implicative in most situations. With all three examples, if the context changed to a classroom setting (for example), the questions would become test questions (§4.L).

Formation

Inapposite questions are determined by the semantic and pragmatic qualities of the question. Since any question formation can be inapposite, there are no restrictions on the syntactic formation of inapposite questions. Inapposite questions can equally be positive or negative polarity, and have a reasonable amount of bias. There are also little restrictions on the pragmatic qualities of inapposite questions; they can appear in any dialogue turn. A speaker can also use an inapposite question in any dialogue position with the caveat that an opening- or middle-position use can make the question seem spurious or condescending (as if it is fully intended to mock the audience) since there is no window for a response.

The primary factor in the formation and identification of an inapposite question is explained below.

1) Inapposite Questions Contain Obvious References to an Asker-Known Answer

Many questions that are traditionally included in the category of "rhetorical question" can appear inapposite at first glance. This is because their rhetorical effects make them appear as if the asker already knows an answer. However, to be notably inapposite, what the question asks should be perceptibly known by the asker. This knowledge situation needs to be apparent to the audience. Furthermore, it is not enough that the asker could guess at a reply; the asker must know (or be perceived to know) an answer in an obvious way. For example:

(4) Τί οὖν ὁ νόμος; (GAL 3:19)

A first reading of (4) indicates the question is primarily a proof question (§4.G). When Paul asks his readers, "Then why the law?" he asks them to consider the rationale for the law and wants them to reflect on the fact that "the law was given + *because*..." However, a deeper reading leads to a second semantic quality—an inapposite quality. After all, this is the same Paul about whom the audience knows (Gal 1:13), about how his zeal for Pharisaical Judaism drove him to be against Christians until God's call of grace (vv. 13–24), and about how he was able to debate circumcision with other Jews in Jerusalem (2:3–12). This Paul, a Pharisee and zealot, should *obviously* and *apparently* know why the law was given, and what the purpose of the law is. In fact, even asking a question such as "why the law?" in general is inherently inapposite given its religious and cultural role. In this case, Paul uses an inapposite question to take a jab at the Galatians—they should already know the purpose of the law without having Paul need to ask. The Galatians should already know about the law as they knew about Christ (2:15–16).

Rhetorical Effects

Informational
Rhetorical

Inapposite questions are mildly information seeking and moderately rhetorical in their asking. They give hearers pause about how to respond appropriately. Because hearers presume that the question asker should know the answer to the question, these types of questions put hearers in *i-predicaments* (§2.C.7). Inapposite questions are related to test questions (§4.L) in that with both types of questions, the asker should know the answer to the question. The difference (and overlap) between test questions and inapposite questions is complex semantically and pragmatically; the most notable difference is pragmatic, as an asker uses test questions for a narrow reason whereas an asker may have many different reasons for asking an inapposite question.

Two of the most notable rhetorical effects of inapposite questions are described below.

1) Inapposite Questions Can Embarrass the Asker

An inapposite question can reveal that the asker is not as aware of something as they should be. This happens when the asker doesn't realize that they know something—or when they should know something, and the audience agrees that they should indeed know the something. Often when a speaker asks an inapposite question, the reaction from the audience comes across as "how could you ask that?" For example:

(5) Τίς ἐστιν ἡ μήτηρ μου καὶ οἱ ἀδελφοί [μου]; (MARK 3:33)

In Mark 3, Jesus is told by the crowd sitting around him that his mother and brothers have arrived. Surprisingly, Jesus responds to this information by asking the inapposite question (5), "Who are my mother and my brothers?" To both hearers and readers, this is a bizarre question as almost everyone is very aware of who their mother and brothers would be. In fact, it would be shocking and embarrassing to hear someone ask such a question. Readers often see this as a dig at or disavowal of his family.[66] The reason the question can seem to be a dig at his family is that the question has a repair function (§5.B.4), which means

66. For example, Thurston, *Preaching Mark*, 42; Juel, *Mark*, 65.

at first glance the question comes across as Jesus needing clarification (and it is therefore insulting). Yet a conversation cannot be repaired if the knowledge needed for repair is already generally known. Because the question is so obvious, the semantics grate against the repair function, resulting in the *opposite* of Jesus taking a dig against his family. By asking this question, Jesus makes himself look absurd—no person in their right mind would ask something so inane as who their family is.[67] Jesus then turns the "embarrassment" of not appearing to know who his family is back on the crowd to persuade them that his family is whoever does the will of God (v. 35). Because Jesus is willing to embarrass himself to ask an obvious question, it persuades those with him to embarrass themselves a little to ask themselves also who might be their family and to ask whether fellow believers might better be thought of as their family after all.

2) Inapposite Questions Can Ridicule a Hearer

Because inapposite questions are known in an obvious way to the asker, and they cause an effect of making the audience wonder why the asker is bothering to ask the question, the audience may conclude that the asker is asking such a question to trick or ridicule the audience. For example, an adult asking (1) to other adults will come across in an insulting way to the audience. Likewise, if a seminarian asks (3), the audience will not believe the question is legitimate and will wonder if there is some trick involved. For example:

(6) Οὐκ ἀνέγνωτε ὅτι ὁ κτίσας ἀπ' ἀρχῆς ἄρσεν καὶ θῆλυ ἐποίησεν αὐτούς; (MATT 19:4)

In example (6), Jesus responds to the Pharisees' opening question with his own question, "Haven't you read that from the beginning the Creator made them male and female?" Here Jesus forms the question as a negative polar question, but the pragmatic and semantic intent of the question supercedes its syntax. The most important feature of this question is its pragmatics, as Jesus's question functions as an opposing-turn question (§5.B.1). Thus, Jesus's primary intent is to push back against the Pharisees' question. Yet the most striking feature is its semantics, as the wording of the question indicates that Jesus uses this question as an inapposite question. Thus, he is neither asking if they have read these texts nor asserting that they have not read these texts nor suggesting that they do read these texts. Instead, he is asking about their reading of these texts in such an obvious way that both Jesus and the audience know the answer. (Of course, they have read these texts.) But by asking this inapposite question, Jesus not only pushes back on them through opposing-turn pragmatics but amplifies the pushback by questioning their reading skills. After all, during this time period even small children would have read the beginning of Genesis (reading in the

67. Or someone who is "demented"; Hooker, *Saint Mark*, 118.

sense of what we would today call public reading), and so this question is both inapposite and belittling to the Pharisees.

Case Study JOHN 18:35A

Μήτι ἐγὼ Ἰουδαῖός εἰμι;

PILATE: I'm not a Judaean?

During the trial before Pilate, Jesus and Pilate engage in question-and-answer dialogue that is reminiscent of Greek disputation in its structure, even if it comes across as abbreviated and informal to the modern reader. The trial begins when the Judaean leaders take Jesus to stand before Pilate, the Roman governor (John 18:28). Because of Passover considerations, the first part of the dialogue takes place outside (vv. 29–32), but when it became obvious that the Judaean leaders were seeking execution for Jesus, Pilate takes Jesus inside the palace where the Judaean leadership cannot go (v. 33). Pilate begins his disputation with Jesus with a classic dialectical question, "You are the king of the Jews?" meant to establish the grounds for the enquiry.[68] While this question may seem unusual to modern readers, it was a common strategy for handling legal cases in the ancient world. From Pilate's perspective, he would begin the disputation (with a polar question), and Jesus would pick which side of the question he wanted to defend. This is not what happens; Jesus does not "play the game" and instead responds with an opposing-turn question (v. 34). Not only is Jesus oppositional, he actually almost phrases his question in a dialectical format also, strong enough that many ancient readers would have considered Jesus to be putting himself in the disputant's seat instead of Pilate. We can expect that this would be unusual under the circumstances. This situation leads us to the third question in a row, where Pilate responds to Jesus with another opposing-turn question, "I'm not a Jew?" (Cf. §2.B.9.)

Pilate's question functions pragmatically as an opposing-turn question (§5.B.1), is formed syntactically as a polar question with a negative polarity item, and is an intentional pushback against Jesus's prior question. Like all good questions in rhetorical debates, it not only has the pragmatic function, but its semantic qualities also create an amplified sense of pushback against Jesus. The question has strong rhetorical qualities and weak informational qualities—it is not primarily seeking an answer. When Pilate puts the question to Jesus, it was patently obvious to Jesus (and any hearers present) that Pilate was not Judaean (in either ethnicity or religion). Because the question is inapposite, it has the rhetorical effect of condescension and mockery. By asking this question, Pilate pushes back against Jesus by letting Jesus know that his question asking

68. Aristotle, *Topics* 101b29–33.

is unwarranted (the pragmatic function of an opposing-turn question) and that any attempt to dispute him would be met with scorn (the semantic function of an inapposite question). Pilate is not asking the question to assert that he is not Judaean; he asks the question to remind the audience how much *not* Judaean he really is.

FURTHER EXAMPLES
Mark 12:10–11; Rom 7:7b; 9:14b.

Key Bibliography
Estes, *Questions*, 88; Heinemann, "Inapposite Inquiries."

N. Riddle Questions

Riddle questions—or as they are more generally known, *riddles*—are asked to puzzle an audience through vague wordplay. Riddles are an unusual language phenomenon that show up in many, but not all, languages.[69] Riddle questions use semantics to intentionally create ambiguous situations that are then posed to the audience to see whether an answer can be given. They are often short and easily remembered with a few indefinite words or phrases. They often use simple ideas and mythic, poetic, or archetypal language. However, riddles do not require a certain sound or look to qualify as a riddle (though at times they may look and sound similar to each other).[70] Usually the archetypal nature of the subject matter of the riddle makes the question appear as if it could be easily answered (when it is not). Riddle questions may rely on humor with the motive of creating play, but they may also rely on deception with the motive of embarrassing or putting down a hearer. Riddle questions are highly information seeking, though the information they seek is known to the asker. They do possess unique rhetorical effects among hearers. Even though riddles take on interrogative force (they seek an answer), they may appear in the form of a declarative in written discourse. Riddles are implicative, as they ask for something not overtly found in the question asking. For example:

(1) What has an eye but cannot see? (RIDDLE)
(2) A box without hinges, key or lid, yet golden treasure inside is hid.[71] (RIDDLE)

69. For the sake of our work here, I avoid technical discussions of riddles and take *riddle* in the broadest sense of the word. Our interest lies more in the questioning and rhetorical effects of riddle questions than riddles, riddle play, and folklore.
70. Thatcher, *Jesus the Riddler*, 68.
71. Tolkien, *Hobbit*, 86.

In (1), the speaker asks a riddle question that seeks an answer from the audience. Since hearers will know that any creature with an eye should be able to see, the "trick" of the question becomes clear. The word *eye* is broad enough that it allows for the speaker to exploit its many meanings to create ambiguity in the questioning. This ambiguity encourages hearers to puzzle over the question until they can attempt a reply (e.g., "a needle"). However, other hearers may come up with other, equally persuasive replies ("a hurricane") or replies that may seem to work but do not feel satisfactory ("a person born blind" or "a doll"). Example (2) is a riddle that is not formed as a question but still expects a reply. In this case, the pragmatics of the riddle trump syntax; every hearer who hears this riddle will search for an adequate reply.

In some sense, riddle questions are a subset of test questions. In both cases, an asker asks one of these types of questions to gain information, but the information to be gained is not the answer to the question itself but to learn how the hearer responds. Riddle questions share one common trait with retort questions in that both questions usually rely on previously used utterances or "stock" phrases and concepts. Thus they stand in contrast to most other question types in natural language that are created during communication. As with retort questions, some riddle questions will have a long and well-established pedigree.

Formation

Riddles are almost entirely based on their semantic qualities, and they have little established syntactic or pragmatic requirements. There are two semantic qualities that are necessary for a question to be considered a riddle question: (a) it must contain enough semantic clues for a hearer to solve and (b) it must evoke a sense of competition or desire to solve the riddle.[72] With few syntactic requirements, a speaker can form a riddle question with any major formation of question. The one caveat to this is that riddles formed with polar or alternative formations usually represent a simpler type of riddle that can border on a dilemma type of question (§4.O). Though riddle questions have few pragmatic requirements, they do tend to be asked only in certain contexts. (Much depends on the genre of the text and the language culture within which the text was written.) When they are asked, riddle questions are not usually employed as a second-turn question. They are not typically asked in the middle position and are mostly asked in standalone or closing position.

The two primary factors in the formation and identification of riddle questions are described below.

72. Pagis, "Toward a Theory," 81.

1) Riddle Questions Contain Ambiguous Clues to Alert the Hearer to an Answer

Riddle questions must contain just enough clues for a hearer to be able to solve the riddle. This usually involves hiding clues within intentionally ambiguous word choices or meanings. Alerting the hearer to clues is usually not on purpose but is a by-product of riddle asking (as the riddler does not usually want the audience to successfully decode the riddle). For example:

(3) Μήτι δύναται τυφλὸς τυφλὸν ὁδηγεῖν; (LUKE 6:39A)

When Jesus asks (3), "Can the blind lead the blind?" he forms the question as a polar question with bias, as part of a double-question string. Normally these qualities would be enough to diagnose the question, but in the case of (3), there is something else going on. Jesus's use of τυφλὸς is unexpected, and the clause τυφλὸς τυφλὸν ὁδηγεῖν hints at a wordplay. As a result, (3) takes on the semantic feel of a riddle, albeit a simple one, since it is formed as a polar question. The hearer is left to puzzle over whether someone who cannot see can lead another person, but since the other person also cannot see, would not know whether the first person was leading or not. The question is a riddle-like puzzle from which no good answer can come.

2) Riddle Questions Use Wordplay to Tease the Audience

While properly raised questions provoke in hearers a desire to respond, riddle questions provoke in hearers a desire to engage in the wordplay. More than making a request for information, riddle questions tease the audience into playing the game so as to solve the riddle. In example (3), the simple statement about blind people tempts the reader to make a quick guess. Since (3) is not a true riddle question but a hybrid, its ability to tease is limited (mostly by its syntactic formation). However, the puzzling nature of the question is what has led the question to be so frequently repeated throughout Western history. When a reader encounters a more complex riddle, such as (5) below, the complex nature of the riddle goads a response from hearers.

Rhetorical Effects

Informational
Rhetorical

Riddle questions carry strong informational qualities and mild to moderate rhetorical qualities. When a speaker asks a riddle question, it seeks an answer. However, the information they seek is not so much a literal answer to the question asked but whether or not a hearer can muster an acceptable reply (or better, the intended figurative answer) to the question. Riddle questions are also rhetorically persuasive in tempting the audience to respond. In fact, one of the rhetorical effects of riddles is their power to enthrall hearers and include within them an implicit challenge to see if they can answer the question.

The two most common rhetorical effects of riddle questions are explained below.

1) Riddle Questions Are Asked to See if a Listener Can Guess the Answer

As part of the game undertaken in the asking of riddles, the asker wants to see if a hearer can correctly solve the riddle. If the hearer can guess the answer to the riddle, the hearer succeeds. If not, the hearer fails. This is true for questions that are formed as formal riddles and to a lesser extent for questions that have some degree of riddle quality. For example:

(4) Καλὸν οὖν τὸ ἅλας· ἐὰν δὲ καὶ τὸ ἅλας μωρανθῇ, ἐν τίνι ἀρτυθήσεται; (LUKE 14:34)

In (4) during his public teaching, Jesus asks the audience, "Therefore, salt is good; but if salt were to become unsalty, how will it ever become salty again?" At first glance, the reader sees that Jesus asks a conditional question based on counterfactual logic, with a less common type of syntax for the interrogative variable word in the clause that carries the interrogative logic of the question (§4.P). At the same time, the semantic emphasis on ἅλας ("salt") alerts the audience that something else is at play in this question. There is similar wordplay as in (3). While question (4) is not a formal riddle (at least in the sense that English readers may expect), it does have some degree of riddling quality. The quandary that Jesus puts forth has puzzled readers for almost two millennia; most of these readers have experienced something once tasty that has since lost its flavor. However, salt cannot actually become unsalty (the counterfactual argument), and thus the point of the riddle is what to do with something when it is not what it is anymore. As Jesus makes clear, when something that purports to be something no longer is that something, it cannot become that something again; it must be thrown out (v. 35). The answer to Jesus's riddle is actually hidden in the dialogue before it, leading to v. 33 where the reader learns that being a disciple is completely incompatible with being in the world. Jesus's warning in the riddle is that being a disciple is good, but if it were possible for a disciple to lose their saltiness (i.e., mission mindedness), there is no way to regain the saltiness (mission mindedness). A disciple of Jesus who loves his possessions has lost their worth (v. 35).

2) Riddle Questions Are Often Asked to Stump a Hearer

As a close cousin to test questions, riddle questions have the rhetorical effect of stumping or confusing a hearer. If the hearer cannot guess the answer to the riddle, the hearer fails. If this happens, the asker of the riddle succeeds. Thus it is usually in the vested interest of the asker to ask a riddle that the hearer is unlikely to answer. While many types of questions may inadvertently stump a hearer, riddle questions set out to do this intentionally. For example:

(5) ἐν τῇ ἀναστάσει οὖν τίνος τῶν ἑπτὰ ἔσται γυνή; (MATT 22:28)

In Matthew 22:24–28, the Sadducees ask Jesus a riddle that represents one of the few more formal riddles in the GNT. The riddle culminates with (5), "In the resurrection—which of the seven's wife will she be?" Considering the syntax, the utterance is a set question formed with τίνος τῶν ἑπτὰ ("which of the seven's") and is statistically unusual since the question does not front the π-word but instead fronts ἐν τῇ ἀναστάσει ("in the resurrection"). This is to place focus on the situation on which the question depends. In fact, the fronting of ἐν τῇ ἀναστάσει is so striking in GNT syntax that it begs the question as to why the Sadducees asked their question in this way. It seems probable that it was to discount any attempt by Jesus to speak to whose wife she was while on earth (had she still been alive) and work backwards to solve the problem. As the Sadducees are well known in their denial of the resurrection, their goal was for Jesus to try to solve a riddle with a premise (ἐν τῇ ἀναστάσει) they believed impossible or absurd. However, in doing so they unwittingly overplayed their hand, making the intentional ambiguity of the riddle too plain for their audience. By exploiting the premise ἐν τῇ ἀναστάσει, Jesus may now solve the riddle without any deference to earthly law or custom: marriage is simply not an activity for people in the resurrection (v. 30). The riddle collapses, and the audience is astonished that Jesus navigates the puzzle so well (v. 33).

Case Study — MARK 12:37

αὐτὸς Δαυὶδ λέγει αὐτὸν κύριον, καὶ πόθεν αὐτοῦ ἐστιν υἱός;

JESUS: David himself calls him Lord, so in what way can he be his son?

In the Gospel of Mark, Jesus teaches in the temple courts during his public ministry, with crowds of many people listening. In one of those situations, Jesus uses a riddle to capture the attention of his audience (Mark 12:37). To tell the riddle, Jesus opens with a question: "In what way do the teachers of the law say that the Messiah will be the Son of David?" (v. 35) Jesus asks this question as a means to get the audience thinking; it is a way to warm up the audience for the conclusion of the puzzle (v. 37). After Jesus asks this question, he reminds his hearers of what David had to say in the Psalm through the Holy Spirit: The Messiah is Lord to David (v. 36). This evidence then leads Jesus to ask his audience the riddle question, "David himself calls the Messiah Lord, so in what way can the Messiah be his son?"

Before considering the riddle question, let's break down the crux of the riddle. There are three parts—a question, a statement, and a question:

- In what way can teachers of law say: Messiah = son of David?

- David says (BY THE HOLY SPIRIT): Messiah = Lord
- Therefore in what way is: Messiah = son of David?

Jesus produces two testimonial evidences to sustain his riddle: (a) the words of the teachers of the law and (b) the words of David himself under the influence of the Holy Spirit. These two testimonies—the argument that Messiah is both son of David and Lord of David—are contrary to each other. However, since Jesus does not suggest to the audience that one evidence is in error, the argument is not dilemmatic (§4.O). It is paradoxical, as the riddle asks how two competing ideas can both be valid.

Jesus asks his opening question with the interrogative variable word πῶς with the sense of "in what way" (v. 35). This question is a speculative question with an open nature that encourages thinking. Contextually, however, it is the opening of a riddle, and thus its rhetorical purpose is to encourage the audience to start thinking deeply about what Jesus will say next. Care must be taken to remember that Jesus is not *saying* the Messiah is the son of David but is *asking* how the scribes can speak of the Messiah in this way. Due to its use, the question also carries with it the semantic qualities of a riddle question. In asking this, Jesus allows his audience to anticipate the point of the greater riddle. Moving through the paradox, the audience comes to the concluding question that ties up the riddle: In what way can the Messiah be both Lord and son? Jesus forms the question with the propositional premise αὐτὸς Δαυὶδ λέγει αὐτὸν κύριον ("David himself calls him Lord") and forms the clause with interrogative force as a variable question with πόθεν ("in what way"). Jesus's use of πόθεν naturally sets up a sense of speculation which is helpful for riddling an audience when using a paradoxical puzzle. The easily drawn indexical αὐτοῦ ("his") creates a little extra wordplay for the audience. Though the paradox cannot be solved, the crowd enjoyed the riddle (v. 37b).

FURTHER EXAMPLES

Matt 5:13; Mark 9:50; 12:23, 35.

Key Bibliography

Pagis, "Toward a Theory"; Pepicello and Green, *Language of Riddles*; Roberts and Forman, "Riddles"; Weiner and de Palma, "Pragmatic Features."

O. Dilemma Questions

Dilemma questions are asked to put a hearer in a bind between two weak positions. *Dilemma question* is an umbrella term—it covers several related but distinct kinds of questions with strong rhetorical qualities. Of these, the most important two types are (a) the *dilemma* and (b) the *dilemmaton*. These types of questions are related in how they approach their semantic scheme but are distinct in how that scheme is applied. The point of the dilemma is to trap a hearer in the middle, whereas the point of the dilemmaton is to hook a hearer on either prong. A dilemma is more simple than a dilemmaton; the dilemma originates more in everyday culture and conversation whereas the dilemmaton originates in ancient logic and rhetoric. Most of our focus will be on the more technical dilemmaton. When dilemma questions contain archetypal, mythic, or ambiguous language, they can also be heard as riddle questions (§4.N).

The first, the question based on a dilemma, allows the speaker to ask a hearer to choose between two difficult situations. These two situations are difficult because of their semantic or contextual relationship—a relationship that causes the receiver to have difficulty in choosing between the two. A dilemma posed as a question is generally a specialized kind of alternative question (§3.C) wherein the two options are related in that they are equally good or equally bad. The symbol of the dilemma is a two-pronged fork. For example:

(1) Do you want warm brownies or oven-baked cookies? (DILEMMA)
(2) Do you want to go to school or go to the dentist? (DILEMMA)
(3) Do you want to go to school or go have fun? (ALTERNATIVE)

In examples (1) and (2), the asker presents the recipient of the question with two options that are designed intentionally to create a difficulty in choosing between the two options. In (1), both options sound really great, and a hearer will not be able to simply choose between the two. In (2), both options are bad, and the hearer will not want to choose either option. In both cases, these questions have strong informational qualities, but they also are deceptively rhetorical. These types of dilemma questions are found in everyday discourse, as well as in the GNT (e.g., Matt 22:17, and mildly, Mark 10:38).[73] Example (3) is not a dilemma question as it does not contain two equal prongs.

The second, the *dilemmaton* (διλήμματον), is asked as a trap to trick an enemy into a verbal ambush formed from two oppositional but defeatable positions.[74] A dilemmaton is not the same thing as a dilemma—but when a person asks a dilemmaton they are intending to first put the hearer in a dilemma. Unlike the dilemma, where the difficulty between the two options is often apparent, the delimmaton works best if the hearer is unaware that both options are problematic. When asked, a dilemmaton appears as a question the asker uses to present two divergent paths for the hearer. The goal of the dilemmaton is for the hearer to choose to answer one of the two prongs of the question. To set the trap, the

73. We can also interpret Matt 22:17 as a poorly executed dilemmaton.

74. As with most ancient concepts, the dilemmaton had slightly different meanings and uses in different authors and fields of study (e.g., both ancient logic and rhetoric).

asker must have a ready response or rebuttal to both prongs prior to asking the question. When the speaker deploys the dilemmaton on an unsuspecting recipient, the choice of two options will appear to an audience as if the recipient can chose the better option for a response. With either choice, the original asker has a ready response, which makes the recipient appear to have the weaker position. As with any trap, a dilemmaton must be properly set to work effectively—in this case, the asker must be able to beat both options. Neither prong can appear to the audience as easily defeated by the recipient or easily defeated by the asker. The asker must also pull off the asking without making it appear as if it were a trap. Dilemmata were so effective as a rhetorical weapon that over time they began to be featured in *progymnasmata*, the rhetorical handbooks for training students in rhetoric.[75] Dilemmata were sometimes depicted as a two-pronged fork with hooks, a devious device meant to ensnare an unwary opponent.[76] For example:

(4) Do you think it is better to be rich or to be lucky? (DILEMMATON)

Question (4) is a common example of a dilemmaton that occurs in everyday conversation. At first glance, both riches and luck appear to be equally good things (as in a dilemma). A naive hearer will consider this question and pick the one that seems most positive to them. However, this springs the trap for the asker. Once the selection is made, the asker can easily explain why being rich is better than being lucky ("you can make your own luck if you are rich") or can easily explain why being lucky is better than being rich ("with luck you can always get rich again and again"). Example (4) has the effect of ensnaring the person foolish enough to respond with either reply and holding them with the hooks of the fork long enough for the asker to embarrass or ridicule their opponent. According to the rhetorician Hermogenes (flor. late 2nd century AD), these kinds of dilemma questions are meant to shock an opponent and score points (δόξα; "glory").[77]

Formation

A speaker must meet syntactic, semantic, *and* pragmatic requirements to properly ask a dilemma question. Generally speaking, they will satisfy one of two syntactical requirements in their formation: Either they will be formed as (a) an alternative question with the two alternatives in semantic opposition or (b) as a disjunctive question with the two disjunctive clauses in semantic opposition. Semantically, the two prongs of the dilemma question must be in opposition so as to push the hearer into responding to one or the other. Speakers often ask

75. Hermogenes, *Invention* 4.6 (Kennedy, WGRW).
76. Nuchelmans, *Dilemmatic Arguments*, 51–53, 96.
77. Hermogenes, *Invention* 4.6 (Kennedy, WGRW). Here Hermogenes uses δόξα in the Greco-Roman sense; if one pulls off a dilemmaton on their opponent in the ἐκκλησία, their δόξα will live forever.

a dilemma question with an excluded middle (and thus may commit a fallacy, intentional or not). Pragmatically, a dilemma question can appear in any turn in narrative discourse, though they are highly rhetorical and will alter the course of the dialogue. Due to their unique rhetorical and informational effects, they can occur only in the standalone and closing positions. Since a dilemma question requires not just an audience but a dupe, they occur most frequently in narrative; if used in rhetorical discourse, it means the writer is suggesting (to some extent) that the reader is the dupe, able to be caught. Unlike most other question types, a hearer must respond to the question for the trap to work.

The primary factor in the formation and identification of dilemma questions is described below.

1) Dilemma Questions Pose Two Options in Opposition for the Hearer

The tell of the dilemma question is the two equally uncomfortable prongs on the fork of the question. Because of their balanced weight, these two equal prongs create an uncertainty in the hearer. If the hearer does not respond, the asker can goad the hearer into responding. In order to form the question successfully, the audience should not be aware that the question coming is a dilemma question. For example:

(5) ἀπὸ σεαυτοῦ σὺ τοῦτο λέγεις ἢ ἄλλοι εἶπόν σοι περὶ ἐμοῦ; (JOHN 18:34)

In example (5), Jesus responds to Pilate's question with, "Do you say this on your own behalf, or did others say this to you about me?" In asking this, Jesus presents Pilate with two options—neither are particularly good and both would paint Pilate into a rhetorical corner. Since each option is cunningly constructed as the prong of the fork, it is not possible for Pilate to retreat ("Neither?"). The only way for Pilate to defeat this would be to get outside the prongs (perhaps a *deus ex machina* reply: "Actually, Jove told me") or to reject the excluded middle ("both I and others say this"). Not only is this question a dilemma question, it is also an opposing-turn question (§5.B.1).[78]

Rhetorical Effects

Informational
Rhetorical

Dilemma questions are unique among questions in that they possess the strongest degrees of both informational and rhetorical qualities. This is because the question is really nothing more than a rhetorical trap, yet at the same time for the trap to succeed the asker must draw reliable information from the dupe who responds. Dilemma questions are rhetorically complex, and they can convey

78. For further discussion on the logic and rhetoric of John 18:34, see Estes, *Questions*, 120–3.

many rhetorical effects. When asked, they do not tend to be limited to one or two primary rhetorical effects as most questions are. For example, a dilemma question can push a hearer to choose between two equally unpalatable options, expose a major weakness in the responder's argument, create an adversarial spirit between asker and audience, backfire badly on the asker if not set properly, and many more possibilities—potentially all in the asking of just one dilemma question.

The most important rhetorical effect of a dilemma question is explained below.

1) Dilemma Questions Can Trap a Hearer Unable to Dodge the Fork

Dilemma questions exist to capture a hearer between the two prongs of the fork (the dilemma) or to skewer a responder on one of the two prongs of the fork (dilemmaton). In rhetorical strategy, skewering is preferred. Either way pushes the responder into a weak position. For example:

(6) Ἐπερωτῶ ὑμᾶς, εἰ ἔξεστιν τῷ σαββάτῳ ἀγαθοποιῆσαι ἢ κακοποιῆσαι, ψυχὴν σῶσαι ἢ ἀπολέσαι; (LUKE 6:9)

In the Gospel of Luke, Jesus asks (6), "I ask you—if it is lawful on the Sabbath to do good or to do bad; to save a life or to destroy it?" Jesus asks this in response to the watchfulness of the scribes and Pharisees; notably, Luke records no attempt by them to respond. In this case, neither response would fit their agenda, and either response would give a rhetorical point to Jesus in front of the crowds. From Luke's perspective, the scribes and Pharisees refuse to take the bait. Nonetheless, their silence allows Jesus to capture them between the two prongs, rhetorically giving him permission to make his own choice on whether it is lawful to do good or to do bad on the Sabbath.

Case Study — LUKE 20:4

Τὸ βάπτισμα Ἰωάννου ἐξ οὐρανοῦ ἦν ἢ ἐξ ἀνθρώπων;

JESUS: The baptism of John—was it from heaven or was it from man?

As Jesus's public ministry continues, the discussions and debates between Jesus and his opponents in the Judaean leadership grow more and more heated. At one point, Jesus teaches the people in the temple about the good news within earshot of the chief priests, some scribes, and some elders (Luke 20:1). When they hear Jesus teaching the good news, they approach Jesus and ask him, "Tell us: By what authority do you do these things; or, who is the one who gives this authority to you?" (v. 2) In response, Jesus does not answer; instead, he states that he will ask them a question in return. "Tell me," Jesus says, "the baptism of John—was it from heaven or was it from man?" (vv. 3–4) Jesus's question prompts a discussion among the chief priests, scribes, and elders (vv. 5–6).

In this exchange, readers get a glimpse of something in the GNT that is lost on modern readers: Jesus's skilled use of polished rhetoric to score a victory over his opponents using a textbook example of a dilemmaton worthy of record in any *progymnasmata*. When the Judaean leaders confront Jesus at the temple, they ask Jesus a disjunctive question meant to determine his authority to teach. Even though the question is meant to be determinative (in other words, to try to get Jesus to give one clear answer out of the couple of issues the leaders raise), their question comes off as a bit cumbersome (§3.E.2). In response, Jesus does not answer their question but comes back at his interlocutors with an opposing-turn question (§5.B.1) formed as an alternative question (§3.C). Jesus's question is contrastive in both form and function to the leaders' question—in terms of its rhetoric, it is a straight punch (a cross) to their wild haymaker. If the leaders try to answer, Jesus has caught them in a classic dilemmaton.[79] Logically, the argument works as it sets up an ἀντίφασις ("contradiction"), and there is no μεταξύ ("middle position") that the question excludes.[80]

What is fascinating about this rhetorical argument is that Luke records the discussion of the Judaean leaders as they weigh their options that Jesus gives in his question (vv. 5–6). They acknowledge that both prongs of the fork contain hooks on which Jesus will ensnare them. Their only recourse is to pick "neither" and suggest that they do not know where John's baptism came from. This part of Luke's Gospel raises a question for the interpreter: Was one of Jesus's followers privy to the Judaean leaders' conversation? Or was the trap set by Jesus so textbook that someone (a Greek speaker with some education) observing the discussion among the Judaean leaders in the wake of the question would know the logical problem presented by the question? If the latter, does Luke explain the trap for his readers by recreating the conversation? Either way, this argument in Luke demonstrates the importance of the logic and rhetoric of questions in the establishment of Jesus's public ministry as well as the promotion of his teaching among early Christians.

FURTHER EXAMPLES

Matt 21:25a–b; 22:17; Mark 11:30.

Key Bibliography

Estes, *Questions*, 120–23; Kennedy, *Invention*, 168–71; Montefusco, "Rhetorical Use of Dilemmatic Arguments"; Nuchelmans, *Dilemmatic Arguments*.

79. Nuchelmans, *Dilemmatic Arguments*, 33.
80. Cf. Aristotle, *Posterior Analytics* 72a12–13.

P. Counterfactual Questions

Counterfactual questions are asked to propose a possibility based on a premise that runs counter to established truth. Counterfactual questions are a type of conditional question and are sometimes referred to as *subjunctive conditional questions* (though this term is not truly accurate, especially in Koine Greek). They are formed much like conditional questions, but their semantics and logic are more distinct. These questions get their name from their use of counterfactual logic. Counterfactual logic was in regular use in ancient Greek writing predating the GNT.[81] Jesus uses explicit counterfactual logic in his public ministry (e.g., Matt 11:21b; John 5:46; 18:36b), as does Paul (e.g., 1 Cor 15:16, 17). A counterfactual is "a conditional construction in which the conditional clause expresses a condition that [has never been met or] can no longer be met" or will never be met; a counterfactual *question* is a counterfactual affixed to another clause with interrogative force that asks about something that can never be true since the counterfactual condition can never actually be met (*CDL* 114). Counterfactual questions are akin to "what if?" questions but are actually utterances with a complex logic. Unlike most other question types, it is impossible to give a true answer to a counterfactual question—the only option for a hearer is to provide a reply that can never be determined (an "opinion"). For example:

(1) If the cadets had lost, would Hunter have shelled the Institute? (COUNTERFACTUAL)
(2) If the cadets had lost, would flying cars be in service today? (COUNTERFACTUAL)
(3) If God created people, can they be saved? (CONDITIONAL)
(4) If God created aliens, can they be saved? (COUNTERFACTUAL)
(5) If there were no religion, would the world be a better place? (COUNTERFACTUAL)

With (1), we know from history that the cadets did win (the Battle of New Market) and that Hunter did shell the Institute as a response to the victory. Thus, the premise of the conditional clause is not conditional (as the truth of the victory is historically demonstrable) but counterfactual. The question asked in (1) as a result of the counterfactual is closely tied to the counterfactual, and thus the question may cause the audience to reflect on the reasons for the shelling of the Institute. Since it seems unlikely that Hunter would have shelled the Institute as a result of the cadets' loss—though there is no way to know for sure—this creates additional reflection for the audience to think through in regard to the relationship between the victory and the shelling. Further, many readers may not know all the details to which the counterfactual and the question refers; even

81. Tordoff, "Counterfactual History and Thucydides," 101.

if some readers do, this is the reason counterfactual questions are quite tricky in that they usually rely on the expectation of a significant knowledge base and reasoning. But since the cadets did not lose, there is no way to ever know for certain whether Hunter would have shelled the Institute or not. With (2), the question asked is not tied closely to the counterfactual, and thus it is easier to answer—the counterfactual seems irrelevant to the issue of flying cars; there is no relationship for the hearer to explore. When it comes to question (3), since we believe God did create people, it is (at least for theists) not a counterfactual question but a conditional question. Note that a committed atheist could treat (3) as if it were a counterfactual question (though they might not then find the question raised very challenging). Yet if the conditional clause changes, as in (4), since we do not believe in (sentient) aliens, the question raised becomes a counterfactual question. A reader may argue, "But I believe in (sentient) aliens!" and if so, the question would still lean toward the counterfactual side because it is not in any way (currently) a demonstrable or explainable condition. Thus (4) is for all intents and purposes a counterfactual question in all current scenarios. Likewise, (5) is a counterfactual question because there is no imaginable time where the condition could be true based on historical evidence. However, this example is close to the speculative use of standard conditionals and is often read too quickly that way. While the question seems speculative and easily answerable, it is not because it is a counterfactual and requires the hearer to create the counterfactual scenarios *before* trying to answer the question. These examples are rather simple; counterfactual questions in natural discourse are typically more difficult to spot and even more puzzling to reason.

Formation

Counterfactual questions are formed as conditional questions. However, unlike standard conditional questions which we can identify syntactically, counterfactual questions are a type of conditional question that we can only identify semantically. In some cases, the counterfactual may not be readily apparent as such or may be hidden within the premise of the question itself.[82] As a result, identifying counterfactual questions in the GNT is extremely difficult. Much depends on the truth expectations of the speaker and their audience. Counterfactual questions posed with negative polarity in either clause are less common (though see 1 Cor 15:29b), and a speaker may use a counterfactual question in any type of discourse or dialogue position.

The most important factor in the formation and identification of a counterfactual question is described below.

82. Cf. Knight, "Questions and Universals," 571.

1) Counterfactual Questions Must Include a Counterfactual Phrase or Clause

A counterfactual question is a composite question formation that makes use of counterfactual logic coupled with the erotetic logic of the main clause with interrogative force. The tell for counterfactual questions is that the conditional phrase or clause must introduce a counterfactual limitation. Determining when and if a conditional is a counterfactual conditional is subject to interpretation. For example:

> (6) Εἰ μὲν οὖν τελείωσις διὰ τῆς Λευιτικῆς ἱερωσύνης ἦν, ὁ λαὸς γὰρ ἐπ' αὐτῆς νενομοθέτηται, τίς ἔτι χρεία κατὰ τὴν τάξιν Μελχισέδεκ ἕτερον ἀνίστασθαι ἱερέα καὶ οὐ κατὰ τὴν τάξιν Ἀαρὼν λέγεσθαι; (HEB 7:11)

Question (6) is a complex question from Hebrews that asks, "Indeed, if perfection was possible through the Levitical priesthood—for based on this the people had been given the law—why was there still need for another priest to arise, from the order of Melchizedek, and not from the order of Aaron?" Here the use of an εἰ ("if") conditional clause, coupled with the subject matter and τίς ("why?"), steers the question toward a subjective semantic type. Breaking down the question grammatically, the εἰ conditional clause serves as a protasis to the variable question fronted by τίς (in this case, "why?" or "what?"). The question also contains a strong bias word, ἔτι ("still"; cf. §4.U). Since it is not possible—it never was and will never be possible—for perfection to be achieved through the Levitical priesthood, the question presupposes a counterfactual condition. Since the question is contingent on a counterfactual claim, the rhetorical goal of the question is to push the reader toward deeper consideration of the need for another priest to arise.

Rhetorical Effects

Informational
Rhetorical

Counterfactual questions are a staple of thought-provoking discussion and argumentation. Though their logic is unique, they are useful for generating several mundane rhetorical effects, most notably for encouraging the audience to look at an old issue in a new way. Counterfactual questions explore causality, and a speaker may use them to suggest new methods where old methods did not work.[83] Simplistically, they are a kind of "what if?" question, which allows a speaker to use them to open up new lines of discussion or establish distance between themselves and the audience by questioning norms.[84] They can occur in

83. Spellman, Kincannon, and Stose, "Relation between Counterfactual and Causal Reasoning," 28.
84. Cf. Chariton, *Callirhoe* 2.9.

both narrative and rhetorical discourse, and in either case their rhetorical effect is to use a falsehood to create new takes on truth.

One of the most notable rhetorical effects of counterfactual questions is described below.

1) Counterfactual Questions Create New Avenues for Reasoning and Argumentation

Speakers raise counterfactual questions by conditioning them upon contrary-to-fact claims; as a result, these claims challenge the audience to contemplate the question through a new or wholly different lens. They can use counterfactual questions to reevaluate past actions and decisions or simply to riddle their audience (§4.N). Speakers can also use counterfactual questions to challenge conventions or unfounded assumptions by asking the audience to assume their position is incorrect without directly stating that their position is incorrect. For example:

(7) εἰ ὅλως νεκροὶ οὐκ ἐγείρονται, τί καὶ βαπτίζονται ὑπὲρ αὐτῶν; (1 COR 15:29B)

In (7), Paul uses a counterfactual question to raise a question that has perplexed readers since it was written. Our goal here is not to address the forty or fifty interpretive options for the "baptism of the dead" phrase,[85] but to see what light the interrogative logic can shed on the question. Paul asks, "If dead people are not actually raised, why then are they baptized for them?" Before we can unpack Paul's argument, we must recognize that Paul does intend to raise a counterfactual argument here. Paul's theology and belief held that people are raised (Rom 8:11; 1 Cor 6:14; Col 2:12); yet beyond this, his use of ὅλως ("actually") suggests that Paul understands that dead people are actually raised (and that it is an indisputable truth). Thus the complement clause is a not conditional clause or a speculative clause (as readers may treat it). In fact, the counterfactual clause in (7) is almost identical to the counterfactual clause in 1 Corinthians 15:16 (εἰ γὰρ νεκροὶ οὐκ ἐγείρονται). From this, Paul's use of the counterfactual indicates that this issue of baptism of the dead is important, and in this case, its importance is to get Paul's readers to reevaluate their position on the resurrection of the dead. In other words, Paul asks a counterfactual question to try to get his readers to consider why people would baptize for the dead if there is no resurrection for the dead. If we can remove the baptism-for-the-dead idea, it seems that we can reconstruct the logic of Paul's counterfactual question this way: "If God is not really real, why then do people pray to him?" Thus the rhetorical force of Paul's question is to box in his audience—to make them realize that their practices disprove their beliefs (or that their beliefs are inconsistent). Why this works as a rhetorical strategy must be that Paul's audience most likely were

85. Thiselton, *First Epistle to the Corinthians*, 1240.

firmly entrenched in (a) their doubt in the resurrection (1 Cor 15:12) *and* (b) their unexamined cultural practices that point to a resurrection. Because of these contrasts, a counterfactual question works better than a more ordinary question to help Paul's readers see a new path through their inconsistencies.

Case Study — MATTHEW 5:13

ἐὰν δὲ τὸ ἅλας μωρανθῇ, ἐν τίνι ἁλισθήσεται;

JESUS: But if salt could become saltless [dumb], with what will it be salt [again]?

One day, seeing the crowds drew near, Jesus went up on the shoulder of a mountain to sit down (Matt 5:1). After his disciples came to him, Jesus began to teach one of his most famous messages. Jesus started with the qualities of those who are blessed (vv. 3–12). Next, Jesus told those gathered around, "You are the salt of the earth." After Jesus asserted this, he then followed this assertion up with a question: "But if salt could become saltless [dumb], with what will it be salt [again]?" As Matthew records no response or interruption to Jesus's question, Jesus then finished his point, saying, "It is no longer good for anything, except for throwing it out to be trampled by people."

Jesus's question in Matthew 5:13 is one of the great counterfactual questions of all time. Unfortunately, readers today skip over the question without realizing either its counterfactual or erotetic logic. Partly, this is because the question is deceiving; it is quite complex and difficult to unpack though it speaks of something that seems so simple—salt. This is also because the question is intended to riddle the audience (see §4.N for a related take on Luke 14:34). There are several aspects that we need to highlight. First, the question is a counterfactual question, and the ἐάν plus the subjunctive μωρανθῇ reinforces this syntactically. We can also confirm this semantically, because salt that is not salty is contrary-to-fact. While scholars have tried to look for historical explanations for saltless salt (especially weak salt from the Dead Sea area),[86] a historical explanation misses the logic and rhetoric of the question.[87] Second, Jesus's use of ἅλας is not meant to refer to literal salt; rather, it is a conceptual metaphor that he employs just as he does with "light" in Matthew 5:14. Thus, to understand Jesus's argument, we must see salt metaphorically and not draw literal or exact parallels between salt and whatever the meaning is of Jesus's figurative language. While readers debate the exact meaning of the metaphor, we do note that the metaphor is tied to the followers of Jesus (Ὑμεῖς ["you"] at the beginning of 5:13). This is validated to some degree by the inclusion of the article τό, but perhaps more so by Jesus's use

86. For example, Hagner, *Matthew 1–13*, 99; Morris, *Matthew*, 104.
87. Nolland, *Matthew*, 213.

of μωρανθῇ which most likely points to the underlying human implication of the metaphor. Third, the question clause does not follow typical Koine Greek grammar, as the interrogative pronoun is fronted only as part of a phrase. Jesus uses the dative construction ἐν τίνι, "with what" or "by what," to emphasize in asking the hearer what are the immediate actions that would cause salt to be salty again. The passive "be salt [again]" is preferable to an active translation (cf. T. Levi 9:14). Finally, the pragmatics of the question is expository (§5.A.2) in that Jesus uses the question to give a type of reply and continue speaking.

It is possible that without knowing how to decode the metaphor, we may not be able to accurately determine what Jesus meant. However, instead of approaching this through the metaphor as is always done, we will approach the utterance through its interrogative logic. Let's consider two parallel constructions. The first is: "If light could become lightless, with what will it brighten again?" This is a counterfactual question, because the complement clause raises a contrary-to-fact condition: light cannot become lightless (as salt cannot become saltless).[88] Therefore, as it is a counterfactual, and salt is a metaphor, the implication that Jesus uses this metaphor as part of the counterfactual condition means that it is not possible for the condition to be true—in this case, it is not possible for light to become lightless or salt to become saltless. In other words, *it is contrary-to-fact for whatever the metaphor means to not apply to the followers of Jesus*. So, if for example the salt is a metaphor for faith, then the second parallel construction might be: "If faithful disciples become faithless, what would cause faith to grow again?" Just as it is contrary-to-fact for faithful disciples to become faithless, it is contrary-to-fact for salt to become tasteless (cf. b. Bek. 8b). Following the second parallel construction, Jesus uses the question to presuppose what would happen if one had faithless disciples—with what could those disciples be made faithful again?

One of the primary rhetorical effects of counterfactual questions is to push prevention—to raise questions that are based on a contrary-to-fact condition to help the hearer to think through what could be done differently. In this case, Jesus uses a counterfactual to condition his hearers that whatever quality salt conveys in terms of discipleship, it can't be lost by (real) disciples. Yet Jesus asks his hearers to suppose for a minute that this quality could be lost; what would it take for this quality to ever come back? While we don't know if the crowd or disciples attempted any replies, we do know that Jesus continues with his own indirect response, indicating that there is *nothing* that can do this. Thus, such disciples are only worth being thrown out. Jesus asks his counterfactual question to push his audience to think through what it means for a disciple to not be a disciple with the intent to persuade them (and box them in) that once discipleship is lost, it cannot be regained.[89]

88. Cf. Betz, *Sermon on the Mount*, 159.
89. For a related conclusion, see Basser, *Gospel of Matthew and Judaic Traditions*, 130.

FURTHER EXAMPLES
Mark 9:50; Luke 14:34; Rom 2:26; 1 Cor 15:32; Gal 5:11.

Key Bibliography
Byrne, *Rational Imagination*, 1–14; Evans and Over, *If*, 113–31; Knight, "Questions and Universals"; Rescher, *Conditionals*, 89–102.

Q. Decision Questions

Decision questions are asked to encourage a hearer to make a decision or choose a selection. Decision questions are also called *choice questions* in that the purpose of the question is to ask for a hearer to make a choice through an answer. They are also called *open polar questions* in that no preference is made between the options presented. Semantically, decision questions are similar to open questions in that both questions are rhetorically unrestricted. What this means is that a true decision question does not and will not try to persuade the audience in one direction or another. At the same time, decision questions are a closed question type since they have a narrow set of answers (§2.E).[90] To be a decision question, the question under consideration must be asked with little or no rhetorical pretense on the part of the asker. They are a common kind of question found in all discourse forms, as they represent vanilla forms of polar questions (§3.A), alternative questions (§3.C), and set questions (§3.D). For example:

(1) Do brownies taste good? (DECISION QUESTION)
(2) Do you want steak or chicken? (DECISION QUESTION)
(3) Which team are you rooting for? (DECISION QUESTION)
(4) What is your favorite rugby team? (OPEN QUESTION)
(5) Can we go skiing tomorrow? (CONFIRMATION QUESTION)

Sample questions (1), (2), and (3) are all decision questions constructed from different question formations. In each case, the question does not lean in either direction, and so the audience cannot anticipate a preferred answer. Sample question (4) is not a decision question; even though it is free from semantic spin, the question is open and does not call for an actual decision (and thus answers can be extremely broad, from "Munster!" to "I don't have one"). Sample question (5) does ask for a decision to be made by the hearer, but the rhetorical force is not neutral, and so the question is better analyzed as a confirmation question (§4.R).

90. The distinction between open and closed depends on perspective—polar questions are open if no reply is predicated, but are closed since only two options (yes/no) are available; cf. Fiengo, *Asking Questions*, 53.

Formation

Decision questions are formed from polar-, alternative-, or set-question formations. They cannot be formed from variable questions, as variable questions do not have sufficient limits over their set of answers to call for a decision. When set questions are asked with minimal rhetorical force, if they are open (and without a strict set of implied answers) they can be treated as open questions, but if they are closed (with a more strict set of implied answers) they can be treated as decision questions. Decision questions are positive in polarity; negative polarity or the presence of bias words would push this type of question into a more rhetorical type of question. An asker can only ask a decision question when there are not any notable semantic or pragmatic influences shaping the question. For example, while a decision question could occur in any turn or position within discourse, it generally cannot be asked as a middle-position question, since the pragmatic influence on those types of questions is too rhetorical for the decision question. As a result, it is difficult to ask a decision question within a highly rhetorical form of discourse (such as most of the letters in the GNT) without the question taking on a more persuasive effect.

Two factors in the formation and identification of decision questions are explained below.

1) Decision Questions Should Not Contain Any Semantic Spin

For a speaker to ask a decision question, the question asked should not contain any semantic spin that alters the question for the audience. One of the most common ways of prejudging the audience is to put semantic limiters that bias or lead the hearer toward or away from some desired reply (or lack of reply) from the asker. For example:

(6) ἢ Ἰουδαίων ὁ θεὸς *μόνον*; (ROM 3:29A)

Example (6) is *not* a decision question. At first glance, this question may appear to be Paul merely asking his reader to decide, "Is God the God of Jews only?" It is true that Paul does ask a polar question and does want his reader to ask themselves whether this is true or false, yes or no. However, Paul's use is not neutral; most notably, he includes the strong bias word μόνον ("only") in an attempt to influence the reader's response toward "no." Example (6) also has the rhetorical effect of being part of a double question. While Paul wants a decision, (6) is actually a biased question (§4.U) with a strong rhetorical push.

2) Decision Questions Should Not Contain Any Pragmatic Spin

Likewise, for a speaker to ask a decision question, the question asked should not contain any pragmatic spin that leans the question toward one choice or another for the audience. One of the most common ways of tainting the audience is to put pragmatic limiters that push or condition the hearer toward or away from some desired reply (or lack of reply) from the asker. For example:

(7) δέδεσαι γυναικί; (1 COR 7:27A)

Example (7) is *not* a decision question. Here Paul asks his readers, "You've been pledged to a woman?" At first glance, it may appear to be a candid yes-or-no polar question, but the pragmatics of the question are too influential here for us to read it as a decision question. First, because the question is embedded within rhetorical discourse, this alone adds more rhetorical force than what would normally be comfortable for decision questions. Second, the polar question is actually Paul speaking to his readers about something they know and Paul does not know—meaning a B-event (§2.C.7) occurs. Thus, these tells reveal that (7) is actually a confirmation question (§4.R).

Rhetorical Effects

Decision questions have little rhetorical effect on the audience. The purpose of the asker in asking a decision question is to be as neutral as possible in the asking so the hearer can make an unbiased decision. Decision questions are strongly informational and have weak rhetorical qualities. This type of question should have little or no persuasive power (except as defined in the asker-supplied set of answers) and are formed to assert as little influence as possible over hearers. To remain rhetorically weak, shorter questions tend to make better decision questions.

Two mild rhetorical effects of decision questions are explained below.

1) Decision Questions Admit Ignorance on the Part of the Asker

While all questions (even test questions) admit some degree of ignorance on the part of the asker, decision questions presume by their nature that the asker does not know the decision that a hearer may make in response to the question asked. Thus, the weak rhetorical force of a decision question hinges on its ability to ask a hearer to decide for themselves between the options given and that this decision can be seen by the audience as a legitimate and unforced decision. For example:

(8) Κύριε, πρὸς ἡμᾶς τὴν παραβολὴν ταύτην λέγεις ἢ
καὶ πρὸς πάντας; (LUKE 12:41)

Example (8) occurs within one of Jesus's parables. Here Peter asks a question formed as an alternative question (§3.C), "Lord, are you telling this parable to us, or to everyone?" Since Luke does not record a response to Peter's question, this question may seem odd, placed as it is between parables.[91] Peter's question is a

91. For example, Nolland, *Luke 9:21–18:34*, 702.

decision question in that he asks Jesus to decide (and tell him) whether the parable is intended πρὸς ἡμᾶς ("to us") or πρὸς πάντας ("to everyone"). By asking the question this way, Peter tacitly admits he does not know the answer. Because Luke does not have Jesus supply a direct answer, the history of interpretation argues that the answer is implicit in the following parable.[92] While this may be true, the importance of the question is that Peter still is not at a point where he understands much of what Jesus teaches. Even more so, what is often missed is that Jesus responds to Peter's question with a question (an opposing-turn question; §5.B.1) which serves as a rebuttal to Peter's question. In Peter's question the reader glimpses Peter's ignorance of what Jesus hoped to accomplish through his teaching.

2) Decision Questions Ask Hearers to Choose between Two or More Equally Viable Options

Decision questions ask hearers to make a fair decision. To be a decision question, the options presented by the asker in the asking of the question must be equally viable *in the ears of the audience*. It is possible that one of the options will not be as viable as another, but if the asker is aware of this or pushes a preference in the asking of the question, the question will carry too many rhetorical effects to be considered a decision question. For example:

(9) Εἴ τι βλέπεις; (MARK 8:23)

Example (9) is a decision question asked by Jesus in a narrative (not a rhetorical) dialogue. After putting a cure on the eyes of a blind man, Jesus asks him, "Can you see anything?" In this case, the question is formed as a polar question, and Jesus's use of εἰ emphasizes his openness to hearing any valid reply from the blind man. The question does not appear to telegraph to the audience—either semantically or pragmatically—any indication from Jesus as to which answer would be preferable. Therefore, the blind man can choose for himself how to answer from among a set of equally viable answers.

Case Study — 1 CORINTHIANS 1:13A

μεμέρισται ὁ Χριστός;

PAUL: Is Christ divided?

After Paul conveys his greetings to the church of God in Corinth (1 Cor 1:1–9), he opens his letter with an appeal to the church that there not be division among them. His appeal is made διὰ τοῦ ὀνόματος τοῦ κυρίου ἡμῶν Ἰησοῦ

92. For example, Bovon, *Luke 2*, 237.

Χριστοῦ ("in the name of our Lord Jesus Christ") in the hopes of perfect unity. Then Paul gets specific in the quarrels he has heard about: some claim to follow Paul, some claim to follow Apollos, some claim to follow Cephas, and some claim to follow Christ (v. 12). After presenting the problem, Paul raises questions to challenge his readers to consider their situation more deeply. The first question Paul asks is, "Is Christ divided?"

Paul's question is short, simple, and to the point for his readers. It is the lead-off question in a question string (where the first question is often the least rhetorical; §5.D.2). Paul's use of μεμέρισται brings a little bias into the polar question, but it is mild given the context in which the question is asked. All in all, the question leans informational with only mild rhetorical effect. Paul asks the question because he wants an answer back from his readers. His rhetorical goal is that they will read the questions and ask themselves to decide whether Christ is really divided or not. Given the way Paul asks the question, he is tacitly admitting that he does not know if the Corinthians may actually feel that Christ is divided—certainly their actions would lead Paul to believe they would say yes! The Corinthian readers must decide what they believe and how they will act. As the question string proceeds, Paul introduces greater degrees of bias into the questions to persuade the Corinthians to reevaluate their lack of unity.

FURTHER EXAMPLES

Matt 8:29b; 18:21b; Mark 11:32; Luke 7:20, 24b, 25b, 26b; 9:54; 23:3; Acts 8:34b; 2 Cor 11:7.

Key Bibliography

Fiengo, *Asking Questions*, 48–53.

R. Confirmation Questions

Confirmation questions are asked to verify knowledge or belief for the asker on behalf of the hearer. Confirmation questions are also called *check questions*. They get their name from the fact that the asker seeks to confirm something that the asker believes the hearer knows or should know. Confirmation questions are closely related to polar questions and are close in rhetorical effect to standard polar questions, but they arise when a vector from the semantic and pragmatic environment interacts epistemically with the asker of a polar question.[93] As a result, the contrast in the knowledge about the subject and the audience is what allows for a confirmation question. For example:

93. Here I deviate a little from my previous work by distinguishing confirmation questions from the larger umbrella of polar questions; see Estes, *Questions*, 113.

(1) Do brownies taste good? (DECISION QUESTION)
(2) Do brownies taste good to you? (CONFIRMATION QUESTION)
(3) Everett sees a brownie. "Can I have the brownie?" (PRAGMATIC DETERMINATION)

Example (1) is a polar question, and it asks a general question about brownies that could be answered yes or no (even if a no answer seems terribly unlikely). However, "to you" in (2) introduces a new semantic element that implies that the hearer knows something that the asker does not (i.e., a mild B-event occurs), which pushes this question into the realm of a confirmation question. Example (3) is more complex. If the question "can I have a brownie?" appeared naked in artificial discourse, it would be a vanilla kind of polar question. However, in the situation in (3), new semantic (and possibly pragmatic) factors intersect the asking of the question such that pragmatics will determine for certain whether this question is a polar question or a confirmation question. If Everett sees a brownie appear on his now-empty supper plate, it will be heard as a confirmation question, but if Everett sees a brownie in the window of a sweets shop downtown, it remains a polar question. Thus, confirmation questions are akin to request questions (§4.5). The difference between the two questions is mostly pragmatic; requests fulfill certain social and dialogue functions that make them distinct from confirmation questions. There is enough overlap between the two, however, that it is possible to consider request questions as a subset of confirmation questions.

The difficulty in identifying confirmation questions comes from the ebb and flow between strong semantics and strong pragmatics in the asking of these questions. One of the most important kinds of confirmation questions has its own unique pragmatic situation and its own name in linguistic literature—the *similar polarity question* (or SPQ). Though the general rule of polar questions and negation is that a polar question leans toward receiving a reply in the reverse polarity of that which the question is asked, in some situations askers subvert this rule in order to push a hearer toward confirmation. Let's look at an extended example:

Jason sees Su-Anne eating pizza. Jason could say to Su-Anne, "Do you like pizza?" Normally, this question would be asked as a polar question where the answer could go either way (or ever so slightly leaning negative, as it is positive). But in this situation, Jason knows Su-Anne is eating pizza, and Su-Anne knows Jason knows she is eating pizza, creating an epistemic problem for the question. In this case, the asker has evidence that the answer to his question is yes but for some reason asks for confirmation. (Perhaps the knowledge generated by seeing Su-Anne eating pizza contrasts with past knowledge about Su-Anne and pizza.) We can illustrate a more rhetorically powerful use of an SPQ by recasting the situation and using negative polarity in the question: Jason sees pizza but sees that Su-Anne is not eating any pizza (perhaps she is eating salad). Jason could say to Su-Anne, "Don't you like pizza?" In this situation, Jason knows Su-Anne is not eating pizza, so he could have asked, "Do you like pizza?" which would have indicated his lack of knowledge either way (and so we would treat it as a normal polar question). Instead, Jason uses an SPQ to confirm that she doesn't like pizza, and her response to "don't you like pizza?" would be, "No, I don't, actually." This scenario indicates that a B-event is at play, because Su-Anne knows whether she likes pizza, but Jason does not, though he has enough evidence not to simply ask but to call for a confirmation.

Formation

Confirmation questions must follow syntactic and semantic requirements. With syntax, only polar and alternative questions can serve as confirmation questions. This is not to say that a speaker cannot use variable questions and set questions to confirm something (with the right semantic situation and pragmatic force, almost anything is possible), but they are not asked or thought of in the same way as polar-built confirmation questions. Confirmation questions can occur with both positive and negative polarities, but the rhetorical force of a negative confirmation question is more pronounced than a positive or SPQ confirmation question. One of the most important possible tells for confirmation questions occurs when the question is asked in the second person (e.g., "Do *you* like...?" is a common form of mild confirmation question), though not all second-person polar questions are confirmation questions. However, to determine that a question is a confirmation question, there must be additional tells in the semantic and pragmatic spheres beyond simple syntax. With semantics, a confirmation question requires a semantic link between what the asker is asking and what the hearer knows or believes. With pragmatics, a confirmation question typically will not be asked in the first turn of dialogue but can occur in any other turn. They also can occupy any dialogue position, though the more they move toward the middle of a dialogue turn, the weaker their sense of confirmation becomes.

The most important factor in the formation and identification of confirmation questions is explained below.

1) Confirmation Questions Point to Something the Hearer Knows or Believes

Confirmation questions reveal an epistemic issue between question and asker—the asker asks a question where a) an answer to the question is not known for certain by the asker, b) there is some evidence of an answer known to the asker, and c) the asker believes the hearer can give an answer that substantiates the evidence. Confirmation questions are not impersonal; they focus on some perceived knowledge base within the audience. For example:

(4) Πιστεύετε ὅτι δύναμαι τοῦτο ποιῆσαι; (MATT 9:28)

Here in (4) Jesus asks two blind men who had been following him, "Do you believe that I am able to do this?" At first glance, we may read this as a typical open polar question where the answer could go either way. However, there are two reasons why this is not the best reading. First, Jesus asks πιστεύετε ("do you believe?"), a deeply personal question whose answer is merely a guess to someone else. Second, the two blind men have already shown evidence that they believe that Jesus is able to do this in that they (a) followed Jesus, (b) called out to Jesus, c) expected that Jesus could show mercy to them, and d) followed Jesus once more inside (Matt 9:27–28). As a result, Jesus does not ask in general whether or not the two blind men believe Jesus has the power to show mercy on their blindness but asks to confirm all the evidence coming out of these two men's hearts and actions that they do believe Jesus can do this. Though the question carries a positive polarity, it fully expects a positive response.

Rhetorical Effects

Informational
Rhetorical

Confirmation questions have multiple rhetorical effects that drive their interrogative logic. On one hand, they are strongly informational; they push the hearer to reply with either a positive or negative confirmation. As with most polar questions, they are decisive and encourage the speaker to answer. On the other hand, they have (at minimum) a moderate rhetorical effect in persuading the audience to agree with the focus of the question. Confirmation questions set up a weak B-event because the asker assumes the audience has an answer that would clarify the uncertainty in the asker. Except for decision questions (§4.Q), these are the least rhetorical and the most open toward receiving information of the polar questions we will study. Rhetorically, there is a fine line between confirmation questions and decision questions.

Three significant rhetorical effects of confirmation questions are explained below.

1) Confirmation Questions Suggest the Hearer Agree with the Asker

The most powerful rhetorical effect of confirmation questions is that they are often veiled attempts to get the hearer to agree with the presupposition of the asker. A speaker may use confirmation questions to get a hearer to admit to something that is not well established. For example:

(5) Σὺ εἶ ὁ βασιλεὺς τῶν Ἰουδαίων; (JOHN 18:33)

In (5), the first question Pilate asks Jesus is, "You are the king of the Jews?" With this question, Pilate clearly suspects the answer is yes and poses his question in such a way as to suggest to the audience that the answer is yes. It is likely that he asks his question in this way as the first premise of a dialectical argument. Thus, Pilate is merely trying to confirm what the evidence suggests, but to do so will require Jesus to make an admission that would create problems for Jesus. The situation is tense, but the form of Pilate's question suggests his approach his logical and matter-of-fact. Even today, readers think through this question and get the sense that Pilate is probably stating something we all know, even if it is not immediately admitted. Pragmatically, readers can almost visualize Pilate's assertive confidence in what he feels is an evident truth of Jesus's self-belief.

2) Confirmation Questions May Summarize an Argument

When confirmation questions are asked outside of a simple question-answer dialogue pair, they can have the rhetorical effect of capping or summarizing a lengthier argument. As noted in the *Rhetorica ad Herennium*, this was a common tactic in ancient rhetoric to reinforce the argument.[94] In this case, they can either push the audience to accept the argument (perhaps without allowing enough time for reflection), or they can persuade the audience to agree to the merits of the argument (cf. Matt 13:51). For example:

(6) οὐχὶ τοῖς ἁμαρτήσασιν, ὧν τὰ κῶλα ἔπεσεν ἐν τῇ ἐρήμῳ; (HEB 3:17B)

At the end of Hebrews 3, the author uses a question string to emphasize the danger of unbelief. The pattern of the string is test question (v. 16a), confirmation question (v. 16b), test question (v. 17a), confirmation question (v. 17b), test question (v. 18), and statement (v. 19). The pattern here is classic—the author asks a series of test questions (to see if the reader is awake and understands the point of the argument), followed by a series of confirmation questions to make sure the reader understands. Since (6), "Wasn't it to those who sinned, whose bodies fell in the wilderness?" is a polar question with negative polarity, the interpreter may wonder whether the question is not better understood as a negative polar question (§4.T). Because of (6)'s placement in the question string and the rhetorical use of test questions, the author of Hebrews is not using (6) to assert something about ὧν τὰ κῶλα ἔπεσεν ἐν τῇ ἐρήμῳ ("whose bodies fell in the wilderness") but to check and make sure the reader understands the significance of their deaths.

3) Confirmation Questions Betray a Doubt or Lack of Knowledge on the part of the Asker

Although a speaker can use confirmation questions to substantiate their argument, they also can work against the speaker by betraying to the audience that the speaker is uncertain about an answer to the question. In (5) above, Pilate may suggest that Jesus go ahead and admit that he is the king of the Jews, but in doing so Pilate also admits that he is perhaps not quite certain as to whether this is really true or not. For another example:

(7) οὐχ οὗτός ἐστιν ὁ τοῦ τέκτονος υἱός; (MATT 13:55A)

94. *Rhetorica ad Herennium* 4.15.22.

The question in (7) is one asked by the crowds in Jesus's hometown: "Isn't this one the carpenter's son?" Formed as a polar question with negative polarity, this question could be read as if the crowds were asserting that Jesus was the carpenter's son (or better, *merely* the carpenter's son). However, this reading does not take into account the fact that this question is part of a question string that is opened with a rather open question (Matt 13:54). As a result, the crowd uses this question more as a way to confirm their suspicions, that there is "no where" (πόθεν, v. 54) that Jesus could have gotten this wisdom and powers. But in asking a confirmation question, the townspeople are admitting that they really don't know for certain who Jesus is, whether he really is the carpenter's son or something much more.

Case Study JOHN 7:31

Ὁ Χριστὸς ὅταν ἔλθῃ μὴ πλείονα σημεῖα ποιήσει ὧν οὗτος ἐποίησεν;

CROWD: When the Messiah comes, will he perform even more signs than this man?

While Jesus teaches in the temple courts in Jerusalem, a debate arises as to who Jesus is and where he comes from. As Jesus teaches, he speaks to the crowd and tells them that they do in fact know who he is and where he is from. He tells them that he is not there on his own authority but on God's authority, a God that the crowd does not know, but Jesus knows because he was sent by God (John 7:28–29). These words cause a furor, and an unsuccessful attempt is made to seize Jesus. But many in the crowd believe the teaching and testimony of Jesus, asking, "When the Messiah comes, will he perform even more signs than this man?" These kinds of questions spur the Pharisees even more in their desire to arrest Jesus (v. 32).

John records this question in standalone position, as a representative of the kinds of questions that the crowd asked upon seeing the words and actions of Jesus. The question is a polar question, ultimately seeking a yes or no answer. It also contains an ἔνδοξα, in this case the belief that the Messiah would do miracles (§4.J). In the Greek, the question carries with it the NPI μή, which helps to demonstrate that the question is a confirmation question rather than a less rhetorical open polar question or a more rhetorical negative polar question.

Though the Pharisees may not like it, the crowd believes that the Messiah will do miracles, and they have evidence that Jesus himself has done a number of miracles (in the sense of σημεῖα, "signs"). Thus, the crowd suspects that Jesus could, in fact, be the Messiah—but they are not for certain. As a result, they go around asking questions to determine whether or not Jesus is the Messiah. These questions are not open, as if they were guessing, but based on the evidence of the signs he has done. The crowd asks the confirmation question with a negative polarity, asking if the Messiah won't do more signs than Jesus and expecting the answer, "No, he will not do more signs than this one did."

Thus the crowd forms the question with SPQ pragmatics. This is evidenced in the many modern English translations that convert the polarity of the question in translation so that new readers will be sure to surmise the answer is no. However, in the original Greek, casting the question as an SPQ points to the fact that these folks were trying to confirm with (and persuade) each other that the Messiah would not do more miracles than Jesus.

When many in the crowd started asking these kinds of confirmation questions, it reveals that while they may not yet be fully convinced that Jesus is from God, they do have enough evidence now to ask Jesus to confirm this belief for them. This is why the Pharisees make a second attempt to move against Jesus (v. 32), even though the first attempt failed. The enemies of Jesus cannot take the chance of the crowd moving from suspecting Jesus to be from God to having their suspicions confirmed and fully believing that Jesus actually is sent from God.

FURTHER EXAMPLES

Matt 9:28; 13:51, 55b; 15:12, 16; 20:13; Mark 14:37b; Luke 22:70; 24:32; John 7:41; Acts 23:4; 26:27; Rom 7:1; 1 Cor 7:27a, 27b; Heb 3:16b.

Key Bibliography

Estes, *Questions*, 111–13; Fiengo, *Asking Questions*, 53–63; Heinemann, "Questions of Accountability."

S. Request Questions

Request questions are asked to encourage a hearer to respond with a corresponding action. Because of the unique nature of this type of question, Western languages usually have a term for these kinds of questions; in English linguistics, they are simply called *requests*. Requests are a unique form of interrogative in that instead of asking for a reply through words they ask for a reply through actions. Requests ask hearers to *do* something. Requests are almost always intentional, though certain situations do arise when the utterance of a speaker is heard by the audience as an unintended request. Even though requests seek a response from a hearer and carry some degree of interrogative force, requests are not always punctuated as a question. For example:

(1) Can you pass the butter? (REQUEST QUESTION)

(2) Please pass the butter. (REQUEST "QUESTION")

(3) Pass the butter! (REQUEST "QUESTION")
(4) Who can pass the butter? (VARIABLE QUESTION)

In (1), the speaker asks a request question. While the question looks for a reply and is in a sense information seeking ("Yes, I can pass the butter"), what it really seeks is not the verbal reply but an active reply—the action of passing the butter. Even though (2) and (3) do not look like questions, they still perform a similar function with a similar sentential force. The reply to (2) could be, "Sure, happy to," but the request seeks the action of passing the butter. The reply to (3) could be, "Ok, I will! Here!" but the request still seeks the action of passing the butter. Thus, no matter how the speaker "asks" the request question, the desired reply is essentially the same.[95] In contrast, (4) is not a request; it is actually a variable question, but because of semantic factors and phatic expectations it would probably be heard as a request if the speaker and hearers were sitting around a supper table. There is much debate in erotetics as to whether request questions are really questions at all or politely disguised assertions or commands.[96]

Request questions are semantically related to confirmation questions (§4.R) and, occasionally, pragmatically related to repair questions (§5.B.4). In most natural-language situations, request questions will have some degree of phatic influence in their asking (§4.K) and will quite often implicate meaning about the syntactic and semantic level (§2.D.4).

Formation

Request questions are utterances with interrogative force that a speaker can mold as a question, a declarative, an imperative, or an exclamative. However, as examples (1), (2), and (3) reveal above, their syntactic formation and rhetorical effect is essentially the same regardless of the mold in which the utterance is cast. This is the reason some linguists do not feel requests are true questions but are a special kind of utterance. At the same time, a speaker may ask a request question in much the same way as any other question. Requests are always formed as polar questions or (in less common circumstances) alternative questions. This is the reason why (2) and (3) are requests (and in a sense, request questions) same as (1), while (4) is not a request question. In the GNT, askers sometimes form request questions with aposiopesis, meaning a conditional conjunction plus a polar-formed question without a complement clause (as in (5) below, which seems incomplete when translated literally into English).[97] In making the request, the speaker may use the imperative mood (cf. John 4:7). Request questions are usually positive in polarity, but they can be negative in polarity. When a speaker

95. Fava, "Questioning," 97.
96. Groenendijk and Stokhof, "Questions," 1069–72.
97. Cf. Fiengo, *Asking Questions*, 9.

asks a request question with negative polarity, the negative polarity changes the rhetorical effects of the request significantly.[98] A negative-polarity request question will have a similar rhetorical effect as a request molded by the speaker as an exclamative. A speaker may ask a request question in any turn of dialogue. They also may ask a request question in any dialogue position within a turn, but a request question is most common in standalone or closing positions; it is very unusual for it to be in the middle position. In most cases, request questions only occur in certain types of narrative discourse.

The primary factor in the formation and identification of the request questions is explained below.

1) Request Questions Ask a Hearer to Perform an Action in Lieu of a Verbal Reply

Request questions call for a response in the form of an action from a hearer. In some cases, the action called for by the asker of the request question is obvious (as in (1) above), but other times the request is made more obliquely. For example:

(5) Εἰ ἔξεστίν μοι εἰπεῖν τι πρὸς σέ; (ACTS 21:37A)

Question (5) from Acts is a great example of a certain type of request question. When Paul asks, "If it is possible for me to say something to you?" he makes a request of the Roman χιλίαρχος ("commander"). Here Paul's question is implicative, as it is certainly possible for Paul to say something to the commander. Although Paul asks the question in such a way that it could be information seeking, seeking a yes or no from the commander, what Paul really is asking is that the commander stop and listen. Paul wants the commander to complete an action (so he can be allowed to speak). Paul forms his question as a conditional question, presumably to make his request more polite. (After all, Paul is requesting the *Roman commander* to *stop* and *be quiet*). As we can see from Luke's writing, the commander's response is to ask a set of opposing-turn questions back at Paul, ignoring Paul's request (but presumably because of Paul's quality of spoken Greek, he doesn't beat him).

Rhetorical Effects

Informational
Rhetorical

Requests questions have, in a sense, informational qualities in that the information they seek is relayed to the asker through the performance of an action. Requests are also rhetorical, in a sense, because they persuade the hearer to perform the action. When request questions possess strong rhetorical force, an audience may hear them more as an order than a question. This is what happens when the speaker molds the request in a declarative, imperative, or exclamative

98. Heinemann, "'Will You or Can't You?,'" 1092–1102.

sentence or when the speaker asks a request question with negative polarity. Request questions are good indicators of power structures in discourse; the asking of request questions and the evaluation of the replies to request questions can reveal a great deal about the power relationships between the dialogue partners. They are often directed at specific hearers rather than opened to an audience.

The two most important rhetorical effects of request questions are explained below.

1) Request Questions Persuade a Hearer to Do What the Speaker Asks

The unique performative aspect of the request question results in a unique rhetorical effect: the request question is highly efficient at persuading a hearer to act. In one sense, request questions are the most effective rhetorical question available to a speaker. The caveat to this statement is that most request questions in natural-language situations are asked for mundane things (like passing the butter, which has a very high probability of success at most supper tables). Because of the effectiveness of a request question, sometimes speakers create hybrids with other types of questions. For example:

(6) Εἰ ἄνθρωπον Ῥωμαῖον καὶ ἀκατάκριτον ἔξεστιν ὑμῖν μαστίζειν; (ACTS 22:25)

Unfortunately, the GNT has few request questions, and (6) is only a request question in part.[99] Luke records that at the moment that Paul was to be flogged in Jerusalem, Paul says to the Roman ἑκατοντάρχης ("centurion"), "If it is possible for you to flog a man both Roman and innocent...?" As in (5), Paul again finds himself politely making a request of a Roman commander, using highly implicative language. However, unlike (5) which is a request question, here in (6) Paul adds a bit of bias that ups the rhetorical force of the question. Still, (6) is at base a type of request question; as with (5), although Paul asks the question in such a way that it could be information seeking, seeking a yes or no from the commander, what Paul really is asking is that the commander stop the flogging. In the case of (6), Paul's argument works better, as the commander *does* in fact do what Paul wants him to do—he stops the flogging.

2) Negative Request Questions Intimidate the Hearer into Compliance

Negative-polarity request questions come across as harsh to their hearers (e.g., "Can't you pass the butter?"). In some cases, the force of a negative request

99. This is not unexpected, as request questions are usually only found in narrative discourse that includes representation of everyday conversational patterns; for example, 2 Macc 7:7; 4 Macc 18:17; Dan 10:20 LXX.

question will cow the hearer into submission (and the hearer will complete the request), but in other cases the force of the request will cause a backlash against the asker. Because request questions are formed from polar questions, negative request questions have similar rhetorical effects as negative polar questions (§4.T). There do not appear to be any negative request questions in the GNT.

Case Studies — LUKE 22:49

Κύριε, εἰ πατάξομεν ἐν μαχαίρῃ;

JESUS'S DISCIPLES: Lord, can we strike with a sword?

Near the end of Jesus's public ministry, Jesus goes out after supper and prays near the Mount of Olives. During Jesus's time of prayer, the disciples fall asleep out of misery (Luke 22:45). As Jesus returns, he asks the disciples, "Why are you sleeping?" At that moment, a crowd appears with Judas at the forefront. When Judas sees Jesus, he comes over and tries to kiss Jesus. Jesus responds to this aggression with the question, "Judas, with a kiss you betray the Son of Man?" Watching these events unfold, the disciples then raise the question, "Lord, can we strike with a sword?" Before anyone replies, one disciple swings his sword at a servant of the high priest and severs the servant's ear.

The disciples' question in v. 49 comes at a pivotal moment in the narrative of the arrest of Jesus. To tell the story, Luke engages in compelling representational discourse that includes direct speech, such as this question. As a result, one issue that always comes in to play is the type of representation involved. In the case of this question, much is made of this question being unique to Luke. However, this question is more important to the narrative chain of events than often understood. The disciples' question is a polar question, and they employ it in a standalone position that signals the next turn. Though it is not technically a first-turn question, Luke records an event that breaks the dialogue so that the question is not read by the reader as an opposing-turn question (§5.B.1), thereby giving the question appropriate pragmatics for a topic shift into a new turn. In English, translators render the question as a typical polar question, as if the disciples are using the question to ask Jesus to decide what to do (as a decision question; §4.Q). Since this sounds odd, commentators often try to gloss over it as merely a "rhetorical question" or, worse, try to interpret it as a deliberative question (as if the question contained a subjunctive or did not expect an answer).[100] However, the syntactic construction of the question does not allow this: πατάξομεν is not subjunctive but future active indicative, and coupled with

100. For example, Burton, *Syntax*, 36; and from this Tiede, *Luke*, 393; Nolland, *Luke 18:35–24:53*, 1088; Marshall, *Gospel of Luke*, 836–37.

the direct, vocative Κύριε plus εἰ, this question is strongly informational and only mildly rhetorical. The disciples ask a question to Jesus to which they want an answer, and the question is not hesitant or uncertain.[101]

The key to identifying the interrogative logic of the question is not in the verb but in Κύριε, εἰ ("Lord, if"). The presence of these two conversational devices indicate that this question is a request question. Thus, the disciples are asking Jesus if he will give them permission to use their swords. Even more so, request questions ask a hearer to perform an action in lieu of a verbal reply. "Can you please pass the salt?" is a request question because the asker is asking a hearer to complete the action more than say yes. Request questions often begin with εἰ in the GNT to indicate a condition for action, not possibility.[102] They do expect an affirmative reply, especially when used to make a request.[103] The problem with the question of the disciples is that they are not asking the action of someone else; rather, they are asking the action of themselves. As a result, the disciples are asking Jesus to give them permission to take the action.[104] Adding to this is the disciples use of πατάξομεν—interpreters usually assume the "we" to refer to the disciples, based on implicit assumptions made about Jesus's character, but if the disciples thought it was proper for them to strike there is no reason to believe that they did not *also* think it was proper for Jesus to fight also (making the "we" to include Jesus). Either way, the disciples are making a request for their group to fight with the full expectation of action.

So clear is the request for action that one of the disciples does exactly what the question intends and strikes a member of the arresting party. The request is made and the disciple acts. To this, Augustine notes that Jesus responds to the disciples' question—not their actions—with a request to stand down: ἐᾶτε ἕως τούτου ("Leave it be!"; v. 51).[105] Luke includes this question because the disciples' request for their group to take action is a clear and visceral response to the situa-

101. Cf. Porter, *Verbal Aspect*, 420, 425.

102. And at times outside the GNT, such as Dan 2:26 Theodotion; Tobit 5:10. In this case εἰ functions more as a discourse particle than a conditional particle (§2.B.7). Caragounis argues that the εἰ in direct questions in the GNT is a misspelling of the adverb ἦ ("truly"), brought about because of the close or identical pronunciations of the two words since ἦ was dying out from the language. The argument hinges on several circumstances that cannot be debated in this space. If Caragounis is correct, it would only alter the coloring and not the substance of my analysis. If not, my analysis stands. See Caragounis, *Development of Greek*, 208–16.

103. Bock, *Luke 9:51–24:53*, 1770. Also, it is socially more acceptable to affirm a request than to deny a request.

104. An example of this type of request occurs in modern language. If I were to ask someone, "Can we go to the store?" in most situations I do not want a verbal response; I simply want the person to get in the car and go to the store. The question is meant as a request for action.

105. Augustine, *Harmony of the Gospels* 3.17.

tion they were enduring, even while it signals to Luke's readers that the disciples still do not fully understand Jesus's mission.

MATTHEW 15:15

φράσον ἡμῖν τὴν παραβολὴν [ταύτην];

PETER: Explain the parable to us?

In Jesus's public ministry, he often told parables to the crowds, and because his speech was in parables, he was often not well understood by the crowds or his disciples. In one situation, as Jesus is trading barbs with the Pharisees over eating practices, he tells the disciples a short parable that compares the Pharisees to plants and blind guides (Matt 15:13–14). Peter, at least, does not understand Jesus's metaphorical speech and says to Jesus to φράσον ("explain") the parable to them. Matthew records Peter's request with a verb in an imperative mood, φράσον, which could cause a misunderstanding for readers that Peter is ordering Jesus to explain the parable. In every major English translation, this utterance is translated as a declarative. Is Peter telling or instructing Jesus to explain the parable? Or is there more going on here?

Though the utterance is short, the interrogative logic of this request question is complex. There are three major factors. First, Peter's use of φράζω in the question semantically marks the question as a repair question (§5.B.4). A speaker asks a repair question when something in the prior dialogue turn does not make sense and needs to be clarified. When a speaker initiates dialogue repair, the speaker may not form the utterance with a traditional question form, yet the utterance is still a request by the speaker for the previous-turn speaker to reply and clarify their turn. Second, Peter's lack of understanding of the parable sets up a B-event scenario (§2.C.7). A B-event occurs when a speaker makes an utterance about something that only a hearer would know, and therefore that utterance from the speaker is heard as a question by the hearer. Because Peter makes an utterance about Jesus's parable—a parable that is reflective of Jesus's internal understanding of spiritual matters—his utterance will be heard by an audience as a question regardless of whether or not it is formed as a question. Finally, Peter makes a request of Jesus, much in the same way typical requests are made. He asks Jesus to perform an action, which in this case is Jesus stopping his teaching to go back and explain the parable to the disciples. Matthew's use of the imperative here serves to distinguish Peter's use from the standard indicative. The imperative has several functions, one of which is to make requests.[106] The formation of the question leads the reader to believe that Peter made his request

106. BDF §387.

in earnest, and this is the most probable reason why Matthew records φράσον. Thus, Peter is not being rude or demanding; rather, he asks a question of Jesus to explain the parable.[107] The question has multiple effects, which we read as Peter's emphatic desire for Jesus to repair, to clarify, and to respond so that Peter might truly understand what Jesus really meant by this parable.

FURTHER EXAMPLES
John 4:7; Acts 22:27; 25:9.

Key Bibliography
Estes, *Questions*, 112; Holmberg, "Whimperatives"; Macaulay, "Asking to Ask"; May, "Questions as Suggestions," 237.

T. Negative Polar Questions

Negative polar questions are asked to persuade or coerce the hearer into a position favorable to the position of the asker. A negative polar question is often called a *negative polar interrogative* by linguists. As with polar questions and confirmation questions, they are a common question type; they are also one of the most discussed question types in linguistics. In their purest sense, negative polar questions are simply polar questions with a negative polarity. This may make it seem that we should treat NPQs under the syntax heading. However, while we can identify NPQs primarily by their syntax, it is their unique and powerful rhetorical nature that makes a bigger impact on us. This is especially true once we take into consideration their semantic and pragmatic influences. Negative polar questions are one of the most "assertive" of all question types. For example:

(1) Doesn't Wyatt have homework to do? (NPQ)
(2) Can't Bridget help around the house? (NPQ)
(3) Can Violet go and not play anymore? (NOT NPQ)

Examples (1) and (2) both represent typical negative polar questions. In both situations, the speaker asks a question that the hearer is persuaded to answer with an affirmative. In fact, (2) is coercive enough that it may result in more than just an affirmative; it may also result in a call to action. However, (3) is not a negative polar question in the fullest (syntactic/semantic) sense, mostly because the negation does not occur in the verbal phrase that carries the interrogative force of the question. Since (3) has negative polarity items ("not" and "anymore"), it still creates a situation where the asker hopes the answer is yes. But it does not coerce

107. Luz, *Matthew 8–20*, 327; Nolland, *Matthew*, 625; Talbert, *Matthew*, 188; Smith, *Matthew*, 192.

or assert as a true NPQ does. Most, but not all, polar questions with negative polarity do work as negative polar questions (the most obvious exception being SPQs; see §4.R). While we can find negative polar questions in many environments, they are especially common in rhetorical discourse in the GNT.

Formation

Negative polar questions have strict formation guidelines: a speaker must form them from a polar question, and the question must be negated. The negation must occur in the primary interrogative clause (not a subclause or phrase), and it must be a singular negation or equivalent. Typically this means that the negative polarity item doing the negating will negate the verb. Since Koine Greek handles negation differently than English, care must be taken in interpreting negative polar questions (§2.B.9). One example of this is the difference between the use of οὐ-forms and μή-forms of negative particles. Both particles are negative polarity items and can create negative polarity. However, in some questions in the GNT, μή functions as a negative polarity item (creating a strong, negative bias) but does not switch the polarity of the question (at least, with the same strength as οὐ does). This nuance is often difficult to translate into English, since English does not use a nuanced negative particle like μή. In contrast, οὐ always seems to switch the polarity of the question when the οὐ-form negates the clause bearing the interrogative force. Negative polar questions cannot be formed with other syntactic formations nor with a positive polarity. In addition, negative polar questions usually carry a semantic quality that feels as though they are foisting their opinion on the audience. It must be strong enough; if not, the polar question with negative polarity could be more of a decision question or a similar polarity question (as can occur when a question uses μή instead of οὐ). In fact, NPQs are so strong rhetorically that they seem not to expect a positive reply as much as to assert what should be the positive reply, yet still phrased as a question seeking a response. NPQs have no pragmatic limits; they can be asked in any dialogue turn and from any position. However, because of their rhetorical effects, they are more likely to be asked in the standalone or closing position.

The most critical factor in the formation and identification of NPQs is explained below.

1) NPQs Are Formed from a Polar Question That Is Negated Syntactically and Semantically

Negative polar questions must possess a clear negative polarity to pull off the rhetorical effects of this type of question. One indicator that a question is a NPQ is the placement of the negative particle—in Koine Greek, it will usually appear near the beginning of the sentence (and usually before the main verb).[108] In the

108. Cf. Levinsohn, *Discourse Features*, 51.

GNT, it is also common to see NPQs front their negative particle (§2.B.11). For example:

(4) μὴ *οὐκ* ἔχομεν ἐξουσίαν φαγεῖν καὶ πεῖν; (1 COR 9:4)

Example (4) sees Paul defensively asking his readers, "Don't we [even] have the right to eat and to drink?" Paul uses the negative polarity item οὐκ to negate the sentence and then uses the negative polarity item μή to push emphasis on the verb ἔχομεν, much in the way that the English word "even" would work if included. In asking this, Paul raises a question that needs to be answered, with the strong expectation that the answer is yes. But just as much as Paul is asking this, he is also asserting that he expects the audience to know that they *do* have this right.

In contrast, see this example:

(5) ἁμαρτήσωμεν ὅτι *οὐκ* ἐσμὲν ὑπὸ νόμον ἀλλὰ ὑπὸ χάριν; (ROM 6:15B)

Question (5) presents a different scenario, even though at first glance this question may appear to be a negative polar question. Paul asks, "Should we sin because we are not under the law but under grace?" This question is an example of a polar question that has a clear negative polarity item in it (οὐκ), but the clause that carries the interrogative force is not syntactically or semantically the recipient of this negation. The clause that carries the interrogative force is ἁμαρτήσωμεν ("should we sin?"). What is negated in this question is the premise that "we are not under the law." Thus, Paul asks whether it is possible that they should consider sinning while keeping in mind the premise of no longer being under the law but under grace. Therefore, (5) is an example of an open polar question with positive polarity and not a negative polar question.

Rhetorical Effects

Informational
Rhetorical

Negative polar questions are one of the most recognized question types with regard to their rhetorical effects. Typically, NPQs have weak informational qualities and strong rhetorical qualities. While it is easy for the rhetorical qualities of negative polar questions to overshadow their informational qualities, interpreters must remember that NPQs are no different than any other question in that they do ask more than they say. Negative polar questions ask for agreement, and they ask for it so strongly that it feels to the audience that the asking is really a telling (or if strong enough, a yelling). With weak rhetorical qualities, an NPQ may come across as a pleading or a slightly manipulative request. With strong rhetorical qualities, an NPQ will come across as harsh and demeaning.[109] A speaker

109. For greater discussion of the rhetorical impact of NPQs on the audience, see Estes, *Questions*, 145–47.

may ask a negative polar question in almost any pragmatic situation with almost any degree of strength from weak to strong.

The two most important rhetorical effects of negative polar questions are explained below.

1) Negative Polar Questions Are Highly Assertive

NPQs are one of the most assertive of all question types. Askers raise them as if they are taking the point of the question and asserting it toward the audience. Their negation combines with their interrogative force to give this sense of assertion alongside the question's native bent toward seeking information. Yet the assertive force present in a negative polar question is categorically different from the assertive force of a proposition; in the question, it is a secondary force, but in the proposition it is the one and only force. For example:

(5) Οὐχὶ σὺ εἶ ὁ Χριστός; (LUKE 23:39)

The question in (5), "Aren't you the Christ?" is made by one of the criminals who was crucified with Jesus (Luke 23:39). Prior to the question, the criminal witnessed the soldiers mocking Jesus's plight, given that he is ὁ βασιλεὺς τῶν Ἰουδαίων ("the king of the Jews"; v. 38). In asking (5) as a negative polar question, the criminal raises a legitimate question as to whether Jesus is the Christ, but does so with such strong rhetorical force that it overtakes the informational qualities of the question. The question is designed to ἐβλασφήμει ("to slander") Jesus by implying to the audience that he is (supposedly) the Christ. Thus, Jesus should be able to save himself (v. 39). Because of their strong rhetorical effects, negative polar questions are often used in an accusatory way to suggest and imply hurt to others.

2) Negative Polar Questions Can Be Strongly Coercive

With their assertive effect, NPQs can combine this with their questioning force to create a strongly coercive question. In English, questions that begin with clauses like "can't you even..." or "don't you still..." are indicative of highly coercive negative polar questions. These kinds of strong NPQs occur in highly charged debates or difficult arguments, not pleasant discourse. Speakers often use them in double questions as the *two* part of a *one-two combination* (§5.D.1), or as the final punch of a longer question string (§5.D.2). For example:

(6) οὐ νοεῖτε ὅτι πᾶν τὸ εἰσπορευόμενον εἰς τὸ στόμα εἰς
τὴν κοιλίαν χωρεῖ καὶ εἰς ἀφεδρῶνα ἐκβάλλεται; (MATT 15:17)

In Matthew 15:16, Jesus asks the disciples, "And yet you still don't understand?" as a confirmation question with mild bias from ἀκμήν ("yet"), and follows it up with a second question (6), "Don't you see that ...?" For the reader, Jesus establishes what we already suspect: the disciples are clueless. Jesus follows this with a strong, even harsh, negative polar question, asking—or in a sense, asserting—that they can't see the obvious principle of external trappings and internal realities. The problem for Jesus is *not* the principle itself; it is the disciples' failure to understand. Jesus asks the question to force them to rip away their spiritual blindness. This second question is the powerful hook in this *one-two combination* (cf. §5.D.1).

Case Study 1 CORINTHIANS 1:20D

οὐχὶ ἐμώρανεν ὁ θεὸς τὴν σοφίαν τοῦ κόσμου;

PAUL: Hasn't God made foolish the wisdom of the world?

Near the beginning of Paul's first extant letter to the Corinthians, Paul starts a memorable argument based on the cross as μωρία ("foolishness") to those dying and δύναμις ("power") to those being rescued (1 Cor 1:18). Paul cites Isaiah as a reference to the fact that the power of the cross will one day be the end of the wisdom of the world (v. 19). Then Paul does something rather dramatic: he introduces a question string that begins with three aporetic questions (§4.E). "Where is the wise one? Where is the scholar? Where is the speaker du jour?" (v. 20). These questions are ironically aporetic. Paul is not really at a loss in the face of these magnificent thinkers but asks these questions to point out that they are not as wonderful as people in the world might think they are. They certainly are not as wise as the world thinks they are.

Paul caps the question string with the question, "Hasn't God made foolish the wisdom of the world?" As a question with both negative polarity and semantic bias in ἐμώρανεν ("made foolish"), the rhetorical qualities are too strong for it to be merely a decision question, but nothing indicates that it is intended to trap the reader (as in a loaded or leading question, cf. §4.V and §4.W). It is also not a confirmation question, as the argument does not seem personal; Paul is not trying to confirm with his audience that God hasn't made foolish the wisdom of the world (as in a SPQ, cf. §4.R). Instead, Paul writes a negative polar question to ask (tell) his reader that God has made foolish the wisdom of the world. By leading into this question with three aporetic-yet-ironic questions, Paul scorns the greatness of those considered paragons of worldy wisdom to show how adrift his readers in Corinth are by looking to the wise, the writers, and the philosophers. He then rips the glory of this worldly wisdom away from these authorities by emphasizing that God has made each of them foolish. Paul coerces his audience to see it this way, too.

FURTHER EXAMPLES

Matt 21:42; 22:31–32; 26:40, 62a; Mark 4:21b; Luke 23:40; Acts 7:50; Rom 10:18, 19; 1 Cor 9:1a, 1b, 1c; 2 Cor 12:18b, 18c; Jas 2:6, 7, 21, 25.

Key Bibliography
Estes, *Questions*, 152–57; Golka, "Semantics and Pragmatics," 149–150; Guerzoni and Sharvit, "Question of Strength," 361–91; Reese, "Meaning and Use," 331–54; Romero and Han, "Negative *Yes/No* Questions," 609–58; van Rooy, "Negative Polarity Items," 239–73.

U. Biased Questions

A *biased question* is asked to provide a strong rhetorical push at the audience. The primary intent of asking a biased question derives from the strong bias embedded in the question. Biased questions "convey an expectation, or bias, on the part of the speaker toward a specific answer to the question."[110] To some degree, almost all utterances have some bias (§2.C.2). Bias is one quality of questions that help them feel rhetorical. However, in this section we consider biased questions, not questions with some bias. The difference between a question with bias and a biased question is that the bias present in the question with bias does not overwhelm the semantic focus of the question, but the bias present in a biased question does overwhelm the semantic focus of the question. Of course, the exact distinction between the two does not always hold in natural-language situations. As so many questions have some degree of bias in them, the type of question we identify as a biased question is one with both a high degree of bias and one where the primary force is inexorably tainted by the bias. To qualify as a biased question, the question must not only show bias internally but be asked primarily to export the bias in the direction of the audience. For example:

(1) Where the *hell* are you going? (BIASED QUESTION)
(2) Can't you *ever* take out the trash? (BIASED QUESTION)

Examples (1) and (2) show how bias breaks into the different question formations and taints the questions to the point that they are no longer able to be considered open questions (as in (1)) or negative polar questions (as in (2)). In (2), "ever" is also in English a unique type of negative polarity item which creates a great deal of bias. Because of the prominence of bias in questions, biased questions are related to negative polar questions (§4.T), loaded questions (§4.V), and leading questions (§4.W). As a result, it is usually better to see if a question under consideration is a loaded, leading, or negative polar question first; if not, and it seems to be a strongly opinionated question, it is likely a biased question.

110. Asher and Reese, "Intonation and Discourse," 3.

Formation

Biased questions can be formed from any other formation (or even type) of question without regard to any syntactic, semantic, or pragmatic qualities. Thus, any question can be turned into a bias-type question with the addition of sufficient bias. The way bias shows up in questions is through meaning; yet one of the challenges of reading from an ancient language such as Greek is knowing exactly what words would create bias (and exactly how much bias it would create). For example, in the above examples we can be relatively confident that a question such as (2) will exhibit bias in most IE languages, including Koine Greek and English. However, even though (1) may appear more biased than (2), the semantic inference created by "hell" may create different degrees of bias in different languages and in different situations. In addition, Koine Greek has bias words such as ἄρα that are not always easily translatable into English (e.g., Matt 19:25). Another challenge in identifying bias words is that a speaker can create bias in questions in at least four different ways: A speaker can create bias (a) minimally, using syntactic constructions such as particles and adverbs (for example, ἄρα); (b) semantically, using words that have pejorative or negative meanings; (c) implicatively, using idioms and expressions that indicate bias to the audience even if not stated directly; and (d) pragmatically, if a speaker takes a word or phrase that does not normally add bias but adds spoken or written emphasis to artificially create bias. Of these, (a) and (b) are the most common and easiest to identify in the GNT; (c) and (d) are much more difficult. Interpreting bias in the GNT is not an exact science. In addition, some questions are strongly bent toward bias; for example, negative tag questions and some negative polar questions are (by their formation) a type of biased question. A speaker may employ biased questions in any dialogue turn or any dialogue position, though a strongly biased question will present problems for a speaker if it is placed in the middle position (as it usually will elicit a strong response from the audience).

The primary factor in the formation and identification of biased questions is explained below.

1) Biased Questions Contain Overt Bias Words or Phrases

The telltale sign of a biased question is the inclusion of an overt bias word (or words or phrase) that shapes (or often seems to take control over) the interrogative force of the question. By overt, this simply means that the bias word is literally present—it doesn't mean that the hearer has to recognize the bias word as a bias word (in fact, in many cases, the hearer does not, not explicitly anyway). However, the bias word must fall within the primary clause that carries the interrogative force. For example:

(3) *Οὐκ* ἀποκρίνῃ *οὐδέν*; (MARK 14:60A)

Question (3) contains two bias words (οὐκ and οὐδέν) in a short clause. Both bias words are negative polarity items and therefore exhibit strong bias, but what makes this question more a biased question than a negative polar question is the use of οὐδέν. In this case, when the high priest asks, "You won't answer with anything?" the bias of οὐδέν changes the interrogative logic of the question so that instead of asserting that Jesus won't answer (as a NPQ would here), the bias words create a rhetorical push around οὐδέν. Thus, the high priest is not asking why Jesus won't respond; rather, he is pushing against Jesus's refusal to respond at all. The question telegraphs the high priest's expectation that Jesus will continue to refuse to respond. In English, rendering the high priest's question along the lines of "have you no answer?" (NRSV) is too weak to capture the explicit bias present in the Greek and weakens the interrogative logic of the question.

Rhetorical Effects

Informational
Rhetorical

Biased questions have some of the strongest rhetorical effects of any question type. These effects occur when the asker uses the bias to telegraph their opinions and expectations about the focus of the question. Even though biased questions may have strong rhetorical qualities, it does not eliminate them from being information seeking. Quite the contrary, biased questions may actually have strong informational qualities, though the information being sought may not be limited to the literal question itself. So strong is their bias that this type of question has the side effect of seeming to be directed at certain hearers rather than being asked in general to an audience. This can create tension between the speaker and hearer(s). Scholars have recognized the rhetorical effect of bias in questions since at least the time of Quintilian.[111]

Two of the most important rhetorical effects of biased questions are explained below.

1) Biased Questions Frequently Take Jabs at the Audience

If the degree of bias in a question is mild, the question may cause the hearer to twinge a little, but if the degree of bias in a question is strong, the question will feel like an attack on the hearer (as in (2), above). The stronger the bias, the greater the rhetorical strength of the question and the more pushy these questions can seem. Sometimes the hearer on the receiving end of the question will simultaneously think about how to answer the question and how to retaliate against the negative push. For example:

(4) Ὦ *ἀνόητοι* Γαλάται, τίς ὑμᾶς *ἐβάσκανεν*, οἷς *κατ' ὀφθαλμοὺς*…; (GAL 3:1)

When Paul asks in (4), "O foolish Galatians, who has bewitched you, that before

111. Quintilian, *Institutio oratoria* 8.3.89.

your eyes...," he uses three distinct bias words to convey his frustration at the audience in Galatia: ἀνόητοι ("foolish"), ἐβάσκανεν ("has bewitched") and likely the expression κατ᾽ ὀφθαλμοὺς ("before ... eyes"). At its base, Paul forms this complex question with a variable formation, as if asking "who" has done this thing to them. Yet Paul inserts his concerns about their lack of sense (through the adjectival bias in ἀνόητος) and their lack of sophistication (through the verbal bias in βασκαίνω) before modifying his "open"-seeming question with the expressive κατ᾽ ὀφθαλμοὺς that telegraphs Paul's expectation that even if the Galatians would see something, they are not necessarily savvy enough to figure it out or believe it. Thus, in asking the Galatians about their sorry state, Paul takes a real shot at their capacity and maturity as fellow believers.

2) Biased Questions Can Reveal Underlying Assumptions of the Asker

Questions with strong rhetorical effects are often two-way streets. Because biased questions telegraph the opinions and expectations of the asker to the audience, these questions can also reveal underlying assumptions of the asker. With biased questions, this is usually obvious; in (4) Paul makes no attempt to hide his assumptions about the Galatians. In (2), the clear underlying assumption is that the asker believes the hearer never takes out the trash. The stronger the bias, the easier this is to spot. For example:

(5) *Ἀκμὴν καὶ ὑμεῖς ἀσύνετοί ἐστε;* (MATT 15:16)

In example (5), Jesus includes two bias words, ἀκμήν ("yet") and ἀσύνετοί ("don't understand"), when he asks the disciples, "And yet you still don't understand?" It's not hard for readers to catch Jesus's underlying assumption: he thinks the disciples are quite cotton headed. In fact, what makes this question humorous is that Jesus—by asking a biased question rather than an accusatory NPQ—is not simply telegraphing his opinion about their lack of understanding but is inviting the disciples to agree with him that they, in fact, do have heads stuffed with cotton.

Case Study — MATTHEW 19:20

τί *ἔτι* ὑστερῶ;

YOUNG MAN: What do I *still* lack?

In a well-known and poignant story in Matthew's Gospel, a young man with great wealth approaches Jesus to ask what good must be done to receive eternal life (Matt 19:16). Jesus responds to this question with an opposing-turn question (§5.B.1), meant to push back against the premise of the young man's question.

Jesus then answers the young man's question by saying he is to keep the commandments (v. 17). Next follows an exchange where the young man clarifies that he has kept the greater commandments and asks, "What do I still lack?" In response, Jesus tells him that to achieve τέλειος ("completion"), he must sell his possessions, give the proceeds to the poor, and follow Jesus (v. 21).

The question from the young man plays an interesting role in the dialogue exchange. Let's consider the dialogue movements. First, the young man asks a question, then (eventually) Jesus provides an answer, then the young man asks a kind of repair question to clarify (which commandments), then Jesus provides an answer, and in response the young man confirms he has done this (i.e., kept all these commandments). At this point in the dialogue, the reader would expect that the dialogue would move forward. However, it does not. Instead, the young man—seemingly unsatisfied with either Jesus's answer or his own life—asks a question that harkens back to the original question ("What good must I do that I can get eternal life?").

This question τί ἔτι ὑστερῶ; has a subtle yet important source of bias in ἔτι that fully taints the question and telegraphs to the audience what the young man is really asking. The question is a simple variable question, and its simple formation hides its semantic importance. (In many cases, the more simple the question, the more subtle the bias can be and the more clever the bias is in shaping the force and meaning of the question.) In this case, the young man is not only asking if there is something he is missing; because it is a biased question, the emphasis on ἔτι creates a strong signal back to Jesus: "There is something you're not telling me." If the young man had asked, τί ὑστερῶ; ("What do I lack?"), readers would know (because it's an open question) the young man asked hoping to find out what could be missing. By adding in the bias ἔτι, the reader can perceive the underlying assumption of the asker that something is missing and that whatever that something is may not be acceptable or palatable. Adding bias to questions like this also creates a slight hedge where the asker can make a genuine request for information but, by including the bias, creates a defense so as to be more readily able to reject whatever the missing information means. In this case, ἔτι reveals the young man knows there's more to the story than Jesus first said and telegraphs his defensiveness or frustration with the possibility of having to accept this new information.

FURTHER EXAMPLES

Mark 7:18; 14:63; Luke 14:5; John 1:46; 8:10b; Rom 3:29a; 11:1; Jas 2:20.

Key Bibliography

Estes, *Questions*, 157–62; Progovac, *Negative and Positive Polarity*, 97–103; Reese, "Bias in Questions"; Reese and Asher, "Biased Questions"; Walton, *One-Sided Arguments*, 230–33.

V. Loaded Questions

Loaded questions embed an unproven assumption in the asking of the question. The usual goal of the implicit assumption in a loaded question is to trap or trick the hearer into confirming the assumption of the question as asked by the speaker. The rhetorical result is that if the addressee responds to the loaded question without addressing the implicit premise of the question, the addressee will either (a) appear guilty or (b) appear to be "protesting too much" (and therefore, appear guilty). To some degree, all utterances have some type of embedded or implicit presupposition(s).[112] The difference between a question with an implicit assumption and a loaded question is that the implicit assumption present in the unloaded question does not overwhelm the semantic focus of the question, but the implicit assumption present in a loaded question does overwhelm the semantic focus of the question. Of course, the exact distinction between the two does not always hold in natural-language situations. With so many questions containing implicit assumptions, the type of question we identify as a loaded question is one with both a strong and overt implicit assumption *and* one where the primary force is inexorably tainted by the assumption. To qualify as a loaded question, the question must not only make an assumption but be asked primarily to push the assumption onto the addressee and in the direction of the audience. Loaded questions rely heavily on implicated meaning (§2.D.4). For example:

(1) When did Nadine stop texting while driving? (LOADED QUESTION)
(2) Don't you ever come to work on time? (LOADED QUESTION)

Example (1) is a reworking of the classic example of a loaded question. The question is fully loaded as it implies to the audience that there was a time that Nadine was texting while driving, even if that implication is not true or even valid. However Nadine tries to answer, she will look guilty. In fact, so loaded is this question that if Nadine had never driven a car in her life and was asked this question, she would still appear guilty in the eyes of the audience. Example (2) is a more subtle loaded question, because the question asks about tardiness, but it also implies to the addressee that they are lacking in quality as an employee—they are almost always late. As with (1), even if the receiver of this question was never late to work, there is no answer to this question that does not make them appear guilty of being late when asked before an audience.

Loaded questions are similar to biased questions (§4.U) and leading questions (§4.W). The difference between a loaded question and a biased question is that a biased question contains a word or phrase with overt bias and a loaded question contains a (usually) implicit hidden assumption. Sometimes bias creates a presuppositional condition, so there can be overlap between these two types.

112. Widdowson, *Text, Context, Pretext*, 103.

Likewise, there is a great deal of overlap between loaded and leading questions; a leading question is usually loaded, and many loaded questions can function in a leading capacity. The difference between the two often comes down to motive—the loaded question uses deception to confuse or trap an addressee, whereas the leading question uses coercion and browbeating to force agreement with an addressee.

Formation

Loaded questions cannot be identified by syntax, as a speaker can effectively form a loaded question from any of the major question formations. Even conditional questions can be used to create loaded questions. Loaded questions can be either positive or negative in polarity. In artificial dialogue, examples of loaded questions are often formed with positive polarity, but loaded questions tend toward negative polarity in most natural-dialogue situations. The key to the formation of loaded questions is in their semantics. Hearers must consider all that is presupposed by the asking of the question. If the presupposition is deceptive, erroneous, or fallacious and the point of the question is contingent on the presupposition, then the question likely has loaded semantic qualities. Pragmatically, a loaded question is provocative and inflammatory and is often found in heated rhetorical discourse. They can be found in any type of discourse, in any dialogue turn, and in any dialogue position. Because they are meant to be answered, they should be asked in either the standalone or closing dialogue position.

The primary factor in the formation and identification of a loaded question is explained below.

1) Loaded Questions Embed an Unsubstantiated Presupposition

Loaded questions contain an implicit assumption that creates the condition for the loaded question used against the addressee. This assumption can be mild or strong, overt or disguised. The transparency of the presupposition is directly proportional to the rhetorical force of the question. Key to understanding the question is identifying the implicit assumption. For example:

(3) μοιχαλίδες, οὐκ οἴδατε ὅτι ἡ φιλία τοῦ κόσμου ἔχθρα τοῦ θεοῦ ἐστιν; (JAS 4:4)

Example (3) is a variation on the classic example of a loaded question, as James asks his readers, "Adulterers, don't you know that the love of the world equals hostility to God?" First, there is the bias word μοιχαλίδες ("adulterers") that alerts the reader that something critical is coming. Then James asks about love of the world creating hostility to God. (Surely this is something to be avoided!) Notice, James uses the factive-verb construction οὐκ οἴδατε ὅτι ("don't you know?") to create a loaded question. James never actually asks his readers if they are choosing love of the world; instead, he coyly asks them if they *know* that love of the world means hostility to God. Why bring it up if James's readers are not loving the world? By asking the question, the embedded presupposition of James's loaded question indicates James believes that his audience does love the world. No matter which way they would try to answer, it would seem that they were either (a) ignorant of what God wanted them to do or (b) guilty in some way of what James claims.

Rhetorical Effects

Informational
Rhetorical

All questions are built on implicit premises, but what makes a loaded question different is that it employs its implicit premise against both the addressee *and* the audience. Loaded questions are a strongly rhetorical type of questioning. Their substantial rhetorical effects are very effective at persuading the audience (and demoralizing the addressee). If they can be successfully asked without challenge, they are one of the most persuasive types of questions. Even with all of their coercive rhetorical effects, they are still mildly information seeking as one of their goals is to see how a hearer may respond. In fact, the request for information is very much a part of the rhetorical strategy of loaded questions—any reply can further persuade the audience.

Three of the most important rhetorical effects of loaded questions are explained below.

1) Loaded Questions Attempt to Entrap Their Addressee

When a speaker asks a loaded question, the speaker put the addressee in a bind. The speaker's hope is to coerce a reply that will trap the addressee in the ears of the audience. In this sense, while loaded questions are not formed similar to dilemma questions (§4.O), they do possess a similar rhetorical function. Due to their presupposition(s), loaded questions do not allow an addressee to respond in a favorable way—they create a no-win scenario for anyone attempting to answer. Even refusing to answer seems suspicious to the audience, as the rhetorical force of the loaded question appears to validate the presupposition in the minds of the audience. For example:

(4) τί ἄρα ἔσται ἡμῖν; (MATT 19:27)

In example (4), Peter asks what seems syntactically to be a simple question: "What will be for us?" In fact, the simplistic feel of the question makes it appear as an open question, as if Peter is asking with full sincerity (and perhaps he is). Yet this strategy is what makes this open question all the more loaded (and deceptive). Prior to this question, Peter heard Jesus tell the rich young man that to be complete he must sell his possessions, give the proceeds to the poor, receive treasure in heaven, then come and follow Jesus (Matt 19:21). Then Peter hears

Jesus's remark at the exit of the grieving rich young man that it was hard for the rich to enter the kingdom of heaven. Finally, Peter hears the disciples ask something of a loaded repair question about who can actually be rescued from death, to which Jesus offers a euphemistic answer about God who can make the impossible possible. Now it is Peter's turn, and he makes a statement about what the disciples have left behind and also asks a loaded question to establish what will be for them. Peter's use of ἄρα creates a mild bias. First, we have Peter's propositional premise: ἰδοὺ ἡμεῖς ἀφήκαμεν πάντα καὶ ἠκολουθήσαμέν σοι ("See, we left everything and followed you"; v. 27a). This is in itself an implicit assumption, at least for the reader, as there is no way to know if Peter's πάντα ("everything") is literal or euphemistic or whether Peter's definition of πάντα would be at odds with Jesus's definition. Logically, it is not possible for Peter to have actually left πάντα (some things he surely still held). Second, Peter's question includes the implicit assumption that there will be (something) for him and the disciples. Based on Jesus's remarks in v. 21, the reader is aware that some type of reward is at play, but Peter asks his question with the implicit assumption that he and the disciples should get something. In this, Peter makes a false equivalency between what people in the world get to what he thinks he should get for forsaking a worldly life. Thus, by appealing to his great sacrifice, Peter tries to trap Jesus into admitting that the disciples should get something for their efforts. Fortunately for Peter, Jesus does admit that those who follow him will receive a reward (vv. 28–29), but then concludes his answer by warning Peter that many who assume they are first will actually be last.

2) Loaded Questions Are Antagonistic toward Their Addressee

In dialogue, no addressee wants to be the recipient of a loaded question. They are often hostile, condescending, and inflammatory. Unlike strongly informational questions, strongly rhetorical questions such as loaded questions are often asked *at* people rather than asked *to* people. When a speaker asks a loaded question, the presupposition in the question is forced on the addressee regardless of whether they accept the presupposition or not. For example:

(5) Ποῦ ἐστιν ἡ ἐπαγγελία τῆς παρουσίας αὐτοῦ; (2 PET 3:4)

Example (5) occurs when Peter predicts how mockers in the last days will question the return of Jesus. "Where is the promise of his return?" they will ask. Given that Peter's question has proven remarkably accurate over the last two millennia, it is all the more important to see that this question is actually a loaded question. While it is true that Christians believe Jesus did promise his return (2 Pet 3:8–12; Rev 22:20), the mockers' question presupposes that Jesus's coming will be in the timeframe of their—not God's—expectations. Thus, their implicit assumption renders the question fallacious (based on Christian evidences and belief; see Matt 24:44). This loaded question is antagonistic toward

Christians because of the embedded implicit assumption that Jesus has not and will not return.

3) Loaded Questions Try to Score Points against the Addressee with the Audience

A speaker can employ loaded questions quite effectively in a number of different ways within persuasive discourse. However, the danger of the loaded question is not just trapping the addressee but also making the addressee look bad in front of the audience. Because the implicit assumption embedded in loaded question has the force of an unstated proposition, but is concealed within the greater interrogative utterance, the audience is susceptible to confirming the proposition unintentionally. Thus, no matter how the addressee answers the loaded question, the audience prejudges the addressee based on the unsubstantiated presupposition. The result is a point scored for the asker within an argument. For example:

(6) Σὺ πιστεύεις εἰς τὸν υἱὸν τοῦ ἀνθρώπου; (JOHN 9:35)

Example (6) is Jesus asking the man born blind, whom he just healed, "Do you believe in the Son of Man?" This simple question belies the fact that it is a mild loaded question. On the surface, Jesus forms the question as a positive polar question with test qualities and an indexical; but more than this, Jesus loads the question with the theologically significant phrase, τὸν υἱὸν τοῦ ἀνθρώπου ("the Son of Man"). This phrase is used a hundred and seven times in the Old Testament, ensuring that the man born blind would have at least heard the phrase at some point in his life. Thus, Jesus puts the man in a bind by asking him if he believes in something he has heard (and quite possible already believed) to be true. Jesus doesn't ask the man if he believes that Jesus is the Son of Man; he just asks the man if he believes in the Son of Man in general. This is a question to which the man born blind cannot say no. Of course, the implicit assumption that Jesus is the Son of Man is made by the question, making it loaded. For those who hear this dialogue (the reader), Jesus's argument is persuasive and successful, though the man born blind is no fool. Instead of answering, he follows Jesus's question with a repair question (John 9:36), and once Jesus speaks more clearly, the man born blind believes (v. 38).[113]

113. For a lengthier discussion of the interrogative logic of John 9:35, see Estes, *Questions*, 149–52.

Case Study MATTHEW 15:33

Πόθεν ἡμῖν ἐν ἐρημίᾳ ἄρτοι τοσοῦτοι ὥστε χορτάσαι ὄχλον τοσοῦτον;

JESUS'S DISCIPLES: From where in this desert can we get so much bread that would satisfy so great a crowd?

As Jesus teaches publicly throughout Galilee, the crowds continue to follow him. At one point Jesus goes up on the shoulder of a mountain near the Sea of Galilee and sits down (Matt 15:29). With Jesus resting, great crowds of people come to him, bringing with them many who were sick. As the crowd brings the sick to Jesus sitting on the mountainside, he begins to heal those who are infirm. As the crowd sees Jesus healing people, they are amazed, and many in the crowd praise God because of the miracles they see. Then Jesus asks his disciples to come over. When the disciples arrive, Jesus tells the disciples that out of compassion for the crowd and their time with him that he does not want to release the crowd in their weakened state while they are still hungry. In response, the disciples ask, "From where in this desert can we get so much bread that would satisfy so great a crowd?"

At first glance, the disciples' question comes across as a rather mundane dialogue question that commentaries, sermons, and exegetical discussions often quickly skip over. Even though the disciples in Matthew form this question as a variable question with πόθεν ("from where?"), its semantic focus pushes it toward having mildly informational yet strongly rhetorical qualities. One tell that the question has significant rhetorical play is the repetition of the superlative τοσοῦτος ("so much," "so great"). When coupled with ἐν ἐρημίᾳ ("in this desert") the question takes on a negative and antagonistic tone. (After all, there is no food in a desert.) The reason for this is that the question is a mild loaded question, as it contains a rather clear embedded presupposition: contrary to what Jesus suggests, the crowd is too large and needs too much food for it to be fed in the desert. The disciples also imply that the crowd is so weak (not due to duration on the mountain but to infirmities and poverty) that the amount of food they need is not attainable. The question contains a great deal of semantic bias, but the reason that this is a mildly loaded question is that the disciples' presupposition is so strong that it drives the overall interrogative logic of the question more than any of the individual biases drive it. Perhaps most importantly, the disciples' question contains the presupposition that Jesus's request is impossible (even after they have seen miracles occur throughout all of the last three days). In response to the disciples' loaded question, Jesus handles their embedded presupposition by ignoring the question completely with the use of an opposing-turn question (§5.B.1), pushing back on these assumptions about him and the crowd.

FURTHER EXAMPLES

Matt 19:25; Mark 10:26; 11:17; 12:24; Luke 24:18; John 1:38a; Jas 4:1a, 1b, 5.

Key Bibliography
Clayman, "Questions," 266–68; Dillon, *Practice of Questioning*, 131–36; Estes, *Questions*, 147–52; Litwack, "Classification," 182–83; Walton, *One-Sided Arguments*, 230–33.

W. Leading Questions

Leading questions are asked so as to allow the asker to imply the expected answer in the wording of the question. This implication of a leading question is made in an overt way before an audience. Leading questions are so named in that they try to lead an audience to an answer predetermined by the asker. Borrowing langauge from popular legal culture, these questions are related to what it means to "lead a witness." Given their coercive power, leading questions possess some of the strongest rhetorical qualities a question may have. For example:

(1) Isn't it true that you stole the ring? (LEADING QUESTION)
(2) Don't you have the ring that you stole? (LOADED QUESTION)
(3) You have the stolen ring, don't you? (LEADING QUESTION)

The question in example (1) is a classic use of a leading question. This question contains a great deal of coercive power designed to force the addressee to affirm that they did in fact steal the ring. Example (1) is a leading question in that it "leads" the addressee by including the overt complement "it is true that you stole the ring" and (formed as a negative polar question) expects the answer yes. Example (2) is a loaded question, and the difference between (2) and (1) is that (2) deceives the audience into believing that the addressee stole the ring rather than using an overt premise to ask whether the most likely truth is that the addressee in fact stole the ring (as in (1)). Example (3) is a leading-question type that is formed as a *tag question*. In both questions (1) and (3), the premise of the question is overt, and the asker is coercing the addressee to agree to the premise.

Leading questions are similar to biased questions (§4.U) and loaded questions (§4.V). The difference between a leading question and a biased question is that a biased question contains a word or phrase with overt bias, and a leading question contains an overt premise meant to be affirmed by the audience. Likewise, there is a great deal of overlap between leading and loaded questions; a leading question is usually loaded (though overt), and many loaded questions can function in a leading capacity. The difference between the two often comes down to motive—the loaded question uses deception to confuse or trap an addressee, whereas the leading question uses coercion and browbeating to force agreement with an addressee.

Formation

Leading questions can be formed from any syntactic formation of question as they rely on semantic tricks to qualify as leading questions. Thus, any question formation can be turned into a leading question with the addition of leading semantic qualities. However, leading questions formed with a polar formation are the most common. By their nature, leading questions are most commonly negative in polarity and usually display notable bias. Depending on the language in use, leading questions can often be formed as *tag questions*. When it comes to semantics, the leading question must contain an overt premise that the asker uses to lead the audience toward the desired answer. When it comes to pragmatics, a speaker can employ leading questions in any dialogue turn or dialogue position. However, leading questions are most effective when the addressee can respond, and therefore they seem to work best in a closing dialogue position.

The primary factor in the formation and identification of a leading question is explained below.

1) Leading Questions Embed the Preferred Answer within the Question

What creates the condition that allows a question to lead an audience is the expected answer to the question placed within the question itself. The expected answer can be more or less clear and more or less pronounced, but it should be overt enough that it is distinguishable as such in the asking of the question. Typically, leading questions are not known for their subtlety, and speakers use them with a great deal of pragmatic force to try to push, pull, and coerce the addressee and audience into compliance. For example:

(4) Τίς ἐστιν ὁ ψεύστης εἰ μὴ ὁ ἀρνούμενος ὅτι Ἰησοῦς οὐκ ἔστιν ὁ Χριστός; (1 JOHN 2:22)

A strongly coercive question occurs in (4) when John asks, "Who is the liar if not the one denying that Jesus is the Christ?" John forms the question with the rather obvious tell of an overt premise: The liar is the one who denies that Jesus is the Christ. With this embedded premise, the question strongly leads the reader to agree that a person who denies that Jesus is the Christ is, in fact, a liar. As a leading question, (4) does not give the reader any room to negotiate. Because John forms the question as a variable question instead of a polar question, the question takes on a certain rhetorical openness that suggests that any person who denies that Jesus is the Christ is a liar.

Rhetorical Effects

Informational
Rhetorical

Leading questions are rhetorically conditioned to reject any counterclaims or negotiations. Even though they are strongly rhetorical, they still have moderate information-seeking qualities in that leading questions are typically asked to evoke a response from the audience (albeit the response already embedded within the question). While the semantics and pragmatics of any question type can telegraph the speaker's expected answer to the question, leading questions are rhetorically charged to go far beyond this. Leading questions do not merely telegraph the answer; they state it clearly for the audience to hear.

The primary rhetorical effect of leading questions is explained below.

1) Leading Questions Introduce a Considerable Amount of Interrogative Pressure

By asserting the expected answer as a part of the premise of the question, leading questions put a considerable amount of interrogative pressure on the audience.[114] *Interrogative pressure* is the tension felt by an addressee of a question that persuades the addressee to answer the question and in many cases compels the addressee to answer in a way the asker intends. To put pressure on their hearers, leading questions also use multiple kinds of strong bias to set up their question. For example:

(5) Οὐ διὰ τοῦτο πλανᾶσθε μὴ εἰδότες τὰς γραφὰς μηδὲ τὴν δύναμιν τοῦ θεοῦ; (MARK 12:24)

When the Sadducees try to trap Jesus in a famous exchange about the resurrection, Jesus responds with (5), "Aren't you being deceived because you haven't known the Scriptures nor the power of God?" This question is a paragon of rhetorical force, as syntactically it is a negative polar question, semantically it works as both a leading- and a loaded-question type, and pragmatically Jesus employs the questions as an opposing-turn question. The question is loaded as it includes the unproven assumption that the Sadducees don't know the Scriptures nor the power of God. However, its primary rhetorical goal is as a leading question, and thus it is similar to (1), leading the audience to affirm the premise that "yes, the Sadducees are clearly deceived."

114. Baxter, Boon, and Marley, "Interrogative Pressure," 89.

Case Study 1 JOHN 5:5

τίς [δέ] ἐστιν ὁ νικῶν τὸν κόσμον εἰ μὴ ὁ πιστεύων ὅτι Ἰησοῦς ἐστιν ὁ υἱὸς τοῦ θεοῦ;

JOHN: But who is the one overcoming the world if not the one believing that Jesus is the Son of God?

As John moves through the arguments of his first letter, two of his major concerns is for his "dear children" to continue to affirm Jesus as the Christ and, in affirming this, to continue to love each other as God loves them (1 John 4:7 – 15). John explains to his readers that everyone who believes that Jesus is the Christ is born of God (5:1) and overcomes the world (5:4). This overcoming of the world comes through loving God, loving his children, and keeping his commands (which are not encumbering). John explains that it is the readers' faith that is the victorious aspect of overcoming the world. In response to this assertion, John then asks, "But who is the one overcoming the world if not the one believing that Jesus is the Son of God?"

Here John asks a complex question to seek a strong affirmation from his readers. At first glance, the variable word τίς ("who") could indicate some type of open question, as if John wants his readers to consider a suitable answer. After the main clause carrying the interrogative force, John uses a restricted (exceptive) conditional with εἰ μή ("if not") to make a premise for the question (§3.E.3). Typically, εἰ ("if") marks a conditional question, but in the case of εἰ μή, the restricted conditional (often translated as "except") instead has the semantic effect of creating an assertive premise that works to lead the audience in the overt direction John intends. It is likely this premise carries a confessional overtone.[115] John phrases the question as a leading question to coerce the reader into adopting the view that the only victors in life are those who believe that Jesus is the Son of God. Because John forms the question as a variable question instead of a polar question, as with (4) above, the question takes on a certain rhetorical openness that suggests that any person who does not believe that Jesus is the Son of God cannot overcome the world. John's goal in placing interrogative pressure on his readers is to prod them into full acceptance that victory only comes through faith in Jesus. This confession is not optional or secondary to anyone who wants to be victorious.

FURTHER EXAMPLES

Matt 18:33; Luke 24:26; Acts 5:3; Rom 9:21; 1 Cor 6:15; Jas 3:11, 12.

115. Bultmann, *Johannine Epistles*, 79; Smalley, *1, 2, 3 John*, 276.

Key Bibliography

Baxter, Boon, and Marley, "Interrogative Pressure"; Dickson and Hargie, "Questioning," 131–35; Swann, Giuliano, and Wegner, "Leading Questions."

Chapter 5

Questions Driven by Pragmatics

In New Testament Greek, questions may be driven by *syntax*, *semantics*, and/or *pragmatics*. The third category, pragmatics, is the most rhetorically powerful of all three but also the hardest to identify within a written text (especially a text written in a language that is no longer spoken). As a result, almost all the pragmatic clues for interpreting New Testament questions are lost to modern readers. Only a few remain as reconstructions, developed in the course of the working out of modern-language and text studies. Since pragmatics is tied to the sociocultural part of communication, our lack of fluency in Greek culture also limits our ability to accurately read the text for pragmatic features. However, we can reconstruct these clues based on the way that the questions are placed and positioned within the larger discourse. With questions driven by pragmatics, it is tempting for the reader to evaluate the pragmatic qualities of the question by way of replies. This, however, is an interpretive fallacy, since there is no way to know what kind of reply is actually being offered (§2.E). For the sake of our study, there are essentially three main areas where we will look to discern the pragmatics of a question embedded within a text: *turn*, *position*, and *repetition*. While there are other ways in which we could consider pragmatic factors, these basic textual moves are well established and relatively accessible even for beginning students.

The first, the turn in which the question falls (§2.D.7), is an effective indicator of latent pragmatic effects set up within discourse. In the narrative discourse parts of the GNT, the challenge of determining turn is related to the challenge of determining the accuracy of the words and events. For example, just as there is the discussion over the actual words of Jesus and the narrated words of Jesus, there also will be a discussion over the actual turns that Jesus and his dialogue partners took and the narrated turns that Jesus and his dialogue partners took. However, the narrated turns are as valuable as any of the other parts of the Gospels for portraying the narrated characters for readers today—the discourse is neither more or less valuable than the words. In the rhetorical discourse of the GNT, the role of turn is more oblique and nuanced, and a different way of thinking is required. In either case, determining turn is often not an exact science. Often, the text must be read carefully for clues. For example, a quick reading of Mark 15:9 might suggest that it is a first-turn question. It is, however, second-turn; the first turn is the unspoken (but noted by the narrator) words of the crowd. In this study, we will only consider first- and second-turn questions. Though the pragmatics of questions in the third turn, fourth turn, and beyond are important, the level of nuance increases significantly for each turn past the second. Thus, late-turn questions tend to have much weaker pragmatic effects (based on their turn). As a result, we will focus solely on the implications of questions within first-turn and second-turn utterances.

The second, the position of the question within its dialogue turn or argument structure (§2.D.7), is also an effective indicator of potential pragmatic effects in discourse. In the GNT, the position in which the question is asked often shapes the discourse around the question, which in turn shapes the purpose and goals of the question. When it comes to evaluating questions based on their turn in discourse, sometimes it is not just the turn but also the placement in the turn that matters. For the short turns of conversation, the turn is most important; but for long dialogues that include speeches, the placement within the turn can trump the pragmatic influence of the turn on the question. For example, Jesus asks a question from the cross in Mark 15:34 without any discussion before or after, which emphasizes certain possible pragmatic effects. If Jesus had launched into a monologue after asking the question, it would change the way readers apprehend the question and the overall narrative progression.

The third, the repetition of questions, is also another indicator of strong pragmatic effects within discourse. This pragmatic effect occurs whenever there is the occurrence of more than one question in an extended sequence. It does this in two ways. First, the repetition of questions in discourse creates a cumulative effect on each of the questions asked. For example, the question in John 1:21b takes on a whole new feel because of the question in John 1:21a. Second, these questions amplify their rhetorical force across the sequence, which creates powerful pragmatic effects impacting the greater discourse. Question repetition is a widely used rhetorical strategy in the GNT as well as throughout similar genres of ancient Greek literature.

One factor in the pragmatics of question asking is the determination of the type of discourse in which the question appears. If the question appears in the direct discourse of reported speech, as in the narrative sections of the GNT, then pragmatic expectations for the question play a significant interpretive role. But if the question appears in rhetorical discourse, as in much of the letter writing in the GNT, the pragmatic expectations for the question play a more nuanced interpretive role. And in the case of rhetorical discourse, how the reader understands the genre and use of the discourse will significantly impact the nuanced pragmatic expectations of questions (§2.D.5). As an example, if (as I believe) the letters of Paul are highly rhetorical, with the ideas and arguments developed over the course of years of oral, public proclamation and formed into a letter that could be sent and read aloud to various churches, then the pragmatic expectations of Paul's questions will be oratorical, and they will have a higher persuasive push than in a typical person-to-person letter.

Finally, not all questions have strong pragmatic effects. This occurs whenever a question does not appear to have any notable pragmatic feature. In those cases, we generally refer to their pragmatic value as weak. For example:

(1) Πιστεύετε ὅτι δύναμαι τοῦτο ποιῆσαι; (MATT 9:28)

The question in Matthew 9:28, "Do you believe that I have the power to do this?" is a question with weak pragmatic qualities. The reason is not so much the question itself but the clues from its setup within the narrative discourse. For one, Matthew is vague about whether the question is meant as a response to the blind men's cries or whether there is a set change and Jesus initiates a new conversation after a pause (or both). For another, by using a simple polar question as a means of confirmation, Jesus's question is driven most by its syntactic formation and its semantic quality; it has little pragmatic value.

The question types considered below represent merely some of the possibilities for interpretation when the study of pragmatics is taken into account.

A. First-Turn Questions

A *first-turn question* is any question asked by the first speaker within the first utterance of a dialogue sequence. Any utterance(s) made by the first speaker—after any scene setting and prior to any subsequent speaker or break in dialogue—becomes the *first turn* or *turn 1* of the dialogue sequence (§2.D.7). Turn-taking is the mechanism that allows for orderly dialogue to occur (whether in discussion or debate). Subsequent turns follow subsequent speakers and their utterances. For example:

(1) The phone rang and he hurried to reach for it. Seeing the name of the caller on the screen, he hesitated, but then quickly pushed the answer button.

"What do you want?" he said with a thickness in his voice. (TURN 1)
"I just wanted to talk," she said, slow and measured. (TURN 2)
"Sure, fine, whatever," he replied. (TURN 3)

Above, the scene is set by the narrator, who then introduces the first speaker in the dialogue. As each speaker speaks, the dialogue follows the expected turn-taking sequence. The narrator assertively sets up the male speaker for the first-turn utterance, and since this is purely artificial dialogue, there is nothing exceptional about the utterance in this turn. In representational dialogue (§2.D.8), the reader may discover clues about the dialogue beyond the turn-taking sequence. Even so, writers of the representational dialogue in the GNT fully shape their dialogue sequences.

Pragmatics play an immense role in the asking of questions. The pragmatics of first-turn questions often trump the syntactic and semantic values within those questions. The defining pragmatic feature of first-turn questions is that they guide the subsequent sequence of dialogue. There are essentially two notable types of first-turn questions: *governing questions* (§5.A.1) and *expository questions* (§5.A.2). We can map the differences between the two different kinds of first-turn questions as:

Variations among Turn 1 Question Types

	Syntactic	Semantic	Pragmatic
Governing	None	Linked to Next Speaker(s)	Introducing
Expository	None	Linked to Original Speaker	Self-Completing

As an identifiable rhetorical strategy, the use of first-turn questions can reveal traits about the author of a text. We can see how this rhetorical strategy plays out by comparing the general frequency of first-turn questions within each of the four Gospels:

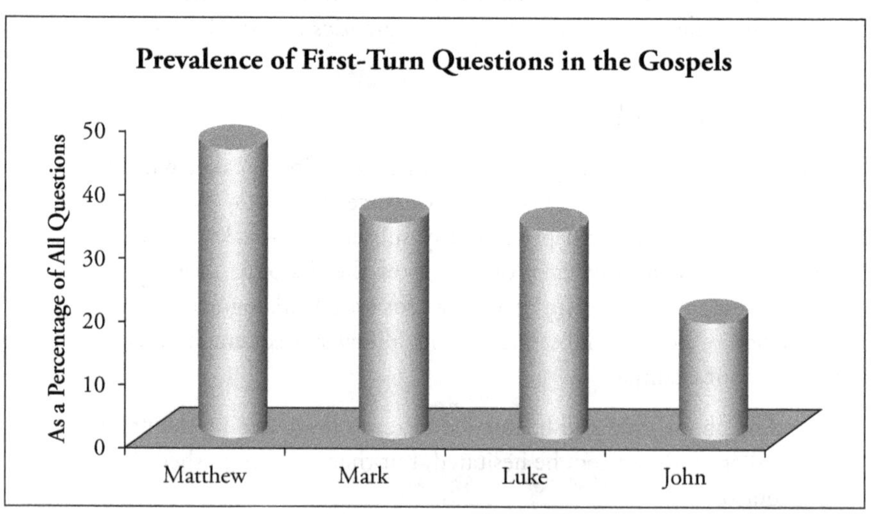

Even with the overarching similarities between the Synoptic Gospels, the writer of Matthew exhibits a clear preference for setting up dialogue with first-turn questions. In fact, nearly 50% of Matthew's questions come as first-turn questions. In contrast, the writer of John uses the lowest percentage of first-turn questions—less than half as many as Matthew—even while using the greatest number of total questions. Thus, the writer of John relies on a different rhetorical strategy than the first-turn question to use questions and guide dialogue (while keeping in mind that John's dialogue sequences are far more nuanced than any of the Synoptic Gospel's sequences). Of course, this chart represents a broad-brush approach, as it does not reveal finer details (such as what position each first-turn question occupies).

Furthermore, we can consider the prevalence of first-turn questions as a rhetorical strategy from the depiction of Jesus in each of the four Gospels. We can see in the chart that this distribution is even more pronounced:

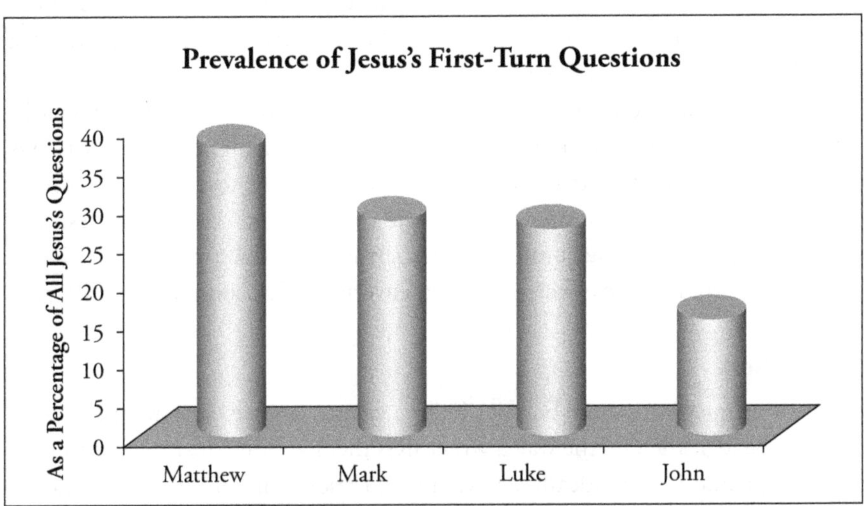

Among the Gospels, the writer of Matthew uses Jesus's asking questions as the opening technique to further dialogue. Based on the evidence from the use of questions, the Matthean Jesus is far more interested in setting parameters on the dialogue sequence from the beginning than the Johannine Jesus. It is interesting to note that Luke and Mark possess almost identical percentages in both graphs.

1. Governing Questions

Governing questions are asked as an attempt to assert control over the future direction of the dialogue. Governing questions get their name from the fact that they "govern" the next parts of the dialogue. Many, if not most, first-turn questions are mildly governing—of which many are so mild that we treat them without considering their pragmatic function in the text (e.g., Matt 2:2). Governing questions are those questions used by speakers in an overt way to kick-start conversation, create debates, or identify a subject to be discussed. Occasionally this governance is unintentional; in most cases it is an intentional move by the asker. For example, if one were to stop and ask for directions, and the first turn of the conversation was:

(1) "Excuse me, do you know the way to San Jose?" (GOVERNING QUESTION)

This example is a common governing question, as it attempts to direct the next steps in the dialogue sequence. In the case of (1), if for some reason the next speaker was not amenable to conversation (as in their asking an opposing-turn question [§5.B.1], or they just ran off), the lack of expected response does not invalidate (1) as a governing question. Thus, governing questions work in much the same way as test questions do; just because a test question is not answered or not answered as expected does not make the question any less a test question.

Governing questions are also similar to focus-shifting questions (§5.B.2), a second-turn-question type. Aside from their turn requirements, the difference between a governing question and a focus-shifting question is that a speaker asks a governing question to start or shape dialogue in a particular direction, whereas a focus-shifting question is more broad in that it merely changes the direction of the dialogue. Open questions (§4.A) often make good governing questions, and the semantics of some question types such as riddle questions (§4.N) almost guarantee the pragmatic effects will be to govern the direction of the dialogue.

Formation

A governing question cannot be identified via syntax. Instead, governing questions can only be identified by the way a writer uses them within a text (their pragmatics and semantics). Semantically, a governing question will most likely be topically related to the ensuing dialogue; in many cases, the following utterances will in some way answer the governing question. Pragmatically, a governing question is mildly provocative and picks at the audience in such a way that discussion is started. As a general rule, governing questions occur only in narrative discourse; they do not occur in persuasive discourse. They often follow immediately after a scene-setting device—this is especially prevalent in the GNT. More times than not, governing questions are formed from variable questions (especially open-question types), but as semantics play a factor, in those cases a speaker can use polar questions. For example:

(2) As the guys settled in their seats, Chuck asked,
"Do you think the Cowboys could
win the Superbowl?" (GOVERNING QUESTION)
This created a stir, with Gary quickly saying, "Yes..."

Even though question (2) is not an open question or typical of the formation of governing questions, the debate-oriented semantic values it introduces is sufficient to create a great deal of discussion (and most likely end whatever dialogue occurred before the question). The scene is set beforehand, making the question first turn and creating space for the new dialogue sequence to begin.

Technically, a governing question can be asked in later turns, but these situations are less common; when it does happen, the governing question will create a narrative break by its fundamental interrogative force.

Several factors in the formation and identification of governing questions are explained below.

1) Governing Questions Introduce a New Topic

For a question to be considered a governing question, it must introduce a new topic from within the first turn. Quite frequently in written texts, the author will "set the scene" with characters and movement to create a narrative break for the reader wherein the first speaker can then ask a governing question designed to carry the narrative progression forward for another dialogue sequence. For example:

(3) ῥαββί, τίς ἥμαρτεν, οὗτος ἢ οἱ γονεῖς αὐτοῦ, ἵνα τυφλὸς γεννηθῇ; (JOHN 9:2)

In (3), the disciples start a new discussion concerning the origin of sin, asking, "Rabbi, who sinned, this one or his parents, that caused him to be born blind?" Even though the narrator sets the scene for the reader that there was a man born blind who happened to be along the way (John 9:1), the question still serves well as a governing question to raise the topic through the disciples' question. The semantics of this question helps to give Jesus space to answer at length on a difficult topic.

2) Governing Questions Are Followed by Deliberative Conversation

Governing questions can fall into either the opening, middle, or closing position, but middle position would be rare. In the opening position, the interpreter has to ensure that the question asked in the first turn—if followed by additional utterances from the first-turn speaker—is not more of an expository question than a governing question.

(4) διδάσκαλε ἀγαθέ, τί ποιήσω ἵνα ζωὴν αἰώνιον κληρονομήσω; (MARK 10:17)

Example (4) contains a classic use of the rhetorical feature of governing questions. After setting the scene by telling the reader about Jesus's travels, a member of the crowd approaches the protagonist in order to ask a question. This question results in a deliberative conversation (and is strong enough that Jesus's initial response is a rebuttal by means of an opposing-turn question). In many cases, the strength of the rhetorical effect of the question may be unknown to the asker—the asker is not always privy to how strongly an audience will react to the governing question.

Rhetorical Effects

As typical of first-turn questions, governing questions tend to have strong informational qualities and weaker rhetorical qualities. Given their mild provocative nature, governing questions are akin to test questions in that both push the audience for a response (governing push for dialogue, test push for answers). Governing questions are used to set the stage for further discussion and should remain open and neutral in their asking, as they are not designed to persuade the audience toward one side or the other of the issue. They create dialogue space to discuss an issue. Where the strength of the rhetorical qualities play a role is whether the governing question is mildly governing or strongly governing; if mildly, the question becomes merely a discussion starter, but if strongly, the question starts an argument or debate. The stronger the rhetorical quality, the more deliberative the governing question becomes.

The two most important rhetorical effects of governing questions are explained below.

1) Governing Questions Provoke Further Discussion and/or Action

Governing questions are phrased and asked to cause discussion, deliberation, or debate. Because complete pragmatic information is not available for written texts, the interpreter must rely on all available semantic and pragmatic clues to determine whether a question is provoking dialogue. For example:

(5) κύριε, εἰ ὀλίγοι οἱ σῳζόμενοι; (LUKE 13:23)

At first glance, question (5), "Lord, if only a few are going to be saved ...?" seems to be best understood as a conditional question (based on the use of εἰ [often translated as "if"]). It is a conditional question, but the goal of the question is more than determining a possibility. Instead, the conditional question is asked by the speaker to raise a possibility that would result in greater dialogue. It works; Jesus takes the bait. There are four factors that point to (5) as a governing question. First, while the question does not result in a literal dialogue, it does provoke the Lukan Jesus enough to enter into a longer monologue. Second, the question occurs in a first-turn, standalone position. Third, Luke uses the question to shift focus from Jesus's teaching on the kingdom of God to the concern of how many σῳζόμενοι ("going to be saved"). This switch introduces a slightly philosophical bent to the discourse. Last, the speaker's inclusion of ὀλίγοι ("few") creates a negative bias, which in this case serves to encourage subsequent discussion. As a result, this question has a strong governing quality, making it very tempting for hearers to want to answer and discuss.

2) Governing Questions Shift Focus from Previous Events

Because governing questions are asked to guide future dialogue, these questions have the rhetorical effect of shifting the focus away from the previous event. A narrator may use a governing question in the mouth of a character to help make this shift happen; governing questions are one of many devices within narrative discourse that help keep the story moving. For example:

(6) σὺ τίς εἶ; (JOHN 1:19)

Prior to this question, "Who are you?" the writer of John's Gospel has introduced two primary characters (the Word and John) in an epic opening exposition. To bring the text down to earth and into the world of human interaction, John's narrator leads with a brief scene-setting device and a governing question to transition toward the discussion between John and the priests and Levites (John 1:19–28). This discussion occurs to let the reader know more precisely who John is, and the transition is made through the use of a governing question.

Case Study MATTHEW 16:13

Τίνα λέγουσιν οἱ ἄνθρωποι εἶναι τὸν υἱὸν τοῦ ἀνθρώπου;

JESUS'S DISCIPLES: Who do people say the Son of Man is?

As Jesus nears the region of Caesarea Philippi, he broaches an important but delicate topic of conversation with his disciples: his identity (Matt 16:13). Jesus asks them, "Who do people say the Son of Man is?" As the question opens up discussion, the disciples try to guess at Jesus's identity by throwing out what others say. After they speak, Jesus again tries to narrow them down to what they believe about who he is (v. 15).

Here Jesus demonstrates the rhetorical power of questions to govern conversations and discourse. The question Jesus asks is a variable question (§3.B), and an open one (§4.A), that invites a wide range of responses. Generally speaking, this type of question will be strongly informational and mildly rhetorical; thus, it invites replies and discussion. Pragmatically, however, it does more than this—it functions as a governing question. In this case, Jesus is not asking the question just to receive a useful reply. Rather, he asks to generate discussion and bring all focus on to the topic of his question.

From the perspective of the reader, there is no significant correlation between their arrival in Caesarea Philippi and the issue of Jesus's identity.[1] All the reader knows is that the previous topic (guarding against the teaching of the Pharisees and Sadducees) is over and the scene has shifted. What makes Matthew's question overshadow the scene even more is the enigmatic "Son of Man" (τὸν υἱὸν τοῦ ἀνθρώπου), absent in Mark and Luke (Mark 8:27; Luke 9:18), a phrase that naturally leads the hearers to discuss further. The dialogue that follows the governing question is shaped by it (as in the turn exchanges in Matt 16:14–16) and also provides an answer to it as the dialogue progresses (vv. 16–17). The combination of focus shift plus open variable question not only causes a dialogue to occur within the text but invites the reader to engage the question as

1. Nolland, *Matthew*, 658.

well. Jesus's question is so artful and compelling that it did not result in just one answer—instead, it started an important dialogue among his disciples, much in the same way as it does for readers today.

FURTHER EXAMPLES

Matt 9:11, 14; 11:3; Mark 6:24; 12:23; Luke 6:2; 20:22; John 1:38a; 6:5; Acts 9:4; 10:29; 17:19; 19:2; 23:19; Rom 3:7; Rev 5:2; 6:10; 7:13.

Key Bibliography

Walton, *Dialog Theory*, 22–33.

2. Expository Questions

Expository questions are asked so that a speaker may introduce a topic and then provide information (or exposition) about the new topic. In the ancient world, rhetoricians referred to expository-type questions as either αἰτιολογία, ἀνθυποφορά, ὑποφορά, *percontatio*, *rogatio*, *subiectio*, or any other number of related terms based on a variety of circumstances. To be an expository question, the question under consideration must be followed by exposition from the asker—not another speaker or member of the audience. To put it another way, an expository question is asked and then answered by the same speaker. If a question seems like an expository question but is answered by another speaker, it is most likely a kind of governing question.

Expository questions get their name from the fact that they are a device to introduce exposition into the discourse. The introduction of exposition by the speaker is almost always an intentional rhetorical move. For example:

(1) The pastor approached the group gathered by the door.

"Who knows what the Bible says about Lois? Well, let me tell you, she must have been one special lady to have impressed the apostle Paul that way. I bet her name means "awesome granny" in the Greek. Did you know..."

The question in example (1) functions as an expository question in that it is asked by the speaker and then answered by the speaker. As (1) is artificial dialogue (§2.D.8), we can tell that the speaker obviously has no intention of letting anyone else answer the question. In reading texts with representational dialogue, such as the GNT, it is not always obvious whether the expository question is simply a narrative device, a truncation of reported speech, or something other. Even if we cannot ascertain the exact pragmatics of these questions, we can clearly see their rhetorical effects.

Expository questions are not *only* first-turn questions—in that they can be asked in other turns—but they are prevalent in the first turn, especially in the GNT. They also have qualities that are closer to first-turn questions than second-turn questions. As such, they have the power to guide subsequent dialogue similar to governing questions (§5.A.1). A shorthand view of this is that governing questions guide dialogues, while expository questions direct monologues. With the unique texts of the GNT, the Gospel writers sometimes use expository questions (or expository-like questions) to introduce Jesus's parables (e.g., Luke 13:18, 20; 15:4) or a speech (Acts 3:12). Furthermore, many times second-turn (and beyond) questions that seem like expository questions are actually more closely aligned with actual second-turn-question types. A great example of this is Luke 5:34, which seems to introduce exposition (and it does) but is more properly interpreted first as an opposing-turn question (§5.B.1).

Formation

As a type of question defined by its pragmatics, an expository question cannot be identified via syntax. Instead, we can only identify expository questions by the way a writer uses them within a text (pragmatics) and by their relation to subsequent discourse (semantics). Expository questions have several tells which make them relatively easy for a reader to spot. In a sense, any type of question could be used by a speaker as an expository question. The pragmatic tell is that the expository question is followed immediately after with further utterances, and the semantic tell is that these utterances are topically related to the expository question.

Several factors in the formation and identification of expository questions are discussed below.

1) Expository Questions Require Subsequent Exposition from the Asker

For a question to be used as an expository question, the question requires subsequent and related exposition in the form of continued utterances from the asker. In the classic formation of the expository question, the question asked is broad and philosophical or hypothetical, and the subsequent exposition is lengthy (think a speech, especially in a political or legal situation; e.g., Cicero, *Philippics II*). However, place or topic of the question and length of exposition are not factors in determining whether a question is an expository question or not. For example:

(2) τίνι ὁμοιώσω τὴν βασιλείαν τοῦ θεοῦ; (LUKE 13:20)

Reading question (2), "To what will I compare the kingdom of God?" in the context of Luke 13 makes it easy for the reader to quickly pass over the question.

The exposition that follows the question is short and cryptic; the question almost seems superfluous to the reader, merely a variable question. However, since the speaker expounds upon the topic in the same turn after the question is asked, it does fall within the category of an expository question. While it does not appear to be a classic example, it is actually a notable expository question as it raises an important topic and then is responded to forcefully in the following utterance. Not all immediately answered questions by the speaker are expository questions, however (e.g., Mark 5:39).

2) Expository Questions Never Occur in the Closing or Standalone Positions

As expository questions require subsequent exposition, they can never be asked in such a way as to end a speaker's turn. Thus, expository questions may occupy the opening and middle positions within a turn but never the closing or standalone position. Except in rare circumstances, they are also not usually a part of a double question. In monological texts or one-speaker discourse (such as the letters in the GNT), expository questions can occur in a weakened sense as they are used to introduce a new topic to the reader. In these cases, they are not first-turn questions even though they act like first-turn questions in that they can occur almost as headwords or subtitles to a new section. For example:

(3) Λέγετέ μοι, οἱ ὑπὸ νόμον θέλοντες εἶναι, τὸν νόμον οὐκ ἀκούετε; (GAL 4:21)

Question (3) is a middle-position question (§5.C), but its rhetorical effect is extremely close to that of an expository question. Here Paul uses the question to shift focus in his discourse and then raises this question, only to launch a subsequent exposition that responds to the question. Galatians 4:21 is not an expository question in the purest sense, but it does show how the position of the question in the utterance (or discourse) determines whether exposition is possible. In Paul's letters, it is especially common to see him use a middle-position question in a set of double questions with expository purposes.

Rhetorical Effects

Expository questions tend to have strong informational qualities and weaker rhetorical qualities. However, expository questions are unique among questions in that instead of seeking information and/or trying to persuade an audience, they also overtly introduce information from the asker (in the hopes of trying to persuade the audience). According to Quintilian, expository questions may have a pleasing effect on an audience.[2] Due to the idiosyncratic rhetorical effects of

2. Quintilian, *Institutio oratoria* 9.2.14.

expository questions, they can also frustrate an audience if not used cautiously and sparingly. This is less true in written texts than in natural discourse.

The two most important rhetorical effects of expository questions are discussed below.

1) Expository Questions Introduce the Asker's Opinions

Expository questions are devices designed to subtly introduce the asker's views on a subject. However, they are not "normal" questions that are asked by the speaker, left unanswered by the audience, and then fielded by the speaker to prevent awkward silence or to continue the conversation. Rather, expository questions are created and asked for the purpose of allowing the speaker to expound on their topic. For example:

(4) γινώσκετε τί πεποίηκα ὑμῖν; (JOHN 13:12)

After a dialogue and a pause to perform a lengthy action, Jesus resumes the dialogue by asking expository question (4), "Do you understand what I have done for you?" Though this question comes in turn seven of a complex dialogue, the lengthy and interruptive action of Jesus in John 13:12 is enough to make the question read as if it were a first-turn dialogue opener (and we may count it that way legitimately).[3] Here Jesus uses this question to introduce to his disciples his reasons for washing their feet as well as to open the disciples up to consider his next words of explanation.

2) Expository Questions Shift Focus from Previous Events

Because expository questions are asked to give the speaker a chance to expound on a subject, the rhetorical effect is to almost always shift the focus away from a previous topic or event. Narrators who want to shift focus often combine a brief scene change with an expository question. This is a common technique for first-turn questions (§5.A). Other times, the change is more abrupt. For example:

(5) Τίνι οὖν ὁμοιώσω τοὺς ἀνθρώπους τῆς γενεᾶς ταύτης
καὶ τίνι εἰσὶν ὅμοιοι; (LUKE 7:31)

Here in (5) Jesus desires to speak to the faithlessness of this generation, and asks, "To what, then, can I compare the people of this generation—to what are they like?" Since the prior dialogue was about John the Baptist, the expository question is a rhetorical device to draw the audience's attention away from John and to the present situation. By introducing the topic interrogatively rather than assertively, the speaker raises the chance that the audience will listen (even though it is critical of the audience members). Shortly afterward, Jesus ties his previous and

3. McKay notes that John's use of the perfect is "much more effective in preparing for the explanation"; see McKay, "On the Perfect," 315.

current thoughts together by mentioning John and himself (Luke 7:33–34). The writer of Luke even uses an aside (vv. 29–30) to juxtapose the two dialogues.

Case Study HEBREWS 2:6

Τί ἐστιν ἄνθρωπος ὅτι μιμνῄσκῃ αὐτοῦ,
ἢ υἱὸς ἀνθρώπου ὅτι ἐπισκέπτῃ αὐτόν;

SOMEONE (PSALMIST): What is man that you are mindful of him,
or a son of man that you care for him?

The writer of Hebrews begins his epistolary argument by making the claim that Jesus, the Son of God, is the culmination of the speech of the prophets and messengers in these last days (Heb 1:1–2). As a result, the Son is superlatively superior to the angels, as his inherited name is to theirs (v. 4). The writer then develops this line of reasoning further (vv. 5–14), concluding with the rhetorically persuasive, negative polar question, "Aren't all [of them] ministering spirits, sent for the service of those destined to inherit salvation?" (v.14). From this, the writer of Hebrews warns his readers not to ignore but to pay careful attention to what they have heard about salvation and to recognize the confirmation that God provided in signs, wonders, miracles, and gifts of the Holy Spirit (2:1–4). In fact, God did not make the world subject to angels (as the argument went); in fact, didn't someone long ago already argue for this very truth? At this point, the writer of Hebrew quotes the question from the LXX of Psalm 8:5–6, asking his readers about themselves and the Son, "What is man that you are mindful of him, or a son of man that you care for him?" followed by an answer (of sorts) as a direct quotation from Psalm 8:7 (Heb 2:7–8).

Hebrews 2:6 is a fascinating case of not only intertextuality but also the adaption and rhetorical transformation of the Old Testament in the New. Looking at the question itself, the syntax of the question is a bit difficult, but consideration of the Hebrew and LXX originals indicates that the question is a composite question rather than a double question. The asker forms the question with the variable word τί ("what?"), and semantically the question is speculative (§4.B), bordering on the lyrical (§4.C). From this, the purpose of the question is to encourage big-picture thinking on the part of the audience. However, what makes Hebrews 2:6 interesting for the interpreter is not only the much-discussed semantic issues (e.g., ἄνθρωπος ["man"] and υἱὸς ἀνθρώπου ["son of man"]) within the question but also the overlooked pragmatics of the question. In this case, the author of Hebrews turns to Psalm 8, a song of praise of the majesty of God. If we look at this question in Psalm 8, it is used as a middle-position question in the midst of what is in essence a type of strong rhetorical discourse (a psalm). It is used by the psalmist to bolster the claims made about God and to encourage the reader to consider and accept the truth of this. Conversely, the author of Hebrews does not co-opt the entire psalm; instead, the first movement of Psalm 8 is excised, and only several clauses from the middle of the psalm are included. The writer of Hebrews promotes the middle-position question of the psalmist to the beginning of the quotation, and while the question is still in essence a middle-position question, it becomes the first question of a longer quotation, which imbues it with similar pragmatics as an expository question.[4] Thus, the hearer of Hebrews 2:6 comes to the quotation, hears the introductory διεμαρτύρατο δέ πού τις λέγων ("but somewhere someone urged, saying"), hears the pause, and then hears a question asked.[5] With the question coming first, before the hearer may attempt their own response the writer of Hebrews carries on with more monologue (vv. 7–8a). Thus, the writer of Hebrews has taken the question out of its original pragmatic context and put it into a new pragmatic context. Though the words are the same, the movement causes the question to move from a question designed to rhetorically reengage the hearer during a time of worship to a question asked to prompt the hearer to accept the rhetorical argument of the writer. Therefore, given the debate over the semantic issues within the question,[6] the clue to their interpretation lies closest to the follow-up to the expository question, which has been reinterpreted by the writer of Hebrews as a reply. While ἄνθρωπος may refer to human beings in general, the composite ἤ ("or") plus the pragmatic expository shift points the reader toward a more christological reading of υἱὸς ἀνθρώπου.[7]

FURTHER EXAMPLES

Mark 4:30; 12:9; Luke 13:18; Acts 3:12; 4:16; 13:10; Rev 17:7; 18:18.

Key Bibliography

Blakemore, *Understanding Utterances*, 114; Estes, *Questions*, 107–10; Ilie, "Question-Response," 975–99; Wilson and Sperber, *Meaning and Relevance*, 222–27.

4. As a quotation, the question exists on a higher diegetic level that helps to create the insular feel. Evidence of this occurs in the dropping of the extraneous-to-the-argument clause (καὶ κατέστησας αὐτὸν ἐπὶ τὰ ἔργα τῶν χειρῶν σου; Ps 8:7a LXX) in many early manuscripts.
5. Fuhrmann's suggestion that the introductory clause could itself be a question is interesting. On the one hand, πού does not front, so the statistical evidence weighs strongly against this possibility. On the other hand, the syntax indicates to me that the interrogative strength of the indirect question is likely to be more pronounced than modern readers assume and is not (as per Lane) intentionally vague to emphasize the divine character of oracular pronouncements; see Fuhrmann, "The Son, the Angels and the Odd," 89; Lane, *Hebrews 1–8*, 46.
6. For example, Blomberg, "'But We See Jesus.'"
7. Cf. De Wet, "Messianic Interpretation."

B. Second-Turn Questions

A *second-turn question* is any question asked by the second speaker within the second utterance of a dialogue sequence. Any utterance(s) made by the second speaker—after any explicit or implicit utterance(s) from a previous speaker and prior to any utterance(s) from subsequent speakers (or break in dialogue)—becomes the *second turn* or *turn 2* of the dialogue sequence (§2.D.7). Turn-taking is the mechanism that allows for orderly dialogue to occur (whether in discussion or debate). Subsequent turns follow subsequent speakers and their utterances. For example:

(1) The phone rang, and he hurried to reach for it. Seeing the name of the caller on the screen, he hesitated, but then quickly pushed the answer button.

His voice was thick as he opened the call. (TURN 1)
"Can we just talk?" she responded, slow and measured. (TURN 2)
"Sure, fine, whatever," he replied. (TURN 3)

Above, once the scene is set, the dialogue starts to follow a typical turn-taking sequence. However, identifying each turn is often more art than science. For example, it is tempting to consider the direct speech from the female speaker as a first-turn question (it certainly could act as a *governing question*; §5.A.1). Yet the first actual turn is the male speaker who opens the call with some type of greeting—albeit unspoken and implicit to the reader of the text. Thus, the female speaker is responding in some way to whatever the male speaker said during the opening turn, and her question is better interpreted as a second-turn question. Because (1) is an example of artificial dialogue (§2.D.8), the pragmatics are shaped by the author more than any represented event.

While pragmatics can play an immense role in the meaning of questions, the defining pragmatic and semantic features of second-turn questions are that they complete, oppose, or push back against the original first-turn utterance. Speakers can use second-turn questions as a response to any type of first-turn utterance, but they are at their most dramatic against first-turn questions. Thus they can be identified via pragmatics (in the reading) and, to a much lesser degree, via semantics (in its relationship to the original question). There are essentially six notable types of second-turn questions: *opposing-turn questions* (§5.B.1), *focus-shifting questions* (§5.B.2), *echo questions* (§5.B.3), *repair questions* (§5.B.4), *retort questions*, and *nonsensical questions*. The last two of these types are unusual; they are rarely found in natural and representational dialogue, with only one retort question and zero nonsensical questions in the GNT.[8] We can map the differences between the different types of second-turn questions in the chart below:

8. I examine the only retort question (John 11:9) in my previous book; see Estes, *Questions*, 140–44.

Variations among Turn 2 Question Types

	Syntactic	Semantic	Pragmatic
Opposing-Turn	None	Loose Relationship with Turn 1	Confronting
Focus-Shifting	None	No Relationship with Turn 1	Diverting
Echo	None	Matching Relationship with Turn 1	Mimicking
Repair	None	Close Relationship with Turn 1	Clarifying
Retort	None	No Relationship with Turn 1	Scorning
Nonsensical	None	No Relationship with Turn 1	Confusing

In some uncommon dialogue situations, the semantics of a question may make it well suited for a second-turn question with minimal pragmatic factors (and low rhetorical effect). Examples of this are phatic questions (§4.K), request questions (§4.S), and confirmation questions (§4.R).

Key Bibliography
Estes, *Questions*, 128–31; Levinson, *Pragmatics*, 306–8, 332–39; Yule, *Pragmatics*, 78–82.

---

1. Opposing-Turn Questions

Opposing-turn questions are asked in response to a question asked in the preceding dialogue turn. These types of questions violate normal dialogue practice and thus require an extra interpretive step to discover their purpose in a text. One of the foundational expectations of dialogue in natural language is the *question-answer pair*: When a question is asked, an assumption is made by hearers that the next utterance will be an answer to that question (§2.D.7). When a responder violates the expectations of a question-answer pair, the greater discourse pattern and interpretation is affected. For example, in a standard question-answer pair:

(1) Bridget: Where are my shoes? (QUESTION)
Dad: By the front door. (ANSWER)

This discourse follows the expected rules of dialogue, but if Dad asks an opposing-turn question, the question disrupts this:

(2) Bridget: Where are my shoes? (QUESTION)
Dad: Why should I tell you? (OPPOSING-TURN QUESTION)

In sample (1), Bridget asks a normal question in conversation, and Dad follows a similarly normal pattern of replying to her question. If Dad did not respond, it would perhaps be rude but not disruptive. However, in sample (2), when Bridget asks a normal question, Dad responds with a question that serves to disrupt the dialogue. At this point, the original speaker is unsure whether to wait for a reply to their original question or to try to reply to the second speaker's question (even though their question remains unanswered).

Opposing-turn questions are akin to focus-shifting questions (§5.B.2) in that they tend to disrupt the natural flow of dialogue. They are akin to echo questions (§5.B.3) and repair questions (§5.B.4) in that all three are second-turn questions that relate back to the previous utterance.

Formation

The formation criteria for opposing-turn questions are almost entirely pragmatic. An asker may form an opposing-turn question with any syntactic formation. There are also little semantic requirements for an opposing-turn question other than it be loosely related in context to the question it is opposing. Because of the pragmatics of the question, however, it is unusual for a speaker to form an opposing-turn question with a composite question form or with complex semantics—as with most turn-two questions, opposing-turn questions tend to be short and blunt. By definition, an opposing-turn question must always occur in *turn two* or equivalent (§2.D.7). They also occur in response to a direct question in the subsequent utterance; there should not be a break in the narrative sequence. An asker cannot form an opposing-turn question as a response to a statement. An opposing-turn question must be asked by a different speaker than the asker of the first question. As a result, opposing-turn questions only occur in dialogues (narratives); they do not occur in rhetorical texts such as the NT letters. These types of questions are not naturally arising; rather, they are intentional rhetorical acts designed to affect dialogue.

The primary factor in the formation and identification of opposing-turn questions is explained below.

1) Opposing-Turn Questions Must Be the Response Given to a Previous Question

An opposing-turn question must respond to a question asked in the previous turn. While the relationship between the two questions does not have to be close, the questions cannot be completely foreign, either. It is this not-too-close, not-too-far tension that allows opposing-turn questions to challenge the previous question pragmatically and semantically. For example:

(3) διδάσκαλε, τί ἀγαθὸν ποιήσω ἵνα σχῶ ζωὴν αἰώνιον;
ὁ δὲ εἶπεν αὐτῷ· τί με ἐρωτᾷς περὶ τοῦ ἀγαθοῦ; (MATT 19:16–17)

A young man asked Jesus, "Teacher, what good may I do that I may have eternal life?" Instead of answering his question, Jesus responds with (3), "Why do you ask me about goodness?" The young man broaches the conversation with a simple variable question. Any reader hears this pleasant request from the young man for information and clarification and will expect any response to provide an answer. In fact, anything other than a reply will violate the question-answer pair and breaks trust with the audience. Yet Jesus does this very thing by asking an opposing-turn question. In asking this question, Jesus rhetorically returns the question to the original asker. The pragmatic effect is to refocus everyone around the issues originating in the first question, namely, "goodness." This turnabout undermines the original question and emotionally affects the reader to be suspect of claims of "goodness." Semantically, the question is a quite meaningful proof question (§4.G). Therefore, the question Jesus raises is *not* "what good is for the rich young man" but "why the rich young man focuses on good" in his question. Jesus wants the rich young man to reflect on the reason why he would ask this question about goodness. Likely, this is because the young man secretly knew he was not generous (Matt 19:22).

Rhetorical Effects

Opposing-turn questions have a number of rhetorical effects that deserve careful consideration. Generally speaking, opposing-turn questions can be quite forceful. Because the turn-two speaker violates the rules of dialogue, the reader will react to this violation in a number of ways, including pausing in reading, feeling uncertain as to the discourse direction, rereading the turn-one question, and reconsidering or even rejecting the turn-one question. And because opposing-turn questions often convey animosity, they will evoke a small emotional response in the reader. As a result, the hearer must gauge how forceful the opposition is to the first question. Speakers may use an opposing-turn question as either an attack or a defense, and when used correctly they can be quite strategic. In some cases they can exert a great deal of interrogative pressure on the original speaker (to the point of browbeating). Linguists call these *weak face-threatening devices* in that they interrupt dialogue without shutting it down or ending it.[9] For reading the GNT, we follow the EGH (§2.C.6) and rhetorical-shift principles (§2.D.9): most of the opposing-turn questions may come across mild in English translations, but their actual performance would in most cases be quite strong.

The two main rhetorical effects of opposing-turn questions are explained below.

1) Opposing-Turn Questions Challenge the Previous Question

Opposing-turn questions represent a fundamental challenge to a previous question. In a sense, an opposing-turn question shifts focus back on the original question. Even when they have mild rhetorical effects, they still are a rhetorical jab back at the original asker and their question. With their challenging nature, opposing-turn questions allow the asker to avoid replying to the original

9. Gruber, "Questions," 1816.

question. In ancient rhetoric, speakers used opposing-turn questions to mount a defense before dealing with the original question and to circumvent any potential charge or attack from that question.[10] A speaker may also use them as a ploy to trick the previous speaker into forgetting the original question. Opposing-turn questions are useful in challenging presuppositions embedded in the original question. For example:

(4) πῶς δύναται ταῦτα γενέσθαι;... σὺ εἶ ὁ διδάσκαλος τοῦ Ἰσραὴλ καὶ ταῦτα οὐ γινώσκεις; (JOHN 3:9–10)

In example (4), Nicodemus asks Jesus, "How is it possible for these things to be?" Instead of answering, Jesus responds with his own question: "You are the teacher of Israel and you don't understand these things?" In this dialogue sequence, Nicodemus opens with a sequence question (§4.F). The question leans open due to the variable word πῶς (syntax; "how?"), plus δύναται (semantic; "is it possible") and ταῦτα (indexical; "these things"). These open characteristics betray that Nicodemus asks a question to which he plainly does not know the answer. Readers expect the next utterance to be an answer to Nicodemus's question, but it is not. Instead, Jesus responds to Nicodemus's question with a syntactically complex question: an opposing-turn, conjunctive, positive/negative polar question with an indexical. Given the linguistic complexity of Jesus's question, we start with its strongest rhetorical effect (the EGH principle): its standing in opposition to Nicodemus's question. From this, Jesus asks the question back at Nicodemus not as a statement or as a rebuke but as a challenge to reevaluate the assumptions of the original question. The most obvious result of challenging the original question is to undermine Nicodemus's presupposition; it is entirely possible for these things to be.[11]

2) Opposing-Turn Questions Undermine the Original Question or Asker

An opposing-turn question undercuts the previous question not only by not answering the question but by replacing the question with a new question. It is asked to push back against the previous question, which has the effect of encouraging the audience to reconsider the validity, purpose, or significance of the original question. Rather than giving the original question a pass—by answering it and then asking the next question—the opposing-turn question turns the issue back around and past the original question. When a speaker employs an opposing-turn question, it signals implicit disrespect for the original question or the asker of the question. The opposing-turn question can make it seem as if the original question is weak, unwarranted, or undeserved. For example:

10. Quintilian, *Institutio oratoria* 9.2.13.
11. For lengthier discussion of John 3:10, see Estes, *Questions*, 131–36.

(5) *Διὰ τί* οἱ μαθηταί σου *παραβαίνουσιν τὴν παράδοσιν* τῶν πρεσβυτέρων; …
Διὰ τί καὶ ὑμεῖς *παραβαίνετε* τὴν ἐντολὴν τοῦ θεοῦ διὰ *τὴν παράδοσιν* ὑμῶν; (MATT 15:2–3)

In (5), when the Pharisees and scribes from Jerusalem ask Jesus, "Why do your disciples break the tradition of the elders?" followed by their short explanation of the transgression, Jesus asks back at them, "And why do you break the command of God by your traditions?" This exchange is a remarkable bit of wordplay between these interlocutors. Jesus's question functions as both a mild opposing-turn question and an echo question (§5.B.3). It is mild because the Pharisees and scribes get off an explanatory statement in between their question and Jesus's question. In most cases, this would ruin much of the rhetorical effect of the opposing-turn question, but in this case Jesus uses the echo to force the audience to *skip back over* the explanatory statement to the original question and pushes back against that. This strong pragmatic force creates several effects for the audience. First, Jesus completely skips over the explanation given by the Pharisees (οὐ γὰρ νίπτονται τὰς χεῖρας [αὐτῶν] ὅταν ἄρτον ἐσθίωσιν, "they do not wash their hands when they eat"; v. 2b). Rhetorically, this has the effect of erasing this issue completely from the audience's mind. Second, Jesus not only opposes the original question but explicitly mocks it because he echoes it. Jesus takes the original question and puts it right back in the face of his antagonists. With the echo (noted above in italics), we can see clearly the issue that Jesus takes umbrage with: "Why do you break the command of God?" Third, after asking the question, Jesus makes yet a third pragmatic shift and turns the question into an expository question by not letting up on the Pharisees and scribes. By doing so, Jesus is bluntly calling their authority into question in a way that signals he has no respect for them. Here Jesus's turnabout reveals sophisticated rhetorical skill that would make a trained rhetor take notice.

Case Study — ACTS 9:4–5

Σαοὺλ Σαούλ, τί με διώκεις;

JESUS: Saul, Saul, why are you persecuting me?

Τίς εἶ, κύριε;

PAUL: Who are you, Lord?

Saul continues to make threats of persecution toward the disciples of Jesus. So as to have the legal right to have Jesus's followers tried, he visits the high priest and asks him for letters to be used in the synagogues in Damascus (Acts 9:1–2). After receiving the letters, Saul heads toward Damascus with persecution in his heart. On the road, a light from heaven shines around him (v. 3). Saul falls to the ground, overwhelmed by the light (v. 4a). On the ground he hears a voice say to him, "Saul, Saul, why are you persecuting me?" Saul's blunt response is simply, "Who are you, Lord?"

Paul's experience on the Damascus road makes for an intriguing theological investigation into his relationship with Jesus.[12] Aside from visions and the like (e.g., Acts 18:9–10; 22:18–21), this is the only place in the GNT where Jesus and Paul seem to interact with direct speech. What happens in this interaction is both important and interesting as Luke records the encounter. First, φῶς ἐκ τοῦ οὐρανοῦ ("a light from heaven") shined around him, and falling to the ground Paul heard a voice. The voice asked a question: "Why are you persecuting me?" The voice's question is actually a proof question (§4.G), which means that the voice desires a reply something in the form of "subject + question complement + *because* + proof." By phrasing the question this way, Jesus intends Paul to explain the causality behind his persecutions, such as: "I + am persecuting you + *because* + . . ." In this situation, however, we cannot estimate Paul's emotional state, especially with the semantics of such a question. (Proof questions are at times just that; they are requests for proof, and the hearer is at times being asked to justify or prove themselves. In such cases, the proof question may not be well received by the hearer.) So, right off the bat, Jesus's question to Paul is open but rhetorically strong. With the flashing light, it might have felt inquisitional.

"Fascinating" is one way to describe Paul's response. Paul does not try to give a response or justify himself; he doesn't even try to apologize or explain. In fact, Paul is downright *rude*.[13] In response to Jesus's question, he asks the opposing-turn question, "Who are you, Lord?" We could argue that Paul's question was intended as a repair question (§5.B.4); under the light-from-heaven, heavenly-being-is-talking-to-me circumstances, this theory is possible even if the question is not semantically a close match. Yet in context Paul doesn't seem to want to repair any part of Jesus's question; instead, he asks a question intending to ignore and challenge Jesus's question for the sake of his own question. We could also argue it is a focus-shifting question (§5.B.2) on the basis that Paul wants to get away from where Jesus's question is leading. The problem with this is that Paul's question is too oppositional as it is, violating the rules of dialogue.

Inexplicably, Jesus allows Paul to ask his question and then answers Paul's question. In answering Paul's question, Jesus identifies himself and restates plainly (and humbly) that he is being persecuted by Paul.[14] Still, Jesus does allow his question to be challenged by Paul and then dropped completely from

12. Repeated twice more throughout the book of Acts, in each case undergoing a little rhetorical transformation in the retelling; see 22:7–8 and 26:14–15.

13. The traditional Hebraic custom for epiphanies is for those confronted to say, "Here I am, Lord" or the equivalent; see Pervo, *Acts*, 241.

14. In his study on representational dialogue in Acts, Adrian Smith notes that Jesus's response to Paul's question elides the verbal direct speech cue to show tight comparison and con-

the dialogue. Paul never offers up a response to Jesus's question. The most probable rhetorical reason for this occurrence of an opposing-turn question is either (a) the first question was successfully challenged and defeated or (b) the first question was rendered moot by the second (or later dialogue). Since (a) is not the case here, the reader is left to wonder if (b) is what has occurred. To recap, Jesus asks Paul to account for his behavior; Paul responds rudely by ignoring Jesus's request and asking Jesus to identify himself; Jesus acquiesces to Paul's question and identifies himself, noting the question he asked is true (even if Paul won't answer), and then gives Paul some instructions. From this, we tentatively interpret Paul's words and action as tacit compliance, so much so that Jesus drops his case (request for proof) against Paul. Jesus may overlook Paul's challenge and accept his tacit compliance as acceptance of responsibility for the persecution. Jesus's question presumably rendered moot by Paul's actions, Jesus moves forward with Paul as his chosen instrument to carry his name among the gentiles (v. 15).

FURTHER EXAMPLES

Matt 3:14; 9:15; 12:11; 15:34; 19:4; 21:16b; 22:18; Mark 2:19, 12:15b; Luke 5:22; 6:3; 20:4; 22:49; John 6:61, 68; Acts 8:31.

Key Bibliography

Estes, *Questions*, 131–36; Gruber, "Questions," 1829–41; Liddicoat, *Introduction*, 74; Mastronarde, *Contact*, 37–38; Sacks, *Lectures*, 49–55; Smith, "'I Will Ask You a Question'"; Walton, *Informal Logic*, 61–64.

2. Focus-Shifting Questions

Focus-shifting questions are asked to move the dialogue away from the topic or theme introduced within the first-utterance turn of the dialogue. They get their name from their rhetorical ability to change the subject of the discourse. Focus-shifting questions are a common type of second-turn question; many second-turn (or later) utterances fall into the category of focus-shifting. This is partly due to the innate properties of interrogatives to set or break the movement of dialogue or argument.[15] For example:

(1) After the game, Ken said, "Let's go get something to eat." (TURN 1)
"Whom do you want me to invite?" asked Jason. (TURN 2)

---

trast; I add to Smith's argument by suggesting it reveals how definitively Jesus answers Paul's question in the face of Paul's challenge; see Smith, *Representation*, 531–40.

15. Quintilian recognized this effect of questions to naturally create transitions; see Quintilian, *Institutio oratoria* 9.3.25.

In sample (1), the focus-shifting question in turn two moves the dialogue away from the subject of the characters going out to eat and toward the topic of who should go. In this situation, the shift is mild and part of regular dialogue. However, this is not always the case; for example:

(2) After the game, Ken said, "Let's go get something to eat." (TURN 1)
"Can we go play video games?" asked Jason. (TURN 2)

In sample (2), the focus-shifting question creates a greater degree of separation between the original topic of dialogue and the new topic, presuming that playing games has nothing to do with eating. If the degree of separation gets too great, the turn-two question can drift into being nonsensical.

Focus-shifting questions are similar to opposing-turn questions (§5.B.1); the main difference between the two is semantic. The opposing-turn question is related to and pushes back against the first-turn utterance; it is a question following a question. The focus-shifting question is not related to and is a deflection of the first-turn utterance; it is a question following any type of utterance. In addition, focus-shifting questions are semantically dissimilar to echo questions (§5.B.3) and repair questions (§5.B.4), both of which are related to the original utterance.

Formation

As a type of question defined by its pragmatics, a focus-shifting question cannot be identified by syntax. Instead, we can only identify focus-shifting questions by the way a writer uses them within a text (pragmatics) and to a lesser degree by its relationship to the previous utterance (semantics). Focus-shifting questions have several tells which make them possible for a reader to spot. They cannot follow a question without becoming an opposing-turn question (§5.B.1). While any question formation can be employed as a focus-shifting question, variable and set questions make for the best type of focus-shifting questions. When a speaker uses a polar or alternative question to shift focus, it can come across as brash or disjointed with the rest of the dialogue. The main pragmatic tell of focus-shifting questions is their change in direction within the discourse.

Several factors in the formation and identification of focus-shifting questions are explained below.

1) Focus-Shifting Questions Must Turn the Topic Away from the Original Utterance

The shift perpetuated by a focus-shifting question does not have to be great, but it should be noticeable. If the shift is too great, the question moves from being a focus-shifting question to a nonsensical question. If the shift is too close to the original utterance, the question moves toward an echo question or repair question. While it is possible for the change in direction to be unintentional, usually it is an intentional move on the part of the asker. For example:

(3) Τί σοι ὄνομά ἐστιν; (LUKE 8:30)

Question (3) comes after Jesus is met by a multidemon-possessed man, who asks Jesus what he wants and to not torture him (v. 28). In v. 30, Jesus responds and asks the man, "What is your name?" Since (3) follows immediately after the man's statement in v. 28, not his question, we do not treat Jesus's question as an opposing-turn question. Instead, this question is a strong focus-shifting question. While the man wants to talk about what Jesus will do to him, Jesus wants to talk about who he is. Thus, Jesus uses a focus-shifting question to change the topic from Jesus's possible actions to the man's name.

2) Focus-Shifting Questions Only Occur in the Opening or Standalone Positions

When it comes to dialogue, focus-shifting questions will only occur in the opening or standalone positions. This is because the focus-shifting question is relative to the previous utterance. Typically, when a speaker asks a question in the middle or closing position of the second turn, the pragmatic effect is too weak to elicit much effect on the dialogue (though of course syntactic and semantic rhetorical effects still apply). But when the question is at the opening, it interacts directly with the previous utterance, even if it is a springboard to other movements in the dialogue. For example:

(4) Τί σημεῖον δεικνύεις ἡμῖν, ὅτι ταῦτα ποιεῖς; (JOHN 2:18)

The question in example (4), "What sign do you show us that you can do this?" follows this rule of formation by keeping the question simple, in a standalone position. The Judaeans ask this question in response to Jesus's outburst in the temple courts. Their focus-shifting question is meaningful rhetoric; it is meant to stymie the validity of Jesus's concerns about the temple courts being turned into a marketplace. This type of question is common in political discourse where the second person may ask something to the effect of "What right/position/standing do you have to object?" in response to a prior criticism.

One exception to this rule occurs within rhetorical discourse when a question is asked by the speaker to extend the argument or move the argument in a new direction. In this case, the question would fall in the middle position (occurring anywhere except the first or last utterances of the argument), and is not therefore a turn-two question. In this situation, the pragmatic effect is not present; the focus shift occurs solely on the semantic plane.

Rhetorical Effects

Focus-shifting questions are a common second-turn question type that have a wide range of rhetorical effects. When the shift in focus is mild (e.g., Matt 12:3), focus-shifting questions act as simple rebuttals that subtly change the point of the conversation. When the shift in focus is strong (e.g., Matt 26:10), focus-shifting questions act dramatically to wrest the direction away from the first speaker. As a result, focus-shifting questions tend to have strong rhetorical qualities and less strong informational qualities. In one sense, the rhetorical and informational qualities are interconnected when a speaker asks a focus-shifting question. If a speaker asks a focus-shifting question that is too weak rhetorically, the dialogue may not shift, and the informational quality suffers (because the question is not answered in subsequent dialogue). If a speaker asks a focus-shifting question that is too strong rhetorically, the informational quality also suffers because the focus-shifting question abruptly ends the previous topic, which could bring the dialogue to a halt, or introduce confusion, or be used by the turn-two asker to seize control of the direction of the dialogue.

The two most important rhetorical effects of focus-shifting questions are explained below.

1) Focus-Shifting Questions Are Used to Deflect Attention from the Original Topic

Whether subtle or not, focus-shifting questions move the attention of the audience away from whatever topic preceded it. There are many motives that can cause a second-turn (or later) speaker to feel the need to shift the focus of the topic, but the two motives that *cannot* be at play are (a) to better understand the original utterance (this is a repair or echo question) or (b) to ridicule the asker (this is a retort or nonsensical question). In some cases, focus-shifting questions can serve as quite the riposte to the original speaker. For example:

(5) Τί ἐμοὶ καὶ σοί, γύναι; (JOHN 2:4)

Example (5), "Woman, what do you want with me?" is a classic case of a speaker employing a focus-shifting question to change the subject, deflect attention away from the original subject, and serve as a rejoinder. In John 2, Jesus is at a wedding in Cana during which his mother comes to him and informs him that the party is out of wine. Instead of talking about wine, Jesus tries to shift the focus away from the concern over wine to himself and his role. Jesus's question comes off strong rhetorically not just because of Jesus's use of the word *woman* (γύναι) but also because it is a phatic utterance (§4.K).[16] This is confirmed by Jesus's next

16. The LXX of 2 Kgs 3:13 and 2 Chr 35:21 also contains the phatic question, Τί ἐμοὶ καὶ σοί; On the possibility that the phatic clause is originally Hebraic, see Turner, *Grammatical Insights*, 43–44.

utterance where he continues to talk about himself (and his hour), not the wine or the party.[17] However, Jesus's mother (because it was his mother?) is unfazed by Jesus's attempt to use the question to turn the direction of the conversation and returns to her original topic focused on the party. Jesus is only partially successful in deflecting attention away from the wine and toward himself.

2) Focus-Shifting Questions Can Allow a Subsequent Speaker to Seize Control

Focus-shifting questions are a rhetorical device that allow the asker to go on the initiative. In many cases, this is without completely disrupting the flow of dialogue. In extreme cases, the asker uses the focus-shifting question to wrest control of the dialogue from the earlier speakers. In these cases, often the asker of the focus-shifting question follows up the question with a monologue or creates enough of a disturbance that other speakers will chime in (if successful, in relation to the question, not in relation to the original course of dialogue).

(6) Τί κόπους παρέχετε τῇ γυναικί; (MATT 26:10)

Jesus's question in (6), "Why make trouble for this woman?" comes immediately following inflammatory comments by the disciples about wasting a precious commodity. Rather than respond to the disciples' concerns over wasting perfume, Jesus challenges the disciples' argument by moving away from the material to the personal. Jesus's question highlights the fact that the disciples' may think they are arguing about perfume, but really they are arguing about the actions of a person (in a personally hurtful way to the woman). Jesus uses the question as a springboard to teach the disciples about people issues: (a) the poor (v. 11), (b) sacrificial acts by people who love Jesus (v. 12), and (c) remembering those who followed Jesus during his ministry (v. 13). Even though this question serves as a prompt for a small monologue from Jesus, this question is not an expository question—not only because it is not in turn one but also because Jesus continues to speak without ever actually answering the question. This disjunction highlights the rhetorical effect of the focus-shifting question and its ability to seize control of a conversation.

17. Though see the thought experiment in §1.A.

Case Study — MATTHEW 8:26

Τί δειλοί ἐστε, ὀλιγόπιστοι;

JESUS: Why are you fearful, faithless ones?

During Jesus's public ministry, crowds would often surround him, and on one particular day of this situation Jesus chooses to try to cross to the other side of a lake (Matt 8:18). After some individual discussions (vv. 19–22), Jesus finally gets into the boat with his disciples to cross to the other side (v. 23). During the journey, Jesus falls asleep. Yet a storm arises, and with Jesus fast asleep the disciples decide to wake him, crying out in fear of drowning (vv. 24–25). Rather than address their fear, Jesus responds with a question: "Why are you fearful, faithless ones?"

Matthew records the story of the disciples focused on the storm and their impending death, and as a result they wake Jesus to ask him to save them. Jesus responds to their exclamations with a question, which is a little unusual under the circumstances. The question is a variable question, most likely a mild proof question (§4.G). However, it also carries a clear and negative bias in the descriptor ὀλιγόπιστοι ("faithless ones"). The result is a question formed with a mild rhetorical quality that includes a highly rhetorical bias element. Yet what locks in the strong rhetorical flavor is the pragmatics of the question—it is uncommon for a proof question to appear in turn two unless the asker is attempting to aggressively counter the first speaker. In this case, whereas the focus of the first utterance is different than the focus of the second utterance and the question is a second-turn response to a first-turn utterance, Jesus uses the question in an attempt to shift the focus away from their immediate physical concerns (drowning) and toward the bigger spiritual concerns (not trusting Jesus over against the weather). For the reader, the reason the question is so effective is that a question that leans informational is subverted through semantic bias and then subverted again by second-turn pragmatics to make the question so strong and forceful that the question comes off as if it were an assertion. However, it is not an assertion, and the strong rhetoric causes the disciples to try to avoid the question by responding with their own focus-shifting question—to try to shift blame away from their lack of faith to questioning the identity of Jesus: "What kind of man is this?" (v. 27).

FURTHER EXAMPLES

Matt 27:4; Mark 8:4; Luke 20:5; John 1:46; Acts 9:21; 19:15.

Key Bibliography

Gruber, "Questions," 1826–29; Stewart and Maxwell, *Storied Conflict Talk*, 23–24.

3. Echo Questions

Echo questions are asked to mimic some or all of the previous utterance to draw further attention to the mimicked part of the utterance. They get their name from the "echo" they produce when asked. Echo questions are questions that are asked intentionally as a type of response to a previous utterance. In most cases, they are asked as a response to statements; they cannot serve as a response to a question (except in the special case of (2), below). Echo questions are not common, and they do not occur in rhetorical discourse nor in indirect discourse. They only occur in direct-speech sequences. For example:

(1) Jason: "Don't *run near the train tracks*."
Ken: "Why can't I *run near the train tracks*?" (ECHO QUESTION)

(2) Everett: "*What is that*?"
Violet: "Why are you asking, '*What is that?*' " (ECHO QUESTION)

(3) Young man: "Teacher, what *good* thing must I do to get eternal life?"
Jesus: "Why do you ask me about what is *good*?" (NOT AN ECHO)

In example (1), the echo question in turn two is a close mimic of the original proposition uttered by the previous speaker. In this example, the replication of the entire clause makes the question feel formal and more inquisitive than the more common "why can't I?" or "why not?" While most *why* questions are open, in the special case of an echo question the *why* (or similar variable) becomes limited not only by the remainder of the sentence but also by the intent of the original utterance. With (2), the echo question in turn two is constructed differently than (1), with the second speaker reiterating the entire question from turn one. These kinds of echo questions are less common and are often less rhetorical and more reparative than those like (1). Example (3) is not an echo question, as the amount of mimicking is insufficient for the audience to hear the effects of an echo question.

As a second-turn question, echo questions are closely related to repair questions (§5.B.4). Often echo questions initiate repair, and many repair questions necessarily use some degree of echo to make their repair. However, the key difference between echo questions and repair questions is rhetorical effect: repair questions are always strongly informational, whereas echo questions can run the gamut between being strongly informational (and thus a kind of repair question) to strongly rhetorical. Most of the echo questions in the GNT are formed from a weak echo. In the GNT, John has the most within the narrative sections; the Synoptics have less and Acts has none. (This is due to the much stronger dialogical and dialectical nature of John compared to the Synoptics, and especially to Acts). Echo questions are a well studied phenomenon in IE languages.

Eroteticians can distinguish between various forms of echo questions (but this is beyond our scope here).

Formation

Echo questions have strict syntactic and semantic formation guidelines. Syntactically, a speaker can form an echo question from any question formation—yet the wording of the question must mimic the previous utterance (which typically requires a syntactical relationship between the two). The mimicked phrase or clause can be a paraphrase, but echo questions work best when the phrase or clause is an exact repetition. Echo questions are most commonly formed from polar formations and secondarily from variable formations. Semantically, they must mimic the previous utterance not only in form but also in meaning. In fact, if the question mimics the meaning of the previous utterance but does not mimic the wording, then the question is *not* an echo question. Pragmatically, echo questions are always turn-two (or later) questions and cannot be asked in turn one (as there would be nothing to echo). They have to echo direct discourse, not indirect discourse. With their need for dialogue, echo questions generally cannot occur in rhetorical discourse.

The primary factor in the formation and identification of echo questions is explained below.

1) Echo Questions Must Mimic the Previous Turn Utterance with a Repeated Phrase or Clause

To qualify as an echo question and not merely a type of repair question, the question must precisely mimic the wording from a phrase or clause in the previous turn. Normally the amount of utterance echoed is more than merely a word or two; in some cases, a phrase may be enough, but a clause is more representative of a strong echo. As a general rule, the longer and more specific the echo, the stronger the echo becomes. For example:

(4) *τὴν ψυχήν μου ὑπὲρ σοῦ θήσω. . . .*
Τὴν ψυχήν σου ὑπὲρ ἐμοῦ θήσεις; (JOHN 13:37B–38)

The question in (4) is the sharpest example of an echo question in the GNT. In this dialogue, Peter states that he will lay down his life for Jesus. Instead of Jesus accepting Peter's claim, Jesus responds with a question, asking Peter, "You will lay down your life for me?" Here Jesus does not alter Peter's words but puts them back on him. It is strongly rhetorical and minimally informational. Jesus does not mock Peter; rather, by repeating Peter's own words back to him, Jesus allows Peter to really hear what Peter is saying. Peter may then better evaluate his strong statement.[18]

---

18. For more discussion of John 13:38, see Estes, *Questions*, 138–40.

Rhetorical Effects

The rhetorical effects of echo questions are limited to their ability to refocus attention on the original utterance. Echo questions do not shift the focus away from the original utterance; rather, they cast a brighter light on the original utterance. Echo questions are akin to repair questions in that speakers can use them to repair a conversation, though usually with an extra push or tinge of emotional reaction to initiating repair. They are also akin to opposing-turn questions in that speakers can use them to push back against the first utterance, though they usually are not as forceful. Echo questions often use their mimicry to raise questions about or reveal weaknesses in the original utterance. A speaker may use an echo question to apply interrogative pressure; as a general rule, the more repetitive the echo, the stronger the pressure.[19] This may cause them to be assertive or exclamatory in feel.

Two of the most important rhetorical effects of echo questions are discussed below.

1) Echo Questions Can Clarify or Initiate Repairs with Precision

With their pragmatic refocusing of dialogue back onto a previous utterance, a speaker can use an echo question to clarify the previous utterance. In doing so, echo questions often do not simply initiate a repair but add a rhetorical effect that can call into question the usefulness or validity of the previous utterance. This makes echo questions good at eliciting responses; pragmatically, they are very tempting. For example:

(5) ἐκεῖνός μοι εἶπεν· *ἆρον* τὸν κράβαττόν σου *καὶ περιπάτει*...
Τίς ἐστιν ὁ ἄνθρωπος ὁ εἰπών σοι, *Ἆρον καὶ περιπάτει*; (JOHN 5:11–12)

From (5), the man who is made well by Jesus explains to the Judaean leaders that he was simply instructed to "pick up your mat and walk." This repetition of Jesus's words (John 5:8) is also echoed in the question from the authorities, "Who is the person that said to you, 'Pick up and walk?'" In this case, the authorities are not simply asking the man what happened in order to clarify the events in a general way; instead, they are echoing back his exact wording as a prosecutor might do to a person on trial, in order that the exactness of his words (and the possible guilt therein) may be preserved and presented as evidence to those in the audience. The question is highly informational, but the rhetorical effect is to push the original speaker to confirm the evidence.

2) Echo Questions Can Mirror or Mock the Words of the Original Utterance

With their mimicry of the previous utterance, echo questions return the focus of the dialogue sequence back toward the previous utterance (at least to

19. Cf. Baxter, Boon, and Marley, "Interrogative Pressure," 89.

some degree). This return focus results in several possible rhetorical effects. One example is the *mirror effect*; this occurs when the asker of the echo question wishes to push the original speaker and/or the audience to carefully listen again to the original utterance. This is a useful rhetorical strategy when the original utterance is problematic or indefensible (if carefully reconsidered). Another example is the *mocking effect*; this occurs when the asker of the echo question wishes to ridicule the original speaker in the ears of the audience. This is a useful rhetorical strategy when the original utterance is strange or unbelievable (again, if carefully reconsidered). For example:

(6) *ἀλλ' εἴ τι δύνῃ...*
τὸ εἰ δύνῃ; (MARK 9:22–23)

In example (6), Jesus responds to a distraught father who asks Jesus, "But if you can do anything ..." Jesus responds to the father with, "'If you can'?" echoing back the same words that the father used to ask Jesus to help. By repeating the words back to the father, Jesus (gently) reproves the father's lack of faith or lack of understanding about his person. The audience hears Jesus's echo question as ironic, as they are well aware that Jesus has the power to heal the child. Here Jesus uses an echo question to chide the father toward faith.

Case Study — JOHN 2:19–20

λύσατε τὸν ναὸν τοῦτον καὶ *ἐν τρισὶν ἡμέραις ἐγερῶ αὐτόν.*

JESUS: Destroy this temple and *in three days I will raise it.*

Τεσσαράκοντα καὶ ἓξ ἔτεσιν οἰκοδομήθη ὁ ναὸς οὗτος,
καὶ σὺ *ἐν τρισὶν ἡμέραις ἐγερεῖς αὐτόν;*

THE JUDAEANS: Forty-six years it took to build this temple—and you—
in three days you will raise it?

Jesus's trips to Jerusalem are a common occurrence during his public ministry. In one instance, woven into the beginning of John's narrative and at the end of the Synoptic accounts, the trip results in Jesus clearing the temple courts of people selling livestock and exchanging money. According to John, it occurs during the season of Passover (2:13). When Jesus sees what is happening, he makes a whip and begins to drive out all the livestock and people acting as if it were a market. As Jesus clears the temple courts, he reminds his audience that the temple is his "Father's house" (v. 16). (Later this remark will trigger a realization for the disciples that Jesus's actions were prophetic.) In response to Jesus's claim, the Judaean leaders ask him if he can produce a sign that shows he has the authority to turn out the livestock and people from the temple courts (v. 18). Jesus replies to the Judaeans, "Destroy this temple and in three days I will raise it" (v.19). In response to Jesus's assertion, the Judaeans ask another question, "Forty-six years it took to build this temple—and you—in three days you will raise it?" (v. 20). At this point, the narrator of the Fourth Gospel interrupts to explain the spiritual significance of the exchange for his readers and uses this interruption to shift the scene elsewhere.

During the dialogue with the Judaean leaders, Jesus makes a claim about the temple that appears to be about his ability to raise the temple in Jerusalem in short order if it were to be destroyed. However, John informs his readers that Jesus creates a play on words, indicating to the Judaean leaders that if they destroy "this temple"—meaning his body—that Jesus will raise "this temple" in three days. After Jesus makes this claim, the Judaean leaders respond to the claim with an echo question: "Forty-six years it took to build this temple—and you—in three days you will raise it?" The echo is mild, but it repeats the seemingly impossible part of Jesus's earlier claim. The Judaeans form the question as a polar question, most likely a confirmation question (§4.R). Their use of a confirmation question with an echo effect makes the point of their question clear: they are incredulous about Jesus's claim, they cannot believe he would make such a claim, and they feel that if they can go back and hold Jesus's claim up to the light of day (the ears of the audience), no one would take Jesus's claim seriously. In forming the polar question, the Judaeans front σύ ("you"), and while not unusual, it probably is heard with some emphasis on the preposterousness of who Jesus thinks he is. In fact, John also uses the Judaeans' echo question with rhetorical effect in his Gospel. Just as the Judaeans tried to mimic Jesus's claim to show how ridiculous it sounded, so too does John want his readers to hear Jesus's claim again—contrasted against the lack of understanding of the Judaean leaders and alongside John's push for his readers to believe that Jesus really is the Messiah, the Son of God.

FURTHER EXAMPLES

Matt 15:3; 16:8; Mark 3:23, 33; 8:17a; 10:36; Luke 2:49a; 7:49; John 7:20, 36; 8:22; 13:37; 14:5, 9; 16:17a, 17b, 18, 19.

Key Bibliography

Brown et al., "Questions and Answers," 508–9; Carlson, *Dialogue Games*, 133–36; Comorovski, *Interrogative Phrases*, 55–81; Dumitrescu, "Rhetorical vs Nonrhetorical"; Estes, *Questions*, 136–40; Iwata, "Echo Questions," 185–254; Noh, "Echo Questions," 603–28; Sobin, "Echo Questions," 131–48.

4. Repair Questions

Repair questions are asked to clarify the previous utterance. Repair questions get their name from the fact that the asker seeks to "repair" the conversation and are asked because the asker of the repair question does not understand the previous utterance. They are usually asked so that the asker may be a productive partner in the dialogue. Repair questions can be asked in response to any type of first-turn utterance, though they are most commonly raised in response to a proposition. While any speaker may attempt to repair dialogue, repair questions are only asked by someone other than the speaker of the trouble source. For example:

(1) "Don't cross your skis," exclaimed Dad. (TURN 1)
"Huh?" asked Violet. (TURN 2)

(2) "Don't cross your skis," exclaimed Dad. (TURN 1)
"What do you mean?" asked Bridget. (TURN 2)

(3) "Don't cross your skis," exclaimed Dad. (TURN 1)
"How do you want me to not do that?" asked Wyatt. (TURN 2)

Each second-turn question in samples (1), (2), and (3) are repair questions. The question in sample (1) is an example of a common, gut-level indicator of the need for repair that occurs constantly in natural language. Sample (2) is another strong example of a repair question that specifically targets the confused part of the original utterance (in this case, "cross"). Likewise sample (3) has some tendencies of a repair question, but since its request for repair is weak and indirect, it may not be capable of starting a full repair. The speaker in the first turn cannot ask a repair question (cannot self-repair). Unlike some questions based on pragmatics, repair questions are heavily dependent on their semantic relationship with the previous utterance. While a repair question may request that the previous speaker repair the conversation, no repair is required on the part of the previous speaker in order for a question to be considered a valid repair question.

The inclusion of repair questions presents a unique problem for interpretation of the GNT. Why are repair questions even included? Is their inclusion based on created dialogue, source reconstruction, or eyewitness testimony? Either way, why include repair questions when they are not necessary and could be edited out? While we cannot answer all of these questions here, we can say that the existence of repair questions reveals the strength of the narrative dialogue in creating a real world within the text and engaging the reader in being a part of that world.

Formation

As a type of question expressed primarily by its pragmatic qualities, a repair question cannot be identified by syntax. Instead, repair questions can only be identified by the way a writer uses them within a text (pragmatics) and by their relation to the previous discourse (semantics). Because repair questions only occur within the dynamics of conversation, they are only found in narrative discourse and not in rhetorical discourse. These kinds of questions are not always easy to spot. Strong repair questions ask for direct clarification, whereas weaker examples may only seem like a general question in response to a previous utterance. When a speaker forms a repair question using a variable word, the variable typically indicates what element needs to be repaired in the dialogue.[20] Repair questions are always turn-two (or later) questions and cannot be asked in turn one (as there would be nothing to repair). Repair questions occur only in the opening or standalone dialogue positions and never in the middle or closing positions. Repair questions are semantically related to echo questions in that repair questions "echo" some of the information from the previous utterance (though not necessarily the exact wording as echo questions do). In some cases, repair questions are similar to requests (§4.S). They are a type of question highly susceptible to sluicing (§3.E.4).

The most important factor in the formation and identification of repair questions is explained below.

1) Repair Questions Must Initiate Repair Based on the Previous Utterance

A repair question points the dialogue back toward the trouble spot. Since the asker of the repair question uses the question to identify the trouble spot in the previous utterance, there is some semantic link between the original utterance and the repair question. This link can sometimes be literal in that exact words are echoed back, and sometimes the link can be referential (e.g., John 9:36) in that the hearer must make an association with the previous utterance (e.g., Luke 24:19). For example:

(4) Ποῦ θέλεις ἑτοιμάσωμεν; (LUKE 22:9)

Prior to question (4) from Luke 22, on the day of Unleavened Bread, Jesus tells Peter and John to go make preparations (πορευθέντες ἑτοιμάσατε ἡμῖν; v. 8). Instead of doing this, Peter and John believe Jesus's statement was unclear, and thus they initiate a repair question ("Where do you want us to prepare it?" v. 9). To initiate repair, they ask a question that echoes back the wording of the original utterance. The use of the semantic link generated by the literal duplication of the verb ἑτοιμάζω ("to prepare") allows the reader to associate the repair question with the source of the trouble: the preparations. Likewise, the disciples' use of ποῦ ("where?") alerts the reader that the misunderstanding comes from a lack of spatial knowledge about the preparations. After the disciples' question, Jesus agrees to the repair by giving more details about where the preparations were to be made (vv. 10–12).

20. Sidnell, *Conversation Analysis*, 117.

2) Repair Questions May Be Followed by Repair Attempts

A speaker asks a repair question without any guarantee that the previous utterance will be repaired. As the speaker has no control over the previous speaker, the asking of a repair question is not predicated on the action or response of the previous speaker. However, since social rules of dialogue usually oblige a dialogue partner to assist in repair, it is rare for a repair question to be raised and the previous speaker not in some way to engage in the request (even if just to deny the request). As a result, one helpful tell in identifying a repair question is to look for a repair attempt immediately following the asking of the repair question. For example:

(5) Μήτι ἐγώ εἰμι, κύριε; (MATT 26:22)

In Matthew 26:21, Jesus makes an inflammatory statement on his imminent betrayal by a disciple. As a response, question (5) is asked by the disciples as a weak repair initiator based on Jesus's statement. They ask the question because they do not understand to whom Jesus is referring and seek clarification. As a result of their question, Jesus has a choice to either (a) ignore their attempt at repair or (b) interact in some way with their repair request. Jesus chooses (b), the socially acceptable choice, and clarifies whom he refers to by way of his follow-up statement in v. 23. Because of Jesus's predilection for ambiguous or dramatic discourse, he makes the repair, but on his terms, with a symbolic answer rather than simply giving the name of the person. Nonetheless, a repair question was asked, and the repair was granted in the course of the dialogue.

Rhetorical Effects

Repair questions are usually strong, information-seeking questions, but their rhetorical qualities can range from very weak to relatively strong. In the case of their rhetorical effects, much depends on how the question is asked and what kind of repair is sought. For example, a repair question that initiates repair on an easily understood utterance may carry a strong rhetorical quality that is heard by the audience as belittling the speaker of the original utterance. In extreme cases, a speaker may use repair questions as a rhetorical device to stymie an argument (cf. Abbott and Costello's "Who's on First" routine). Repair questions do not oppose or shift the focus away from the original utterance; instead, they return focus to the original utterance.

The two most important rhetorical effects of repair questions are explained below.

1) Repair Questions Reveal a Lack of Understanding in the Asker

Repair questions not only point to a trouble spot in the dialogue, but they also indicate that the asker does not understand the last utterance. When an asker asks a repair question, it tips off the rest of the audience that the asker is not following the first speaker. In everyday conversation, this is not significant; but in dramatic dialogue it can reveal a weakness in a character or a type of bluff or other deception. For example:

(6) τί θέλεις; (MATT 20:21)

In example (6), Jesus responds to the mother of the sons of Zebedee's request for a favor with a mild repair question, "What do you want?" This makes for an interesting gambit on Jesus's part and introduces a great deal of ambiguity for readers. First, the reader is not privy to what the original favor request was nor whether the request was similar or different to the restatement of the request in Matthew 20:21. (In fact, the restatement of the request is strong evidence that Jesus's question does initiate repair in some way.) Second, while Jesus's request is heard by the mother of the sons of Zebedee as a repair request—which is why she repeats the request in v. 21—it is also possible that Jesus is less interested in repair and more interested in testing her.

2) Repair Questions Refocus the Topic Back to the Previous Turn

As with all other turn-two questions, repair questions have the effect of reflecting attention back on the previous utterance. The primary reason for the asker to do this is a result of misunderstanding, but there are other reasons why the asker may do this. Perhaps the original utterance was nonsensical, or it was intentionally confusing, or it was simply outside the scope of the hearer and audience. In all these circumstances, the results are the same—the audience is pushed to reconsider the original utterance. For example:

(7) Μήτι ἀποκτενεῖ ἑαυτόν, ὅτι λέγει,
Ὅπου ἐγὼ ὑπάγω ὑμεῖς οὐ δύνασθε ἐλθεῖν; (JOHN 8:22)

In John 8:21, Jesus tells the Judaeans who are present that he is going away, they will look for him, they will die, and they cannot go where he goes (ὅπου ἐγὼ ὑπάγω ὑμεῖς οὐ δύνασθε ἐλθεῖν). By any measure, Jesus's words are cryptic. As a result, the Judaeans respond with a question: "Will he really kill himself, because he says 'Where I go, you cannot come'?" The question in v. 22 is complex, as it is formed from a polar question with bias (μήτι) yet possesses the pragmatic qualities of repair, echo, and focus shift all in one utterance. In asking this question, the Judaeans offer up a weak repair question that includes part of an indirect echo question (§5.B.3) to try to decipher what Jesus means. This has the effect of refocusing the dialogue on Jesus's original utterance (note the exact echo of ὅπου ἐγὼ ὑπάγω ὑμεῖς οὐ δύνασθε ἐλθεῖν). By couching the echo within a polar question, the question's primary effect is repair. However, the bias word pushes the question away from the feel of a typical repair question; perhaps this is why Jesus does not give a repair of his original statement but proceeds to talk about the

Judaeans. As a result, the Judaeans' repair question fails to gather information from Jesus but succeeds in creating an ironic, rhetorical effect for the audience.

Case Study JOHN 9:36

καὶ τίς ἐστιν, κύριε, ἵνα πιστεύσω εἰς αὐτόν;

MAN BLIND FROM BIRTH: And who is he, Lord, that I may believe in him?

As Jesus engages in his public ministry, John records that Jesus heals a man born blind from birth (John 9:6–7). Because the day the healing occurred is a Sabbath, this act sets off an investigation of Jesus by the Pharisees (vv. 14–34). After the investigation, Jesus finds the man that he healed and asks him, σὺ πιστεύεις εἰς τὸν υἱὸν τοῦ ἀνθρώπου; ("Do you believe in the Son of Man?"; v. 35). Instead of answering Jesus's question, the man born blind responds with a question. He asks a variable question: "Who is he?" (v. 36a). This question is an earnest request for information. Yet the pragmatics of the question provide an additional spin on the effect of the question.

As a variable question, "Who is he?" is an open question seeking an answer. However, this question is a second-turn question, asked in response to a previous utterance. As with all second-turn questions, it is a bit disruptive to the flow of dialogue. In this case, the question follows a question, which breaks the traditional rules of dialogue. The man born blind should have answered Jesus's question, not responded with a question. At first, we may read the man's question as an opposing-turn question (§5.B.1). It certainly is an oppositional question and does show the man's impatience bordering on rudeness, but in this case the opposition is a special kind: it is a request to initiate repair. Thus the semantics of the question in relation to the previous utterance means it has a stronger repair function than an opposing function—but *it still is mildly oppositional.* The man born blind hears Jesus's question about belief, and instead of answering yes or no, he opposes the question based on his lack of understanding of exactly who is the Son of Man. The man born blind initiates the repair by asking Jesus to identify this Son of Man. As a result, the man born blind is not merely asking Jesus to tell him who the Son of Man is but is informing Jesus that he is not following the dialogue and opposes moving forward until the information is given to him by Jesus. As a result, the pragmatic indicators reveal the man does not ask for the identity of the Son of Man out of curiosity or general interest but out of a lack of understanding and a strong desire to decipher the riddle.

FURTHER EXAMPLES

Matt 12:48; Mark 3:33; Luke 17:37; John 6:42; 12:34b; 13:25.

Key Bibliography
Estes, *Questions*, 151–52; Koshik, "Alternative Questions," 193–211; Schegloff, "Repair," 1295–345; Sidnell, *Conversation Analysis*, 110–38.

C. Middle-Position Questions

Middle-position questions are asked within the middle of a monologue or dialogue turn. Middle-position questions exist between other utterances made by the same speaker, with no breaks in the dialogue turn. They get their name from the fact that they always occupy a middle position within their utterance. In many ways, middle-position questions are most representative of true "rhetorical questions" as they are popularly understood, since they are asked in such a way that no response can immediately follow them. Within persuasive discourse, the middle-position question is the standard question. As a result, the middle-position question encompasses a wide range of minor rhetorical effects. A speaker can employ middle-position questions to heighten rhetorical intensity, shift focus, restate ideas, bridge topics, or refocus the audience. For example:

(1) To argue my next point, I will keep writing about questions.
And yet, what are questions? (MIDDLE-POSITION QUESTION)
Certainly they are peculiar things...

This example makes use of a typical middle-position question. Here in (1) the speaker interrupts their own argument or dialogue turn to insert a question (italicized). The appearance of the question is mildly disruptive in the sense that the question is unexpected by the audience—and as the speaker continues to speak after the question is asked, this also is mildly unexpected. This interrogative peak that occurs in the midst of a string of propositions is what creates the rhetorical effect of middle-position questions.

Middle-position questions can be chameleons, sharing features with all of the other pragmatic qualities of questions. Often in dialogue these questions are static, not dynamic. They can appear one-dimensional or trite, but when used well they are quite important features of speech that can subtly or profoundly affect an argument or dialogue.

Formation

Middle-position questions can be formed from any of the basic formations for questions, and they can relate to previous utterances in almost any way. Therefore, they cannot be identified by syntax or semantics, only pragmatics. Among questions they are one of the most independent of syntactic and semantic factors. A speaker can ask a middle-position question within any dialogue turn.

1) Middle-Position Questions Occur in the Middle of Any Monologue or Dialogue Turn

The one and only formation requirement for a middle-position question is that it be asked in the middle of a monologue or dialogue turn. This may seem an overly broad formation requirement, but the middle position is a severely limiting factor in overall rhetorical effect. An example of this broad formation possibility includes:

(2) καὶ ὅτι πᾶν ψεῦδος ἐκ τῆς ἀληθείας οὐκ ἔστιν.
Τίς ἐστιν ὁ ψεύστης εἰ μὴ ὁ ἀρνούμενος ὅτι Ἰησοῦς οὐκ ἔστιν ὁ χριστός;
οὗτός ἐστιν ὁ ἀντίχριστος, (1 JOHN 2:21–22)

In (2), the middle-position question is a common example in texts; it is especially common in the letters of the GNT where middle-position questions are often placed into question strings for greater rhetorical effect. In the case of 1 John, the subject is knowing the truth in relation to who Jesus is. John then asks, Τίς ἐστιν ὁ ψεύστης εἰ μὴ ὁ ἀρνούμενος ὅτι Ἰησοῦς οὐκ ἔστιν ὁ χριστός; ("Who is the liar if not the one denying that Jesus is the Christ?"). He then follows the question with a description of such a liar. Here the middle-position question is a rhetorical peak that punctuates the point of the argument and refocuses the audience on the issue at hand.

Rhetorical Effects

Middle-position questions possess the purest rhetorical qualities of almost any question that a speaker can ask. It is for this that they are known. Because of their limited positioning, middle-position questions have only one overarching rhetorical effect, which is to adjust the perception of the audience. This can happen in many different ways. These questions can create a segue to a new line of argumentation or a pause in the argument for the audience to catch up. Or they can restate an argument for the audience. Yet because of their wide usage in natural language, they can be coaxed into having numerous, mild secondary rhetorical effects.

Several of the rhetorical effects of middle-position questions are explained below.

1) Middle-Position Questions Can Shift the Focus of an Argument

In the course of a speech, a speaker may wish to move on to a new point or idea. In this situation, a speaker may use a middle-position question to shift the focus on to the new area for discussion. In doing so, the speaker can use the middle-position question to introduce a new argument (e.g., Rom 3:1) or as a rhetorical capstone to the current line of argumentation. For an example of the latter:

(3) εἷς ἐστιν [ὁ] νομοθέτης καὶ κριτὴς ὁ δυνάμενος σῶσαι καὶ ἀπολέσαι
σὺ δὲ τίς εἶ ὁ κρίνων τὸν πλησίον;
Ἄγε νῦν οἱ λέγοντες … (JAS 4:12–13)

In example (3), James comes to the end of a segment on spiritual exhortation for God's people by correcting those who would slander a fellow believer. To elucidate this principle, James notes that this is against the law, and to take a position against the law causes one to sit in judgment of the law—but only God can do that. Only God is Judge. Then, to make the point and encapsulate the argument, James asks the question: σὺ δὲ τίς εἶ ὁ κρίνων τὸν πλησίον; ("But you—who are you to judge your neighbor?"). Not only is this question a middle-position question, but it is a π-*in situ* question as well (§2.B.11). This rare question formation repurposes the normal word order of Koine Greek to front the σύ ("you"), leaving a ringing warning to not judge in the ears of the reader. This is followed by the transitional Ἄγε νῦν οἱ λέγοντες· ("Come now, you who say") which initiates the next phase of James's argument.

2) Middle-Position Questions Can Still Solicit a Response from the Audience

It is possible to overstate the rhetorical qualities of a middle-position question, especially when a middle-position question retains some mild degree of information seeking. They are not unanswerable questions as often assumed. Responses to information-seeking middle-position questions can come not only from the audience but also the speaker in the form of later monologue. In narrative discourse, this can happen if the asker still intends a hearer to answer a question even though it occurred in the middle position. This can occur if the asker is a loquacious speaker, or if the asker has caveats to embed around the question, or if the question is particularly provocative. Yet such information seeking may not always be particularly obvious to the audience. These occurrences are uncommon; for example:

(4) καὶ ἐν κρυπτῷ ἐλάλησα οὐδέν.
τί με ἐρωτᾷς;
ἐρώτησον τοὺς ἀκηκοότας τί ἐλάλησα αὐτοῖς (JOHN 18:20C–21)

Question (4) comes amidst Jesus's response to the high priest during his pretrial inquiry. While John does not record the high priest's questions, the reader hears Jesus respond with a statement of activity, then the question τί με ἐρωτᾷς; ("Why question me?"), followed by a suggestion to call further witnesses. Jesus's dialogue turn infuriates the gathering enough that one official slaps Jesus in the face. Certainly Jesus's opening declaratives would not be welcome, and his concluding call for new witnesses would come across as condescending, but it is the question that provokes the response by the official. Jesus's question is a middle-position question, hiding between two propositions, but it is not a question that does not seek an answer. This question very much seeks an answer from its audience, which implicitly suggests to the hearers that it is not the high priest who will do the asking, but Jesus. Such gall on the part of Jesus to raise a legitimate question (hidden as it were among propositions) and to expect a response results in a strong response—a slap in the face.

3) Middle-Position Questions with Polar Formations Are Often Personal

While an asker may fashion middle-position questions from any type of syntactic formation, polar formations generate a unique rhetorical effect when they are placed in the middle position. The reason for this is their innately closed nature (§3.A). When a variable question, which is innately open, is placed in the middle position, it creates a rhetorical peak that allows for a relatively smooth transition to the next proposition (excepting other factors, such as bias, of course). In contrast, the innate logic of a polar question makes it much more rhetorically disruptive in the middle position, which causes the audience to perceive the question as directed more at them than otherwise would be the case. To say this another way, polar questions generally seek confirmation, and to ask one in the middle position does not eliminate that confirmation-seeking quality. For example:

(5) Οὐ καλὸν τὸ καύχημα ὑμῶν.
οὐκ οἴδατε ὅτι μικρὰ ζύμη ὅλον τὸ φύραμα ζυμοῖ;
ἐκκαθάρατε τὴν παλαιὰν ζύμην, ἵνα ἦτε νέον φύραμα,
καθώς ἐστε ἄζυμοι·
καὶ γὰρ τὸ πάσχα ἡμῶν ἐτύθη Χριστός. (1 COR 5:6–7)

In example (5), Paul is in the process of arguing against how the church in Corinth is dealing with the sin of an incestuous relationship. After making a point about the Corinthians' boasting (1 Cor 5:6), Paul asks a middle-position question using an Old Testament metaphor. It is based on a negative polar form with a strong rhetorical effect designed to make the reader pause and consider whether this is true. By using a negative polar form, Paul makes the question more personal and directed toward his reader than another formation would otherwise allow.

Instead of οὐκ οἴδατε ὅτι μικρὰ ζύμη ὅλον τὸ φύραμα ζυμοῖ; ("Don't you know that a little yeast leavens the whole batch of dough?") consider the alternatives Paul could have used:

- τίς οὐκ οἶδεν ὅτι μικρὰ ζύμη ὅλον τὸ φύραμα ζυμοῖ; ("Who doesn't know that a little yeast leavens the whole batch of dough?")
- τίς ἐξ ὑμῶν οὐκ οἶδεν ὅτι μικρὰ ζύμη ὅλον τὸ φύραμα ζυμοῖ; ("Which of you doesn't know that a little yeast leavens the whole batch of dough?")

As a middle-position question, the polar form still comes across as more pointed to the reader than the variable- or set-question form. Note, this personal effect is not simply because Paul uses second person instead of third person, it is because the internal logic of the question moves from open—"who" could be anyone, so it is open (cf. 1 John 2:22)—to closed—"don't you" is an attempt to get the hearer to confirm their answer. The occurrence of a polar question in the middle plays a rhetorical trick of engagement on the audience.

Case Study — ACTS 26:27

πιστεύεις, βασιλεῦ Ἀγρίππα, τοῖς προφήταις;

PAUL: Do you believe, King Agrippa, in the prophets?

In Acts 26, Paul gets the opportunity to plead his case before King Agrippa. What follows is a long speech by Paul where he testifies to who Jesus is, especially as it relates to his call on the Damascus Road. After a brief interruption by Festus, Paul uses the interruption to turn the discussion away from the past history of his experiences to present concerns arising from his defense before Agrippa. After speaking about Agrippa to Festus (in the presence of Agrippa), Paul rhetorically turns by way of a middle question to Agrippa, asking him if he believes in the prophets. Before Agrippa can speak, Paul answers the question for Agrippa. Paul's strategy is rhetorically savvy and bold in the way that he structures his argument toward Agrippa.

The challenge of lengthy speeches before those who sit in judgment is usually the conclusion. In these situations, the beginning is forced (as the defender must start speaking upon request; hence Demosthenes's prepared introductions for orators),[21] and the middle is the line of evidence, but the ending involves phrasing the response request or initiating a call to action. In this situation, Festus's interruption provides Paul the opportunity to move his argument from the middle to the conclusion, transitioning from evidence to appeal. At the rhetorical peak of Paul's appeal he asks Agrippa, πιστεύεις, βασιλεῦ Ἀγρίππα, τοῖς προφήταις; ("Do you believe, King Agrippa, in the prophets?").

There are several parts to Paul's rhetorical strategy. By asking a pointed question as a middle-position question, Paul is able to blunt the question some, hiding it among propositions. Paul forms the question syntactically as a polar question (§3.A), and semantically it carries the qualities of a confirmation question (§4.R). As such, the question has notable rhetorical qualities to begin with, but when placed in the middle position, it still has enough force to engage the hearer. This is especially true in this case, as Paul embeds Agrippa's name within

21. Cf. Worthington in his introduction to *Prologues*, 57–58.

the question. This allows Paul to ask for a confirmation without seeming as though he is—even as he very much is, in fact, asking for a confirmation. Most importantly, Paul uses the middle-position question as a means to adjust the perception of the audience by switching the focus of his argument away from truth and reasonableness and toward Agrippa's faith, while raising the pitch of his argument (without directly offending Agrippa). By answering his own middle-position question, Paul completes the rhetorical push, only to have Agrippa object to this strategy with a question himself (v. 28).

FURTHER EXAMPLES

Matt 6:25; 22:31–32; Mark 8:36, 37; 9:12; Rom 3:31; 1 Pet 4:17.

Key Bibliography

Meynet, "Question."

D. Question Strings

Question strings are any occurrence of two or more questions in close succession. Within narrative discourse, a question string is the succession of two or more questions made by the same speaker within the same dialogue turn. Within rhetorical discourse, a question string is the succession of two or more questions within the same argument. Question strings are a unique feature of ancient literature and are not limited to the GNT. They occur in both ancient Hebraic and Greek literature.[22] For example, the popular novel *Callirhoe*, written most likely within a couple decades of the New Testament and in a similar vein of Koine Greek, includes question strings such as:

> What if it should be a boy? What if he should be like his father? What if he should be luckier than I? Are you, his mother, going to kill him when he has been saved from the tomb and from pirates?[23]

This exemplifies the drama and rhetoric of the question string in ancient discourse. In the first-century AD, Quintilian recognized the use of question strings as a form of accumulation where the argument is amplified by way of repeated asking.[24] By as early as the fifth century, there were two types of noted questions strings in the Western rhetorical tradition, *erotema* and *pysma*.[25] Question strings

22. For example, Job 6:11–12; Eccl 6:11–12; Homer, *Odyssey* 1.170–77.
23. Chariton, *Callirhoe* 2.9.4–5 (Goold). Note the very standard and effective open-, open-, open-, closed-question types (the *one-one-one-two combination*), similar in formation to 1 Cor 1:20a–d.
24. Quintilian, *Institutio oratoria* 8.4.26–27.
25. Martianus Capella, *De nuptiis Philologiae et Mercurii*; cf. Peacham, *Garden of Eloquence*.

are a prominent feature of both narrative discourse and rhetorical discourse in the GNT:

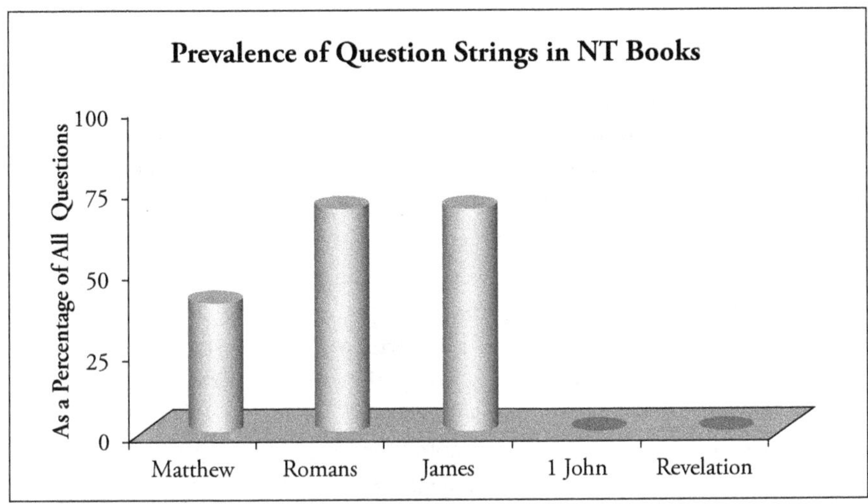

The above chart gives a snapshot of the use of question strings in several books of the GNT. Even though Matthew is a βίος-type narrative, the prevalence of question strings points to a moderately persuasive kind of βίος-type narrative. Romans and James have a greater percentage of question strings but perhaps not as great as one might expect in contrast to a narrative such as Matthew. One interesting feature in this chart is that Romans and James use an identical percentage of question strings in the construction of their text. In contrast to Matthew, Romans, and James, 1 John and Revelation use no question strings at all.

Since a speaker can use question strings to create a complex argument, one question that always arises is: Do questions have to "touch" to be considered part of the same string? Can some phrase, clause, or sentence occur between questions or in the middle of a question string? This is a difficult question that cannot be answered with a unilateral rule; each situation will be unique depending on a myriad of factors. However, the working rule I use is this: *If a string of questions is broken up by a complete thought, then it is not a question string; if a string of questions is broken up by an expression, exclamation, or short phrase, then it may be a question string.*[26] Furthermore, it is technically possible that multiple strings juxtaposed may not be a question string (or may be more than one question string)—this is especially true in the *scriptio continua* of ancient literature where there are no section breaks.

26. Exceptions exist to every rule. In the GNT, Gal 4:15–16 takes the classic form of the open/closed rhetorical combination, even though Paul expresses a complete thought in between.

Another question that regularly arises with the use of question strings is this: What types of questions can a speaker use to create questions strings? While there are no solid rules, there do seem to be several guidelines that make for better (and more persuasive) use of question strings. First, a speaker can use any formation or type of question as part of a question string. However, two factors influence how well certain question types can be used in questions strings. On the one hand, short, simple questions tend to work better than long, composite questions. This is because the interrogative logic stays simple enough that when these questions begin to amplify the argument, the argument does not become too complex for the audience to follow. On the other hand, open-question types with mild rhetorical value tend to work better than closed-question types that are already highly rhetorical. The reason for this is that the persuasive push of question types with strong rhetorical qualities are already strongly rhetorical, and when this becomes amplified in a question string it can quickly become too much for the audience. Second, a speaker is not constrained to use only one type of question. Ancient rhetoricians noted that question strings can occur even when the questions are συναθροισμός, a string of unrelated questions that move the audience toward a similar point.[27] However, the more the variety in the question types, the more chance the speaker takes in fielding a confusing and nonworking question string. This is the reason why most question strings are composed of similar question types with similar syntactic and semantic qualities. They are eminently stackable.

There are, in a sense, two types of question strings: *double questions* and *multiple questions*. These two types can share many similarities and are rarely distinguished as such. However, double questions and multiple questions have distinct pragmatic goals within ancient texts. In short, double questions tend to *encapsulate* an argument, whereas multiple questions tend to *sustain* an argument. In less common circumstances, some double questions can function pragmatically like multiple questions, and some multiple questions can constitute several iterations of double questions. Since Koine Greek in the GNT places a higher prominence on syndeton, the adverbial and conjunctive connections between questions may also augment their rhetorical goals.[28]

1. Double Questions

Double questions are asked to amplify the rhetorical goal(s) of a speaker through a combination attack. A double question is not actually a question but two questions pragmatically linked and asked in succession. Any form or type of question can be a part of a double question; what makes them a double question is that

27. Quintilian, *Institutio oratoria* 8.4.27.

28. For example, see Buth, "Οὖν, Δέ, Καί, and Asyndeton."

they must work in tandem to accomplish the rhetorical goal(s) of the speaker, which is usually to bring greater attention or interest to the speaker's concerns. Therefore, certain forms or types of questions will work better as a part of a double question than others, and certain forms or types may or may not work well with other forms and types. Because double questions work in the pragmatic plane, much depends on the skill of the asker to create double questions that effectively amplify their utterance goals. For example:

(1) How busy is Bridget? Can she clean up her room now? (DOUBLE QUESTION)
(2) Where did the young goat come from? Surely it is stolen?[29] (DOUBLE QUESTION)

Example (1) is a typical double question both in its construction and its rhetorical effect. Here two questions are asked successively. The first question is more of an open-question type, formed with a variable question. The second question is more of a closed-question type, formed with a polar question. This kind of argument structure is extremely common with double questions—an open question is asked first to establish the issue, and the second closed question amplifies the issue to meet the rhetorical goal of the asker. To use an example, the typical double question follows the pattern of the *one-two combination*. In boxing, the *one-two combination* is the most basic combination attack strategy that a boxer learns. The *one* (or first punch) is a jab made at less than full strength that momentarily stuns the opponent, and the *two* (or second punch) is a cross or hook that carries the force of the boxer's attack. To use this analogy, perhaps the most common double-question argumentation strategy involves the *one* (an informational-leaning question that makes the hearer stop to think), followed immediately by the *two* (a stronger, rhetorical-leaning question that lands the weight of the asker's rhetorical goal). However, this is only one possible combination that a speaker may use. Argumentation, as with boxing, depends a great deal on technique, and a speaker with a great combination such as (1) will land a devastating argument that will result in the speaker's goal being met (in this case, someone moving Bridget to clean up her room now rather than later). Example (2) is a nearly identical constructed combination from the book of Tobit.

Formation

Double questions can be formed from any of the basic formations for questions, and there can be a great deal of variation semantically and pragmatically. With the *scriptio continua* style of the GNT, it is not always possible to know whether two subsequent interrogative clauses are double questions or one

29. Tob 2:13.

composite question (either conjunctive or disjunctive). Typically, it is easier to distinguish conjunctive questions from double questions than it is easier to distinguish disjunctive questions from double questions. For example, the NIV translates Revelation 13:4 as a double question, but Revelation 13:4 is more likely a conjunctive question (and punctuated as such by NA^{28} and UBS^{5}). Unfortunately, this uncertainty does affect interpretation. If Revelation 13:4 is a double question, it is like a *one-one* (jab-jab) *combination* of two weak questions, but if a conjunctive question then it is a widening question, which seems to be the case since the question is also an aporetic question type (§4.E). Pragmatically, a speaker can ask a double question within any dialogue turn and from any position within the turn. However, with their role in argumentation, double questions are uncommon in the first turn.

The sole factor in the formation and identification of a double question is explained below.

1) Double Questions Are Two (And Only Two) Related Questions in Succession

In the most simple sense, double questions are two questions asked in succession. To be useful, the two questions must be related, and the more related to similar rhetorical goals that they are, the more effective they become within discourse. For example:

(3) τί ἡμῖν καὶ σοί, Ἰησοῦ Ναζαρηνέ;
ἦλθες ἀπολέσαι ἡμᾶς; (MARK 1:24A–B)

The double question in (3) is another classic example as in examples (1) and (2). Here a man with an impure spirit asks, "What do you want with us, Jesus of Nazareth? Have you come to destroy us?" Whether the man realized it or not, he attempts a standard one-two combo on Jesus. The first question is an open (somewhat phatic) question (§4.A; §4.K), designed to make Jesus pause to think of a reply, while the second question is a decision question (§4.Q) with moderate bias in ἀπολέσαι ("to destroy"), designed to push Jesus to respond. The double question is followed by something of a threat in revealing Jesus's identity. The man delivers his argument effectively, as Jesus does not waste time talking to the spirit but just simply exclaims: φιμώθητι καὶ ἔξελθε ἐξ αὐτοῦ ("Quiet! Come out of him").

Rhetorical Effects

Double questions are a pragmatic feature of question asking that are employed purely for rhetorical effect. Even when a double question contains a question type that would be considered rhetorically weak outside of a double question, the inclusion of the question raises the rhetorical effect of the question by linking it with another question. Thus, double questions are a strongly rhetorical form of question as each question included amplifies the other included question. In this, double questions are effected by both the EGH principle (§2.C.6) and the rhetorical-shift principle (§2.D.9). Though double questions are strongly rhetorical, their use is often more strategic and less aggressive than the typically blunt rhetorical force that comes with negative polar questions (§4.T), leading questions (§4.W), or loaded questions (§4.V). As a result, double questions retain mild informational qualities that do allow for constructive dialogue. Unlike other questions shaped by their pragmatic features, double questions are less influenced by the type of discourse they are embedded in—they tend to have similar rhetorical effects in both narrative discourse and rhetorical discourse.

The two most significant rhetorical effects of double questions are explained below.

1) Double Questions Can Amplify the Argument Made by the Speaker

Double questions are related to other types of question strings in that they amplify the rhetorical effects of the questions included. This is a standard effect for any questions placed in proximity to each other. With double questions, often the first question is slightly amplified and the second question is moderately amplified. For example:

> (4) μήτι ἔρχεται ὁ λύχνος ἵνα ὑπὸ τὸν μόδιον τεθῇ ἢ ὑπὸ τὴν κλίνην; οὐχ ἵνα ἐπὶ τὴν λυχνίαν τεθῇ; (MARK 4:21A–B)

According to Mark, Jesus asks, "Do you ever bring in a lamp to put it under a bowl or under a bed? Don't you put it on a lampstand?" as a double question to introduce his next teaching segment. Here, both questions are syntactically similar, being formed as polar questions, and the main difference between the two is the strength of the negative polarity item. The first question uses the weaker μήτι, while the second question uses the stronger οὐχ. Thus, the second question naturally amplifies the first. Since both questions start off with strong rhetorical qualities, these questions form a *two-two combination* (cross-cross). Jesus asks the first question for the audience to consider whether they would ever hide a lamp, only to have the second question raise the stakes by pushing the audience to agree that there is surely a public place for the lamp to sit. Working together, the questions take on a highly convincing argumentation strategy that sets the audience up to be pliable to Jesus's next utterances.

2) Double Questions Create Rhetorical Combinations That Power Argumentation

Double questions are constructed by the asker as rhetorical combinations meant to apply strong rhetorical pressure toward the audience. These combinations when constructed with precision can be quite effective at persuasion. However, some combinations prove to be more effective than others. As there are many different forms and types of questions, there are many, many combinations that speakers can create to execute their rhetorical strategy. For example:

(5) δέομαί σου, περὶ τίνος ὁ προφήτης λέγει τοῦτο;
περὶ ἑαυτοῦ ἢ περὶ ἑτέρου τινός; (ACTS 8:34A–B)

In (5), the Ethiopian eunuch asks Philip, "I beg you, about whom does the prophet say this? About himself or about someone else?" This double-question sequence creates a rhetorical combination that allows the eunuch to succeed in his rhetorical goal. Syntactically the combination is built on a variable question coupled with an alternative question. Semantically the asker uses an open question type (§4.A) followed by a decision question type (§4.Q). Thus, it is a kind of *one-two combination*—the most popular rhetorical strategy for question strings. Generally speaking, neither of these types alone are strongly rhetorical. Together, however, the double-question sequence amplifies the rhetorical force of each. The open question raises a question that Philip can answer, and the decision question entices Philip to provide an opinion (and get into the discussion). The *one-two combination* makes it seem that the Ethiopian is both earnestly open to any reasonable answer and yet at the same time is gently pushing Philip to choose between two specific answers.

Case Study — MARK 9:19A–B

ὦ γενεὰ ἄπιστος, ἕως πότε πρὸς ὑμᾶς ἔσομαι; ἕως πότε ἀνέξομαι ὑμῶν;

JESUS: O unbelieving generation, how long shall I be with you?
How long shall I endure you?

After the transfiguration event, Jesus, along with Peter, James, and John, return down the mountain to rejoin the other disciples (Mark 9:2–14). There they find the disciples and some teachers of the law engaged in a row over the healing of a demon-possessed man, with a large crowd gathered around. When the crowd sees Jesus, they run to meet him, and Jesus asks them, "What are you arguing about with them?" (vv. 15–16). At this point, a man comes forward and tells the story of his son who, possessed by a demon, cannot talk and is seized regularly by the evil spirit. He tells Jesus that he asked the disciples to drive out the spirit, but they could not (vv. 17–18). Hearing this, Jesus asks the audience, "O unbelieving generation, how long shall I be with you? How long shall I endure you?"

Jesus's response to the scene in which he finds the disciples after the transfiguration is a unique double-question construction with strong rhetorical effects on the audience. Before asking the questions, Jesus prefaces his utterance with the pejorative ὦ γενεὰ ἄπιστος ("O unbelieving generation"), surely meant as a strong pushback against all of those in the audience (i.e., the disciples, the teachers of the law, the crowd, and the father). When a speaker begins their turn with pejorative language, the audience expects to be upbraided. However, in this situation Jesus does not *actually* say anything else about the crowd. Instead, he coyly asks himself two deliberative questions (§4.D) in tandem. Normally, these questions would be moderately informational, but the pragmatics in the question create a sizeable shift in the rhetorical force of the question (§2.D.9). It is also interesting that Jesus does not choose a more commonly expected open/closed combination (such as a deliberative + negative polar question), but one factor in this decision could be that deliberative questions are less frequently formed as polar questions. One of the primary rhetorical effects of deliberative questions is to admit weakness in the asker. In the first question, Jesus uses the verb ἔσομαι ("shall I be"), which does not introduce bias into the utterance. But in the second question, Jesus asks virtually the same question but introduces stronger bias into the utterance by using the verb ἀνέξομαι ("shall I endure").

Jesus's combination relies on a rhetorical sleight-of-hand to shame the audience into understanding its mistakes. Jesus opens with a pejorative, only to raise a double-deliberative question that on the surface seems to suggest a weakness or struggle within Jesus (revealed for the benefit of the audience). The first part of that struggle is Jesus asking openly until when he must be with "these people," and then Jesus amplifies his argument to himself by asking himself until when he has to endure "these people." Jesus expresses his exasperation toward himself, admitting his weakness in remaining with "these people," which has the effect of shaming the audience into hearing Jesus express his regrets. From Jesus's perspective, it is not enough *to be* with them, but *to endure* them also. By eschewing a closed second question and asking a deliberative or more-deliberative combination, Jesus's questions heighten the tension in the audience, causing them to also ask themselves, "How much longer *will* Jesus remain with us?"

FURTHER EXAMPLES

Matt 5:46a–b, 47a–b; 8:29a–b; 18:21a–b; 20:15a–b; 21:23a–b, 25a–b; 22:42a–b; 26:53–54; Mark 2:7a–b; John 6:30a–b; 7:47–48; 20:15a–b; Rom 3:3a–b; 8:35a–b; 9:19a–b; 10:6–7; 14:10a–b; 1 Cor 1:13a–b; 5:12a–b; Gal 4:15–16; Jas 2:6–7; 3:11–12; 4:1a–b.

Key Bibliography

Minchin, "Rhythm and Regularity"; Poole and White, "Question Repetition," 975–86.

2. Multiple Questions

Multiple questions are asked to amplify the rhetorical goal(s) of a speaker by overwhelming the audience. A multiple question is not actually a question but three or more questions pragmatically linked together and asked in succession. Any form or type of question can be a part of a multiple question; what makes them a multiple question is that the questions must work in tandem to accomplish the rhetorical goal(s) of the speaker, which is usually to overpower any opposition to the speaker's concerns. Therefore, certain forms or types of questions will work better as a part of a multiple question than others, and certain forms or types may or may not work well with other forms and types. Because multiple questions work solely in the pragmatic plane, much depends on the skill of the asker to create constructions that are effective. For example:

(1) Who are you? What do you want?
Why are you here? Don't you need to be moving on?
[Yes, you do.] (MULTIPLE QUESTION)

Here the speaker uses a multiple-question construction to overpower the hearer, enforcing the speaker's rhetorical goals and trying to prevent the addressee from replying before the point is made. In (1), the speaker uses three variable questions (open-, open-, and proof-question types) followed by a polar question (negative polar-question type) to amplify the already considerable rhetorical force. In some circumstances, the speaker may elect to include a concluding remark—as in this case, the "Yes, you do" utterance.[30] When this occurs, the multiple question resembles what ancient rhetoricians sometimes considered as a form of ὑποφορά.[31] Unlike double questions where the speaker usually uses two different forms and types of questions to create a rhetorical combination, multiple questions tend to be comprised of similar or related forms and types of questions. Thus, while double questions often encapsulate an argument, multiple questions often extend and prolong an argument (and frustrate a would-be replier). Multiple questions are a common rhetorical device that dates to at least the time of the Old Testament (cf. Job 35:6a–7b; Isa 40:12a–14b) and Demosthenes (e.g., *Mid.* 97–98) and a common narrative device that dates to at least the time of Homer (*Od.* 1.170–72) and the writing of Genesis (cf. 4:6–7; 12:18–19).[32] Multiple questions may have served as an introductory device in ancient lyric tragedies.[33]

---

30. Aristotle notes it is stronger argumentation to conclude with a proposition; Aristotle, *Topics* 158a7–9.
31. *Rhetorica ad Herennium* 4.23.33–24.34.
32. Minchin, "Rhythm and Regularity."
33. Hutchinson, *Greek Lyric Poetry*, 428.

Formation

Multiple questions can be formed from any of the basic formations for questions. Among question types, they are one of the most independent of syntactical factors. A speaker can ask multiple questions within any dialogue turn and from any position within the turn. However, multiple questions are rare in turn one (unless part of a one-act monologue). When a speaker uses similar syntactic constructions to create a multiple question, the constructions do not need to be exactly the same; sometimes grammar will trump style (though, vice versa is true also).

Two notable factors in the formation and identification of multiple questions are explained below.

1) Multiple Questions Are Three or More Related Questions in Succession

Since conversational expectations are built on the question and answer pair, two questions in a row by the same speaker may be manageable, but three or more are not. At that point, the questions take on an argument structure of their own that is distinct from the normal purpose and roles of question asking. As a result, multiple-question strings are relatively easy to form and to identify (though if not formed well, they can fail to accomplish their goal and their audience will find them confusing). For example:

(2) ποῦ σοφός;
ποῦ γραμματεύς;
ποῦ συζητητὴς τοῦ αἰῶνος τούτου;
οὐχὶ ἐμώρανεν ὁ θεὸς τὴν σοφίαν τοῦ κόσμου; (1 COR 1:20A–D)

In example (2), Paul creates a multiple-question string and asks, "Where is the wise? Where is the teacher of the law? Where is the pop philosopher? Hasn't God made foolish the wisdom of the world?" In this case, each of the questions are related both syntactically and semantically, which creates a style of persuasive appeal centered around overwhelming the hearer into believing Paul's view. Paul believes that a person can ask where wise people may be found, but in doing so it does no good because their wisdom is, in the end, less even than the foolishness of God (1 Cor 1:25). Paul's multiple questions are an interrogative barrage that leads to an inability to mount a successful counterreply on the part of his readers.

2) Multiple Questions Are So Strong They Often End with a Punctuating Point

Because multiple questions present a sustained line of argumentation that are meant to overwhelm an audience, the force of a multiple-question string can result in confusion at the end with the audience feeling blown away by the flurry of questions. As a result, one common trick in using multiple questions is for the speaker to conclude the multiple-question asking with a brief statement that punctuates the point of the argument. This point can be an utterance following any sentential function, though an assertion or exclamation is most common. For example:

(3) ὁ οὖν διδάσκων ἕτερον σεαυτὸν οὐ διδάσκεις;
ὁ κηρύσσων μὴ κλέπτειν κλέπτεις;
ὁ λέγων μὴ μοιχεύειν μοιχεύεις;
ὁ βδελυσσόμενος τὰ εἴδωλα ἱεροσυλεῖς;
ὃς ἐν νόμῳ καυχᾶσαι, διὰ τῆς παραβάσεως τοῦ νόμου τὸν θεὸν ἀτιμάζεις;
τὸ γὰρ ὄνομα τοῦ θεοῦ δι' ὑμᾶς βλασφημεῖται ἐν τοῖς ἔθνεσιν,
καθὼς γέγραπται. (ROM 2:21–24)

In (3), Paul asks his readers, "Therefore, those who teach others, do you not teach yourself? Those who preach not to steal, do you steal? Those who say not to commit adultery, do you commit adultery? Those who hate idols, do you rob temples? Those who boast in the law, do you dishonor God by breaking the law? For as it is written: 'The name of God—because of you—is blasphemed by the gentiles.'" This multiple-question set, composed of polar questions, is a strong, rhetorical attack on the unfaithfulness of people who claim to be for God and yet do not live for God. So strong is the attack that Paul risks losing his reader—both heart and attention—so he concludes the question with a punctuating point that resolves the argument for his readers. In this case, he does so by adapting Isaiah 52:5 as the point, saying τὸ ὄνομα τοῦ θεοῦ δι' ὑμᾶς βλασφημεῖται ἐν τοῖς ἔθνεσιν ("The name of God—because of you—is blasphemed by the gentiles"). This does not negate Paul's desire for the reader to raise these questions themselves to ask themselves how they may be party to this, but the pragmatic effect of the multiple-question attack is so strong as to severely limit the informational force of the individual questions.

Rhetorical Effects

Multiple questions are created from a barrage of interrogative utterances that unleash a battery of rhetorical effects on their audience. While each question in a multiple question will have different individual rhetorical effects typical for their form and type, the pragmatic effects of the multiple-question string as a whole trumps any of these individual effects. The overall effect is both dramatic and overwhelming. It is meant to cover a range of issues at once, and in many cases, to create an oratorical shield that will at best give pause to the audience or at worst cause a great deal of frustration. These types of questions are not a natural occurrence in conversation; they are created by speakers purely for rhetorical and persuasive effect.[34]

34. Minchin, "Rhythm and Regularity," 35.

Three of the most notable rhetorical effects of multiple questions are explained below.

1) Multiple Questions Can Overview a Situation or Shape a Larger Argument

The limits inherent in both rhetorical and narrative texts require a writer or speaker to engage in summarization that will quickly outline a situation at hand (narrative) or position to be taken (rhetoric). In the ancient world, multiple questions were sometimes used as a narrative and rhetorical device to quickly abridge a much larger occurrence or discussion. For example:

(4) Ποῦ οὗτος μέλλει πορεύεσθαι ὅτι ἡμεῖς οὐχ εὑρήσομεν αὐτόν;
μὴ εἰς τὴν διασπορὰν τῶν Ἑλλήνων μέλλει πορεύεσθαι
καὶ διδάσκειν τοὺς Ἕλληνας;
τίς ἐστιν ὁ λόγος οὗτος ὃν εἶπεν, Ζητήσετέ με καὶ οὐχ εὑρήσετέ [με],
καὶ ὅπου εἰμὶ ἐγὼ ὑμεῖς οὐ δύνασθε ἐλθεῖν; (JOHN 7:35A–36)

The multiple questions in (4) come from a lively narrative section of the Gospel of John. Here Jesus makes a rather bold statement publicly about his future plans (7:33–34). After this, the narrator tells us that the Judaeans asked themselves a series of multiple questions, "Where does this man intend to go that we cannot find him? Will he go where our people live scattered among the Greeks, and teach the Greeks? What did he mean when he said, 'You will look for me, but you will not find me,' and 'Where I am, you cannot come'?" These questions help to quickly express the confusion of some within the Judaean leadership about Jesus's plans. Not only do they offer a summary, they also raise questions that the implied reader may also ask. John uses these questions rhetorically to shape the larger argument of Jesus's departure to return to the Father.

2) Multiple Questions Increase in Rhetorical Strength as the String Progresses

As with all types of question strings, multiple questions can amplify the rhetorical argument made throughout the question string. When a hearer encounters a question string, the rhetorical push grows stronger as the argument is heard. In many cases, the last question is the strongest and packs the biggest rhetorical punch of the question string. Conversely, many times the first question in the question string is the least rhetorical—it may actually be primarily information seeking so as to get the reader to begin to consider the issue at hand. For example:

(5) Τολμᾷ τις ὑμῶν πρᾶγμα ἔχων πρὸς τὸν ἕτερον κρίνεσθαι ἐπὶ τῶν ἀδίκων, καὶ οὐχὶ ἐπὶ τῶν ἁγίων;
ἢ *οὐκ οἴδατε* ὅτι οἱ ἅγιοι τὸν κόσμον κρινοῦσιν;
καὶ εἰ ἐν ὑμῖν κρίνεται ὁ κόσμος, ἀνάξιοί ἐστε κριτηρίων ἐλαχίστων;
οὐκ οἴδατε ὅτι ἀγγέλους κρινοῦμεν, μήτιγε βιωτικά; (1 COR 6:1–3)

Multiple question (5) is a case of a question string that is both a multiple question, in one sense, and two double questions fused together, in another sense. Here Paul asks "Do some of you dare the practice of taking a dispute to be judged before the ungodly and not before the holy [people of God]? Or haven't you known that the holy will judge the world? And if by you the world is judged, are you unworthy to judge the least of disputes? Don't you know that we will judge angels, not just mundane concerns?" The logic of the multiple questions works together to create a *one-two, **one-two** combination* to persuade the reader of the ridiculousness of their perceived position. Paul forms all four questions as polar questions, but in order they are used semantically as (i) a confirmation question (note the lead-in bias of τολμᾷ ["dare"]) (ii) a negative polar question (very forceful with οὐκ οἴδατε ["don't you know"]), (iii) another confirmation question (with conditional lead-in, not weaker than the first, just a bigger setup for the final question), and (iv) a final negative polar question (doubly forceful with οὐκ οἴδατε). Paul's rhetorical questioning greatly amplifies his intention to ask and challenge his readers to reconsider their use of lawsuits in the strongest possible terms.

3) Multiple Questions Are Asked to Overwhelm Their Audience

Multiple questions are often a rhetorical attack meant to bewilder and disable an oratorical opponent. They "are as it were like unto a courageous fighter, that doth lay strokes upon his enemy so thick and so hard that he is not able to defend or bear half of them."[35] Even as a defense is readied for the first question, the asker continues to raise more. For example:

(6) τίς γάρ σε διακρίνει;
τί δὲ ἔχεις ὃ οὐκ ἔλαβες;
εἰ δὲ καὶ ἔλαβες, τί καυχᾶσαι ὡς μὴ λαβών; (1 COR 4:7A–C)

Example (6) captures Paul's concluding remarks over the issue of following individuals such as Apollos or himself. Paul's final challenge to his readers asks, "For who makes you distinct? What do you have that you have not received? And if you have received, why do you brag as if you have not received?" This is launched to overwhelm any final objections. Paul's questioning is as personal as it is blistering, designed to lay to rest the particular issue at hand.

35. Peacham, *Garden of Eloquence.*

Case Study ROMANS 10:14A–15

Πῶς οὖν ἐπικαλέσωνται εἰς ὃν οὐκ ἐπίστευσαν;
πῶς δὲ πιστεύσωσιν οὗ οὐκ ἤκουσαν;
πῶς δὲ ἀκούσωσιν χωρὶς κηρύσσοντος;
πῶς δὲ κηρύξωσιν ἐὰν μὴ ἀποσταλῶσιν;

PAUL: Now, how can they call on one in whom they have not believed?
How can they believe in one whom they have not heard?
How can they hear without one who preaches?
How can they preach unless they should be sent?

In Romans 10, Paul turns his argument toward the congruence of faith for both Israelite and gentile. Paul wants to see Israel be saved, but the problem for some of Israel is that while they have zeal for the law and zeal for God, that zeal is based on their attempt to establish their own righteousness rather than rely on the righteousness that comes from God. In fact, the Messiah is the end and goal of righteousness from the law (v. 4). From this, Paul builds a case from Old Testament citations and rhetorical argumentation that faith is what saves a person—and that this salvation is available to everyone, both Jew and gentile, because of God's great grace for all people (v. 12). Paul concludes this thought by referencing Joel 2:32 (3:5 LXX), "For everyone who should call on the name of the Lord will be saved" (v. 13). Paul then transitions to the ramifications of this calling out to God, by asking a question string that moves the thoughts of his audience away from the call itself to how the call can go out. The result is one of the most notable question strings in the GNT: "Now, how can they call on one in whom they have not believed? How can they believe in one whom they have not heard? How can they hear without one who preaches? How can they preach unless they should be sent?"

Many question strings (especially double questions, but some multiple questions) move from beginning to end by raising the intensity of the interrogative logic of later questions in the string, which creates a cumulative effect on the reader (e.g., (5) above). In these cases, the questions are not necessarily poetic; instead, they rely on brute force and hard argumentation to make their case. Here Paul takes a slightly different tact. First, Paul uses the same question type, a series of four means questions (§4.H) that repetitiously raise the possibilities for the audience. Second, the questions create a notable poetic feel based on a rhythmic pattern and some rhyme.[36] For example, the repetitive δὲ (often translated "and" but really here a pragmatic connective particle) extends the feel of the

36. The questions create a "chain" of parallel ideas; see Moo, *Epistle to the Romans*, 663; Barrett, *Epistle to the Romans*, 189–90; Käsemann, *Commentary on Romans*, 293. On the oral implications for hearers, see Kelber, *Oral and Written Gospel*, 149.

argument for the hearer (which would be more pronounced in an oral recitation of this letter). Third, Paul progresses semantically from one tangential concept to the next, creating links between each of his subject foci. The main verbs are subjunctive, which has the effect of modally emphasizing the means semantics of the interrogative logic (even though the question is as strongly rhetorical as it is informational). The end result is a list of questions that seem to point in reverse even as they push the audience forward.

Because this is a rather artful use of multiple questions, Paul is actually building toward the point of his argument. First, he uses the multiple-question attack to fence the reader into his intense argument.[37] Then Paul follows through with jab after jab, constraining the reader to follow his rhetorical focus. As the argument amplifies, Paul raises the possibility at each point as to the *means* by which this can happen. At the crescendo of Paul's argument, his final rhetorical attack reveals the point of the argument: How can one preach (if not sent)?[38] Paul's multiple questions are progressive in their force, building up an argument to overwhelm its hearers with the need to make a way for people to be sent to preach. This is evidenced by the concluding rhetorical flourish, "As it is written: 'How beautiful are the feet of those preaching the good news.'"[39]

FURTHER EXAMPLES

Matt 25:37–39; Luke 17:17a–18; John 16:17a–18; Rom 8:31a–34; 1 Cor 3:4–5b; 2 Cor 11:22a–23; Heb 3:16a–18; Jas 5:13a–14.

Key Bibliography

Karttunen and Peters, "Interrogative Quantifiers," 181–205; Mastronarde, *Contact*, 39–44; Minchin, "Rhythm and Regularity."

37. Cf. Chrysostom, *Romans* 18.
38. Witherington, *Paul's Letter to the Romans*, 264; contra, for example, Hultgren, *Paul's Letter to the Romans*, 389.
39. Barrett, *Epistle to the Romans*, 190.

Chapter 6

The Function of Questions in the Greek New Testament

As a speech act, questions are unbounded in their usefulness for gathering information, creating dialogue, prompting action, and persuading an audience. As we have seen throughout this book, the number of possible logical goals and rhetorical effects are also seemingly without end. Questions are a striking contrast to propositions, as questions are malleable enough to communicate almost anything communicable short of outright assertion (though questions can essentially do that too). In a sense, questions are the salt of communication; they make everyday conversation and texts varied and interesting.

Within the texts of the GNT, as would be the case with any compilation of significant yet related texts, the questions asked take on a variety of functions, often with similar goals. While this book raises many questions that are beyond its scope—such as why one author favors one type of question and what this indicates about the rhetoric of the book—we can note, in passing, several important functions of the questions in the GNT.

A. Narrative Function

Many of the most notable questions in the GNT occur in sequences of narrative dialogue. Within narrative dialogue, questions perform several important functions, of which only three are noted here: *structure*, *flow of information*, and *imagination*. The narrative dialogue in the GNT is an example of representational discourse, as it is not a live recording of the dialogue. This is true even if we consider the representation fully accurate or authentic. Where representational discourse can conflict with natural discourse is when it does not accurately represent the natural discourse on which it is based. Real, everyday dialogue is messy: it is not just statement after statement or question, answer, question, answer, question, answer. When representational discourse seems too neat and tidy, it is often the sign of an overzealous narrator. One way a writer can use questions in representational discourse is to help structure the dialogue. For example, when a writer goes to commit an event (witnessed or heard about) to writing, the writer will naturally "trim the fat" to make the conversations fit within the scope of the narrative. (The writer must do this in order to have a narrative.) While it may be tempting to eliminate the questions, for example, and only include the points the speaker made in the dialogue, this will result in poor writing. As a result, including questions helps the writer to organize the dialogue, create breaks, and give the narrator the opportunity to shape the dialogue so the reader better understands it. Thus, questions in narrative dialogue will greatly contribute to the flow of information—not only between characters, but also between the narrator and the reader. When a reader reads statement after statement, their attention drops as the monotony begins to inhibit the flow of information. In contrast, when the text regularly prompts the reader to answer questions (even if the questions are intended for the characters), it wakes the reader and improves their understanding of what they are reading. Finally, one rhetorical effect of questions on the reader of narrative dialogue is to spur the imagination of the reader. The reader may quickly pass over statements, even profound ones, but some questions are not just profound in what they ask; they evoke an image in the reader's mind that must be engaged before the reading can continue.[1]

B. Dramatic Function

A challenge for modern readers of the NT is not to read "through" the questions in the New Testament as if they were simply statements or asked merely as "rhetorical questions." This is the opposite of how ancient-world readers would have handled the questions in the GNT. Ancient readers read aloud, and any reading of the GNT whether public or private would have been read for the ears and not as much for the eyes. With ancient-world writing styles and reader expectations (e.g., *scriptio continua*), a reader reading out loud would need to quickly decipher the extent and force of the sentence during the reading process. As a result, readings of texts in the ancient world would be closer to a performance than what we think of a reading today. Each sentence would be emphasized. Questions especially would be read so as to increase the dramatic tension. (This is not much different than a skilled public speaker today, who "performs" their message by making each sentence work together by emphasizing their force in the appropriate way.) The questions throughout the GNT will add a dramatic element to the reading if they are read as they were intended (i.e., as they were written). One example of this is the question strings in the letters of Paul; they seem long

1. As the same may be said about rhetorical ornaments that can occur in statements such as ἔκφρᾰσις ("lucid description"), it is the rhetorical effect as much as the interrogative itself that fosters imagination.

when read silently, but if performed the amplification and combinations would be more readily apparent. Another example is the interrogation scenes in the Gospels; the questions asked show the dramatic tension between the speakers in the events that are recorded (e.g., Matt 22:41–46).

C. Rhetorical Function

As a speech act, the potency of questions to persuade an audience is unmatched. In the GNT, the most important function of a question is its rhetorical function. Within texts, questions persuade on a number of different levels. In representational discourse found within historiographical texts, the people characterized within presumably persuaded each other through the use of questions. Within these narratives, the characters try to persuade each other every time the narrative is read. As the narrative is read, the questions of the characters come alive for the reader, and the reader asks the same questions of themselves that the characters ask each other. In rhetorical discourse, it is somewhat simpler since the writer simply asks questions for the reader to answer. This, then, creates the myth of the "rhetorical question": The writer of rhetorical discourse (such as most of the letters in the GNT) does not ask a question without seeking an answer; the writer asks the question very much wanting the reader to answer and respond (even if the answer is not aloud). Writers can use questions in strategic places, such as at the beginning or end of an argument, or to structure the argument in general.[2] For the writers of the GNT, their primary rhetorical goal in their use of questions is to persuade the reader to agree with them in almost all cases. Thus, many of the questions in each book serve something of a metafunction in that they work in tandem to push the reader in the writer's intended direction. This should not be a surprise to most readers of the GNT.

D. Dialectical Function

The dialectical function of questions is often overlooked and misunderstood by modern readers. When we speak of the dialectical function of questions, we are *not* referring to the modern philosophical term *dialectical*. Rather, we are referring to the ancient Greek word for dialectical, διαλεκτική, which roughly means "the art of dialogue." In its everyday sense, dialectic was the ancient practice of examination; it would be akin to what we might today call an interview or a hearing or a diagnostic. One of the original, telltale signs of dialectic was the frequent use of the polar question to ferret out the truth of something by means of examination. By the time of the writing of the GNT, dialectical discussion was more broadly applied. Part of understanding ancient dialectic is the recognition that the speaker would carefully order their argument, specifically

2. Cf. Burggraff, "Corpus Linguistic Verb Analysis," 92–93.

their questions, for maximum interrogative impact. Aristotle discusses this in the eighth book of his *Topics* where he argues that the three major steps to dialectic are (a) choose the area for attack, (b) create the questions and mentally organize them for the attack, and (c) deliver them to the antagonist.[3] Of these steps, the arrangement of questions is the unique province of the dialectician.

In the Gospels, we can see the excerpted remains of not just questions in representational conversation but rhetorically determined lines of attack from both proponents and opponents. Even more, in both the Gospels and most of the Epistles, the writers of these texts intentionally included questions (either directly or in the mouths of characters) in a preselected, systemized way to persuade the hearer/reader of the point of the text. While most Western readers do not have a lot of practice organizing a list of questions for an oral speech, most of the writers of the GNT would have had at least some informal practice in this. As I have shown throughout the book, some of those writers possessed notable dialectical skill derived from both training and practice. While there is much more we could say about this overlooked art, the simple fact is that ancients were as concerned about what they wanted to ask their readers as they were about what they wanted to say to their readers. However, in true dialectical style, the GNT writers often asked their questions with obfuscation so as to persuade their hearers and readers without putting all their cards on the table.[4]

E. Concluding Thoughts

In this book I have set out to explain the way questions and their rhetoric affect the reading of the GNT in several important ways. One by-product of this is the recognition that the ancient Greek language was highly logical and organized, in many ways not terribly different from many other IE languages. However, there is a warning in this. Questions by their nature resist neat categorization, and so the forms, types, kinds, and categories in this book are all intended to be permeable. When we study questions, there will always be new insights for and new ways of looking at them that will shape future readings and interpretations. While questions typically have a fixed syntax and a primary semantic or pragmatic effect, there are many shades of interpretation beyond these two descriptors. My hope is that no reader will use this book to look at a question in the GNT and state matter-of-factly that the question is "this semantic type" or has "this pragmatic effect" and nothing more. Limited by the normal constraints of a book, there are many topics that this work could not explore or develop to the length deserved. As a result, this book is intended as one of the first words on questions in the GNT, but it is not intended in any way to be the last.

3. Aristotle, *Topics* 155b3–8.
4. Ibid., 156b6–9.

Appendix

Semantic Types of Questions

Open Question	Does the *wh*-question ask something without any spin, bias, or leading?
Speculative Question	Does the question ask a hypothetical, or is it not easily answered ("Why")?
Lyric Question	Does the question ask about something mythic, or evoke a feeling of wonder?
Deliberative Question	Does the question ask the asker something (use "I")?
Aporetic Question	Does the question hint at loss or doubt in the face of the impossible?
Sequence Question	Does the question ask for a step-by-step process ("How")?
Proof Question	Does the question ask the reason for something or because of something ("Why")?
Means Question	Does the question ask to explain a possibility ("How")?
Indexical Question	Does the question contain an indexical as the focus of the complement?
Endoxical Question	Does the question contain an appeal to "everyone believes that"?
Phatic Question	Does the question fulfill a social function?
Test Question	Does the question test the audience and allow the asker to evaluate?
Inapposite Question	Does the question asked have an answer known to the asker?
Riddle Question	Does the question contain a semantic puzzle (and is implicative)?
Dilemma Question	Does the question contain a two-pronged scheme ("fork")?

Counterfactual Question	Does the question contain a contrary-to-fact conditional?
Decision Question	Does the question ask yes/no without any spin, bias, or leading?
Confirmation Question	Does the polar question ask the audience to agree (SPQs)?
Request Question	Does the question push the hearer toward an action (often both phatic and implicative)?
Negative Polar Question	Does the question persuade/coerce/assert with a negative polar form?
Biased Question	Does the question contain a notable bias word or phrase?
Loaded Question	Does the question contain a hidden assumption (implicative)?
Leading Question	Does the question ask disingenuously (i.e., it contains the "correct"answer)?

Glossary

Throughout this book there are a number of terms that relate to the interpretation of questions that may not be familiar to all readers. The most common of these terms are below, with basic definitions. These definitions are not intended to be exhaustive, nor are they meticulously precise; rather, they provide a broad meaning for the reader. We will hold to these meanings gently, recognizing there is space for overlap of meaning as well as situations where more than one of these words may apply.

Answer: Any utterance that satisfies what a question asks. When more than one answer can satisfy a question, all of these answers form the *set of answers*. An answer is always a reply, though a reply is not necessarily an answer (and in natural-language situations, frequently is not). Answers are often entailed by their question (§2.E).

Artificial Discourse: Invented utterances used as examples in language studies. Useful for basic analysis (such as syntax), but beyond this is limited due to an absence of context (§2.D.8).

Assertive: The force applied to any utterance that *says*. When one communicates with assertive force, the resulting utterance is a proposition (at least of a basic sort). Sometimes called *declarative*.

Bias: The semantic coloring of an utterance so as to predispose the audience toward a certain attitude or outcome. Bias most often occurs in a negative sense, though positive bias is possible. Most languages have key words that are pervasively used by speakers to create bias (§2.C.2).

Combination: In rhetoric and boxing, a series of attacks that work together to defeat an opponent. A *jab* is a quick, disorienting attack. A *cross* is a strong attack that follows a jab. A *hook* is a power attack meant as the final blow. Conversely, a *haymaker* is a wild, undisciplined attack.

Dialectic: The art of clarifying an issue through dialogue, usually involving question and answer. From the Greek word διαλεκτική. Here we define this term in the way that most ancient Greek-speakers would have understood it; we are not using the term in the modern philosophical sense.[1] Dialectic was intimately related to the art of rhetoric in the ancient Greek philosophical and rhetorical traditions.

Dialogue: A set of two or more turns of related utterances between two or more people. A dialogue usually has more than one speaker across the two or more turns (§2.D.8).

Direct Question: Any question that expresses its interrogative force directly and openly. Stands in contrast to an indirect question (see Indirect Question). The rhetorical quality of a question does not bear on whether a question is direct or indirect.

Discourse: Any group of related utterances that work together to create meaning as a whole. Different styles of discourse (such as rhetorical discourse and narrative discourse) are the building blocks of genre (§2.D.6).

EGH Principle: When considering the rhetorical effects of a question, the reader should assume the strongest rhetorical option is the intent of the asker; a guideline for investigating the rhetorical quality of interrogatives (§2.C.6).

Erotetics: The study of question asking or interrogative theory; from the Greek word ἐρώτησις, which probably came from the more common word ἔρως in its sense of given over to a love for knowledge and truth.

Force: Any semantic or pragmatic effect applied to an utterance in order that the utterance performs as the speaker wishes. It is also called *illocutionary force* (§2.C.1).

Fronting: The movement of a part of an utterance to the beginning of the full utterance. This movement is syntactical, but it also may be made to influence semantic and pragmatic effects (§2.B.11).

Gapping: A specific type of omission in syntax. Gapping occurs when a clause subsequent to the main clause omits a verb (and any potential objects) that is the same as in the first clause, usually to avoid repetition or for stylistic effect. The verb is implied in the second clause of the sentence.

Implicative: A linguistic quality that describes when the meaning of an utterance comes from something beyond the literal syntactic and semantic meaning of the utterance. Related to the word *implied*. An implicative utterance is one that uses implicature to communicate meaning (§2.D.4).

Indexical: A word that gains its meaning (creates an index to) a word outside of the immediate context of the utterance. While any part of speech can serve an indexical function, the most common part of speech used indexically in natural-language questions is the pronoun. Weak indexi-

1. Spranzi, *Art of Dialectic*, 17–21.

cals (such as the definite article) can still affect erotetic logic in small ways. Indexicals are also referred to by a variety of other names such as *deictic*, *anaphora*, and *cataphora*, depending on the circumstance. Here we only use the term *indexical* in a general sense, without differentiation.

Indirect Question: Any question that expresses its interrogative force indirectly or conceals it within the utterance. Stands in contrast to a direct question (See Direct Question). Sometimes is called an *embedded question*.

Informational Quality: One of the two primary qualities that questions possess. By nature, every question possesses some degree of informational quality (no matter how mild) (§2.C.4).

Informational Question: A popular term for a type of question that primarily seeks information in return for the act of asking. The informational question is usually contrasted with the rhetorical question (see Rhetorical Question). The problem with the term is that it is one-dimensional and has little value in understanding the logic and rhetoric of a question. All questions both seek information and have rhetorical effects.

Interrogative: The force applied to any utterance that *asks*. When one communicates with interrogative force, the resulting utterance is a question (at least of a basic sort).

Interrogative Pressure: The feeling of coercion experienced by the audience when a speaker asks a question. Some question types exert no interrogative pressure, while others exert a great deal of pressure.

Interrogative Variable Word: Another name for an interrogative adverb, pronoun, or particle used to start variable questions. In English they are often referred to as *wh*-words and in Greek as π-words (§2.B.10).

Narrative Discourse: A type of discourse that portrays actions and events in time. Narrative discourse is not the same as dialogue; dialogue is the narrativization of conversation that is embedded within narrative discourse.

Natural Language: A real human language as it is used in its habitat with all of the commitments and contexts that come with a living, changing form of communication. Natural language contrasts with language in general, as natural language does not always try to conform to exact standards. As an example, natural language may contain questions that are not well formed.

Π-word: An umbrella term for interrogative pronouns in Koine Greek, most of which start with the letter π (§2.B.10). In English, linguists call these interrogative pronouns *wh*-words since most start with the letters *wh*. This phenomenon is not limited to Greek and English; it is a unique but unresolved feature of most Indo-European languages.

Polarity: The syntactic property of an utterance that represents a polar opposition between affirmation and negation. Utterances may have a positive polarity or a negative polarity. An elemental form of polarity is found in the particles yes and no. Most languages cast utterances in a base positive polarity; to indicate negative polarity, a negative polarity item must be included (§2.B.8).

Position: Where an utterance occurs within a dialogue turn. In this study, we identify four dialogue positions: opening, middle, closing, and standalone.

Proposition: Any utterance with declarative force. The utterance can be spoken, written, nonverbal, or delivered through any other human means of communication to still register as a proposition. A proposition is what one *says*, not what one *asks*. From the Greek idea of ἀπόφανσις.[2] A proposition is similar to a *statement* and *declarative*, and in this book these terms will be used interchangeably.

Question: Any utterance with interrogative force. The utterance can be spoken, written, nonverbal, or delivered through any other human means of communication to still register as a question. A question is what one *asks*, not what one *says*.

Repair: The utterance or action by which a breakdown in the meaning of an utterance is restored. When a person hears an utterance they do not understand and asks for clarification, they are initiating a repair. The repair is made if the original utterance is clarified.

Reply: Any verbal or nonverbal communication following a question from a hearer of the question. A reply does not have to be semantically related to the question, but it does have to be in some way in reaction to the question. A reply is not necessarily an answer, though an answer is always a reply. Alternatively, known as a *response* (§2.E).

Rhetoric: The art of persuasive speech. From the Greek word ῥητορική. Here we use the term in its most general sense and not to refer to one particular form or system of rhetoric (such as what we today call Greco-Roman rhetoric). This is in keeping with how ancient Greek speakers would have used the term, as they would not have recognized the idea of rhetoric as a specific system in contrast to other systems (though they would have understood the differences in the various approaches to persuasion based on all the work given to perfecting a rhetorical system in ancient Greek and Latin culture). Rhetoric was related to the art of dialectic in the ancient Greek philosophical and rhetorical traditions.

Rhetorical Discourse: A type of discourse that is monological and often argu-

2. Aristotle, *Interpretation* 17a1–8.

mentative. Rhetorical discourse is not the same as rhetoric; rhetoric is a style of speech which best characterizes rhetorical discourse.

Rhetorical Quality: One of the two primary qualities that questions possess. By nature, every question possesses some degree of rhetorical quality (no matter how mild) (§2.C.5).

Rhetorical Question: A popular term for a type of question that does not seek information in return for the act of asking (and may seem to be making a statement or not need a reply). The rhetorical question is usually contrasted with the informational question (see Informational Question). The problem with the term is that it is one-dimensional and has little value in understanding the logic and rhetoric of a question. All questions seek information and have rhetorical effects.

Rhetorical-Shift Principle: When considering the rhetorical effects of a question, the more information seeking the question appears to be (based on its syntax and semantics), the greater the shift in persuasive power that can occur in a rhetorical context (based on pragmatics); a guideline for investigating the rhetorical quality of interrogatives (§2.D.9).

Sluice: Any question that omits what it is asking about. Sluices have a unique syntactic form that can be based on any of the four major question formations. Because sluices suppress much of what they ask, they must be asked within the middle of dialogue. Many one-word questions are sluices (§3.E.4).

Tell: A sign or indicator of the interrogative features of an utterance.

Turn: In dialogue, the full utterance of one speaker. In orderly dialogue, one speaker will take a turn, and then a second speaker will take a turn. This process is called *turn-taking* (§2.D.7).

Utterance: Any form of communication made by a speaker. This is true without regard for the particulars of the utterance. Utterances can be one-word responses or lengthy speeches; they can be whispered, shouted, spoken out loud or "spoken" by a character in a text. When working with written texts, we still use the word *utterance* to describe any spoken communication by a character in the text.

Variable: A word in a question that is undefined within the logic of the question. A reader or hearer may solve for a variable as one solves for an *x* in algebra. Variables are almost always pronouns or a part of a pronominal phrase.

Bibliography

Abbreviations follow *The SBL Handbook of Style*, 2nd edition

Abioye, Taiwo O. "Typology of Rhetorical Questions as a Stylistic Device in Writing." *International Journal of Language, Society and Culture* 29 (2009): 1–8.

Achtemeier, Paul J. *1 Peter: A Commentary on First Peter*. Hermencia. Minneapolis: Fortress, 1996.

Adger, David. *Core Syntax: A Minimalist Approach*. Oxford: Oxford University Press, 2003.

Akmajian, Adrian, Richard A. Demers, Ann K. Farmer, Robert M. Harnish. *Linguistics: An Introduction to Language and Communication*. 6th ed. Cambridge: MIT Press, 2010.

Allan, Keith. "Mood, Clause Types, and Illocutionary Force." Pages 267–71 in *Encyclopedia of Language and Linguistics*. Edited by Keith Brown. 2nd ed. Amsterdam: Elsevier, 2006.

Allan, Keith, and Kasia M. Jaszczolt, eds. *The Cambridge Handbook of Pragmatics*. Cambridge Handbooks in Language and Linguistics. Cambridge: Cambridge University Press, 2012.

Allan, Rutger J. "Clause Intertwining and Word Order in Ancient Greek." *Journal of Greek Linguistics* 12 (2012): 5–28.

Allen, Spencer L. "Understanding Amos vi 12 in Light of His Other Rhetorical Questions." *VT* 58 (2008): 437–48.

Allen, W. Sidney. *Accent and Rhythm: Prosodic Features of Latin and Greek*. Cambridge Studies in Linguistics 12. Cambridge: Cambridge University Press, 1973.

———. *Vox Graeca: A Guide to the Pronunciation of Classical Greek*. Cambridge: Cambridge University Press, 1968.

Allott, Nicholas. *Key Terms in Pragmatics*. New York: Continuum, 2010.

Aloni, Maria, Alastair Butler, and Paul Dekker, eds. *Questions in Dynamic Semantics*. Current Research in the Semantics/Pragmatics Interface 17. Amsterdam: Elsevier, 2007.

Aloni, Maria, and Paul Égré. "Alternative Questions and Knowledge Attributions." *Philosophical Quarterly* 60.238 (2010): 1–27.

Anagnostopoulos, Georgios. "Aristotle's Methods." Pages 101–22 in *A Companion to Aristotle*. Edited by Georgios Anagnostopoulos. Blackwell Companions to Philosophy 42. Malden, MA: Wiley-Blackwell, 2009.

Aoun, Joseph, and Yen-hui Audrey Li. *Essays on the Representational and Derivational Nature of Grammar: The Diversity of* Wh-*Constructions*. Linguistic Inquiry Monographs 40. Cambridge: MIT Press, 2003.

Apollonius Dyscolus. *The* Syntax *of Apollonius Dyscolus*. Studies in the History of the Language Sciences 23. Translated with commentary by Fred W. Householder. Amsterdam: John Benjamins, 1981.

Åqvist, Lennart. *A New Approach to the Logical Theory of Interrogatives: Analysis and Formalization*. Tübinger Beiträge zur Linguistik 65. Tübingen: Narr, 1975.

Arbini, Ronald. "Tag-questions and Tag-imperatives in English." *Journal of Linguistics* 5.2 (1969): 205–14.

Archer, Dawn Elizabeth. "Verbal Aggression and Impoliteness: Related or Synonymous?" Pages 181–207 in *Impoliteness in Language: Studies on Its Interplay with Power in Theory and Practice*. Edited by Derek Bousfield and Miriam A. Locher. Language, Power and Social Process 21. Berlin: Mouton de Gruyter, 2008.

Aristophanes. *Acharnians*, *Knights*, *Clouds*, and *Wasps*. Translated by Benjamin Bickley Rogers. LCL. Cambridge: Harvard University Press, 1930.

Aristotle. *The "Art" of Rhetoric*. Translated by John Henry Freese. LCL 193. Cambridge: Harvard University Press, 1975.

———. *Categories* and *De Interpretatione*. Translated by J. L. Ackrill. Clarendon Aristotle Series. Oxford: Oxford University Press, 1963.

———. *Posterior Analytics*. 2nd ed. Translated by Jonathan Barnes. Clarendon Aristotle Series. Oxford: Clarendon, 1993.

———. *Posterior Analytics* and *Topica*. Translated by Hugh Tredennick and E. S. Forster. LCL 391. Cambridge: Harvard University Press, 1960.

———. *On Sophistical Refutations*, *On Coming-to-Be and Passing Away*, and *On the Cosmos*. Translated by E. S. Forster and D. J. Furley. LCL 400. Cambridge: Harvard University Press, 1955.

Aronoff, Mark, and Janie Rees-Miller, eds. *The Handbook of Linguistics*. Blackwell Handbooks in Linguistics. Oxford: Blackwell, 2001.

Asher, Nicholas, and Alex Lascarides. "Questions in Dialogue." *Linguistics and Philosophy* 21.3 (1998): 237–309.

Asher, Nicholas, and Brian Reese. "Intonation and Discourse: Biased Questions." *Interdisciplinary Studies on Information Structure* 8 (2007): 1–38.

Athanasiadou, Angeliki. "The Discourse Function of Questions." *Pragmatics* 1.1 (1991): 107–22.

Augustine. *Harmony of the Gospels*. In vol. 6 of *The Nicene and Post-Nicene Fathers*, Series 1. Edited by Philip Schaff. New York: Christian Literature Company, 1888.

Aune, David E. *Revelation 6–16*. WBC 52B. Dallas: Word, 1998.

———. *The Westminster Dictionary of New Testament and Early Christian Literature and Rhetoric*. Louisville: Westminster John Knox, 2003.

Austin, J. L. "Performative-Constative." Pages 13–22 in *The Philosophy of Language*. Edited by J. R. Searle. Oxford: Oxford University Press, 1971.

Babbitt, Frank Cole. *A Grammar of Attic and Ionic Greek*. New York: American Book, 1902.

———. "The Use of μή in Questions." *HSCP* 12 (1901): 307–17.

Bach, Emmon. "Questions." *Linguistic Inquiry* 2.2 (1971): 153–66.

Bach, Kent. "The Top 10 Misconceptions about Implicature." Pages 21–30 in *Drawing the Boundaries of Meaning: Neo-Gricean Studies in Pragmatics and Semantics in Honor of Laurence R. Horn*. Edited by Betty J. Birner and Gregory Ward. Studies in Language Companion Series 80. Amsterdam: John Benjamins, 2006.

Baker, Anne E., and Kees Hengeveld, eds. *Linguistics*. Introducing Linguistics 5. Malden, MA: Wiley-Blackwell, 2012.

Bakhtin, M. M. *Speech Genres and Other Late Essays*. Edited by Caryl Emerson and Michael Holquist. Translated by Vern W. McGee. Austin: University of Texas Press, 1986.

Bakker, Egbert J., ed. *A Companion to the Ancient Greek Language*. Blackwell Companions to the Ancient World. Malden, MA: Wiley-Blackwell, 2010.

Barr, James. "Why? in Biblical Hebrew." *JTS* 36.1 (1985): 1–33.

Barrett, C. K. *The Epistle to the Romans*. Rev. ed. BNTC. London: Continuum, 1991.

Basser, Herbert W., with Marsha B. Cohen. *The Gospel of Matthew and Judaic Traditions: A Relevance-Based Commentary*. BRLA 46. Leiden: Brill, 2015.

Bauer, Walter, Frederick William Danker, William F. Arndt, and F. Wilbur Gingrich. *A Greek-English Lexicon of the New Testament and Other Early Christian Literature*. 3rd ed. Chicago: University of Chicago Press, 2000.

Baxter, James S., Julian C. W. Boon, and Charles Marley. "Interrogative Pressure and Responses to Minimally Leading Questions." *Personality and Individual Differences* 40 (2006): 87–98.

Beale, G. K. *The Book of Revelation: A Commentary on the Greek Text*. NIGTC. Grand Rapids: Eerdmans, 1999.

Beck, Jana E., Sophia A. Malamud, and Iryna Osadcha. "A Semantics for the Particle ἄν in and outside Conditionals in Classical Greek." *Journal of Greek Linguistics* 12 (2012): 51–83.

Bell, Martin. "Questioning." *Philosophical Quarterly* 25.100 (1975): 193–212.

Belnap, Nuel D., Jr. "Declaratives Are Not Enough." *Philosophical Studies* 59.1 (1990): 1–30.

———. "Questions, Answers, and Presuppositions." *Journal of Philosophy* 63.20 (1966): 609–11.

———. "*S-P* Interrogatives." *Journal of Philosophical Logic* 1.3/4 (1972): 331–46.

Belnap, Nuel D., Jr., and Thomas B. Steel, Jr. *The Logic of Questions and Answers*. New Haven: Yale University Press, 1976.

Bengel, Johann Albrecht. *Gnomon of the New Testament*. 5 Vols. Edited by M. Ernest Bengel and J. C. F. Steudel. Translated by William Fletcher. Edinburgh: T&T Clark, 1866.

Betz, Hans Dieter. *The Sermon on the Mount: A Commentary on the Sermon on the Mount, Including the Sermon on the Plain (Matthew 5:3–7:27 and Luke 6:20–49)*. Edited by Adela Yarbro Collins. Hermeneia. Minneapolis: Fortress, 1995.

Black, David Alan, ed. *Linguistics and New Testament Interpretation: Essays on Discourse Analysis*. Nashville: Broadman & Holman, 1992.

Blakemore, Diane. *Understanding Utterances: An Introduction to Pragmatics*. Blackwell Textbooks in Linguistics. Oxford: Blackwell, 1992.

Blank, David L. *Ancient Philosophy and Grammar: The Syntax of Apollonius Dyscolus*. American Philological Association American Classical Studies 10. Chico: Scholars, 1982.

Blankenship, Kevin L., and Traci Y. Craig. "Rhetorical Question Use and Resistance to Persuasion: An Attitude Strength Analysis." *Journal of Language and Social Psychology* 25.2 (2006): 111–28.

Blass, Friedrich. *Grammar of New Testament Greek*. 2nd ed. Translated by Henry Thackeray. London: MacMillan, 1905.

———. *Pronunciation of Ancient Greek*. From the third German edition. Translated by W. J. Purton. Cambridge: Cambridge University Press, 1890.

Blass, Friedrich, and A. DeBrunner. *A Greek Grammar of the New Testament and Other Early Christian Literature*. Translated and Edited by Robert W. Funk. Chicago: University of Chicago Press, 1961.

Blomberg, Craig L. "'But We See Jesus': The Relationship between the Son of Man in Hebrews 2.6 and 2.9 and the Implications for English Translations." Pages 88–99 in *A Cloud of Witnesses: The Theology of Hebrews in Its Ancient Contexts*. Edited by Richard Bauckham, Daniel Driver, Trevor Hart, and Nathan MacDonald. LNTS 387. London: T&T Clark, 2008.

Boas, Evert van Emde, and Luuk Huitink. "Syntax." Pages 134–50 in *A Companion to the Ancient Greek Language*. Edited by Egbert J. Bakker. Blackwell Companions to the Ancient World. Malden, MA: Wiley-Blackwell, 2010.

Bock, Darrell L. *Luke: 9:51–24:53*. BECNT. Grand Rapids: Baker, 1996.

Bolinger, Dwight. *Interrogative Structures of American English*. Birmingham: University of Alabama Press, 1957.

Bortone, Pietro. *Greek Prepositions: From Antiquity to the Present*. Oxford: Oxford University Press, 2010.

Bousfield, Derek. *Impoliteness in Interaction*. Pragmatics & Beyond New Series 167. Amsterdam: John Benjamins, 2008.

Bovon, François. *Luke 1: A Commentary on the Gospel of Luke 1:1–9:50*. Edited by Helmut Koester. Translated by Christine M. Thomas. Hermeneia. Minneapolis: Fortress, 2002.

———. *Luke 2: A Commentary on the Gospel of Luke 9:51–19:27*. Edited by Helmut Koester. Translated by Donald S. Deer. Hermeneia. Minneapolis: Fortress, 2013.

Bradley, Mark Alan. "The Functions of Questions in the Fourth Gospel: A Narrative-Critical Inquiry." PhD diss., Golden Gate Baptist Theological Seminary, 1994.

Bromberger, Sylvain. *On What We Know We Don't Know: Explanation, Theory, Linguistics, and How Questions Shape Them*. Chicago: University of Chicago Press, 1992.

———. "Questions." *Journal of Philosophy* 63.20 (1966): 597–606.

———. "Rational Ignorance." *Synthese* 74.1 (1988): 47–64.

———. "Why-Questions." Pages 86–111 in *Mind and Cosmos: Essays in Contemporary Science and Philosophy*. Edited by Robert G. Colodny. Pittsburgh: University of Pittsburgh Press, 1966.

Brook, Eric C. "The Interrogative Model: Historical Inquiry and Explanation." *Journal of the Philosophy of History* 1 (2007): 137–59.

Brooks, James A. *Mark*. NAC 23. Nashville: Broadman & Holman, 1991.

Brown, H. Paul, Brian D. Joseph, and Rex E. Wallace. "Questions and Answers." Pages 489–530 in *Syntax of the Sentence*. Vol. 1 of *New Perspectives on Historical Latin Syntax*. Edited by Philip Baldi and Pierluigi Cuzzolin. Trends in Linguistics, Studies and Monographs 180.1. Berlin: Mouton de Gruyter, 2009.

Brown, Keith, and Jim Miller. *The Cambridge Dictionary of Linguistics*. Cambridge: Cambridge University Press, 2013.

Brown, Penelope, and Stephen Levinson. "Universals in Language Use: Politeness Phenomena." Pages 56–289 in *Questions and Politeness: Strategies in Social Interaction*. Edited by Esther N. Goody. Cambridge Papers in Social Anthropology 8. Cambridge: Cambridge University Press, 1978.

Bruce, F. F. *The Epistle to the Galatians: A Commentary on the Greek Text*. NIGTC. Grand Rapids: Eerdmans, 1982.

Brueggemann, Walter A. "Jeremiah's Use of Rhetorical Questions." *JBL* 92.3 (1973): 358–74.

Bruin, John. *Homo Interrogans: Questioning and the Intentional Structure of Cognition*. Philosophica 53. Ottawa: University of Ottawa Press, 2001.

Bublitz, Wolfram. "Tag Questions, Transformational Grammar and Pragmatics." Pages 5–22 in *Papers and Studies in Contrastive Linguistics*. Edited by Jacek Fisiak. Poznań: Adam Mickiewicz University, 1979.

Bullinger, E. W. *Figures of Speech Used in the Bible: Explained and Illustrated*. New York: E. & J. B. Young, 1898.

Bultmann, Rudolf Karl. *The Johannine Epistles: A Commentary on the Johannine Epistles.* Edited by Robert W. Funk. Translated by R. Philip O'Hara, Lane C. McGaughy, and Robert W. Funk. Hermeneia. Philadelphia: Fortress, 1973.

Bunt, Harry. "Conversational Principles in Question-Answer Dialogues." Pages 119–41 in *Zur Theorie der Frage: Vorträge des Bad Homburger Kolloquiums 1978.* Edited by Dieter Krallmann and Gerhard Stickel. Forschungsberichte des Instituts für deutsche Sprache 52. Tübingen: Gunter Narr, 1981.

Burggraff, Philip D. "A Corpus Linguistic Verb Analysis of the Pauline Letters: The Contribution of Verb Patterns to Pauline Letter Structure." PhD diss., McMaster Divinity College, 2011.

Burton, Ernest De Witt. *Syntax of the Moods and Tenses in New Testament Greek.* 2nd ed. Edinburgh: T&T Clark, 1894.

Bussmann, Hadumod. *Routledge Dictionary of Language and Linguistics.* Translated and edited by Gregory P. Trauth and Kerstin Kazzazi. London: Routledge, 1996.

Buth, Randall. "Οὖν, Δέ, Καί, and Asyndeton in John's Gospel." Pages 144–61 in *Linguistics and New Testament Interpretation: Essays on Discourse Analysis.* Edited by David Alan Black. Nashville: Broadman & Holman, 1992.

Byrne, Ruth M. J. *The Rational Imagination: How People Create Alternatives to Reality.* Cambridge: MIT Press, 2005.

Cain, Rebecca Bensen. *The Socratic Method: Plato's Use of Philosophical Drama.* Continuum Studies in Ancient Philosophy. London: Continuum, 2007.

Campbell, Constantine R. *Verbal Aspect, the Indicative Mood, and Narrative: Soundings in the Greek of the New Testament.* Studies in Biblical Greek 13. New York: Peter Lang, 1994.

Capella, Martianus. *De nuptiis Philologiae et Mercurii.* Edited by Adolfus Dick. Leipzig: B. G. Teubner, 1983.

Caragounis, Chrys C. *The Development of Greek and the New Testament: Morphology, Syntax, Phonology and Textual Transmission.* Grand Rapids: Baker, 2006.

Carawan, E. M. "*Erotesis*: Interrogation in the Courts of Fourth-Century Athens." *GRBS* 24.3 (1983): 209–26.

Carlson, Lauri. *Dialogue Games: An Approach to Discourse Analysis.* Synthese Language Library 17. Dordrecht: D. Reidel, 1985.

Carter, Ronald, and Paul Simpson, eds. *Language, Discourse and Literature: An Introductory Reader in Discourse Stylistics.* London: Routledge, 1989.

Caton, Charles E. "Essentially Arising Questions and the Ontology of a Natural Language." *Noûs* 5.1 (1971): 27–37.

Chapman, Siobahn, and Christopher Routledge, eds. *Key Ideas in Linguistics and the Philosophy of Language.* Edinburgh: Edinburgh University Press, 2009.

Chariton. *Callirhoe.* Translated by G. P. Goold. LCL 481. Cambridge: Harvard University Press, 1995.

Cheng, Lisa Lai-Shen. *On the Typology of Wh-Questions.* New York: Garland, 1997.

Cheung, Yam-Leung. "The Negative Wh-Construction." PhD diss., University of California, Los Angeles, 2008. UMI.

Chisholm, William S., Jr., Louis T. Milic, and John A. C. Greppin, eds. *Interrogativity: A Colloquium on the Grammar, Typology and Pragmatics of Questions in Seven Diverse Languages.* Typological Studies in Language 4. Amsterdam: John Benjamins, 1984.

Christidis, A.-F., ed. *A History of Ancient Greek: From the Beginnings to Late Antiquity.* Cambridge: Cambridge University Press, 2007.

Chrysostom, John. *Homilies on the Epistle to the Romans.* In vol. 11 of *The Nicene and Post-Nicene Fathers,* Series 1. Edited by Philip Schaff. New York: Christian Literature Company, 1889.

Cicero. *De Inventione, De Optimo Genere Oratorum* and *Topica.* Translated by H. M. Hubbell. LCL 386. Cambridge: Harvard University Press, 1960.

———. *De Oratore.* And other works. Translated by E. W. Sutton and H. Rackham. LCL 348–349. Cambridge: Harvard University Press, 1959–1960.

———. *Philippics I–II.* Edited by John T. Ramsey. Cambridge Greek and Latin Classics. Cambridge: Cambridge University Press, 2003.

Clayman, Steven. "Questions in Broadcast Journalism." Pages 256–78 in *"Why Do You Ask?" The Function of Questions in Institutional Discourse.* Edited by Alice F. Freed and Susan Ehrlich. Oxford: Oxford University Press, 2010.

Coakley, J. F. "An Early Syriac Question Mark." *AS* 10 (2012): 193–213.

Cobb, W. H. "μή Interrogative." *JBL* 4:1–2 (1884): 148–49.

Cohen, Felix S. "What Is a Question?" *The Monist* 39 (1929): 350–64.

Collins, Raymond F. *First Corinthians.* SP 7. Collegeville, MN: Liturgical, 1999.

———. *These Things Have Been Written: Studies on the Fourth Gospel.* Louvain Theological & Pastoral Monographs 2. Louvain: Peeters, 1990.

Colvin, Stephen. *A Brief History of Ancient Greek.* Brief Histories of the Ancient World. Malden, MA: Wiley-Blackwell, 2014.

Comfort, Philip. *Encountering the Manuscripts: An Introduction to New Testament Paleography and Textual Criticism.* Nashville: Broadman & Holman, 2005.

Comorovski, Ileana. *Interrogative Phrases and the Syntax-Semantics Interface.* Studies in Linguistics and Philosophy 59. Dordrecht: Springer, 1996.

Conzelmann, Hans. *1 Corinthians: A Commentary on the First Epistle to the Corinthians.* Edited by George W. MacRae. Translated by James W. Leitch. Hermeneia. Philadelphia: Fortress, 1975.

———. *Acts of the Apostles: A Commentary on the Acts of the Apostles.* Edited by Eldon Jay Epp and Christopher R. Matthews. Translated by James Limburg, A. Thomas Kraabel, and Donald H. Juel. Hermeneia. Philadelphia: Fortress, 1987.

Cooper, Alan. "The Absurdity of Amos 6:12a." *JBL* 107.4 (1988): 725–27.

Cornbleet, Sandra, and Ronald Carter. *The Language of Speech and Writing.* Intertext. London: Routledge, 2001.

Coulthard, Malcolm. *An Introduction to Discourse Analysis*. 2nd ed. Applied Linguistics and Language Study. London: Routledge, 1985.

Coupland, Justine, Nikolas Coupland, and Jeffrey D. Robinson. "'How are You?': Negotiating Phatic Communion." *Language in Society* 21.2 (1992): 207–30.

Craig, Kenneth M., Jr. *Asking For Rhetoric: The Hebrew Bible's Protean Interrogative*. BibInt 73. Leiden: Brill, 2005.

———. "Rhetorical Aspects of Questions Answered with Silence in 1 Samuel 14:37 and 28:6." *CBQ* 56.2 (1994): 221–39.

Crenshaw, James L. "Impossible Questions, Sayings, and Tasks." *Semeia* 17 (1980): 19–34.

Cruse, Alan. *Meaning in Language: An Introduction to Semantics and Pragmatics*. Oxford Handbooks in Linguistics. Oxford: Oxford University Press, 2000.

Cruse, D. A. *Lexical Semantics*. Cambridge Textbooks in Linguistics. Cambridge: Cambridge University Press, 1986.

Crystal, David. *A Dictionary of Linguistics and Phonetics*. 6th ed. Oxford: Blackwell, 2008.

———. *How Language Works: How Babies Babble, Words Change Meaning, and Languages Live or Die*. New York: Avery, 2007.

Culicover, Peter W. *Explaining Syntax: Representations, Structures, and Computation*. Oxford: Oxford University Press, 2013.

Dancygier, Barbara. *Conditionals and Prediction: Time, Knowledge and Causation in Conditional Constructions*. Cambridge Studies in Linguistics 87. Cambridge: Cambridge University Press, 1998.

Davies, Eirian. "Speaking, Telling and Assertion: Interrogatives and Mood in English." *Functions of Language* 13.2 (2006): 151–96.

Davis, Wayne A. *Implicature: Intention, Convention, and Principle in the Failure of Gricean Theory*. Cambridge Studies in Philosophy. Cambridge: Cambridge University Press, 1998.

Dekker, Paul. "Presupposition." Pages 42–52 in *The Routledge Companion to Philosophy of Language*. Edited by Gillian Russell and Delia Graff Fara. Routledge Philosophy Companions. New York: Routledge, 2012.

De Man, Paul. *Allegories of Reading: Figural Language in Rousseau, Nietzsche, Rilke, and Proust*. New Haven: Yale University Press, 1979.

Demosthenes. *Against Meidias, Androtion, Aristocrates, Timocrates, Aristogeiton*. Translated by J. H. Vince. LCL. Cambridge: Harvard University Press, 1935.

Denes, Gianfranco. *Talking Heads: The Neuroscience of Language*. New York: Psychology, 2011.

Denniston, J. D. *The Greek Particles*. 2nd ed. Oxford: Clarendon, 1954.

Devine, A. M., and Laurence D. Stephens. *Discontinuous Syntax: Hyperbaton in Greek*. Oxford: Oxford University Press, 1994.

———. *The Prosody of Greek Speech*. Oxford: Oxford University Press, 1994.

Devitt, Amy J. *Writing Genres*. Rhetorical Philosophy and Theory. Carbondale: Southern Illinois University Press, 2004.

De Wet, Chris L. "The Messianic Interpretation of Psalm 8:4–6 in Hebrews 2:6–9, Part II." Pages 113–25 in *Psalms and Hebrews: Studies in Reception*. Edited by Dirk J. Human and Gert J. Steyn. LHBOTS 527. London: T&T Clark.

Dickman, Nathan. "Dialogue and Divinity: A Hermeneutics of the Interrogative Mood in Religious Language." PhD diss., University of Iowa, 2009.

Dickson, David, and Owen Hargie. "Questioning." Pages 121–45 in *The Handbook of Communication Skills*. Edited by Owen Hargie. 3rd ed. London: Routledge, 2006.

Dik, Helma. *Word Order in Greek Tragic Dialogue*. Oxford: Oxford University Press, 2007.

Dillon, J. T. *The Practice of Questioning*. International Series on Communication Skills. London: Routledge, 1990.

———. "Questioning the Use of Questions." *Journal of Educational Psychology* 83.1 (1991): 163–64.

Dionysius of Halicarnassus. *Critical Essays, Volume II: On Literary Composition, Dinarchus, Letters to Ammaeus and Pompeius*. Translated by Stephen Usher. LCL 466. Cambridge: Harvard University Press, 1985.

———. *Roman Antiquities*. Translated by Earnest Cary. 7 vols. LCL 319, 347, 357, 364, 372, 378, 388. Cambridge: Harvard University Press, 1937–50.

Dionysius Thrax. *Ars Grammatica*. Edited by Gustavus Uhlig. Leipzig: B. G. Teubner, 1883.

Dodson, Joseph R. *The 'Powers' of Personification: Rhetorical Purpose in the 'Book of Wisdom' and the Letter to the Romans*. BZNW 161. Berlin: De Gruyter, 2008.

Drummen, Annemieke. "Discourse Cohesion in Dialogue: Turn-Initial ΑΛΛΑ in Greek Drama." Pages 135–54 in *Discourse Cohesion in Ancient Greek*. Edited by Stéphanie Bakker and Gerry Wakker. Amsterdam Studies in Classical Philology 16. Leiden: Brill, 2009.

Dubis, Mark. *1 Peter: A Handbook on the Greek Text*. Baylor Handbook on the Greek New Testament. Waco: Baylor University Press, 2010.

Dumitrescu, Domnia. "Rhetorical vs Nonrhetorical Allo-repetition: The Case of Romanian Interrogatives." *Journal of Pragmatics* 26.3 (1996): 321–54.

Du Plessis, J. G. "Why Did Peter Ask His Question and How Did Jesus Answer Him? Or: Implicature in Luke 12:35–48." *Neot* 22 (1988): 311–24.

Eemeren, Frans H. van, Rob Grootendorst, and A. Francisca Snoeck Henkemans. *Argumentation: Analysis, Evaluation, Presentation*. Mahwah: Lawrence Erlbaum Associates, 2002.

Elbert, Paul. "An Observation on Luke's Composition and Narrative Style of Questions." *CBQ* 66.1 (2004): 98–109.

Ellingworth, Paul. *The Epistle to the Hebrews: A Commentary on the Greek Text*. NIGTC. Grand Rapids: Eerdmans, 1993.

Elsig, Martin. *Grammatical Variation across Space and Time: The French Interrogative System*. Studies in Language Variation 3. Amsterdam: John Benjamins, 2009.

Engdahl, Elisabet. "Information Packaging in Questions." *Empirical Issues in Formal Syntax and Semantics* 6 (2006): 93–112.

Enzle, Michael E., and Michael D. Harvey. "Rhetorical Requests for Help." *Social Psychology Quarterly* 45.3 (1982): 172–76.

Erp Taalman Kip, A. Maria van. "Η ΓΑΡ in Questions." Pages 151–56 in *New Approaches to Greek Particles*. Edited by Albert Rijksbaron. Amsterdam: J. C. Gieben, 1997.

Estes, Douglas. *The Questions of Jesus in John: Logic, Rhetoric and Persuasive Discourse*. BibInt 115. Leiden: Brill, 2013.

———. *The Temporal Mechanics of the Fourth Gospel: A Theory of Hermeneutical Relativity in the Gospel of John*. BibInt 92. Leiden: Brill, 2008.

Evans, Jonathan, and David Over. *If*. Oxford: Oxford University Press, 2004.

Fahnestock, Jeanne. "*Quid Pro Nobis*: Rhetorical Stylistics for Argument Analysis." Pages 191–220 in *Examining Argumentation in Context: Fifteen Studies on Strategic Maneuvering*. Edited by Frans H. van Eemeren. Argumentation in Context 1. Amsterdam: John Benjamins, 2009.

Fahnestock, Jeanne, and Marie Secor. *A Rhetoric of Argument*. 2nd ed. New York: McGraw-Hill, 1990.

Fălăuş, Anamaria. "Broaden Your Views, But Try to Stay Focused: A Missing Piece in the Polarity System." Pages 81–107 in *From Grammar to Meaning: The Spontaneous Logicality of Language*. Edited by Ivano Caponigro and Carlo Cecchetto. Cambridge: Cambridge University Press, 2013.

———. "Le paradoxe de la double négation dans une langue à concordance négative stricte." Pages 75–97 in *La négation dans les langues romanes*. Edited by Franck Floricic. Linguisticae Investigationes Supplementa 26. Amsterdam: John Benjamins, 2007.

Fales, Walter. "The Phenomenology of Questions." *Philosophy and Phenomenological Research* 4.1 (1943–44): 60–75.

Fava, Elisabetta. "Questioning Interrogative Interpretation in Some Indo-European Languages." *Language Sciences* 18.1–2 (1996): 87–110.

Fiengo, Robert. *Asking Questions: Using Meaningful Structures to Imply Ignorance*. Oxford: Oxford University Press, 2007.

Finch, Geoffrey. *How to Study Linguistics: A Guide to Understanding Language*. 2nd ed. New York: Palgrave Macmillan, 2003.

Floricic, Franck. "Negation and 'Focus Clash' in Sardinian." Pages 129–52 in *Information Structure and Its Interfaces*. Edited by Lunella Mereu. Interface Explorations 19. Berlin: Mouton de Gruyter, 2009.

France, R. T. *The Gospel of Mark: A Commentary on the Greek Text*. NIGTC. Grand Rapids: Eerdmans, 2002.

Frank, Jane. "You Call That a Rhetorical Question? Forms and Functions of Rhetorical Questions in Conversation." *Journal of Pragmatics* 14.5 (1990): 723–38.

Frantz, Donald G. "On Question Word Movement." *Linguistic Inquiry* 4.4 (1973): 531–34.

Freed, Alice F., and Susan Ehrlich, eds. *"Why Do You Ask?" The Function of Questions in Institutional Discourse*. Oxford: Oxford University Press, 2010.

Fromkin, Victoria, Robert Rodman, and Nina Hyams. *An Introduction to Language*. 10th ed. Boston: Wadsworth, 2014.

Frow, John. *Genre*. The New Critical Idiom. London: Routledge, 2006.

Fuhrmann, Sebastian. "The Son, the Angels and the Odd: Psalm 8 in Hebrews 1 and 2." Pages 83–98 in *Psalms and Hebrews: Studies in Reception*. Edited by Dirk J. Human and Gert J. Steyn. LHBOTS 527. London: T&T Clark, 2010.

Gazdar, Gerald. *Pragmatics: Implicature, Presupposition, and Logical Form*. New York: Academic, 1979.

Gempf, Conrad. *Jesus Asked: What He Wanted to Know*. Grand Rapids: Zondervan, 2003.

Ginsburg, Jason Robert. "Interrogative Features." PhD diss., University of Arizona, 2009.

Ginzburg, Jonathan. "Interrogatives: Questions, Facts and Dialogue." Pages 385–422 in *The Handbook of Contemporary Semantic Theory*. Edited by Shalom Lappin. Blackwell Handbooks in Linguistics. London: Blackwell, 1997.

Ginzburg, Jonathan, and Ivan A. Sag. *Interrogative Investigations: The Form, Meaning and Use of English Interrogatives*. CSLI Lecture Notes 123. Stanford: CSLI, 2000.

Givón, T. "The Speech-Act Continuum." Pages 245–54 in *Interrogativity: A Colloquium on the Grammar, Typology and Pragmatics of Questions in Seven Diverse Languages*. Edited by William S. Chisholm Jr., Louis T. Milic, and John A. C. Greppin. Typological Studies in Language 4. Amsterdam: John Benjamins, 1984.

Golka, Maria H. "Semantics and Pragmatics of Negative Polar Questions." *SemDial* 14 (2010): 149–50.

Goodwin, William W. *A Greek Grammar*. Rev. ed. Boston: Ginn, 1892.

———. *Syntax of the Moods and Tenses of the Greek Verb*. Boston: Ginn and Heath, 1879.

Gordis, Robert. "A Rhetorical Use of Interrogative Sentences in Biblical Hebrew." *AJSL* 49.3 (1933): 212–17.

Grice, Paul. *Studies in the Way of Words*. Cambridge: Harvard University Press, 1989.

Groenendijk, Jeroen, and Martin Stokhof. "Questions." Pages 1055–124 in *Handbook of Logic and Language*. Edited by Johan van Benthem and Alice ter Meulen. Cambridge: MIT Press, 1997.

———. "Semantic Analysis of Wh-Complements." *Linguistics and Philosophy* 5 (1982): 175–233.

———. "Studies on the Semantics of Questions and the Pragmatics of Answers." PhD diss., University of Amsterdam, 1984.

Gruber, Helmut. "Questions and Strategic Orientation in Verbal Conflict Sequences." *Journal of Pragmatics* 33.12 (2001): 1815–57.

Guerzoni, Elena. "Why *Even* Ask? On the Pragmatics of Questions and the Semantics of Answers." PhD diss., Massachusetts Institute of Technology, 2003.

Guerzoni, Elena, and Yael Sharvit. "A Question of Strength: On NPIs in Interrogative Clauses." *Linguistics and Philosophy* 30 (2007): 361–91.

Gunlogson, Christine. *True to Form: Rising and Falling Declaratives as Questions in English*. Outstanding Dissertations in Linguistics. New York: Routledge, 2003.

Haegeman, Liliane. "Negative Preposing, Negative Inversion, and the Split CP." Pages 21–61 in *Negation and Polarity: Syntactic and Semantic Perspectives*. Edited by Laurence R. Horn and Yasuhiko Kato. Oxford: Oxford University Press, 2000.

———. *The Syntax of Negation*. Cambridge Studies in Linguistics 75. Cambridge: Cambridge University Press, 1995.

Hagner, Donald A. *Matthew 1–13*. WBC 33A. Dallas: Word, 1998.

———. *Matthew 14–28*. WBC 33B. Dallas: Word, 1998.

Hagstrom, Paul. "Questions." Pages 478–92 in *The Routledge Companion to Philosophy of Language*. Edited by Gillian Russell and Delia Graff Fara. Routledge Philosophy Companions. New York: Routledge, 2012.

Hahn, E. Adelaide. "Apollonius Dyscolus on Mood." *Transactions and Proceedings of the American Philological Association* 82 (1951): 29–48.

Hamblin, Charles L. "Questions." *Australasian Journal of Philosophy* 36 (1958): 159–68.

———. "Questions Aren't Statements." *Philosophy of Science* 30.1 (1963): 62–63.

———. "Questions in Montague English." *Foundations of Language* 10.1 (1973): 41–53.

Han, Chung-hye. "Interpreting Interrogatives as Rhetorical Questions." *Lingua* 112 (2002): 201–29.

Han, Chung-hye, and Maribel Romero. "Disjunction, Focus, and Scope." *Linguistic Inquiry* 35.2 (2004): 179–217.

———. "Negation, Focus and Alternative Questions." Pages 262–75 in *WCCFL 20: Proceedings of the 20th West Coast Conference on Formal Linguistics*. Edited by Karine Megerdoomian and Leora Anne Bar-el. Somerville: Cascadilla, 2001.

Harrah, David. "The Logic of Questions." Pages 1–60 in volume 8 of *Handbook of Philosophical Logic*. 2nd ed. Edited by Dov M. Gabbay and F. Guenthner. Dordrecht: Kluwer, 2002.

———. "A Logic of Questions and Answers." *Philosophy of Science* 28.1 (1961): 40–46.

———. "On Completeness in the Logic of Questions." *American Philosophical Quarterly* 6.2 (1969): 158–64.

———. "Question Generators." *Journal of Philosophy* 63.20 (1966): 606–8.

———. "What Should We Teach about Questions?" *Synthese* 51.1 (1982): 21–38.

Harris, Murray J. *Prepositions and Theology in the Greek New Testament: An Essential Reference Resource for Exegesis*. Grand Rapids: Zondervan, 2012.

———. *The Second Epistle to the Corinthians: A Commentary on the Greek Text*. NIGTC. Grand Rapids: Eerdmans, 2005.

Haugh, Michael. "Conversational Interaction." Pages 251–73 in *The Cambridge Handbook of Pragmatics*. Edited by Keith Allan and Kasia M. Jaszczolt. Cambridge Handbooks in Language and Linguistics. Cambridge: Cambridge University Press, 2012.

Heim, Irene. "A Note on Negative Polarity and Downward Entailingness." Pages 98–107 in *The Proceedings of NELS 14*. Edited by Charles Jones and Peter Sells. Amherst: GLSA, 1984.

Heinemann, Trine. "Questions of Accountability: Yes-No Interrogatives that Are Unanswerable." *Discourse Studies* 10.1 (2008): 55–71.

———. "Two Answers to Inapposite Inquiries." Pages 159–86 in *Conversation Analysis: Comparative Perspectives*. Edited by Jack Sidnell. Studies in Interactional Sociolinguistics 27. Cambridge: Cambridge University Press, 2009.

———. " 'Will You or Can't You?': Displaying Entitlement in Interrogative Requests." *Journal of Pragmatics* 38 (2006): 1081–1104.

Held, Moshe. "Rhetorical Questions in Ugaritic and Biblical Hebrew." *ErIsr* 9 (1969): 71–79.

Henderson, G. P. "On Questions." *Philosophy* 30.115 (1955): 304–17.

Heritage, John. "Epistemics in Action: Action Formation and Territories of Knowledge." *Research on Language and Social Interaction* 45.1 (2012): 1–29.

———. "The Limits of Questioning: Negative Interrogatives and Hostile Question Content." *Journal of Pragmatics* 34.10–11 (2002): 1427–46.

Heritage, John, and Steven Clayman. *Talk in Action: Interactions, Identities, and Institutions*. West Sussex: Wiley-Blackwell, 2010.

Higginbotham, James. "Interrogatives." Pages 195–227 in *The View from Building 20: Essays in Linguistics in Honor of Sylvain Bromberger*. Edited by Kenneth Hale and Samuel Jay Keyser. Cambridge: MIT, 1993.

———. "The Semantics of Questions." Pages 361–83 in *The Handbook of Contemporary Semantic Theory*. Edited by Shalom Lappin. Blackwell Handbooks in Linguistics. London: Blackwell, 1997.

Hintikka, Jaakko. "Questions about Questions." Pages 103–58 in *Semantics and Philosophy*. Edited by Milton K. Munitz and Peter K. Unger. New York: New York University Press, 1974.

———. *Socratic Epistemology: Explorations of Knowledge-Seeking by Questioning.* Cambridge: Cambridge University Press, 2007.

Hintikka, Jaakko, and Ilpo Halonen. "Semantics and Pragmatics for Why-Questions." *Journal of Philosophy* 92.12 (1995): 636–57.

Hintikka, Jaakko, Ilpo Halonen, and Arto Mutanen. "Interrogative Logic as a General Theory of Reasoning." Pages 295–337 in *Handbook of the Logic of Argument and Inference: The Turn Toward the Practical.* Edited by Dov M. Gabbay, Ralph H. Johnson, Hans Jürgen Ohlbach, and John Woods. Vol. 1 of *Studies in Logic and Practical Reasoning.* Amsterdam: Elsevier, 2002.

Hiż, Henry, ed. *Questions.* Synthese Language Library 1. Dordrecht: D. Reidel, 1978.

Hiż, Henry. "Questions and Answers." *Journal of Philosophy* 59.10 (1962): 253–65.

Hoffmann, Ernst G., and Heinrich von Siebenthal. *Griechische Grammatik zum Neuen Testament.* Riehen: Immanuel, 1985.

Hoffman, Kathryn Vitalis, and Mark Vitalis Hoffman. "Question Marks and Turning Points: Following the Gospel of Mark to Surprising Places." *WW* 26.1 (2006): 69–76.

Holmberg, Anders. "On Whimperatives and Related Questions." *Journal of Linguistics* 15 (1979): 225–44.

Holmes, Nigel. "Interrogative *Nam* in Early Latin." *Mnemosyne* 65 (2012): 203–18.

Homer. *The Odyssey.* Translated by A. T. Murray. 2 vols. LCL 104, 105. Cambridge: Harvard University Press, 1919.

Hooker, Morna D. *The Gospel according to Saint Mark.* BNTC. New York: Continuum, 1991.

Hookway, Christopher. "Questions of Context: The Presidential Address." *Proceedings of the Aristotelian Society* 96 (1996): 1–16.

Horn, Laurence R. "Implicature." Pages 3–28 in *The Handbook of Pragmatics.* Edited by Laurence R. Horn and Gregory Ward. Blackwell Handbooks in Linguistics 16. Oxford: Blackwell, 2006.

Horn, Laurence R., and Gregory Ward, eds. *The Handbook of Pragmatics.* Blackwell Handbooks in Linguistics 16. Oxford: Blackwell, 2006.

Horrocks, Geoffrey. "*Ouk Ísmen Oudén*: Negative Concord and Negative Polarity in the History of Greek." *Journal of Greek Linguistics* 14.1 (2014): 43–83.

Huddleston, Rodney. "The Contrast between Interrogatives and Questions." *Journal of Linguistics* 30.2 (1994): 411–39.

Hudson, Richard A. "The Meaning of Questions." *Language* 51.1 (1975): 1–31.

Hultgren, Anna Kristina, and Deborah Cameron. "'How May I Help You?' Questions, Control, and Customer Care in Telephone Call Center Talk." Pages 322–42 in *"Why Do You Ask?" The Function of Questions in Institutional Discourse.* Edited by Alice F. Freed and Susan Ehrlich. Oxford: Oxford University Press, 2010.

Hultgren, Arland J. *Paul's Letter to the Romans: A Commentary.* Grand Rapids: Eerdmans, 2011.

Human, Dirk J., and Gert J. Steyn, eds. *Psalms and Hebrews: Studies in Reception*. LHBOTS 527. London: T&T Clark, 2010.

Hutchinson, G. O. *Greek Lyric Poetry: A Commentary on Selected Larger Pieces*. Oxford: Oxford University Press, 2001.

Hyman, Ronald T. "Esther 3:3: The Question with No Response." *JBQ* 22.2 (1994): 103–9.

———. "God, Abraham, Moses: A Comparison of Key Questions." *JBQ* 19.4 (1991): 250–59.

Ilie, Cornelia. "Question-Response Argumentation in Talk Shows." *Journal of Pragmatics* 31 (1999): 975–99.

———. *What Else Can I Tell You? A Pragmatic Study of English Rhetorical Questions as Discursive and Argumentative Acts*. Stockholm Studies in English 82. Stockholm: Almqvist & Wiksell, 1994.

Isaacs, James, and Kyle Rawlins. "Conditional Questions." *Journal of Semantics* 25.3 (2008): 269–319.

Isocrates. *To Demonicus, To Nicocles, Nicocles or The Cyprians, Panegyricus, To Philip* and *Archidamus*. Translated by George Norlin. LCL. Cambridge: Harvard University Press, 1928.

Israel, Michael. *The Grammar of Polarity: Pragmatics, Sensitivity, and the Logic of Scales*. Cambridge Studies in Linguistics 127. Cambridge: Cambridge University Press, 2011.

Iwata, Seizi. "Echo Questions Are Interrogatives? Another Version of a Metarepresentational Analysis." *Linguistics and Philosophy* 26.2 (2003): 185–254.

Jacobson, Rolf A. *'Many Are Saying': The Function of Direct Discourse in the Hebrew Psalter*. JSOTSup 397. London: T&T Clark, 2004.

Jannaris, A. N. *An Historical Greek Grammar, Chiefly of the Attic Dialect: As Written and Spoken from Classical Antiquity Down to the Present Time*. London: Macmillan, 1897.

Jauss, Hans Robert. *Question and Answer: Forms of Dialogic Understanding*. Edited and translated by Michael Hays. Theory and History of Literature 68. Minneapolis: University of Minnesota Press, 1989.

Jaworski, William. "The Logic of How-Questions." *Synthese* 166 (2009): 133–55.

Jespersen, Otto. *Negation in English and Other Languages*. Copenhagen: A. F. Høst, 1917.

Jewett, Robert. *Romans: A Commentary on the Book of Romans*. Assisted by Roy David Kotansky. Edited by Eldon Jay Epp. Hermeneia. Minneapolis: Fortress, 2006.

Johnson, Raymond E. "The Rhetorical Question as a Literary Device in Ecclesiastes." PhD diss., Southern Baptist Theological Seminary, 1986.

Johnstone, Barbara. *The Linguistic Individual: Self-Expression in Language and Linguistics*. Oxford Studies in Sociolinguistics. Oxford: Oxford University Press, 1996.

Jones, Gordon S. "Studies in the Grammatical Theory of Apollonius Dyscolus." PhD diss., Durham University, 1967.

Juel, Donald H. *Mark*. ACNT. Minneapolis: Augsburg Fortress, 1990.

Karttunen, Lauri. "Implicative Verbs." Pages 285–313 in *Presuppositions in Philosophy and Linguistics*. Edited by János S. Petöfi and Dorothea Franck. Linguistische Forschungen 7. Frankfurt: Athenäum, 1973.

———. "Syntax and Semantics of Questions." *Linguistics and Philosophy* 1.1 (1977): 3–44.

Karttunen, Lauri, and Stanley Peters. "Interrogative Quantifiers." Pages 181–205 in *Time, Tense and Quantifiers*. Edited by Christian Rohrer. Linguistische Arbeiten 83. Tübingen: Niemeyer, 1980.

———. "What Indirect Questions Conventionally Implicate." *Papers from the Twelfth Regional Meeting of the Chicago Linguistic Society* (1976): 351–68.

Käsemann, Ernst. *Commentary on Romans*. Translated and edited by Geoffrey W. Bromiley. Grand Rapids: Eerdmans, 1980.

Katz, Jerrold J., and Paul M. Postal. *An Integrated Theory of Linguistic Descriptions*. Cambridge: MIT, 1964.

Keener, Craig S. *The Gospel of Matthew: A Socio-Rhetorical Commentary*. Grand Rapids: Eerdmans, 2009.

Kekes, John. "Skepticism and External Questions." *Philosophy and Phenomenological Research* 31.3 (1971): 325–40.

Kelber, Werner. *The Oral and Written Gospel: The Hermeneutics of Speaking and Writing in the Synoptic Tradition, Mark, Paul, and Q*. Philadelphia: Fortress, 1983.

Kemp, Alan. "The Tekhnē Grammatikē of Dionysius Thrax: English Translation with Introduction and Notes." Pages 169–89 in *The History of Linguistics in the Classical Period*. Edited by Daniel J. Taylor. Studies in the Histories of the Language Sciences 46. Amsterdam: John Benjamins, 1987.

Kennedy, George A. *Classical Rhetoric and Its Christian and Secular Tradition from Ancient to Modern Times*. 2nd ed. Chapel Hill: University of North Carolina Press, 1999.

———. *Invention and Method: Two Rhetorical Treatises from the Hermogenic Corpus*. WGRW 15. Atlanta: Society of Biblical Literature, 2005.

———. *New Testament Interpretation through Rhetorical Criticism*. Studies in Religion. Chapel Hill: University of North Carolina Press, 1984.

———. *Progymnasmata: Greek Textbooks of Prose Composition and Rhetoric*. WGRW 10. Atlanta: Society of Biblical Literature, 2003.

Kiefer, Ferenc. "Yes-No Questions as Wh-Questions." Pages 97–119 in *Speech Act Theory and Pragmatics*. Edited by John R. Searle, Ferenc Kiefer, and Manfred Bierwisch. Dordrecht: D. Reidel, 1980.

Kirk, Allison. "Word Order and Information Structure in New Testament Greek." PhD diss., Leiden University, 2012.

———. "Word Order Variation in New Testament Greek Wh-Questions." Pages 293–313 in *Historical Linguistics 2009: Selected Papers from the 19th International Conference on Historical Linguistics, Nijmegen, 10–14 August 2009.* Edited by Ans van Kemenade and Nynke de Haas. Current Issues in Linguistic Theory 320. Amsterdam: John Benjamins, 2012.

Kissine, Mikhail. "Sentences, Utterances, and Speech Acts." Pages 169–90 in *The Cambridge Handbook of Pragmatics*. Edited by Keith Allan and Kasia M. Jaszczolt. Cambridge Handbooks in Language and Linguistics. Cambridge: Cambridge University Press, 2012.

Kleiner, Scott A. "Erotetic Logic and Scientific Inquiry." *Synthese* 74.1 (1988): 19–46.

Knight, Thomas. "Questions and Universals." *Philosophy and Phenomenological Research* 27.4 (1967): 564–76.

König, Ekkehard, and Peter Siemund. "Speech Act Distinctions in Grammar." Pages 276–324 in *Language Typology and Syntactic Description: Volume 1, Clause Structure*. Edited by Timothy Shopen. 2nd ed. Cambridge: Cambridge University Press, 1985.

Korta, Kepa, and John Perry. *Critical Pragmatics: An Inquiry into Reference and Communication*. Cambridge: Cambridge University Press, 2011.

Koshik, Irene. "Alternative Questions Used in Conversational Repair." *Discourse Studies* 7.2 (2005): 193–211.

———. *Beyond Rhetorical Questions: Assertive Questions in Everyday Interaction*. Studies in Discourse and Grammar 16. Amsterdam: John Benjamins, 2005.

Köstenberger, Andreas J. " 'What is Truth?' Pilate's Question in Its Johannine and Larger Biblical Context." *JETS* 48.1 (2005): 33–62.

Koura, Antti. "An Approach to Why-Questions." *Synthese* 74.2 (1988): 191–206.

Krifka, Manfred. "The Semantics and Pragmatics of Polarity Items." *Linguistic Analysis* 25 (1995): 209–58.

Krodel, Gerhard A. *Revelation*. ACNT. Minneapolis: Augsburg Fortress, 1989.

Kroeger, Paul R. *Analyzing Grammar: An Introduction*. Cambridge: Cambridge University Press, 2005.

Kubiński, Tadeusz. *An Outline of the Logical Theory of Questions*. Berlin: Akademie, 1980.

Kuno, Susumu, and Jane J. Robinson. "Multiple Wh Questions." *Linguistic Inquiry* 3.4 (1972): 463–87.

Kuntz, J. Kenneth. "The Form, Location, and Function of Rhetorical Questions in Deutero-Isaiah." Pages 121–42 in *Writing and Reading the Scroll of Isaiah: Studies of an Interpretive Tradition*. Vol. 1. Edited by Craig C. Broyles and Craig A. Evans. Vetus Testamentum Supplements 70.1. Leiden: Brill, 1997.

Labov, William. *Sociolinguistic Patterns*. Philadelphia: University of Pennsylvania Press, 1972.

Labov, William, and David Fanshel. *Therapeutic Discourse: Psychotherapy as Conversation*. New York: Academic, 1977.

Ladd, D. Robert. "A First Look at the Semantics and Pragmatics of Negative Questions and Tag Questions." *Proceedings of Chicago Linguistic Society* 17 (1981): 164–71.

Ladusaw, William. "Polarity Sensitivity as Inherent Scope Relations." PhD diss., University of Texas at Austin, 1979.

Lakoff, Robin. "Language and Woman's Place." *Language in Society* 2.1 (1973): 45–80.

Lamari, Anna A. *Narrative, Intertext, and Space in Euripides' Phoenissae*. Trends in Classics 6. Berlin: De Gruyter, 2010.

Lane, William L. *Hebrews 1–8*. WBC 47A. Dallas: Word, 1998.

Lappin, Shalom, ed. *The Handbook of Contemporary Semantic Theory*. Blackwell Handbooks in Linguistics. London: Blackwell, 1997.

Lawler, John M. "Any Questions?" *Papers from the Seventh Regional Meeting of the Chicago Linguistic Society* (1971): 163–73.

Lee, Margaret Ellen, and Bernard Brandon Scott. *Sound Mapping the New Testament*. Salem: Polebridge, 2009.

Lee, Yo-An. "Yes–No Questions in the Third-Turn Position: Pedagogical Discourse Processes." *Discourse Processes* 45 (2008): 237–62.

Lee-Goldman, Russell. "A Typology of Rhetorical Questions." Paper presented at the Syntax and Semantics Circle. University of California-Berkeley, 17 February, 2006.

Leonardi, Paolo, and Marco Santambrogio. "Pragmatics, Language Games, Questions and Answers." Pages 443–72 in *Possibilities and Limitations of Pragmatics*. Edited by Herman Parret, Marina Sbisa, and Jef Verschueren. Studies in Language Companion Series 7. Amsterdam: John Benjamins, 1981.

Levinsohn, Stephen H. *Discourse Features of New Testament Greek: A Coursebook on the Information Structure of New Testament Greek*. 2nd ed. Dallas: SIL, 2000.

Levinson, Stephen C. *Pragmatics*. Cambridge Textbooks in Linguistics. Cambridge: Cambridge University Press, 1983.

Liddell, Henry George, and Robert Scott. *A Greek-English Lexicon with a Revised Supplement*. Revised by Henry Stuart Jones and Roderick McKenzie. 9th rev. ed. Oxford: Clarendon, 1996.

Liddicoat, Anthony J. *An Introduction to Conversation Analysis*. New York: Continuum, 2007.

Lightfoot, David. *Natural Logic and the Greek Moods*. The Hague: Mouton, 1975.

Litwack, Eugene. "A Classification of Biased Questions." *American Journal of Sociology* 62.2 (1956): 182–86.

Llewelyn, John E. "What Is a Question?" *Australasian Journal of Philosophy* 42.1 (1964): 69–85.

López, Luis. "Wh-Movement." Pages 311–24 in *The Bloomsbury Companion to*

Syntax. Edited by Silvia Luraghi and Claudia Parodi. London: Bloomsbury, 2013.

Louw, Johannes P. *Semantics of New Testament Greek*. SBL Semeia Studies. Atlanta: Scholars, 1982.

Louw, Johannes P., and Eugene A. Nida. *Greek-English Lexicon of the New Testament: Based on Semantic Domains*. 2 vols. 2nd ed. New York: United Bible Societies, 1989.

Luraghi, Silvia, and Claudia Parodi, eds. *The Bloomsbury Companion to Syntax*. London: Bloomsbury, 2013.

Luther, Martin. *Luther's Works, Vol. 21: The Sermon on the Mount and the Magnificat*. Edited by Jaroslav Jan Pelikan, Hilton C. Oswald, and Helmut T. Lehmann. Saint Louis: Concordia, 1999.

Luz, Ulrich. *Matthew 8–20: A Commentary*. Translated by James E. Crouch. Hermeneia. Minneapolis: Fortress, 2001.

———. *Matthew 21–28: A Commentary*. Translated by James E. Crouch. Hermeneia. Minneapolis: Fortress, 2005.

Lyons, John. *Introduction to Theoretical Linguistics*. Cambridge: Cambridge University Press, 1968.

———. *Semantics*. 2 vols. Cambridge: Cambridge University Press, 1977.

Macagno, Fabrizio, and Douglas Walton. "The Argumentative Structure of Persuasive Definitions." *Ethical Theory and Moral Practice* 11 (2008): 525–49.

Macaulay, Marcia. "Asking to Ask: The Strategic Function of Indirect Requests for Information in Interviews." *Pragmatics* 6.4 (1996): 491–509.

Maier, Emar. "Switches between Direct and Indirect Speech in Ancient Greek." *Journal of Greek Linguistics* 12 (2012): 118–39.

Malherbe, Abraham J. "ΜΗ ΓΕΝΟΙΤΟ in the Diatribe and Paul." *HTR* 73.1/2 (1980): 231–40.

Maneli, Mieczyslaw. *Perelman's New Rhetoric as Philosophy and Methodology for the Next Century*. Library of Rhetorics 1. Dordrecht: Kluwer, 1994.

Marshall, I. Howard. *The Gospel of Luke: A Commentary on the Greek Text*. NIGTC. Exeter: Paternoster, 1978.

Martin, Ralph P. *2 Corinthians*. 2nd ed. WBC 40. Grand Rapids: Zondervan, 2014.

Mastronarde, Donald J. *Contact and Discontinuity: Some Conventions of Speech and Action on the Greek Tragic Stage*. University of California Publications Classical Studies 21. Berkeley: University of California, 1979.

Matthaios, Stephanos, Franco Montanari, and Antonios Rengakos, eds. *Ancient Scholarship and Grammar: Archetypes, Concepts and Contexts*. Trends in Classics 8. Berlin: De Gruyter, 2011.

May, John D. "Questions as Suggestions: The Pragmatics of Interrogative Speech." *Language & Communication* 9.4 (1989): 227–43.

Mayo, Bernard. "Deliberative Questions: A Criticism." *Analysis* 16.3 (1956): 58–63.

McKay, Kenneth L. *A New Syntax of the Verb in New Testament Greek: An Aspectual Approach*. Studies in Biblical Greek 5. New York: Peter Lang, 1994.

———. "On the Perfect and Other Aspects in New Testament Greek." *NovT* 23.4 (1981): 289–329.

McWhorter, Ashton Waugh. "A Study of the So-Called Deliberative Type of Question (τί ποιήσω;) as Found in Aeschylus, Sophocles, and Euripides." *Transactions and Proceedings of the American Philological Association* 41 (1910): 157–67.

Mealand, David L. "Hellenistic Greek and the New Testament: A Stylometric Perspective." *JSNT* 34.4 (2012): 323–45.

Merchant, Jason. "Sluicing." Pages 271–91 in *The Blackwell Companion to Syntax*. Edited by Martin Everaert and Henk van Riemsdijk. Vol 4. Blackwell Handbooks in Linguistics 19. London: Blackwell, 2006.

Merchant, Jason, and Andrew Simpson, eds. *Sluicing: Cross-Linguistic Perspectives*. Oxford Studies in Theoretical Linguistics 38. Oxford: Oxford University Press, 2012.

Mesthrie, Rajend, Joan Swann, Ana Deumert, and William L. Leap. *Introducing Sociolinguistics*. 2nd ed. Edinburgh: Edinburgh University Press, 2009.

Metzger, Bruce. *Manuscripts of the Greek Bible: An Introduction to Greek Palaeography*. Corrected ed. Oxford: Oxford University Press, 1991.

———. *A Textual Commentary on the Greek New Testament: A Companion Volume to the United Bible Societies' Greek New Testament (4th rev. ed.)*. 2nd ed. London: United Bible Societies, 1994.

Meyer, Heinrich August Wilhelm. *Critical and Exegetical Handbook to the Gospel of Matthew*. 2 vols. Translated by Peter Christie. Critical and Exegetical Commentary on the New Testament. Edinburgh: T&T Clark, 1880–81.

Meyer, Michel. "Dialectic and Questioning: Socrates and Plato." *American Philosophical Quarterly* 17.4 (1980): 281–89.

———, ed. *Questions and Questioning*. Berlin: de Gruyter, 1988.

———. "The Revival of Questioning in the Twentieth Century." *Synthese* 74.1 (1988): 5–18.

Meyer, Michel, and Marlene L. Cushman. "Argumentation in the Light of a Theory of Questioning." *Philosophy and Rhetoric* 15.2 (1982): 81–103.

Meyer, Roland, and Ina Mleinek. "How Prosody Signals Force and Focus—A Study of Pitch Accents in Russian Yes–No Questions." *Journal of Pragmatics* 38.10 (2006): 1615–35.

Meynet, Roland. "The Question at the Center: A Specific Device of Rhetorical Argumentation in Scripture." Pages 200–214 in *Rhetorical Argumentation in Biblical Texts: Essays from the Lund 2000 Conference*. Edited by Anders Eriksson, Thomas H. Olbricht, and Walter Übelacker. Emory Studies in Early Christianity 8. Harrisburg: Trinity Press International, 2002.

Mill, John Stuart. *Inaugural Address: Delivered to the University of St Andrews, 1867.* London: Longmans, Green, Reader, and Dyer, 1867.

Miller, Carolyn R. "Genre as Social Action." *Quarterly Journal of Speech* 70 (1984): 151–67.

Miller, D. Gary. *Ancient Greek Dialects and Early Authors: Introduction to the Dialect Mixture in Homer, with Notes on Lyric and Herodotus.* Berlin: De Gruyter, 2014.

Minchin, Elizabeth. "Rhythm and Regularity in Homeric Composition: Questions in the *Odyssey*." Pages 21–48 in *Oral Performance and Its Context.* Edited by C. J. Mackie. Mnemosyne Supplements 248. Leiden: Brill, 2004.

———. "The Words of Gods: Divine Discourse in Homer's *Iliad*." Pages 17–36 in *Sacred Words: Orality, Literacy and Religion.* Edited by A. P. M. H. Lardinois, Josine H. Blok, and Marc G. M. van der Poel. Vol. 8 of *Orality and Literacy in the Ancient World.* Mnemosyne Supplements 332. Leiden: Brill, 2011.

Modrak, Deborah K. W. *Aristotle's Theory of Language and Meaning.* Cambridge: Cambridge University Press, 2001.

Monro, D. B. *A Grammar of the Homeric Dialect.* 2nd ed. Oxford: Clarendon, 1891.

Montefusco, Lucia Calboli. "Rhetorical Use of Dilemmatic Arguments." *Rhetorica* 28.4 (2010): 363–83.

Moo, Douglas J. *The Epistle to the Romans.* NICNT. Grand Rapids: Eerdmans, 1996.

Morris, Leon. *The Gospel according to Matthew.* Pillar New Testament Commentary. Grand Rapids: Eerdmans, 1992.

Morwood, James. *The Oxford Grammar of Classical Greek.* Oxford: Oxford University Press, 2001.

Moshavi, Adina. "Can a Positive Rhetorical Question Have a Positive Answer in the Bible?" *JSS* 56.2 (2011): 253–73.

———. "Two Types of Argumentation Involving Rhetorical Questions in Biblical Hebrew Dialogue." *Bib* 90 (2009): 32–46.

Moulton, James Hope. *A Grammar of New Testament Greek.* With W. F. Howard and Nigel Turner. 4 vols. London: T&T Clark, 1963–76.

Moulton, William G. "On the Prosody of Statements, Questions, and Echo Questions." *American Speech* 62.3 (1987): 249–61.

Mounce, William D. *Basics of Biblical Greek Grammar.* 2nd ed. Grand Rapids: Zondervan, 2003.

Müller, Mogens. "'Have You Faith in the Son of Man?' (John 9.35)." *NTS* 37.2 (1991): 291–94.

Murphy, M. Lynne, and Anu Koskela. *Key Terms in Semantics.* New York: Continuum, 2010.

Naciscione, Anita. *Stylistic Use of Phraseological Units in Discourse.* Amsterdam: John Benjamins, 2010.

Nagy, Gregory. "Language and Meter." Pages 370–87 in *A Companion to the Ancient Greek Language*. Edited by Egbert J. Bakker. Blackwell Companions to the Ancient World. Malden, MA: Wiley-Blackwell, 2010.

Nässelqvist, Dan. *Public Reading and Aural Intensity: An Analysis of the Soundscape in John 1–4*. Lund: Lund University Press, 2014.

Nestle, Eberhard, Erwin Nestle, Barbara Aland, Kurt Aland, Johannes Karavidopoulos, Carlo M. Martini, and Bruce M. Metzger, eds. *The Greek New Testament*. 27th ed. Stuttgart: Deutsche Bibelgesellschaft, 1993.

Newman, Barclay M., and Philip C. Stine. *A Handbook on the Gospel of Matthew*. UBS Handbook Series. New York: United Bible Societies, 1988.

Neyrey, Jerome H. "Questions, *Chreiai*, and Challenged to Honor: The Interface of Rhetoric and Culture in Mark's Gospel." *CBQ* 60.4 (1998): 657–81.

Niccacci, Alviero. "Marked Syntactical Structures in Biblical Greek in Comparison with Biblical Hebrew." *Liber Annuus* 43 (1993): 9–69.

Nida, Eugene A., and Johannes P. Louw. *Lexical Semantics of the Greek New Testament: A Supplement to the Greek-English Lexicon of the New Testament Based on Semantic Domains*. SBL Resources for Biblical Study 25. Atlanta: Scholars, 1992.

Noh, Eun-Ju. "Echo Questions: Metarepresentation and Pragmatic Enrichment." *Linguistics and Philosophy* 21.6 (1998): 603–28.

———. *Metarepresentation: A Relevance-Theory Approach*. Pragmatics and Beyond: New Series 69. Amsterdam: John Benjamins, 2000.

Nolland, John. *The Gospel of Matthew: A Commentary on the Greek Text*. NIGTC. Grand Rapids: Eerdmans, 2005.

———. *Luke 9:21–18:34*. WBC 35B. Dallas: Word, 1998.

———. *Luke 18:35–24:53*. WBC 35C. Dallas: Word, 1998.

Noveck, Ira A. "Pragmatic Inferences Related to Logical Terms." Pages 301–21 in *Experimental Pragmatics*. Edited by Ira A. Noveck and Dan Sperber. Palgrave Studies in Pragmatics, Language and Cognition. New York: Palgrave Macmillan, 2004.

Nuchelmans, Gabriel. *Dilemmatic Arguments: Towards a History of Their Logic and Rhetoric*. Verhandelingen der Koninklijke Nederlandse Akademie van Wetenschappen, Afd. Letterkunde, Nieuwe Reeks, 145. Amsterdam: North-Holland, 1991.

Nunberg, Geoffrey. *The Linguistics of Punctuation*. CSLI Lecture Notes 18. Stanford: CSLI, 1990.

Nunn, H. P. V. *A Short Syntax of New Testament Greek*. 5th ed. Cambridge: Cambridge University Press, 1976.

Nykiel, Joanna. "Whatever Happened to English Sluicing." Pages 37–59 in *Studies in the History of the English Language V: Variation and Change in English Grammar and Lexicon: Contemporary Approaches*. Edited by Robert A.

Cloutier, Anne Marie Hamilton-Brehm, William A. Kretzschmar, Jr. Topics in English Linguistics 68. Berlin: De Gruyter, 2010.

O'Grady, Gerard. *A Grammar of Spoken English Discourse: The Intonation of Increments*. Continuum Studies in Theoretical Linguistics. New York: Continuum, 2010.

Osborne, Grant R. *Revelation*. BECNT. Grand Rapids: Baker, 2002.

Pagis, Dan. "Toward a Theory of the Literary Riddle." Pages 81 – 108 in *Untying the Knot: On Riddles and Other Enigmatic Modes*. Edited by Galit Hasan-Rokem and David Shulman. Oxford: Oxford University Press, 1996.

Palamountain, J. C. "Notes on the Interrogative." *Modern Language Journal* 29.2 (1945): 117–26.

Park, Ji Seon. "Negative Yes/No Question-Answer Sequences in Conversation: Grammar, Action, and Sequence Organization." PhD diss., University of California, Los Angeles, 2008.

Parodi, Claudia, and A. Carlos Quicoli. "Complementation." Pages 325–40 in *The Bloomsbury Companion to Syntax*. Edited by Silvia Luraghi and Claudia Parodi. London: Bloomsbury, 2013.

Parret, Herman. "La question et la requête: Vers une théorie anthropologique de l'acte de poser une question." *Revue de Métaphysique et de Morale* 86.3 (1981): 326–46.

Parsons, Mikeal C., Martin M. Culy, and Joshua J. Stigall. *Luke: A Handbook on the Greek Text*. Baylor Handbook on the Greek New Testament. Waco: Baylor University Press, 2010.

Pavey, Emma L. *The Structure of Language: An Introduction to Grammatical Analysis*. Cambridge: Cambridge University Press, 2010.

Pavlidou, Th.-S. "Units-Levels of Linguistic Analysis." Pages 65–74 in *A History of Ancient Greek: From the Beginnings to Late Antiquity*. Edited by A.-F. Christidis. Translated by Geoffrey Cox. Cambridge: Cambridge University Press, 2007.

Payne, Thomas E. *Describing Morphosyntax: A Guide for Field Linguistics*. Cambridge: Cambridge University Press, 1997.

Peacham, Henry. *The Garden of Eloquence: Conteyning the Figures of Grammer and Rhetorick*. London: H. Jackson, 1577.

Peetz, Vera. "Disjunctions and Questions." *Philosophy* 53.204 (1978): 264–69.

Pepicello, W. J., and Thomas A. Green. *The Language of Riddles: New Perspectives*. Columbus: Ohio State University Press, 1984.

Perelman, Chaim, and Lucie Olbrechts-Tyteca. *The New Rhetoric: A Treatise on Argumentation*. Notre Dame: University of Notre Dame Press, 1969.

Perkinson, William Howard. "Observations on the Interrogative Sentence in Plautus and Terrence." PhD diss., University of Virginia, 1888.

Pervo, Richard I. *Acts: A Commentary on the Book of Acts*. Hermeneia. Minneapolis: Fortress, 2009.

Petty, Richard E., John T. Cacioppo, and Martin Heesacker. "Effects of Rhetorical Questions on Persuasion: A Cognitive Response Analysis." *Journal of Personality and Social Psychology* 40.3 (1981): 432–40.

Petrus, Klaus, ed. *Meaning and Analysis: New Essays on Grice*. New York: Palgrave Macmillan, 2010.

Philippaki-Warburton, I. "The Syntax of Classical Greek." Pages 590–98 in *A History of Ancient Greek: From the Beginnings to Late Antiquity*. Edited by A.-F. Christidis. Translated by W. J. Lillie. Cambridge: Cambridge University Press, 2007.

Pindar. *Olympian Odes, Pythian Odes*. Edited and Translated by William H. Race. LCL 56. Cambridge: Harvard University Press, 1997.

Pitts, Andrew W. "Greek Word Order and Clause Structure: A Comparative Study of Some New Testament Corpora." Pages 311–46 in *The Language of the New Testament: Context, History, and Development*. Edited by Stanley E. Porter and Andrew W. Pitts. Linguistic Biblical Studies 6. Leiden: Brill, 2013.

Plato. *Clitophon*. Edited and translated by S. R. Slings. CCTC 37. Cambridge: Cambridge University Press, 2004.

———. *Laches, Protagoras, Meno* and *Euthydemus*. Translated by W. R. M. Lamb. LCL 165. Cambridge: Harvard University Press, 1925.

———. *Lysis, Symposium* and *Gorgias*. Translated by W. R. M. Lamb. LCL 166. Cambridge: Harvard University Press, 1925.

———. *The Republic*. 2 Vols. Translated by Paul Shorey. LCL 237, 276. Cambridge: Harvard University Press, 1937, 1942.

Poe, Joe Park. "Word and Deed: On 'Stage-Directions' in Greek Tragedy." *Mnemosyne* 56.4 (2003): 420–48.

Pollock, John L. *Language and Thought*. Princeton: Princeton University Press, 1982.

Pomerantz, Anita. "Telling My Side: 'Limited Access' as a 'Fishing' Device." *Sociological Inquiry* 50 (1980): 186–98.

Poole, Debra A., and Lawrence T. White. "Effects of Question Repetition on the Eyewitness Testimony of Children and Adults." *Developmental Psychology* 27.6 (1991): 975–86.

Pope, Emily. "Answers to Yes-No Questions." *Linguistic Inquiry* 2.1 (1971): 69–82.

Porter, Stanley E. "The Argument of Romans 5: Can a Rhetorical Question Make a Difference?" *JBL* 110.4 (1991): 655–77.

———. *Verbal Aspect in the Greek of the New Testament, with Reference to Tense and Mood*. Studies in Biblical Greek 1. New York: Peter Lang, 1989.

Porter, Stanley E., and D. A. Carson, eds. *Biblical Greek Language and Linguistics: Open Questions in Current Research*. JSNTSup 80. Sheffield: Sheffield Academic, 1993.

———. *Linguistics and the New Testament: Critical Junctures*. JSNTSup 168. Sheffield: Sheffield Academic, 1999.

Potts, Christopher. *The Logic of Conventional Implicatures*. Oxford Studies in Theoretical Linguistics 7. Oxford: Oxford University Press, 2005.

Pratarelli, Marc E., and Adam Lawson. "Conjunctive Forms and Conditional Inference in Questions and Statements." *North American Journal of Psychology* 3.3 (2001): 415–28.

Prior, Mary, and Arthur Prior. "Erotetic Logic." *Philosophical Review* 64.1 (1955): 43–59.

Pritzl, Kurt. "Opinions as Appearances: *Endoxa* in Aristotle." *Ancient Philosophy* 14 (1994): 41–50.

Probert, Philomen. *Ancient Greek Accentuation: Synchronic Patterns, Frequency Effects, and Prehistory*. OCM. Oxford: Oxford University Press, 2006.

Progovac, Ljiljana. *Negative and Positive Polarity: A Binding Approach*. Cambridge Studies in Linguistics 68. Cambridge: Cambridge University Press, 1994.

Quintilian. *Institutio Oratoria*. Translated by H. E. Butler. 4 vols. LCL 124–127. Cambridge: Harvard University Press, 1920–21.

Radford, Andrew, Martin Atkinson, David Britain, Harald Clahsen, and Andrew Spencer. *Linguistics: An Introduction*. 2nd ed. Cambridge: Cambridge University Press, 2009.

Ram, Ashwin. "A Theory of Questions and Question Asking." *Journal of the Learning Sciences* 1.3/4 (1991): 273–318.

Randolph, Charles Brewster. "The Sign of Interrogation in Greek Minuscule Manuscripts." *CP* 5.3 (1910): 309–19.

Rawlins, Kyle. "(Un)Conditionals: An Investigation in the Syntax and Semantics of Conditional Sentences." PhD diss., University of California, Santa Cruz, 2008.

Reddish, Mitchell G. *Revelation*. SHBC. Macon: Smyth & Helwys, 2001.

Reese, Brian J. "Bias in Questions." PhD diss., University of Texas at Austin, 2007.

———. "The Meaning and Use of Negative Polar Interrogatives." *Empirical Issues in Formal Syntax and Semantics* 6 (2006): 331–54.

Reese, Brian J., and Nicholas Asher. "Biased Questions, Intonation, and Discourse." Pages 139–73 in *Information Structure: Theoretical, Typological, and Experimental Perspectives*. Edited by Malte Zimmermann and Caroline Féry. Oxford: Oxford University Press, 2010.

Rescher, Nicholas. *Conditionals*. Cambridge: MIT, 2007.

Rexach, Javier Gutiérrez. "Rhetorical Questions, Relevance and Scales." *Revista Alicantina de Estudios Ingleses* 11 (1998): 139–55.

Rhetorica ad Herennium. Translated by Harry Caplan. LCL 403. Cambridge: Harvard University Press, 1964.

Rijksbaron, Albert, ed. *New Approaches to Greek Particles*. Amsterdam: J. C. Gieben, 1997.

Roberts, John M., and Michael L. Forman. "Riddles: Expressive Models of Interrogation." *Ethnology* 10.4 (1971): 509–33.

Robertson, A. T. *A Grammar of the Greek New Testament in the Light of Historical Research*. New York: Hodder & Stoughton, 1914.

Robins, R. H. *The Byzantine Grammarians: Their Place in History*. Trends in Linguistics Studies and Monographs 70. Berlin: Mouton de Gruyter, 1993.

Rohde, Hannah. "Rhetorical Questions as Redundant Interrogatives." *San Diego Linguistics Papers* 2 (2006): 134–68.

Romero, Maribel. "Concealed Questions and Specificational Subjects." *Linguistics and Philosophy* 28.6 (2005): 687–737.

Romero, Maribel, and Chung-hye Han. "On Negative Yes/No Questions." *Linguistics and Philosophy* 27 (2004): 609–58.

———. "Verum Focus in Negative Yes/No Questions and Ladd's p / $\neg p$ Ambiguity." Pages 204–24 in *Proceedings from Semantics and Linguistic Theory 12*. Edited by Brendan Jackson. Ithaca: CLC, 2002.

Rooy, Robert van. "Negative Polarity Items in Questions: Strength as Relevance." *Journal of Semantics* 20.3 (2003): 239–73.

Rooy, Robert van, and Marie Šafáøová. "On Polar Questions." Pages 292–309 in *Proceedings from SALT 13*. Edited by Robert B. Young and Yuping Zhou. Ithaca: CLC, 2003.

Ross, John Robert. "Guess Who?" *Papers from the Fifth Regional Meeting of the Chicago Linguistic Society* (1969): 252–86.

Rubinelli, Sara. *Ars Topica: The Classical Technique of Constructing Arguments from Aristotle to Cicero*. Argumentation Library 15. Dordrecht: Springer, 2009.

Rudin, Catherine. "On Multiple Questions and Multiple Wh Fronting." *Natural Language and Linguistic Theory* 6 (1988): 445–501.

Runge, Steven E. *Discourse Grammar of the Greek New Testament: A Practical Introduction for Teaching and Exegesis*. Lexham Bible Reference Series. Peabody: Hendrickson, 2010.

———. "Teaching Them What NOT to Do: The Nuances of Negation in the Greek New Testament." Paper presented at the Annual Meeting of the Evangelical Theological Society. San Diego, CA, 13–16 November 2007.

Russell, Gillian, and Delia Graff Fara, eds. *The Routledge Companion to Philosophy of Language*. Routledge Philosophy Companions. New York: Routledge, 2012.

Sabel, Joachim. "Partial Wh-Movement and the Typology of Wh-Questions." Pages 409–46 in *Wh-Scope Marking*. Edited by Uli Lutz, Gereon Müller, and Arnim von Stechow. Linguistik Aktuell 37. Amsterdam: John Benjamins, 2000.

Sacks, Harvey. "An Initial Characterization of the Organization of Speaker Turn-Taking in Conversation." Pages 35–42 in *Conversation Analysis: Studies from the First Generation*. Edited by Gene H. Lerner. Pragmatics & Beyond New Series 125. Amsterdam: John Benjamins, 2004.

———. *Lectures on Conversation*. 2 vols. Edited by Gail Jefferson. Oxford: Blackwell, 1992.

Sadock, Jerrold M. "Queclaratives." *Papers from the Seventh Regional Meeting of the Chicago Linguistic Society* (1971): 223–31.

———. *Toward a Linguistic Theory of Speech Acts*. New York: Academic Press, 1974.

Sadock, Jerrold M., and Arnold M. Zwicky. "Speech Act Distinctions in Syntax." Pages 155–96 in *Language Typology and Syntactic Description: Volume 1, Clause Structure*. Edited by Timothy Shopen. 2nd ed. Cambridge: Cambridge University Press, 1985.

Saeed, John I. *Semantics*. 3rd ed. Introducing Linguistics 2. Malden, MA: Wiley-Blackwell, 2009.

Sandt, Rob van der. "Presupposition and Accommodation in Discourse." Pages 329–50 in *The Cambridge Handbook of Pragmatics*. Edited by Keith Allan and Kasia M. Jaszczolt. Cambridge Handbooks in Language and Linguistics. Cambridge: Cambridge University Press, 2012.

Sarles, Harvey B. *Language and Human Nature: Toward a Grammar of Interaction and Discourse*. Studies in Semiotics 13. Minneapolis: University of Minnesota Press, 1985.

Sauerland, Uli, and Penka Stateva, eds. *Presupposition and Implicature in Compositional Semantics*. Palgrave Studies in Pragmatics, Language and Cognition. New York: Palgrave Macmillan, 2007.

Schaeffer, Nora Cate, and Stanley Presser. "The Science of Asking Questions." *Annual Review of Sociology* 29 (2003): 65–88.

Schaffer, Deborah. "Can Rhetorical Questions Function as Retorts? Is the Pope Catholic?" *Journal of Pragmatics* 37.4 (2005): 433–60.

Schegloff, Emanuel A. "Repair after Next Turn: The Last Structurally Provided Defense of Intersubjectivity in Conversation." *American Journal of Sociology* 97.5 (1992): 1295–345.

Schreiner, Thomas R. *Romans*. BECNT. Grand Rapids: Baker, 1998.

Schrott, Angela. "*Que fais, Adam?* Questions and Seduction in the *Jeu d'Adam*." Pages 331–70 in *Historical Dialogue Analysis*. Edited by Andreas H. Jucker, Gerd Fritz, and Franz Lebsanft. Pragmatics and Beyond: New Series 66. Amsterdam: John Benjamins, 1999.

Schuhmann, Karl, and Barry Smith. "Questions: An Essay in Daubertian Phenomenology." *Philosophy and Phenomenological Research* 47.3 (1987): 353–84.

Scott, Alexander D., and Michael Scott. "The Paradox of the Question." *Analysis* 59.4 (1999): 331–34.

Searle, John R. *Speech Acts: An Essay in the Philosophy of Language*. Cambridge: Cambridge University Press, 1969.

Searle, John R., and Daniel Vanderveken. *Foundations of Illocutionary Logic*. Cambridge: Cambridge University Press, 1985.

Senft, Gunter. "Phatic Communion." Pages 226–33 in *Culture and Language Use*. Edited by Gunter Senft, Jan-Ola Östman, and Jef Verschueren. Handbook of Pragmatic Highlights 2. Amsterdam: John Benjamins, 2009.

Seuren, Pieter A. M. *The Logic of Language*. Vol. 2 of *Language from Within*. Oxford: Oxford University Press, 2010.

Seymour, T. D. "*Hypophora* in Isaeus." *Classical Review* 15.2 (1901): 108–9.

Shopen, Timothy, ed. *Language Typology and Syntactic Description: Volume 1, Clause Structure*. 2nd ed. Cambridge: Cambridge University Press, 1985.

Sicking, C. M. J. "Particles in Questions in Plato." Pages 157–74 in *New Approaches to Greek Particles*. Edited by Albert Rijksbaron. Amsterdam: J. C. Gieben, 1997.

Sider, Theodore. "On the Paradox of the Question." *Analysis* 57.2 (1997): 97–101.

Sidnell, Jack. *Conversation Analysis: An Introduction*. Language in Society 37. Malden, MA: Wiley-Blackwell, 2010.

Simpson, Paul. *Language through Literature: An Introduction*. Interface. London: Routledge, 1997.

Sinclair, John. *Trust the Text: Language, Corpus and Discourse*. Edited with Ronald Carter. London: Routledge, 2004.

Singer, Murray. "Stages of Question Answering." *Canadian Psychology* 30.4 (1989): 706–7.

———. "Toward a Model of Question Answering: Yes-No Questions." *Journal of Experimental Psychology: Learning, Memory, & Cognition* 10.2 (1984): 285–97.

Sintonen, Matti. "On the Logic of Why-Questions." *PSA: Proceedings of the Biennial Meeting of the Philosophy of Science Association* (1984): 168–76.

Slomkowski, Paul. *Aristotle's* Topics. PhA 74. Leiden: Brill, 1997.

Slot, Pauline. *How Can You Say That? Rhetorical Questions in Argumentative Texts*. Studies in Language and Language Use 2. Amsterdam: IFOTT, 1993.

Sluiter, Ineke. "The Greek Tradition." Pages 147–224 in *The Emergence of Semantics in Four Linguistic Traditions: Hebrew, Sanskrit, Greek, Arabic*. Edited by Wout van Bekkum, Jan Houben, Ineke Sluiter, and Kees Versteegh. Amsterdam Studies in the Theory and History of Linguistic Science 82. Amsterdam: John Benjamins, 1997.

Smalley, Stephen S. *1, 2, 3 John*. WBC 51. Dallas: Word, 1989.

Smith, Adrian T. *The Representation of Speech Events in Chariton's* Callirhoe *and the Acts of the Apostles*. Linguistic Biblical Studies 10. Leiden: Brill, 2014.

Smith, Carlota S. *Modes of Discourse: The Local Structure of Texts*. Cambridge Studies in Linguistics 103. Cambridge: Cambridge University Press, 2003.

Smith, Joshua Paul. "'I Will Ask You a Question': A Socio-Rhetorical Study of Opposing-Turn Questions in the Gospel of Luke." MA thesis, Central Baptist Theological Seminary, 2014.

Smith, Robert H. *Matthew*. ACNT. Minneapolis: Augsburg Fortress, 1989.

Snow, Richard E. "What Do We Know About Question-Asking?" *European Scientific Notes* 38.7 (1984): 352–56.

Sobin, Nicholas. "Echo Questions in the Minimalist Program." *Linguistic Inquiry* 41.1 (2010): 131–48.

Somerville, James. *The Epistemological Significance of the Interrogative.* Ashgate New Critical Thinking in Philosophy. Aldershot: Ashgate, 2002.

Sonnenschein, E. A. "Interrogative Commands: A New Theory of οὐ μή (Prohibitive) in the Light of Latin *quin* with Moods of Command." *Classical Review* 16.3 (1902): 165–69.

Sophocles, E. A. *Greek Lexicon of the Roman and Byzantine Periods: From BC 146 to AD 1100.* New York: Charles Scribner's Sons, 1900.

Spellman, Barbara A., Alexandra P. Kincannon, and Stephen J. Stose. "The Relation between Counterfactual and Causal Reasoning." Pages 28–43 in *The Psychology of Counterfactual Thinking.* Edited by David R. Mandel, Denis J. Hilton, and Patrizia Catellani. Routledge Research International Series in Social Psychology 9. London: Routledge, 2005.

Spranzi, Marta. *The Art of Dialectic between Dialogue and Rhetoric: The Aristotelian Tradition.* Controversies 9. Amsterdam: John Benjamins, 2011.

Stahl, Gerold. "The Effectivity of Questions." *Noûs* 3.2 (1969): 211–18.

Stewart, Katherine A., and Madeline M. Maxwell. *Storied Conflict Talk: Narrative Construction in Mediation.* Studies in Narrative 12. Amsterdam: John Benjamins, 2010.

Stivers, Tanya, and N. J. Enfield. "A Coding Scheme for Question-Response Sequences in Conversation." *Journal of Pragmatics* 42.10 (2010): 2620–26.

Stubbs, Michael. *Discourse Analysis: The Sociolinguistic Analysis of Natural Language.* Language in Society 4. Chicago: University of Chicago, 1983.

Suñer, Margarita. "About Indirect Questions and Semi-Questions." *Linguistics and Philosophy* 16.1 (1993): 45–77.

Swann, William B., Jr., Toni Giuliano, and Daniel M. Wegner. "Where Leading Questions Can Lead: The Power of Conjecture in Social Interaction." *Journal of Personality and Social Psychology* 42.6 (1982): 1025–35.

Swart, Henriëtte de. *Expression and Interpretation of Negation: An OT Typology.* Studies in Natural Language and Linguistic Theory 77. Dordrecht: Springer, 2010.

Szabó, Zoltán Gendler, ed. *Semantics versus Pragmatics.* Oxford: Clarendon, 2005.

Szemerényi, Oswald J. L. *Introduction to Indo-European Linguistics.* Oxford: Clarendon, 1996.

Talbert, Charles H. *Matthew.* Paideia Commentaries on the New Testament. Grand Rapids: Baker, 2010.

Tallerman, Maggie. *Understanding Syntax.* 2nd ed. Understanding Language Series. London: Hodder Education, 2005.

Tannen, Deborah. *Talking Voices: Repetition, Dialogue, and Imagery in Conversational Discourse.* 2nd ed. Studies in Interactional Sociolinguistics 25. Cambridge: Cambridge University Press, 2007.

Tarbell, F. B. "The Deliberative Subjunctive in Relative Clauses in Greek." *Classical Review* 5.7 (1891): 302.

Tatham, Mark, and Katherine Morton. *Expression in Speech: Analysis and Synthesis.* Oxford: Oxford University Press, 2004.

Teller, Paul. "On Why-Questions." *Noûs* 8.4 (1974): 371–80.

Temple, Dennis. "The Contrast Theory of Why-Questions." *Philosophy of Science* 55.1 (1988): 141–51.

Thatcher, Tom. *Jesus the Riddler: The Power of Ambiguity in the Gospels.* Louisville: Westminster John Knox, 2006.

Thiselton, Anthony C. *The First Epistle to the Corinthians: A Commentary on the Greek Text.* NIGTC. Grand Rapids: Eerdmans, 2000.

Thomas, Jenny. *Meaning in Interaction: An Introduction to Pragmatics.* Learning about Language. London: Routledge, 1995.

Thomas, Linda, and Shân Wareing. *Language, Society and Power: An Introduction.* London: Routledge, 1999.

Thomas, Robert L. *Revelation 8–22: An Exegetical Commentary.* Chicago: Moody, 1995.

Thompson, G. S. *Greek Prose Usage: A Companion to Greek Prose Composition.* London: Bristol Classical, 1998.

Thomson, George. "The Postponement of Interrogatives in Attic Drama." *ClQ* 33.3/4 (1939): 147–52.

Thrall, Margaret E. *Greek Particles in the New Testament: Linguistic and Exegetical Studies.* NTTS 3. Leiden: Brill, 1962.

Thurston, Bonnie Bowman. *Preaching Mark.* Fortress Resources for Preaching. Minneapolis: Fortress, 2002.

Tichy, Pavel. "Questions, Answers and Logic." *American Philosophical Quarterly* 15.4 (1978): 275–84.

Tiede, David L. *Luke.* ACNT. Minneapolis: Augsburg, 1988.

Titrud, Kermit. "The Function of Καί in the Greek New Testament and an Application to 2 Peter." Pages 240–70 in *Linguistics and New Testament Interpretation: Essays on Discourse Analysis.* Edited by David Alan Black. Nashville: Broadman & Holman, 1992.

Tolkien, J. R. R. *The Hobbit: Or There and Back Again.* Boston: Houghton Mifflin, 1966.

Toosarvandani, Maziar. "Association with Foci." PhD diss., University of California, Berkeley, 2010.

———. "*Wh*-movement and the Syntax of Sluicing." *Journal of Linguistics* 44.3 (2008): 677–722.

Tordoff, Robert. "Counterfactual History and Thucydides." Pages 101–21 in *Probabilities, Hypotheticals, and Counterfactuals in Ancient Greek Thought.* Edited by Victoria Wohl. Cambridge: Cambridge University Press, 2014.

Tottie, Gunnel. "Turn Management and the Fillers *Uh* and *Um.*" Pages 381–407 in *Corpus Pragmatics: A Handbook*. Edited by Karin Aijmer and Christoph Rühlemann. Cambridge: Cambridge University Press, 2015.

Truswell, Robert. *Events, Phrases, and Questions*. Oxford Studies in Theoretical Linguistics 33. Oxford: Oxford University Press, 2011.

Tsantsanoglou, K. "Punctuation." Pages 1326–33 in *A History of Ancient Greek: From the Beginnings to Late Antiquity*. Edited by A.-F. Christidis. Translated by Geoffrey Cox. Cambridge: Cambridge University Press, 2007.

Tupper, Frederick, Jr. "The Comparative Study of Riddles." *Modern Language Notes* 18.1 (1903): 1–8.

Turnbull, Nick. "Rhetorical Agency as a Property of Questioning." *Philosophy and Rhetoric* 37.3 (2004): 207–22.

Turner, Nigel. *Grammatical Insights into the New Testament*. Edinburgh: T&T Clark, 1966.

Urbanová, Ludmila. "On the Status of Declarative Questions in English Conversation." *Brno Studies in English* 21 (1995): 59–65.

Uygur, Nermi. "What is a Philosophical Question?" *Mind* 73.289 (1964): 64–83.

Vanhoye, Albert. "Interrogation johannique et exégèse de Cana (John 2,4)." *Bib* 55.2 (1974): 157–67.

Velissaratou, Sophia. "Conditional Questions and Which-Interrogatives." Master's thesis, University of Amsterdam, 2000.

Wackernagel, Jacob. *Lectures on Syntax: With Special Reference to Greek, Latin and Germanic*. Edited by David Langslow. Oxford: Oxford University Press, 2009.

Wallace, Daniel B. *Greek Grammar Beyond the Basics: An Exegetical Syntax of the New Testament*. Grand Rapids: Zondervan, 1996.

Walton, Douglas. *Dialog Theory for Critical Argumentation*. Controversies 5. Amsterdam: John Benjamins, 2007.

———. *Informal Logic: A Pragmatic Approach*. 2nd ed. Cambridge: Cambridge University Press, 2008.

———. *One-Sided Arguments: A Dialectical Analysis of Bias*. SUNY Series in Logic and Language. Albany: SUNY Press, 1999.

Wang, Jinjun. "A Critical Analysis of Questions in Dialogues." PhD diss., Xiamen University, 2004.

———. "Questions and the Exercise of Power." *Discourse & Society* 17.4 (2006): 529–48.

Wardhaugh, Ronald, and Janet M. Fuller. *An Introduction to Sociolinguistics*. 7th ed. Blackwell Textbooks in Linguistics. Malden, MA: Wiley-Blackwell, 2015.

Watson, Duane F. "1 Corinthians 10:23–11:1 in the Light of Greco-Roman Rhetoric: The Role of Rhetorical Questions." *JBL* 108.2 (1989): 301–18.

Weber, Elizabeth G. *Varieties of Questions in English Conversation*. Studies in Discourse and Grammar 3. Amsterdam: John Benjamins, 1993.

Weigand, Edda. *Dialogue—The Mixed Game*. Dialogue Studies 10. Amsterdam: John Benjamins, 2010.

Weiner, E. Judith, and Paul de Palma. "Some Pragmatic Features of Lexical Ambiguity and Simple Riddles." *Language & Communication* 13.3 (1993): 183–93.

Wellman, Robert R. "Socratic Method in Xenophon." *Journal of the History of Ideas* 37.2 (1976): 307–18.

West, Martin L. *Textual Criticism and Editorial Technique: Applicable to Greek and Latin Texts*. Stuttgart: B. G. Teubner, 1973.

Wharton, Tim. "Pragmatics and Prosody." Pages 567–84 in *The Cambridge Handbook of Pragmatics*. Edited by Keith Allan and Kasia M. Jaszczolt. Cambridge Handbooks in Language and Linguistics. Cambridge: Cambridge University Press, 2012.

Wheatley, J. M. O. "Deliberative Questions." *Analysis* 15.3 (1955): 49–60.

White, Hayden. *The Content of the Form: Narrative Discourse and Historical Representation*. Baltimore: Johns Hopkins University Press, 1987.

Whitelaw, R. "Interrogative Commands." *Classical Review* 16.5 (1902): 277.

Widdowson, H. G. *Text, Context, Pretext: Critical Issues in Discourse Analysis*. Language in Society 35. Oxford: Blackwell, 2004.

Wilce, James M. *Language and Emotion*. Studies in the Social and Cultural Foundations of Language 25. Cambridge: Cambridge University Press, 2009.

Willi, Andreas. "Register Variation." Pages 297–310 in *A Companion to the Ancient Greek Language*. Edited by Egbert J. Bakker. Blackwell Companions to the Ancient World. Malden, MA: Wiley-Blackwell, 2010.

Wilson, Deirdre, and Dan Sperber. *Meaning and Relevance*. Cambridge: Cambridge University Press, 2012.

Wiśniewski, Andrzej. "Erotetic Search Scenarios." *Synthese* 134.3 (2003): 389–427.

———. "On the Reducibility of Questions." *Erkenntnis* 40 (1994): 265–84.

———. *The Posing of Questions: Logical Foundations of Erotetic Inferences*. Synthese Library 252. Dordrecht: Springer, 1995.

Witherington, Ben, III, and Darlene Hyatt. *Paul's Letter to the Romans: A Socio-Rhetorical Commentary*. Grand Rapids: Eerdmans, 2004.

Woods, John. *Aristotle's Earlier Logic*. 2nd rev. ed. Studies in Logic 53. London: College Publications, 2014.

Worthington, Ian. *Demosthenes, Speeches 60 and 61, Prologues, Letters*. Edited by Michael Gagarin. Oratory of Classical Greece 10. Austin: University of Texas Press, 2006.

Yule, George. *Pragmatics*. Oxford Introductions to Language Study. Oxford: Oxford University Press, 1996.

Žegarac, Vladimir. "What is Phatic Communication?" Pages 327–61 in *Current Issues in Relevance Theory*. Edited by Villy Rouchota and Andreas H. Jucker. Pragmatics & Beyond New Series 58. Amsterdam: John Benjamins, 1998.

Zerwick, Maximilian. *Biblical Greek: Illustrated by Examples*. Subsidia Biblica 41. Rome: Gregorian and Biblical Press, 2014.

Zerwick, Max, and Mary Grosvenor. *A Grammatical Analysis of the Greek New Testament*. Rome: Biblical Institute Press, 1974.

Zillman, Dolf. "Rhetorical Elicitation of Agreement in Persuasion." *Journal of Personality and Social Psychology* 21.2 (1972): 159–65.

Zimmerman, Ruben. "Fragen bei Sokrates und Jesus: Wege des Verstehens—Initiale des Weiterfragens." Pages 33–59 in *Schülerfragen im (Religions-)Unterricht: Ein notwendiger Bildungsauftrag heute?!* Edited by Heike Lindner and Mirjam Zimmermann. Neukirchen-Vluyn: Neukirchener, 2011.

Zuber, Richard. *Non-Declarative Sentences*. Pragmatics & Beyond 4.2. Amsterdam: John Benjamins, 1983.

Zwarts, Frans. "Three Types of Polarity." Pages 177–238 in *Plurality and Quantification*. Edited by Fritz Hamm and Erhard Hinrichs. Studies in Linguistics and Philosophy 69. Dordrecht: Kluwer, 1998.

Scripture Index

MARK

LUKE

JOHN

Ancient Literature Index

Greek Word Index

Subject Index

Modern Author Index

Advances in the Study of Greek

New Insights for Reading the New Testament

Constantine R. Campbell

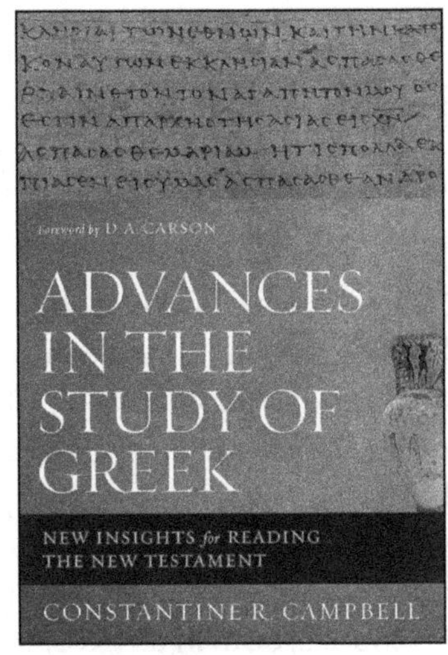

Advances in the Study of Greek offers a much needed introduction to issues of interest in the current world of Greek scholarship. With chapters on a wide range of current issues including linguistic theories, lexical semantics, deponency and the middle voice, verbal aspect, idiolect and genre and register, discourse analysis, and more, Campbell carefully explains these recent advances (and the debates surrounding them) for the study of the Greek New Testament.

Advances in the Study of Greek provides an accessible introduction for students, pastors, professors, and commentators to understand the current issues of interest in this period of paradigm shift.

Available in stores and online!

www.ingramcontent.com/pod-product-compliance
Lightning Source LLC
Chambersburg PA
CBHW070932150426
42814CB00024B/105